Anime, Religion and Spirituality

Reproduction copy of a still from the anime series *The Melancholy of Haruhi Suzumiya*. Image © 2006 Nagaru Tanigawa. Image © 2006 Nagaru Tanigawa • Noizi Ito / a member of SOS. This series was directed by Tatsuya Ishihara and produced by Kyoto Animation. This work is an adaptation of the series of light novels by Nagaru Tanigawa, which were illustrated by Noizi Ito. Image reprinted by kind permission of Kadokawa Corporation.

ANIME, RELIGION AND SPIRITUALITY

Profane and Sacred Worlds in Contemporary Japan

Katharine Buljan and Carole M. Cusack

SHEFFIELD UK   BRISTOL CT

Published by Equinox Publishing Ltd.

UK: Office 415, The Workstation, 15 Paternoster Row, Sheffield S1 2BX
USA: ISD, 70 Enterprise Drive, Bristol, CT 06010

www.equinoxpub.com

First published 2015

© Katharine Buljan and Carole M. Cusack 2015

All rights reserved. No part of this publication may be reproduced or transmitted in any form or by any means, electronic or mechanical, including photocopying, recording or any information storage or retrieval system, without prior permission in writing from the publishers.

ISBN 978 1 78179 109 7 (hardback)
     978 1 78179 110 3 (paperback)

British Library Cataloguing-in-Publication Data

A catalogue record for this book is available from the British Library.

Library of Congress Cataloging-in-Publication Data

Buljan, Katharine, author.
  Anime, religion and spirituality : profane and sacred worlds in contemporary Japan / Katharine Buljan and Carole M. Cusack.
     pages cm
  Includes bibliographical references and index.
  ISBN 978-1-78179-109-7 (hb) -- ISBN 978-1-78179-110-3 (pb)
  1. Animated films--Japan--History and criticism. 2. Animated television programs--Japan--History and criticism. 3. Fantasy comic books, strips, etc.--Japan--History and criticism. 4. Fans (Persons)--Japan--Psychology. 5. Fantasy--Religious aspects. 6. Popular culture--Religious aspects. 7. Popular culture--United States--Japanese influences. 8. Popular culture--Japan--American influences. I. Cusack, Carole M., 1962- author. II. Title.
  NC1766.J3B85 2014
  791.43'340952--dc23
                       2014011991

Typeset by ISB Typesetting, Sheffield, UK

Printed and bound by Lightning Source Inc. (La Vergne, TN), Lighting Source UK Ltd. (Milton Keynes), Lightning Source AU Pty. (Scoresby, Victoria)

Contents

Acknowledgements	vii
Introduction	1
Chapter 1 Japanese Modernity and the Manga and Anime Art Forms	11
Chapter 2 The New Life of Old Beliefs: Religious and Spiritual Concepts in Anime	63
Chapter 3 From Realistic to Supernatural: Genres in Anime	117
Chapter 4 Power Within: The Fan's Embrace of Profane and Sacred Worlds in Anime	163
Conclusion	209
Bibliography	213
Index	232

Acknowledgements

This book grew out of conversations that started in 2007 between Michael Hill (aka 'Doctor Comics'), founding father of the Master of Animation Programme at the University of Technology, Sydney, the first postgraduate course in animation in Australia, and Katharine Buljan. The process of writing a monograph is often slow and difficult, and in 2010 the project expanded to include Carole M. Cusack from Studies in Religion at the University of Sydney. Michael Hill later withdrew from the project due to other commitments, and the final work reached its present form late in 2013.

Many people have assisted the authors during the writing process. Katharine Buljan thanks her beloved parents and brother for their support given to her during the book's long genesis. Carole M. Cusack thanks her research assistant Venetia Robertson, who deserves particular credit for her patience and skill in finding relevant books and articles (both in print and online), her meticulous note-taking, and her considerable talents in identifying crucial issues and highlighting significant arguments. Finance to pay for research assistance was provided by the Macartney Hill Bequest in Studies in Religion, and the School of Letters, Art and Media (SLAM) Roving Research Assistance Programme, both at the University of Sydney. She is also grateful to Don Barrett for his interest in and support of her research.

The authors are both thankful to Mr Takeaki Totsuka, Simon Johnson of the Australian Multilingual Services and to Dr Yuriko Yamanouchi, for their help with English and Japanese translations. They are also grateful to Yasushi Ohshima from Pony Canyon Company, to Kadokawa Corporation, to Mr Daniel Chlebowczyk and Mr Dean Prenc from Madman Entertainment, and to Ms Jude Fowler Smith from the Art Gallery of New South Wales for their kind assistance regarding the images.

The authors are both thankful to Janet Joyce of Equinox Publishing for her interest in and support for their work.

This book is respectfully and affectionately dedicated to Michael Hill.

Introduction

In the early twenty-first century two distinctive, traditional forms of Japanese culture have achieved widespread global status in the world of visual culture. These are manga (comic books) and anime (animated television series and films).[1] This acceptance follows on from the recognition of other Japanese cultural products including *origami* (paper folding), *ikebana* (flower arranging), and *karate* and other martial arts. Anime and manga have achieved considerable resonance and popularity with people, both young and old, and have gained market share in parts of the world far from their homeland. The appeal of Japanese cultural products for the West is predicated upon aesthetic considerations. In Western countries not only its 'design industry press' but also its media in general have been writing in a positive light about design that came from Japan over the last ten years of the twentieth century.[2]

Magazines such as *Time*, *The Face*, and *Wired* have ran cover stories noting the ascendancy of Japanese design in fields ranging from architecture to fashion, cars to cameras, comic books to computers, and from toilets to transport. Innovative architecture, stylish homewares, and new technologies and graphics led the way. Listing '10 reasons why the sun still rises in the East', the *Wired* cover story of September 2001 listed industrial design (Honda cars and Seiko wristwatches), architecture (the design of the theme park Tokyo Disney Seas and the work of architects Tadao Andō, Yoshio Taniguchi, Toyo Ito [Toyoo Itō], Arata Isozaki and Shigeru Ban), branding (*Hello Kitty* and *Pokémon* merchandise), music (DJs, the Technics turntable and the Roland Rhythm Composer machine), robotics (more than half of the world's industrial robots were manufactured and operational in Japan at that time), and comics (at that time manga sales accounted for more than 40% of the publishing industry). The article also referenced the common practice of manga adaptation into anime production, video games (Nintendo Game Boy), demand creation (the rapid cycle of production and consumption

---

1. This study regards manga and anime as words that have become part of colloquial English and do not require italicization as a result.
2. Michael Hill, 'Anime, Art and Design', Arts and Asia Lecture Series, public lecture at the Art Gallery of New South Wales, Sydney (2003).

followed by continuing new product production and consumption), erotica (including BDSM and other specialized sexual tastes), and television game shows that feature the humiliation of contestants.[3]

The dominant item on the list was anime. Animation production surfaced in film and television, in tamagotchi toys and video games, in cosplay (costume role-play) fashion and performances, in fashion itself, and in a large range of supporting merchandise. An important role in this context was played by Japanese artistic heritage, in particular manga, which provided a main source of inspiration for the animations. The terms 'anime' and 'manga' have found their way into modern English. In Australia, for example, the *Macquarie Dictionary* defines anime and manga as follows:

> anime: manga movie...the genre of Japanese animation. [Japanese, from French *animé*, from *animer* to animate], [and] manga: the Japanese form of comic book which has a wide variety of subject areas catering for both children and adults [Japanese, from *man* aimless, involuntary + *ga* (earlier *gwa*) picture; originally *Mangwa*, the title of a sketchbook drawn by Japanese artist Katsushika Hokusai, 1760-1849, in 1812].[4]

It is interesting to note the overlap in these definitions. Anime is a 'manga movie' and presumably this points to the fact that anime is a drawn, graphic medium. Many manga, as noted above, are in fact adapted for production in anime form. There is an intimate affinity of manga for anime that leads to some confusion in the perception of the two media. Western-based anime distributor Manga Entertainment compounded this confusion, as the company distributed anime not manga. Even scholars occasionally err; when discussing Osamu Tezuka's animation, Pauline Moore showed an illustration of a panel from Tezuka's manga of the work complete with word balloons instead of a still frame from his anime.[5]

The popularity of manga and anime was cemented in the 1960s and 1970s, particularly through the dissemination of the cartoons of the medical doctor and prodigiously talented illustrator Osamu Tezuka (1928-1989),[6] the anime adaptations of which included *Astro Boy* (*Tetsuwan*

---

3. Anon, 'Ichiban', *Wired* 9.09 (2001): 120-25.
4. Anon, 'Anime', 'Manga', 'Hokusai', *The Macquarie Dictionary Online* (Sydney: Macquarie Dictionary Publishers, n.d.), at http://www.macquariedictionary.com (accessed 30 December 2011).
5. Pauline Moore, 'When Velvet Gloves Meet Iron Fists: Cuteness in Japanese Animation', in Alan Cholodenko (ed.), *The Illusion of Life II: More Essays on Animation* (Sydney: Power Publications, 2007), 145.
6. The authors have opted to use the Western, rather than the Japanese, form of names (with the given name first and the family name last), except where otherwise

Atomu, 1963), *Princess Knight* (*Ribon no Kishi*, 1967) and *Kimba the White Lion* (*Jungeru Taitei*, 1965). The prolific Tezuka created more than seven hundred manga titles and hand-drew more than 150,000 pages. Although his appeal in the West has chiefly been to

> a young audience...the range of his manga is broader and more complex. He drew inspiration from East and West, turning Fyodor Dostoevsky's *Crime and Punishment* and the lives of Buddha and Beethoven into manga. [Walt] Disney was an influence, as was the society in which he was working, in the aftermath of World War II and the nuclear devastation inflicted on [Japan].[7]

The cultural importance of manga and anime in Japan is significant and consequently, in 2009, 'Meiji University has announced plans to open the world's largest museum of manga and anime, the comic and animation art forms that began in post-World War II Japan and swept the planet'.[8] This has now become a reality and follows the establishment of a Manga Department at the Kyoto Seika University in Kyoto.

The global penetration of manga and anime has been steadily growing since the 1960s, with a significant acceleration since the start of the 1980s, propelled by the success of film directors such as Mamoru Oshii (b. 1951), the director of *Urusei Yatsura 2: Beautiful Dreamer* (1984) and *Ghost in the Shell* (1995), and Hayao Miyazaki (b. 1941), the director of *Nausicaä of the Valley of the Wind* (1984), and *Princess Mononoke* (1997). The work of Oshii and Miyazaki is an important continuation of two of Tezuka's preoccupations: the limits of the human, expressed particularly through robots and cyborgs; and the devastation of the natural environment. Oshii's *oeuvre* is frequently focused on violent crime and death, and the existential question of what human life actually is constantly arises through the interactions of human characters with vampires, demons, extra-terrestrials, cyborgs, and robots, among other non-human persons.[9] Major Motoko Kusanagi, the protagonist of his masterpiece, *Ghost in the Shell* (1995), is a cyborg desperate to hold onto

---

indicated. In some Japanese names and terms macrons are included but not in all and an example of this are the words that have been adopted in English (for example Tokyo). English translations of anime titles are used and romanisation of these is provided only occasionally (for example *Tetsuwan Atomu*).

7. Joyce Morgan, 'Superheroes for a Complex World', *Sydney Morning Herald: Spectrum* (10-11 February 2007), 9.

8. David McNeill, 'A Scholarly Home for Manga', *Chronicle of Higher Education* 55.24 (2009): A6.

9. Tom Looser, 'Gothic Politics: Oshii, War, and Life without Death', *Mechademia* 4 (2009): 55-73; Carlo Silvio, 'Refiguring the Radical Cyborg in Manoru Oshii's *Ghost in the Shell*', *Science Fiction Studies* 26 (1999): 54-72.

the last vestiges of her humanity, until she decides to abandon embodiment to merge with the Puppet Master, an online entity who challenges her, saying 'your effort to remain what you are is what limits you'.[10]

Where Oshii's focus is on the post-human future, Hayao Miyazaki's *oeuvre* is infused with nostalgia, and *Spirited Away* (2001) is a modern folktale, the purpose of which is to remind Japanese young people of the importance of respecting and being connected to the environment, the family and the *kami* (the supernatural beings of the Shintō religion). Chihiro, Miyazaki's child protagonist, starts out ignorant of the meaning and purpose of Shintō shrines, but through her work in the haunted bathhouse, she opens her heart to the *kami* and assumes responsibility for family and community.[11] Miyazaki's use of a child protagonist is also significant; in manga and anime 'children are more open to the kind of fantastical worlds that are portrayed, unencumbered by the materialism that often infects their parents'.[12] In Miyazaki's *My Neighbour Totoro* (1998) this is very clearly spelled out: the sisters Mei and Satsuki are befriended by the forest spirit Totoro because their youth means they have an affinity with and respect for nature. This brief introduction to some themes found in contemporary manga and anime suggest that this field is ripe for an academic examination in terms of its religious and spiritual content.

In support of this contention, in recent years scholarship on manga and anime has developed as an emergent academic field. In 2009 alone, Natsu Onoda Power's *God of Comics: Osamu Tezuka and the Creation of Post-World War II Manga*, Helen McCarthy's *The Art of Osamu Tezuka: God of Manga*, and Colin Odell and Michel le Blanc's *Studio Ghibli: The Films of Hayao Miyazaki and Isao Takahata* were published. In 2010 Josef Steiff and Tristan D. Tamplin's edited volume *Anime and Philosophy: Wide-Eyed Wonder* appeared, and in 2011 Jeremy Robinson released *The Cinema of Hayao Miyazaki*. The majority of these studies concentrate on individual illustrators and animators, although Steiff and Tamplin's (2010) edited volume investigates philosophical issues in manga and anime, and at times touches upon religious themes. Representing part of a general global fascination with contemporary Japanese design and visual

---

10. Sarah Penicka-Smith, 'Cyborg Songs for an Existential Crisis', in Josef Steiff and Tristan D. Tamplin (eds), *Anime and Philosophy: Wide-Eyed Wonder* (Chicago and La Salle, IL: Open Court, 2010), 263.

11. Cari Callis, 'Nothing That Happens is Ever Forgotten', in Steiff and Tamplin (eds), *Anime and Philosophy*, 97-101.

12. Colin Odell and Michel le Blanc, *Studio Ghibli: The Films of Hayao Miyazaki and Isao Takahata* (London: Kamera Books, 2009), 78.

culture, the two media of anime and manga seem set to dominate both Eastern and Western popular culture.[13]

This book investigates anime, focusing on its historical antecedents (graphic and narrative), its religious and supernatural content, its generic and thematic variety, and its popularity and reception among fans. Here it is important to clarify that the reasons for the popularity of anime, both inside and outside of Japan, and the development of emerging consumer behaviours related to anime are not the focus of this book. Having said this, Chapter 4 contains a basic discussion of a number of features of anime that audiences in the West might find attractive, as well as a brief consideration of Western fandom and fan activities, but the unifying thread woven through this chapter is that of the supernatural. It is in the area of the graphic, religious and supernatural content of anime that this study contributes most to scholarly discourse on the subject.

The two dominant religions of Japan are Shintō and Buddhism, although Confucianism, Daoism, Christianity and a variety of new religious movements are also present among the Japanese population. In Japan many individuals adhere to more than one religious tradition. Numerous Japanese people practise both Shintō and Buddhism, and it is the influence of these two religions that is most frequently encountered in anime. The *Kojiki* (Record of Ancient Matters) and the *Nihongi* (Chronicles of Japan), dating from the early eighth century, are considered the earliest Shintō texts, but although they are repositories of mythology and traditions they do not function in the same way as, for example, the Bible does in the context of Christianity.[14] Having said that, they do provide information about Shintō's deities, the *kami*. Unlike the omniscient, omnipotent god of Christianity, *kami* have imperfections, and *kami* can also refer to supernatural forces in addition to specific persons.[15] In the *Kojiki* and the *Nihongi* the 'supernatural' (in terms of phenomena that do not conform to the laws of logic and nature) features prominently. This book highlights an abundance of supernatural content in anime, the majority of which is derived from Shintō, with some Buddhist influences.[16]

---

13. Michael Hill, 'Understanding Manga and Anime Character Design of the Magic Kingdom', public lecture associated with the 'Japan: Kingdom of Characters' exhibition (Sydney: Japan Foundation, 2011).

14. Sokyo Ono, *Shinto: The Kami Way* (Rutland, VT: Tuttle, 1976), 5.

15. H. Byron Earhart, *Japanese Religion: Unity and Diversity*, 4th edn (Victoria and Belmont, CA: Thomson and Wadworth, 2004).

16. Toshio Kuroda, 'Shinto in the History of Japanese Religions', *Journal of Japanese Studies* 7.1 (1981): 1-3.

Chapter 1 situates manga and anime in the context of Japanese modernity and traces the early graphic and narrative precursors (religious and secular) of contemporary manga and anime. This examination commences with Buddhist painted scrolls, the *Chōjū Giga* of the twelfth century, and includes the influence of the Zen Buddhist art known as *zenga* of the seventeenth century and secular graphic works (*ōtsu-e*) of the mid-seventeenth century, through the *ukiyo-e* style of eighteenth-century Edo, *shunga* (graphic erotic works, also from the eighteenth century), and the *kibyōshi*, the illustrated 'yellow cover' books of the late eighteenth century. The book also notes the contributions to the development of the manga form by Katsushika Hokusai (1760–1849), who was noted above in the *Macquarie Dictionary* definition as the originator of the term 'manga' in 1812 and whose artistic practice was in the area of printmaking and painting. In examining manga's long lineage, albeit in forms similar to but not precisely the same as contemporary comic book form, this study offers an alternative view to the more conventional understanding that the modern comic book either originated in the nineteenth century with the work of Swiss schoolteacher Rodolphe Töpffer (1799–1846) and other subsequent European developments, or in the publication of coloured comic strips in the Sunday editions of certain New York newspapers at the end of the nineteenth and the beginning of the twentieth centuries.[17]

The book then examines the recent history and manifestations of the manga form, with its particular range of artwork styles, characters, narrative arcs, graphic content, graphic styles and techniques and generic development. The particular characteristics of Japanese modernity, which has developed since the Meiji Restoration of 1868, are investigated as the backdrop against which the distinctive cultural products of manga and anime emerged. Here the significant influence of Osamu Tezuka (1928–1989) is treated as a case study. The hybrid visual storytelling and performance format, midway between manga and anime, known as *kamishibai*, or paper theatre, is also noted. Manga informs anime by supplying the medium with graphic styles and narratives. The chapter here outlines both the narrative and the graphic influence of manga on anime. The modes of anime production (from hand-drawn to digital), and English translations of manga and anime, are also briefly touched upon, and Mamoru Oshii's *Ghost in the Shell* (1995) is considered as a successful example of adaptation from the manga to anime form.

Chapter 2 explores the religious and supernatural content of anime, which is the principal focus of the book, a theme that makes this medium uniquely distinctive. The Japanese religious context of Shintō and

---

17. Randy Duncan and Matthew J. Smith, *The Power of Comics: History, Form and Culture* (London and New York: Continuum, 2009).

Buddhism is sketched, and the interpretation of anime through notions including animism, anthropomorphism and metamorphosis is linked particularly to the Shintō worldview of a *kami* (spirit)-filled natural world in which all is alive and inter-connected. The idea that not only living creatures but also material things are alive and possess a 'spirit' and that 'spirits' have the ability to change their place of dwelling has persisted in Japan and has been transferred to modern technology so that a spirit presence may be understood to reside not just in natural phenomena such as rocks and trees, but also in domestic items such as furniture, coffee machines, and toothbrushes, as the film director Oshii has asserted.[18] Examples of the use of supernatural characters and themes are provided throughout the chapter, and, as will be demonstrated, some people may be attracted to anime for spiritual reasons, finding some spiritual resonance in their stories and characters. The chapter explores Shintō, Buddhism, and the supernatural world of ghosts and spirit beings. Christian apocalyptic imagery and motifs from European mythology that are featured in anime are also briefly sketched.[19]

Chapter 3 then focuses on anime genres, arguing that these provide a fertile basis from which sprang numerous generic hybrids. They became the norm in anime, with the potential to appeal to various types of audience. The power assigned to female heroines is also investigated and it is argued that rather than reflecting the power of Amaterasu, the Shintō goddess, their power more resembles Western Pagan ideas about the sacredness of the Earth and Gaia as nature goddess. In this chapter we further underline how the generic conventions of the supernatural subgenre permeate a large number of anime films and series, stressing that conventions of this subgenre are also often found in generic hybrids whose dominant themes do not necessarily fit with the supernatural subgenre (and thus, in that context, they have various metaphorical functions). This chapter also analyses the child/young adult anime protagonist in terms of the mythological 'divine child' as a mediator between the supernatural and physical worlds. Chapter 3 argues for the strength of the supernatural subgenre and its close connection with mythology, religion and spirituality.

The final chapter, Chapter 4, focuses on the enthusiasm of anime fans (often referred to as 'anime aficionados' in this study) in the West. In

---

18. At a press conference in Sydney in 2004 to promote his latest film *Ghost in the Shell 2: Innocence*, Mamoru Oshii spoke of his fear of having to confront the six hundred gods he believed to be living in his bathroom, residing in everyday inanimate objects such as combs, soap, toilets and toothbrushes and so on.

19. Michael Broderick, 'Superflat Eschatology: Renewal and Religion in Anime', *Animation Studies – Animated Dialogues 2007* (2007): 29-45.

this context the argument acknowledges that the passing of time does not diminish their devotion to anime, but, rather, that substantial credit for anime's ongoing popularity goes to various initiatives by anime fans themselves. This chapter also briefly discusses various anime characteristics, which might inspire the interest of various members of its non-Japanese audience, and discusses in greater detail the religio-spiritual content of anime drawing on Jin Kyu Park's views that it is this content that some anime aficionados find most interesting.[20] Here this chapter argues that religious/spiritual elements in anime, which are frequently borrowed from world religions such as Christianity, are sometimes stripped of the value and meaning that they had in their original context. Consequently, this can give rise to the formation of an inaccurate understanding of those elements. This would most likely apply to those anime aficionados and viewers who are not familiar with the religious traditions in question. Having said that, the presence of religious and spiritual elements in anime has the potential to awaken the curiosity of anime aficionados and more casual viewers to seek out more information about the particular supernatural elements featured in anime which initially drew their attention. It has been briefly noted in this chapter that anime can inspire fans to familiarize themselves with both Japanese culture and language.

This chapter also sheds light on the subculture of *otaku* (anime enthusiasts or 'nerds'), and the change of the meaning of this term from negative to positive in recent decades. This chapter also focuses on two activities practised by anime aficionados, which are cosplaying and visiting sites in Japan that are portrayed in anime. These trips are often referred to as 'sacred'.[21] This chapter argues that both of these activities perhaps represent anime aficionados' wishes to (in symbolic terms) connect with the diegetic world of anime's narratives, the events and characters that often have otherworldly characteristics.

Consequently this study is a timely publication, both as a resource for anime fans new and existing, young and old, who desire to know more about the religion and mythology of Japan and how it informs the manga and anime genres; and as a worthy addition to the small but growing

---

20. Jin Kyu Park, '"Creating My Own Cultural and Spiritual Bubble": Case of Cultural Consumption by Spiritual Seeker Anime Fans', *Culture and Religion: An Interdisciplinary Journal* 6.3 (2005): 393-413.

21. Susan Napier, 'When Godzilla Speaks', in William M. Tsutsui and Michiko Ito (eds), *In Godzilla's Footsteps: Japanese Pop Culture Icons on the Global Stage* (New York: Palgrave Macmillan, 2006), 9-19; Takayoshi Yamamura, 'Anime Pilgrimage and Local Tourism Promotion: An Experience of Washimiya Town, the Sacred Place for Anime "Lucky Star" Fans', *Web-Journal of Tourism and Cultural Studies* 14 (2009): 1-9, at http://hdl.handle.net/2115/38541 (accessed 7 May 2011).

academic literature on the topic. In particular, it is timely as to date only one monograph that focuses on the religious and spiritual content of manga and anime has been published. Jolyon Baraka Thomas's *Drawing on Tradition: Manga, Anime and Religion in Contemporary Japan* (2012) is a study quite unlike *Anime, Religion and Spirituality: Profane and Sacred Worlds in Contemporary Japan* in that it is based on Thomas's experience of living in Japan. As a scholar, Thomas engages sociologically with fans, manga artists (*mangaka*), and participants in new and fringe religious and spiritual groups, through participant observation and interviews.[22] This study, which like Thomas's seeks to explore in detail both well-known and obscure examples of anime and elucidate the content in terms of Japanese religion and contemporary spirituality, supplies a broad and deep coverage of historical and artistic antecedents, and mythological and religious sources, for manga and anime. Thus it complements Thomas's sociological and popular cultural study, and contributes to the advancement of the scholarly subfield of religion and anime.

---

22. Jolyon Baraka Thomas, *Drawing on Tradition: Manga, Anime and Religion in Contemporary Japan* (Honolulu: University of Hawai'i Press, 2012).

The Heron Maiden by Tsunetomi Kitano (Japan, 1880–1947), made in 1925. Print (colour woodcut), 45.7 × 30 cm. Art Gallery of New South Wales (purchased 1987). Photo: AGNSW. Japanese cultural heritage has many mythological/supernatural stories centred around animal–human relationships. One of these is a story of love between a man and a heron/woman.

Chapter 1

Japanese Modernity and the Manga and Anime Art Forms

Introduction

This chapter examines the emergence of the manga and anime forms in terms of the historical development of Japanese artistic modes that are antecedent to these forms, and also through consideration of the development of Japanese modernity. It is argued that the manga and anime forms and Japanese modernity both retain traditional Eastern religious and aesthetic concerns, while freely appropriating Western religious and aesthetic motifs, which results in a unique new cultural synthesis that is equally appealing to Eastern and Western audiences. The intention of this chapter is to demonstrate that the earliest precursors of manga are a number of centuries old and that manga, and thus anime, is deeply embedded in the history of Japanese art, religion and life.[1] This interpretation is important in that it offers an alternative to the claim that the origins of the comic book aesthetic are European, and that the influence of Walt Disney (1901–1966) on early manga illustrators is more important than their Japanese forebears. This chapter is divided into four sections. The first of these details the historical artistic forms that contribute to the modern manga style in either graphic or narrative ways. The second section sketches an overview of the emergence of Japanese modernity and the manga style of the mid-twentieth century, culminating with the work of Osamu Tezuka (1928–1989). The third section discusses the characteristics of contemporary manga, and traces the anime adaptations of manga stories, again highlighting the importance of Tezuka, and using the celebrated film by Mamoru Oshii (b. 1951), *Ghost in the Shell* (1995), based on the manga by Masamune Shirow (b. 1961) as an example of adaptation. The fourth section briefly investigates the connections between contemporary manifestations of religion and spirituality and popular cultural forms.

---

  1. Fredrik L. Schodt, *Manga! Manga! The World of Japanese Comics*, rev. edn (Tokyo and New York: Kodansha International, 1986).

The Graphic and Narrative Origins of Manga

Tarō Asō (b. 1940) served as Prime Minister of Japan from September 2008 to September 2009. Before his brief elevation to the leadership of his country he was Foreign Minister, and in this role he sought to combine his own interest in manga (which was sufficiently passionate that he had been termed an *otaku*, an extreme fan or 'nerd') with the economic revival of Japan.[2] He advocated the promotion of manga and anime as examples of 'soft power' and their consequent use as a diplomatic tool, and had planned to build an anime and manga museum. However, this was not achieved during his brief one-year tenure as Prime Minister.[3] *Rozen Maiden* is Asō's favourite manga, and this inspired manga fans to call him 'Rozen Asō'.[4] He even complained that being Prime Minister had severely compromised the time he normally allocated to reading manga (he was reputed to read ten magazines per week). As manga culture occupies a special place in contemporary Japan it is not surprising that a Japanese Prime Minister admitted to being a manga fan.[5] Apart from being Prime Minister, Tarō Asō was middle-aged and a putative member of the 'salary man' demographic; since the 1970s magazines for businessmen had included *kyoyo manga* (academic or educational manga), which 'provide readers with special knowledge…about an occupation, historical figure, or event' as well as contain information about 'food, liquor, and annual festivals' among other topics.[6] Japanese people of both sexes and all age groups read manga, and specific age groups are targeted by the industry from three-year-olds to senior citizens, with different genres designed for each age and sex demographic.

In Japan comics have traditionally been accorded the same cultural significance and respect as films and novels. This is quite unlike the situation in the West where graphic novels have only received widespread acclaim as cultural products (particularly in terms of having serious religious or philosophical content) since approximately the turn of the

---

2. Reiji Yoshida, '"Manga" Fans have been Won Over but What about the Rest of Japan?', *The Japan Times* (23 September 2008), at http://www.japantimes.co.jp/text/nn20080923a6.html (accessed 30 December 2011).

3. Roland Kelts, 'Japanamerica: Stray Ambassadors', *3:AM Magazine* (2010), at http://www.3ammagazine.com/3am/japanamerica-stray-ambassadors (accessed 19 March 2012).

4. Jean Snow, 'Akihabara Nerds Rally Behind Likely Japanese PM', *Wired* (September 2008), at http://www.wired.com/gamelife/2008/09/japan-pm-candid/ (accessed 19 March 2012).

5. Anne M. Cooper-Chen, *Cartoon Cultures: The Globalization of Japanese Popular Media* (New York: Peter Lang, 2010), 23.

6. Kinko Ito, 'A History of *Manga* in the Context of Japanese Culture and Society', *Journal of Popular Culture* 38.3 (2005): 471.

twenty-first century. In Japan manga acts as one of the most effective means, not only of drawing the attention of a substantial percentage of the population, but also of influencing public opinion. Kiichi Miyazawa (1919–2007), who was Prime Minister of Japan from 1991 to 1993, used to publish his views in a series in *Big Comic Strips* manga magazine, and the reason for this decision was due to its large male readership, the members of which were also 'potential voters'.[7] This profane and everyday motivation is, however, only part of the picture. As Kinko Ito argues, manga 'reflects the reality of Japanese society' such as 'social order and hierarchy, sexism, racism, ageism, [and] classism', but it also both acts as a conduit for and an expression of 'the myths, beliefs, rituals, traditions, [and] fantasies' of contemporary Japanese people.[8]

Turning to the historical origins of manga, it must be acknowledged that much of the debate about the origins of the comic (and its derivative, the animated cartoon) form is influenced by both national and cultural biases. North American historians often claim the comic book to be a uniquely American creation along with jazz and rock'n'roll music. They claim that comics originated at the turn of the twentieth century with the publication of the comic strip *The Yellow Kid* by Richard Felton Outcault in a New York newspaper, the *New York Sunday World* in 1896.[9] European scholars (and some Americans, to be fair) highlight the contribution of: Rodolphe Töpffer, a Swiss schoolteacher, and his comic-strip narratives that were first published around sixty years previously in 1833; of Wilhelm Busch of Hanover, Germany who drew the comic *Max und Moritz*; and of the German cartoonist resident in New York, Rudolph Dirks, who was clearly influenced by Busch in his creation of the *Katzenjammer Kids* of 1897.[10] In England, attention is drawn to the painter William Hogarth (1697–1764), whose artistic social commentary influenced the satirical cartoonists James Gillray, Thomas Rowlandson, and Isaac and George Cruikshank. The parodic social portraits, narrative engraved works, and caricatures of life in London in the eighteenth century produced by these artists, seem to fit the definition of the sequential graphic nature of comics.[11]

Rather than seeking to establish one or another of these genealogies as the definitive, and authoritatively correct, origin of the comic form,

---

7. Fredrik L. Schodt, *Dreamland Japan: Writings on Modern Manga* (Berkeley, CA: Stone Bridge Press, 1996), 19.
8. Ito, 'A History of *Manga*', 456.
9. Coulton Waugh, *The Comics* (Jackson, MS: University Press of Mississippi, 1947), 1.
10. Duncan and Smith, *The Power of Comics: History, Form and Culture*, 26-27.
11. Mark Wigan, *Sequential Images* (Lausanne: AVA Publishing, 2008), 56.

it is possible, in the case of manga, to point to its graphic and narrative origins in artistic developments that span almost a thousand years in Japan.[12] Japan's cultural heritage abounds with contributions in the field of visual arts,[13] and the roots of manga can be found in this tradition, both distant and recent. It is acknowledged that manga does not have an unbroken genealogy of production, or continuity of creative development, into a singular modern form, yet it may be argued that the popular pictorial trends of various periods in the history of Japanese art have influenced the visual 'look' and narrative style of manga as it appeared in its flourishing evolution following the end of World War II.[14] It has been argued that *Punch*, which first appeared in 1841, is the most obvious forerunner of modern comics, yet there was a comic of sorts, a little yellow-cover book that was popular in Japan almost sixty years before this date, in the late Edo period (c. 1780). Called the *kibyōshi*, it utilized the then-innovative woodblock printing technology to tell stories in graphic narrative form, and is therefore viewed as an early ancestor of contemporary manga.[15]

There is evidence of illustrated texts in Japan from the eighth century (Nara period), when the first written texts, the *Kojiki* and the *Nihon Shoki*, were produced. This was a time of great change, in which written texts, Buddhism, and a new purpose-built capital at Nara, all evidence of the influence of Chinese culture, altered Japanese society dramatically. Shunsuke Tsurumi argues that cartoons in Japan derived from 'stray scribblings' and states that 'the oldest known scribble, dated the first day of the fourth month... A.D. 745 was found on the margin of a *sutra* [Buddhist scripture] among the Emperor's acquisitions in Shōsōin in Nara'.[16] At the same time, wooden slips called *mokkan* (which could be shaved and re-used) were used in place of paper, which was expensive. Joan Piggott, with reference to a cache of *mokkan* discovered in 1989, mentions examples 'with comic sketches of human figures, now considered Japan's earliest *manga*. In one instance, an elegantly tall courtier stands at attention, his official baton (*shaku*) clutched in his respectfully joined hands. But a long nose suggests a humorous attitude on the part of the portraitist,

---

12. Brigitte Koyama-Richard, *One Thousand Years of Manga* (Paris: Flammarion, 2007).

13. Susan Jolliffe Napier, *Anime from Akira to Princess Mononoke: Experiencing Contemporary Japanese Animation* (New York: Palgrave Macmillan, 2001).

14. Ito, 'A History of *Manga*', 458-61.

15. Adam L. Kern, *Manga from the Floating Word: Comicbook Culture and the Kibyōshi of Edo Japan* (Cambridge, MA: Harvard University Asia Center, 2006), 105, 247 and 317.

16. Shunsuke Tsurumi, 'Edo Period in Contemporary Popular Culture', *Modern Asian Studies* 18.4 (1984): 751.

undoubtedly an official himself'.[17] Despite the assertion that these illustrated *mokkan* were 'the first manga', when charting the history of the manga form, it is generally agreed by scholars that the *Chōjū Giga* (animal scrolls) of the twelfth century are the most justifiable starting point.[18] The four volumes of these scrolls, which depict humorous animal images in 'monochromatic narrative pictures',[19] are one of the national treasures of Japan, and are held in the Kōzanji (Kōzan-ji) temple in Toganoo, a Kyōto suburb. According to legend they were painted by the Buddhist monk Toba (1053–1140), and are rolled out laterally, from right to left in manga style, on a paper scroll, called *emakimono*, rather than on sheets of paper in magazine or book format. The protagonists in *Chōjū Giga* scrolls are not humans but rather birds and animals such as frogs, hares, monkeys and foxes. By depicting these animals garbed as clerics and in situations such as playing at games of chance or strip poker, 'the activities and pastimes of members of the clergy and the nobility', these scrolls offer a 'parody and critique of the religious [and social] hierarchy'.[20] Brenner also draws attention to a 'Japanese way of using space' in the *Chōjū Giga* and to the use of calligraphic techniques to capture 'movement, expressions, and figures...' eloquently.[21]

The Buddhist monks who painted scrolls subsequent to Toba's *Chōjū Giga* created content that preached moral lessons using amusing animal characters as a way of catching people's attention and, after their defences against religious instruction had been breached, potentially educating them in Buddhist principles. In the context of Western animation (and this can be also applied to the funny animal characters drawn by the Buddhist monks), the theory was that people would be amused and drawn in by the diverting acts of the animals and respond warmly to them; it was thought that human characters would not be as effective in gaining attention or breaching defences as the 'funny' animal characters were.[22]

It is worth noting that pictures depicting Buddhist subject matter were not only executed by monks and scholars; they were also produced by lay artists who employed comic and satiric elements to represent Buddhist themes, which is taken by art historians to indicate a 'popularization of

---

17. Joan R. Piggott, '*Mokkan*: Wooden Documents from the Nara Period', *Monumenta Nipponica* 45.4 (1990): 467.
18. Schodt, *Manga! Manga!*, 28.
19. Ito, 'A History of *Manga*', 458.
20. Robin E. Brenner, *Understanding Manga and Anime* (Westport, CN: Libraries Unlimited, 2007), 2.
21. Brenner, *Understanding Manga and Anime*, 2.
22. Donald Crafton, *Before Mickey: The Animated Film 1898–1928* (Cambridge, MA and London: MIT Press, 1982), 290, 299.

Buddhism'[23] from the twelfth century onward. The popularity appeal of these scrolls is demonstrated by the fact that such scrolls continued to be produced well into the nineteenth century in various styles.

In the seventeenth century a form of visual expression called Zen painting or *zenga* was developed. *Zenga* was also of Buddhist origin and is another important precursor of manga. Zen painting, like many aspects of Japanese culture including Buddhism and writing, came from China during the Kamakura period (1185–1333). However, the term *zenga* is used specifically to refer to works that were created during the Edo period (1603–1868). Like the *Chōjū Giga* scrolls, *zenga* paintings were executed with a brush and ink, and a calligraphic text accompanied the images. The style was bolder and more abstract than that of *Chōjū Giga*, and although the range of subjects depicted was extensive there were certain recurring motifs, including Mount Fuji, the Zen circular symbol (*ensō*), and sticks. One of the most prominent representatives of *zenga* was the charismatic Rinzai Zen master Ekaku Hakuin (1686–1768).[24] Hakuin exemplifies the style of *zenga*, in that he was broad-minded, tolerant, and popular with lay people, because the Buddhism he taught placed emphasis on action and the achievement of enlightenment through the *kōan* (Zen riddle) system.[25] *Chōjū Giga* and *zenga* are examples of religious influences on the genealogy of manga, as they both stem from Buddhism. Another populist form of graphic cartooning known as *ōtsu-e* also developed in the Edo period. *Ōtsu-e* were inexpensive 'folk sketches and prints' which frequently featured both religious (although generally Shintō not Buddhist) as well as moral content,[26] in the form of rural and agricultural subject matter.

Japanese artists had been exposed to Western influences due to the brief period during which Christianity flourished in Japan. The Jesuit missionary Francis Xavier arrived in Japan in 1549 and by 1600 approximately three hundred thousand Japanese had become Christians (*kirishitan*) of a population estimated at twenty million. From 1587 Hideyoshi Toyotomi (1536–98) and Ieyasu Tokugawa (1543–1616) gradually outlawed Christianity and ordered all priests to leave the country.[27] After 1603 when

---

23. Felice Fischer, 'Japanese Buddhist Art', *Philadelphia Museum of Art Bulletin* 87.369 (1991): 18.

24. Stephen Addiss, *Zenga and Nanga: Paintings by Japanese Monks and Scholars* (New Orleans: New Orleans Museum of Art, 1976), 10.

25. Audrey Yoshiko Seo and Stephen Addiss, *The Sound of One Hand: Paintings and Calligraphy by Zen Master Hakuin* (Boston: Shambhala Publications Inc., 2010).

26. Dianne T. Ooka, 'Ike-no Taiga: Paintings in the Collection', *Philadelphia Museum of Art Bulletin* 66.305 (1971): 28-29.

27. Joseph M. Kitagawa, 'Some Remarks on Shintō', *History of Religions* 27.3 (1988): 238.

Ieyasu Tokugawa assumed the shogunate those Japanese who became Christians fled to Manila or Macao, or went underground. However, in that brief half-century, Portuguese and other European merchant ships commenced trade with Japan through a series of approved port cities, of which the most Westernized was Nagasaki.[28] Among wealthy Japanese there developed a fascination with European culture and the Christian religion, which is in stark contrast to the insularity of the earlier Heian period (794–1185).[29] The Italian Jesuit Giovanni Niccolo, who lived in Japan from 1583 to 1614, taught Western art techniques to Japanese students in a school at Hachirao (Nagasaki), and the resultant artwork of these and other Japanese artists who were influenced by European aesthetics include Christian religious paintings, copperplate engravings for book illustrations, screens on which were painted Western-influenced subjects, including cartographic maps of the known world, and decorated objects including boxes, bowls, gunpowder flasks, church bells, liturgical objects and gravestones.[30] Namban (Nanban) art is not generally acknowledged to be an important source for the modern manga style, but is nevertheless worth noting because it is evidence of Japanese interest in and appropriation of Western aesthetics, a phenomenon that is continued in the twentieth century through manga artists' interest in Disney and Fleischer cartoons. Further, Namban art featured explicitly Christian motifs, which are prominent in modern manga and anime.[31]

Undoubtedly, the secular art form that constitutes the most significant influence on the manga form is *ukiyo-e* (which literally means 'pictures from the floating world'), which also developed during the Edo period in the cosmopolitan city of Edo (later Tokyo).[32] The 'floating world' referred to was a *demi-monde* of courtesans, *geishas*, *kabuki* theatre and other evanescent, transitory pleasures. *Ukiyo-e* as a style included both paintings and woodblock prints, the content of which was connected with the popular culture of the city as its subjects included portraits of actors, *geishas*, courtesans, *sumō* wrestlers, and their workplaces such as the theatres, amusement halls, pavilions and places where these players could be seen.[33] The etymology of *ukiyo-e* involves the fusion of the two

---

28. Yoshitomo Okamoto, *The Namban Art of Japan* (New York and Tokyo: John Wetherill Inc. and Heibonsha, 1972), 69.

29. Ivan Morris, *The World of the Shining Prince: Court Life in Ancient Japan* (New York: Kodansha America, Inc., 1994 [1964]).

30. Okamoto, *The Namban Art of Japan*, 96-156.

31. Adam Barkman, 'Anime, Manga and Christianity: A Comprehensive Analysis', *Journal for the Study of Religions and Ideologies* 9.27 (2010).

32. Tsurumi, 'Edo Period', 747-55.

33. Tadashi Kobayashi, *Ukiyo-e: An Introduction to Japanese Woodblock Prints* (New York: Kodansha America Inc., 1997 [1982]).

meanings of *uki*, the first of which has Buddhist connotations and means 'woeful' or 'sorrowful', whereas the second refers to 'floating' or 'unreliable'; *yo* means 'world'.[34] In addition to the fleeting, ephemeral secular pleasures of the 'floating world', *ukiyo-e* acknowledged the notion of life itself being brief and fundamentally unreal, in the Buddhist sense. This grounding of the graphic content in everyday life, and the inexpensive, mass-produced medium of the woodblock prints, resonated with the population just as the production and publication of manga in cheap comics was to in the twentieth century.[35]

The founder of the *ukiyo-e* school is Matabei Katsumochi Iwasa, also known as Matabei Ukiyo (1578–1650), who began as an exponent of the Tosa style of painting, but through the exercise of artistic individuality in some of his works, developed the distinctive *ukiyo-e* style.[36] Another major artist of this school was Moronobu Hishikawa (1618–1694), another Tosa-trained painter who is hailed by some scholars as one of the 'father[s] of the Japanese print'.[37] Hishikawa came from a family of textile workers, and interestingly, it is likely that *ukiyo-e* stencil patterns were also used for kimono textile design.[38] It is the use of the woodblock printing technique that is most relevant to the graphic development of manga, which will be discussed below, with reference to the development of the *kibyōshi* form.

A subgenre of the *ukiyo-e* style that contributed to the manga form in certain specific ways is *shunga*. *Shunga* images were explicitly sexual and thus pronouncedly secular, and in eighteenth-century Edo they were also known as 'dirty pictures'.[39] To express this more neutrally, *shunga* is the collective term for Japanese 'erotic paintings, prints and illustrated books... [and] literally, it means "spring drawings"'.[40] *Shunga* often feature improbably large male genitalia, and a general exaggeration of the sexual parts of male and female bodies, a stylistic convention still in evidence in manga and anime with strong sexual themes. *Shunga* were in fact the first *ukiyo-e* images to be printed with woodblocks, rather than painted.[41]

---

34. Shigeyosho Mihara, '*Ukiyo-e*: Some Aspects of Japanese Classical Picture Prints', *Monumenta Nipponica* 6.1-2 (1943): 247.
35. Ooka, 'Ike-no Taiga', 28-29.
36. Mihara, '*Ukiyo-e*', 249.
37. Helen C. Gunsaulus, 'A Painted Scroll of the Early *Ukiyo-é* School', *Bulletin of the Art Institute of Chicago* 24.4 (1930): 44.
38. Pauline Simmons, 'Artist Designers of the Tokugawa Period', *Metropolitan Museum of Art Bulletin* (New Series) 14.6 (1956): 147.
39. Koyama-Richard, *One Thousand Years*, 239.
40. Tom Evans and Mary Anne Evans, *Shunga: The Art of Love in Japan* (New York: Paddington Press, 1975), 9.
41. Jeff Yang, Dina Gan and Terry Hong, *Eastern Standard Time: A Guide to Asian*

However, while *shunga* share the same subject matter as modern pornography, they may be distinguished from these on both grounds of artistic merit, and in the liberal sensibility and lack of prurience in their execution.⁴² The 1947 Japanese Constitution bans censorship of any kind, and Timothy Perper and Martha Cornog's comprehensive study of manga that features sex as a major plot line (including rape, sexual violence, fetishes, male and female homosexuality, and other specific sexual interests) reveals a cornucopia of sexual activities and situations that bear out their statement that 'manga draws on very old cultural and aesthetic principles that unify sex with human life elegantly and enjoyably'.⁴³

The penultimate developmental stage in the thousand-year journey from painted scroll to printed contemporary manga was the publication of the little illustrated books called *kibyōshi*, or 'yellow-cover' booklets. Printing technology permitted the production of small booklets, usually illustrated humour or erotica, which were named after the colour of the ink, paper, or covers. Thus, there were *akahon* (red books), *kurohon* (black books), *aohon* (blue books) and the yellow *kibyōshi*.⁴⁴ These small comic pamphlets, printed in black and white, which became popular in the eighteenth century, are important because of their employment of sequential images and narrative.⁴⁵ These images often formed a narrative arc over a number of issues, thus pointing to the serial potential of the comic form. With regards to the link between contemporary manga and *kibyōshi* Adam L. Kern highlights that 'there are probably many more profound differences between the two than similarities',⁴⁶ adding that, 'contrary to the intimations of the proponents of manga culture, the modern manga was *not* the inevitable culmination of the *kibyōshi*'.⁴⁷ However, Schodt holds the opposite view believing that *kibyōshi* is the predecessor, or more precisely, one of the predecessors of manga. Kern also argues that Western comics exercise an influence on the development of the contemporary manga form. This view suggests that Eastern and Western aesthetics continue to the present day to participate in a

---

Influence on American Culture from Astro Boy to Zen Buddhism (Boston and New York: Mariner Original, 1997), 24.

42. Timon Screech, *Sex and the Floating World: Erotic Images in Japan, 1700–1820* (London: Reaktion Books, 1999).

43. Timothy Perper and Martha Cornog, 'Eroticism for the Masses: Japanese Manga Comics and their Assimilation into the U.S.', *Sexuality & Culture* 6.1 (2002): 8.

44. Natsu Onoda Power, *God of Comics: Osamu Tezuka and the Creation of Post-World War II Manga* (Jackson, MS: University Press of Mississippi, 2009), 24.

45. Wigan, *Sequential Images*, 70.

46. Adam L. Kern, 'Manga versus Kibyōshi', in Jeet Heer and Kent Worcester (eds), *A Comics Studies Reader* (Jackson, MS: University Press of Mississippi, 2009), 240.

47. Kern, 'Manga versus Kibyōshi', 241.

mutual cross-fertilization that was evident in the sixteenth century, and that new, original styles such as Namban art and manga are the result. Frederik Schodt, though, argues more strongly for a direct Japanese lineage of manga from *kibyōshi* and *ukiyo-e*.[48]

It is also necessary to briefly note the influence of Katsushika Hokusai (1760–1849) on modern manga, even if it is only to credit him with the origin of the term.[49] Katsushika Hokusai is one of the greatest of *ukiyo-e* printmakers. He developed a distinctive and individual style after being passed over for the headship of the art school of his late master Shunshō Katsukawa in 1792.[50] He is best known for his print series, which include *One Hundred Views of Mount Fuji*, but he is also significant for his publication, in 1812, of a multi-volume collection of everyday studies of people and animals which he called *Mangwa*, a term that meant 'aimless, involuntary...picture'.[51] Hokusai had previously published another lesser-known series in the manga style, this time with the addition of an extended narrative, *Strange Tales of the Crescent Moon*, which was published in twenty-eight volumes from 1807 to 1811, bringing his *oeuvre* even closer to the contemporary manga form.[52] It has also been noted that his celebrated image, *Awabi Fisherwoman and Octopus*, is the first example of the genre later known as 'tentacle *hentai*', in which human women are depicted being sexually penetrated by the tentacles of giant squids.

The artistic influences antecedent to manga and anime that have been discussed to date all derive from static visual forms. Another source of influence on modern Japanese popular cultural forms is the theatre and other entertainments that were developed from the Kamakura period onward. For example, Noh (*Nō*) drama was formalized and institutionalized by innovative artists such as Motokiyo Zeami (1363–1443) in the fourteenth and fifteenth centuries, developing what was essentially a folk art to rarefied aesthetic heights. This theatrical form is best known for its wooden masks, solemn chanting, precise choreography, bare stage design and heroic plots, which often feature supernatural motifs. Noh actors were trained using Buddhist disciplinary techniques, connecting the drama particularly to Zen. However, Noh storylines are

---

48. Ito, 'A History of Manga', 459.
49. Schodt, *Manga! Manga!*, 35. See also Michael Hill, *A Study of Contemporary Australian Alternative Comics 1992–2000 with Particular Reference to the Work of Naylor, Smith, Danko and Ord*, unpublished PhD thesis (Sydney: Macquarie University, 2003), 89.
50. Yang, Gan and Hong, *Eastern Standard Time*, 24.
51. Anon, 'Anime'; 'Manga', 'Hokusai'. See also Mary Grigsby, '*Sailormoon*: Manga (*Comics*) and Anime (*Cartoon*) Superheroine Meets Barbie: Global Entertainment Commodity Comes to the United States', *Journal of Popular Culture* 32.1 (1998): 64.
52. Yang, Gan and Hong, *Eastern Standard Time*, 25.

fundamentally Shintō tales, which often deal with *kami*, transformations between animals and humans, interactions with ghosts and other supernatural beings, and so on.⁵³ It is also important to note that Noh theatres were constructed on the same principles as Shintō shrines and were often located within shrine compounds, and that Noh music was associated with Japanese ritual dances.⁵⁴ This association of Shintō with entertainment forms is also found in *sumō* wrestling, which emerged in the Tokugawa period as a fusion of aristocratic and folk wrestling modes, a contest between two wrestlers conducted in a ring (*dohyō*) demarcated by a *shimenawa* (ritual rope).⁵⁵ The high-ranking wrestlers wear a *mawashi* (loin-cloth) made of silk, where those of the lower ranks wear cotton, and the great champions (*yokozuna*) wear ritual ropes around their waists. Ann Fischer notes that these ropes are of the same 'design made by priests and used to shake over people or objects in purification rituals' and that *sumō* wrestlers are in many ways treated as if they are Shintō priests.⁵⁶ These examples illustrate the absence of a clear-cut division between the sacred and profane in Japan, and the mutual imbrication of Shintō (and to a lesser extent Buddhism) with popular culture, two themes that are expanded upon in Chapter 2.

Once Japan resumed trading with foreign nations in the second half of the nineteenth century, in the wake of Commodore Matthew C. Perry's 1853 mission opening Japan to the West and the rapid industrialization under the Meiji government (1868-1912), other significant developments that led to the emergence of modern manga took place. This included publication of the *Japan Punch* humour magazine in 1862, in imitation of the English satirical journal *Punch*;⁵⁷ *Punch* was established in 1841 by journalist Henry Mayhew and illustrator Ebenezer Landells.⁵⁸ *Japan Punch* was established by the British cartoonist Charles Wirgman (1835-1891) and ran for twenty-five years.⁵⁹ The profound changes that were occurring in Japan at this time were chronicled by Hokusai's great successor, the printmaker Hiroshige Utagawa (1797-1858), in his final masterpiece *One Hundred Famous Views of Edo*, which appeared between 1856 and 1859.

---

53. Thomas P. Kasulis, *Shinto: The Way Home* (Honololu: University of Hawai'i Press, 2004), 46.
54. Kasulis, *Shinto*, 47.
55. Carole M. Cusack, 'Sport', in Richard D. Hecht and Vincent F. Biondo III (eds), *Religion and Everyday Life and Culture* (Westport, CT: Praeger, 2010), 933.
56. Ann Fischer, 'Flexibility in an Expressive Institution: Sumō', *Southwestern Journal of Anthropology* 22.1 (1966): 32.
57. Roger Sabin, *Adult Comics: An Introduction* (London: Routledge, 1993), 200.
58. Paul Martin Lester, *Visual Communication: Images with Messages*, 4th edn (Belmont, CA: Thomson Wadsworth, 2006), 209.
59. Power, *God of Comics*, 25.

This series of prints is described as the depiction of 'an age that was about to disappear, overshadowed by a new age of social change and unstoppable Westernization – a final farewell to a world sinking beneath the waves of progress'.[60] The satirical magazine format caught on in Japan, and the original *Japan Punch* was followed by the *Kiyochika Punch* in 1881, and the *Tokyo Puck* in 1905. Kinko Ito claims that 'the term *ponchi* (stemming from the English word "punch") began to refer to what we call manga today. Words such as *Tobae*, *Otsue*, and *Kyoga* ("crazy pictures"), all of which referred to caricature and witty pictures, were [gradually] replaced by the term manga'.[61] In addition to the work seen in these graphic humour magazines, some newspapers, such as *Jiji Shinpō*, began to include comic strips, especially in the Sunday editions in 1902.[62]

After the Meiji Restoration Japan rapidly modernized and industrialized along Western lines, with the loss of privilege experienced by the *samurai* class being compensated for by its enthusiastic participation in business, which is still evidenced by the number of corporations named after *samurai* families (Honda, Watanabe, and so on). In the 1920s and 1930s a problematic trend in governmental policy became apparent, in which 'artists and editors who harboured subversive and "dangerous" ideas were intimidated, and many were imprisoned', and from 1938 Japanese militarism escalated to intense levels.[63] The production of newspapers featuring manga supplements was interrupted during World War II, and many manga artists either retreated to the countryside to avoid the depredations of war, though others 'died in air raids and from war-related wounds and diseases'.[64] The production of newspapers featuring manga resumed shortly afterwards, amidst the publication of many post-war manga. Ito credits the introduction of American comic and cartoon characters, including Popeye, Mickey Mouse and Donald Duck, with triggering 'the second manga boom after World War II'.[65] This period is also significant for the early work of Osamu Tezuka, including *New Treasure Island* (1947), *Metropolis* (1949) and *Janguru Taitei* (*Jungle Emperor* or *Kimba the White Lion*) in 1950.[66]

This section has demonstrated that there were Buddhist (*Chōjū Giga*, *zenga*) and secular, or at least non-Buddhist, sources (*ōtsu-e*, *ukiyo-e*,

---

60. Yang, Gan and Hong, *Eastern Standard Time*, 25.
61. Ito, 'A History of *Manga*', 461.
62. Sabin, *Adult Comics*, 200-201.
63. Ito, 'A History of *Manga*', 464.
64. Ito, 'A History of *Manga*', 465.
65. Ito, 'A History of *Manga*', 466.
66. Helen McCarthy, *The Art of Osamu Tezuka: God of Manga* (New York: Abrams ComicArts, 2009).

shunga, *kibyōshi*) that influenced the development of manga in its narrative and pictorial forms. It could be argued that the relatively greater importance of the secular antecedents coincided with the national attitude towards Buddhism, in that from the Meiji Restoration in 1868 the Japanese government sought to diminish the importance of Buddhism and to promote Shintō as the 'indigenous religion' of Japan, as opposed to Buddhism, a religion imported into Japan from India by way of China from the sixth century CE onwards.[67] While the official attitude towards Buddhism continued to be hostile until 1912, Buddhist sects managed to survive on the basis of a claim to the authorities that Buddhism had the potential of making the public 'better citizens of the Imperial nation'.[68] The influential Buddhist scholar Enryō Inoue (1858–1919) reformulated Buddhism as a 'philosophy' and stressed its compatibility with modernity and science.[69] He was a monk, but laicized to reinforce his argument that modern Buddhism was more than a 'religion', and in response to the foundation of universities in Japan by Western Christians, he founded what would later become Tokyo University. Inoue's 'modern Buddhism' struck a chord among the Japanese, as it synergized with a prevailing antipathy towards the Protestant missions aiming to convert the Japanese to Christianity after Japan was forced to abandon its isolationist policy. This aggressive policy of Western Christian missions may be viewed largely as a failure, in that the population of Japan in the first quarter of the twenty-first century is approximately 127.3 million and Christians constitute between 0.5 and 1 per cent of the population, and Christianity is compromised as a religious choice for Japanese people as it is perceived as a 'foreign religion'.[70] As will be seen below, the nineteenth century was also crucial for the development of new religions (*shin shūkyō*) in Japan (as it was similarly in the West).

Japanese Modernity and the Emergence of Manga in the Twentieth Century

At the beginning of the twenty-first century manga is having an almost colonial effect in the most discerning international comics markets, including France, Taiwan, South Korea and North America. Manga (and

---

67. Kuroda, 'Shinto in the History of Japanese Religions', 1-3.
68. James Ketelaar paraphrased in, Patricia J. Graham, 'A Heterodox Painting of "Shussan Shaka" in Late Tokugawa Japan: Part II', *Artibus Asiae* 52.1-2 (1992): 134.
69. Judith Snodgrass, *Presenting Japanese Buddhism to the West: Orientalism, Occidentalism, and the Columbian Exposition* (Chapel Hill, NC: University of North Carolina Press, 2003), 137.
70. Harry Thomsen, *The New Religions of Japan* (Rutland, VT: Tuttle, 1963), 18.

its animated form, anime) is now a multi-million-dollar industry, and marketing changes reflect this.[71] In Japan, the Western-derived term *komikkusu* has become popular in an attempt to emulate the perceived success of the Western model. This has resulted in 'manga' coming to mean the comic-strip artistic form, but not a comic book. In addition, *dōjinshi* (a form largely produced by amateurs and fans), represents the cutting-edge form of manga in its home country.[72] It is even possible that the term 'manga' now has more of a foothold outside of Japan, especially in North America and Western Europe, as the export of manga becomes not only increasingly profitable and critically successful but also motivates non-Japanese creators to create works in the manga style and format, resulting in a situation where manga is being produced outside of Japan and comics within.[73]

Thus, ironically, just as the outside world became familiar with the term and the form 'manga', the Japanese started to refer to manga as a 'comic'. In the West non-Japanese creators are making what they call 'manga' and refer to themselves as *mangaka*, the Japanese term for manga artists. The popularity of manga and anime in North America, Australia, Asia, Europe and South America is due to the interest of consumers, rather than because the industry itself attempted to popularize these forms.[74] Manga has become an international phenomenon. Translated into English and initially rearranged into publications with a left-side spine (that has now been replaced with the traditional right-side spine and with printing from rear to front and reading from right to left) manga has established a niche in local Western comics markets.[75] Global manga now incorporates manga that is created outside of Japan by non-Japanese illustrators. There is even an official Japanese Government competition and prize for the best manga created by a non-Japanese person that was implemented by the former Japanese Prime Minister Tarō Asō at the time he was Foreign Minister.[76]

---

71. Morgan, 'Superheroes for a Complex World', 9.
72. Mizuko Ito, 'Japanese Media Mixes and Amateur Cultural Exchange', in David Buckingham and Rebekah Willett (eds), *Digital Generations: Children, Young People, and New Media* (Mahwah, NJ: Lawrence Erlbaum Associates, 2006), 58-61.
73. Duncan and Smith, *The Power of Comics*, 291-314.
74. Antonia Levi, 'New Myths for the Millennium: Japanese Animation', in John A. Lent (ed.) *Animation in Asia and the Pacific* (Eastleigh, UK: John Libbey, 2001); Natsume Fusanosuke, 'Japanese Manga Encounter the World', *Japan Echo* 29.3 (2002).
75. Kaoru Misaka, 'The First Japanese Manga Magazine in the United States', *Publishing Research Quarterly* 19.4 (2004).
76. Yoshida, '"Manga" Fans have been Won Over'.

In addition to the current professional manga market in Japan there is a substantial field of mostly amateur-produced manga known as *dōjinshi*, mentioned above. The growing popular status of the comic-market conventions during the past three decades has had a significant impact on the increase in the making of *dōjinshi* manga.[77] This phenomenon is a direct parallel to the audience participation that is blurring the boundaries in Western forms of popular culture, and which involves such fandom-driven phenomena as slash fiction and amateur films that complement the official *Star Wars* trilogies.[78] Manga produced by fans is increasingly sophisticated and professional, which consequently reduces the distinction between works that are produced by professional artists and those which are not, weakening the demarcation between producers and consumers.[79] Due to the increasing popularity of the manga homages they create, *otaku* ('nerds') are transforming into professional manga artists, selling their work through manga shops and becoming partially professionalized in their activities. Conversely, in order to gain the attention of *otaku*, the professional manga artists are willing to parody their original work. In addition, scouts from the larger publishers scan the comic markets for creative talent, thus creating a potential pathway for some amateurs into the industry. In the majority of cases the fans make their *dōjinshi* for love alone, but Craig Norris draws attention to the '"unspoken, implicit agreement" (*anmoku no ryōkai*) between *dōjinshi* and publishers allowing fans to produce parody-manga based on copyrighted content and characters as this maintains and revives interest and sales in existing titles and sustains a talent pools of manga artists.'[80]

This global industry came into existence because in the mid-twentieth century manga blossomed as Japan developed as an industrial nation and economic power, despite defeat in World War II and the devastating atomic bomb attacks on Hiroshima and Nagasaki. Led by significant innovators such as Osamu Tezuka, who ultimately was accorded the honorific title of *manga no kamisama* ('god of comics'), the *mangaka* pushed

---

77. Tanja Darlington, 'The Queering of Haruhi Fujioka: Cross-Dressing, Camp and Commoner Culture in *Ouran High School Host Club*', *ImageText: Interdisciplinary Comics Studies*, 4.3 (2009), at http://www.english.ufl.edu/imagetext/archives/v4_3/darlington/?print (accessed 2 October 2009).

78. Adam Possamai, 'Yoda Goes to the Vatican: Youth Spirituality and Popular Culture', *Charles Strong Lecture* (Charles Strong Trust, 2007), at http://users.esc.net.au/~nhabel/lectures/Yoda_Goes_to_the_Vatican.pdf (accessed 20 October 2010).

79. Yoko Ono, 'Nostalgia and Futurism in Contemporary Japanese Sci-Fi Animation', *Asiascape.net Occasional Paper Series* 3 (2008): 3.

80. Craig Norris, 'Manga, Anime and Visual Art Culture', in Yoshio Sugimoto (ed.), *The Cambridge Companion to Modern Japanese Culture* (Melbourne: Cambridge University Press, 2009), 254-55.

the possibilities of the range of content and diversity of graphic styles to the limit. Apart from the enormous output of Tezuka, estimated to be in excess of 150,000 pages, not to mention his parallel output in anime,[81] the work of other significant artists has begun to attract notice and critical acclaim outside of Japan. For example, Yoshihiro Tatsumi (b. 1935), a contemporary of Tezuka who is still active today, completed an autobiographical manga of sorts in 2009 titled *A Drifting Life*.[82] This is an eight-hundred-plus-page volume that documents his role (and that of certain others) in the development of the post-World War II manga movement, including meetings with and consequent mentoring from Tezuka.[83] Tatsumi has been acclaimed as a manga pioneer, particularly of the *gekiga* genre of adult-oriented and alternative work.[84] Over time, manga's readership expanded, including not only adults but also small children and teenagers, with specific age and gender-appropriate genres.[85] By the end of the twentieth century manga was being successfully exported to foreign countries and being fêted by critics and scholars as an art form that was providing Japan with cultural and economic power as well as inspiring comics creators and their readers outside of Japan.

Just as manga is an important element of contemporary Japanese pop culture,[86] Osaka is the most important city for the emergence of manga. It was in Osaka that comic drawings (*giga*) first developed as a genre. Secondly, the oldest continuously published manga magazine *Osaka Puck* (*Ōsaka pakku*) originates in that city, rendering it significant for the popularization of manga within Japan. Thirdly, artists such as Osamu Tezuka and Yoshihiro Tatsumi, amongst others, were born in the Osaka area.[87] Tezuka and Tatsumi are two of the most significant postwar creators of manga and both were pioneers of specific genres; Tezuka with girls' manga (*shōjo*) and Tatsumi with *gekiga*, a darker and more adult genre. The seminal work of manga master Osamu Tezuka will be examined later in this section as a case study in the development of the classic manga style (and also his instantly recognizable anime style).

---

81. Hill, *A Study of Contemporary Australian Alternative Comics 1992-2000*, 91.
82. The discerning reader will note the conceptual resemblance between 'a drifting life' and 'the floating world' of *ukiyo-e*.
83. Yoshihiro Tatsumi, *A Drifting Life* (Montreal: Drawn & Quarterly, 2009).
84. Yoshihiro Tatsumi, *Good-Bye* (Montreal: Drawn & Quarterly, 2008), 5-7.
85. Masami Toku, 'What is Manga?: The Influence of Pop Culture in Adolescent Art', *Art Education* 54.2 (2001): 13.
86. Noriko T. Reider, 'Transformation of the Oni: From the Frightening and Diabolical to the Cute and Sexy', *Asian Folklore Studies* 62.1 (2003): 149.
87. Isao Shimizu quoted in, Richard Torrance, 'Literacy and Literature in Osaka, 1890–1940', *Journal of Japanese Studies* 31.1 (2005): 57-58.

After Commodore Perry arrived with a fleet of warships to persuade Japan's ports to open for trade, Japan's policy of isolationism ended through the Convention of Kanagawa in 1854. The Meiji Restoration of 1867–1868 resulted in the end of the Tokugawa Shogunate, the assumption of power by Emperor Meiji, rapid modernization and the promulgation of the Meiji Constitution in 1889. Through trade, Western goods and habits were adopted: meat and dairy foods entered the Japanese diet, wealthy people wore Western clothes, and works of Western literature, philosophy and science were translated. Natsu Onoda Power notes that this rapid Western influence 'caused much panic and confusion among the Japanese...images of the Japanese trying to adjust to the changes in culture and society...circulated in a number of popular prints, called *awatee*, literally "panic pictures"'.[88] European and American journalists came to Japan, and American comics were translated into Japanese. Comic strips were a new form in late nineteenth-century America; in 1893 James Swinnerton's *Little Bears* appeared in the *San Francisco Examiner* and in 1895 Richard Felton Outcoult's *The Yellow Kid* appeared in *The World*.[89] Similarly in 1895 the man considered the first professional *manga shi* (manga artisan), Rakuten Kitazawa (1876–1955), had joined the staff of the English-language magazine *Box of Curios* and was learning to draw cartoons under the tutelage of Australian Frank Arthur Nankivell (1869–1959). At the same time, modern media were also profoundly changed: newspapers and radio took on the lineaments of their twentieth-century forms; and film or 'moving pictures', the ancestor of television, was developed by Louis and Auguste Lumière in 1895.[90] The first cinematograph came to Japan in 1897, the first Japanese film was shot in Tokyo in 1898, and the first permanent cinema opened in 1903. In the 1920s Japan was the most prolific film-making nation in the world.[91] Japanese comic artists rapidly absorbed filmic influences into their work. Ippei Okamoto (1886–1948), who was a great influence on Tezuka, used techniques from literature and film in his work, such as *Onna Hyakumensō* (*One Hundred Faces of a Woman*), published in 1917.[92]

At the same time, as Western entertainment technologies and styles were making inroads into Japan, Japan was entering the Western imagination as a source of sophisticated aesthetics, exotic Eastern religions,

---

88. Power, *God of Comics*, 24.
89. Shunsuke Tsurumi, *A Cultural History of Postwar Japan* (London: Kegan Paul, 1990), 28.
90. Erik Barnouw, *Documentary: A History of the Non-Fiction Film*, 2nd edn (Oxford: Oxford University Press, 1993), 7.
91. Power, *God of Comics*, 49.
92. Power, *God of Comics*, 26.

and exemplary industrialization and modernization that nevertheless preserved elements of traditional culture in a distinctively Japanese version of modernity. The religious consequences of the Meiji Restoration were important; in the later Tokugawa period Buddhism had been under threat in Japan, as nativist scholars such as Norinaga Motoöri (1730–1801) and Atsutane Hirata (1776–1843) promoted Shintō as the indigenous religion of Japan. After the Meiji Restoration Buddhism was disestablished and from 1870 to 1844 the state-sponsored Great Promulgation Campaign (*taikyō senpu undo*) was rolled out, in which Shintō shrines were nationalized and people were required to register with their local shrine. 'State Shintō' resulted in the walling off of Shintō precincts located inside former Buddhist complexes, and the purging of all texts, groups and practices that were deemed inauthentic. This move was partially intended to combat conversion to Christianity (as Protestant missionaries had arrived in Japan after 1854), but also to weaken Buddhism, while incidentally curbing the growth of new religions (*shin shūkyō*), which had been flourishing since the early nineteenth century. A limited number of these new religions managed to gain the classification 'Sect Shintō' under this registration system, despite their divergence from traditional Shintō. This repositioning of Shintō made criticism of the religion identical to criticism of *kokutai* (the essence of the Japanese state), and resulted in hyper-nationalistic developments such as the founding of the Yasukuni Shrine, a shrine to the *kami* of the war dead located in Chiyoda in the Tokyo region. This shrine was founded by Emperor Meiji to commemorate those who sacrificed their lives to bring about the Meiji Restoration. This commemoration was later extended to include those who died in foreign wars; this was a new concept, as prior to the nineteenth century Japan had not participated in foreign wars.[93]

In the early decades of the twentieth century there were developments that directly impacted on the work of Osamu Tezuka. In 1919 the *Asahi Graph* newspaper sent journalist Bunshirō Suzuki (1890–1951) to cover the Peace Conference in Versailles by way of the United States, and he brought back many examples of comic strips. He serialized *Bringing up Father* by George McManus in the *Asahi Graph*, and was responsible for the first Japanese comic strip, *Shōchan and the Squirrel*. In 1925, a Shōchan hat was released for children, and the Osaka headquarters of the *Asahi Graph* held a party for all the Shōchans (a very common name) in the area. Tsurumi argues that 'this episode shows that mass society was already in existence in January 1925, when the party was held. The mass communication media were already well enough developed to spread news

---

93. Kasulis, *Shinto*, 143-44.

instantly to a wide range of people with the income to buy newspapers and comics and Shōchan caps, the aim of the enterprise'.[94] Aggressive marketing, it seems, followed hard upon the comic-strip form.

The adoption of a Western appearance for characters in Japanese comics was one result of developments in the first half of the twentieth century, including the Allied victory in World War II. In the 1920s, when *Bringing up Father* was being serialized, the ideal of beauty became the 'Ziegfeld Follies' showgirl type, embodied by the character of the daughter Nora in the comic strip. Mary Grigsby has noted that before Japanese artists had widespread exposure to either Western people or Western art and popular cultural forms, they depicted Japanese people who looked Asian. This is indisputable, as even a cursory glance at *ukiyo-e* prints will confirm. Many recent examples of manga and anime retain the habit of depicting Japanese people with Western features although some artists have depicted characters with Asian features since the 1970s. The popular manga and anime heroine Sailor Moon, and her four companions, Sailors Mercury, Venus, Mars, and Jupiter, are identical apart from their hair colour, and are Western in appearance, with 'round eyes, blond, red or brown hair, long legs and thin bodies'.[95] The manga and anime characters of Osamu Tezuka were heavily influenced by Walt Disney characters. Tezuka's father often took him to the cinema to see Disney and Max Fleischer animations such as *Bambi* (1942) and *Betty Boop* (which first appeared in 1932), and the cute attributes of the Disney animal characters in particular were not lost on the young Tezuka in the development of his own manga stars. Significantly, these characters all featured child-like faces with very large eyes, which became key motifs in the manga style.[96] Grigsby notes that 'as the windows of the soul, the eyes are one of the first places the emotions are manifested'[97] and Schodt has commented on the habit of artists drawing 'a star next to the pupil [of female characters] that perhaps represents dreams, yearning and romance'.[98] Sapphire, the heroine of *Ribon no Kishi* ('Princess Knight'), Tezuka's pioneering *shōjo* manga, serialized from 1954, exhibits these Western and romantic physical characteristics.

Osamu Tezuka (1928–1989) was born on 3 November in Toyonaka, Osaka Prefecture, which was then under-developed and rural, and famed for its hot springs and bathhouses, which caused him to 'develop a strong

---

94. Tsurumi, *A Cultural History of Postwar Japan*, 30.
95. Grigsby, 'Sailormoon', 69.
96. Christopher Hart, *Manga Mania: How to Draw Japanese Comics* (New York: Watson-Guptil Publications, 2001).
97. Grigsby, 'Sailormoon', 69.
98. Schodt, *Manga! Manga!*, 91.

sense of the relationship humans have with nature'.[99] His family was middle-class, well-educated and affluent, and he grew up surrounded by both Western and Japanese cultural forms. His mother was a regular attendee of performances at the famous all-woman Takarazuka Theatre (discussed in Chapter 2) and his father enjoyed manga, elegant clothes, photography and film.[100] The Tezuka family was linked with Zen Buddhism, but Osamu himself held flexible and agnostic religious views. As a child he was fascinated by the life-cycle of insects, and in his mid-teens he copied an encyclopedia on the subject. Another significant preoccupation of Tezuka's developed logically from his interest in nature; the fact that advances in technology may be beneficial, but nevertheless bring humans closer to the danger of destroying both nature and culture. Tezuka was a teenager during World War II and experienced 'military training, volunteer work and air-raids' as well as witnessing the bombing of Osaka in 1945, an experience he would later draw upon in his manga creations. Tezuka had always drawn cartoons, and in 1947 he became a manga artist while studying for a medical degree. After being defeated in World War II, Japan suffered economically and inexpensive popular entertainments were in high demand. The 'paper theatres' of *kamishibai* operators (discussed below) enjoyed a surge in consumer choice, and the format of published comics changed, as the 'hardback style comics printed by the large publishing houses in Tokyo were too expensive'.[101] In Osaka cheap red-covered comics were printed by new companies, in rented premises in the toy sellers' district, and these magazines were sold by street vendors. Manga artists were in general poorly paid, but had considerable freedom with regard to the subjects they depicted.

Tezuka's manga were often politically subversive and featured strong anti-war themes. Along with his younger contemporary Yoshiharu Tsuge (b. 1937), who published his first manga in 1955 at eighteen under the influence of Tezuka, he offered an alternative vision from that promulgated by the post-war Occupation Government, with its slavish worship of modernity, science, and technological development. As a condition of the surrender of Japan after World War II, the Allies required Emperor Hirohito to announce on radio on 1 January 1945 that he was not a divine being, which was a great blow to the Shintō orthodoxy of the time and profoundly affected Japanese identity, both individual and

---

99. Jane Somerville, 'Japanese *Manga*: Not Just Funny Pictures for Children', *Look: Art Gallery Society of New South Wales* (February 2007), 38.

100. Frederik L. Schodt, *The Astro Boy Essays: Osamu Tezuka, Mighty Atom, and the Manga/Anime Revolution* (Berkeley, CA: Stone Bridge Press, 2007), 24.

101. Somerville, 'Japanese *Manga*', 38.

collective.[102] The Allies then occupied Japan until 1952, and Tsuge in particular expressed opposition to this in his manga, which won him an enduring youth following throughout the 1960s and 1970s, as he was perceived to be a counter-cultural figure.[103]

Tezuka's career began with boys' adventure stories such as *New Treasure Island* (1948). Later he created manga for girls that inaugurated the genre known as *shōjo* with *Ribon no Kishi*; designed cute, appealing characters such as *Jungle Emperor* (*Kimba the White Lion*) and *Tetsuwan Atomu* (*Astro Boy*), discussed below; and adapted such challenging literary classics as Fyodor Dostoyevsky's *Crime and Punishment* (1953) and Johann Wolfgang von Goethe's *Faust* into the manga format. Late in his life, during the 1970s and 1980s, he produced fictionalized historical tales about famous people, including Nazi dictator Adolf Hitler and spiritual *savant* Siddhartha Gautama, the Buddha; and created several dark-themed manga for adults in the *gekiga* genre, including *1001 Nights*, which contains a depiction of human–crocodile sex, recalling Hokusai's famous image of the fisherwoman and octopus coupling.[104] The wide-ranging creativity of *mangaka* has also led to the introduction of subgenres and generic hybridity. The range of genres visible in anime (many of them derived from manga) is dealt with in Chapter 3.

Tezuka's breakthrough came in 1951, with *Atomu Taishi* (*Ambassador Atom*), the first appearance of the character later known as Astro Boy, who featured in a manga that ran from 1952 to 1968. Interestingly, in 1950 Tezuka had floated the idea of creating a manga of Japanese mythology from the *Kojiki* and *Nihon Shoki*, but when he was told that this had little commercial appeal, he turned his attention to the science fiction and fantasy genres, because America was engaged in nuclear testing and the post-war mood was influenced by the Cold War arms and space races, though in fact Tezuka himself abhorred violence and feared nuclear weapons.[105] This is of particular interest because science fiction is the twentieth-century literary form that most resembles mythological and theological discourse, in that it posits other worlds, interrogates the notion of human personhood, and proposes either a perfected future or an eschatological conflict (or in some cases, both). *Ambassador Atom* is significantly different to later stories featuring Astro Boy. Inuhiko Yomota argues that this is because it was conceived of as a stand-alone piece and it fails to resolve the conflict between two groups of near-identical

---

102. Kasulis, *Shinto*, 140.
103. Tsurumi, *A Cultural History of Postwar Japan*, 41.
104. Teddy Jamieson, 'Orient Excess', *Sunday Herald* (8 November 2009), 15.
105. Schodt, *Astro Boy Essays*, 19.

people, those who reside on Earth and their *doppelganger* aliens who invade. He argues that:

> *Ambassador Atom* concludes by expelling the extraterrestrials from Earth rather than enacting a well-crafted peace treaty, and this should be understood as a symptom of Tezuka's failure to truly envision a peaceful co-existence between the two humanities according to Atom's ideals. It may not be a simple coincidence that the San Francisco Peace Treaty was signed around the time of the publication of *Ambassador Atom*.[106]

This perceptive comment draws attention to the fact that Tezuka and his fellow *mangaka* were struggling in their comics with Japan's defeat in the war, the post-war technological threat, the increased and colonialist influence of the West in Japan, and the great questions of life and death, what it means to be human, and how to act morally and ethically in a world in which atom bombs had been dropped on Hiroshima and Nagasaki. Popular cultural forms became a way for Japanese people to rebuild their identity and find shared concerns that did not echo the tainted and troubled militarism, nationalism and fierce Shintō emperor-worship of the period leading up to World War II. This also was a time of social changes; pre-war Japanese cartoonists were almost all men, and post-1945 there was only one notable woman, Machiko Hasegawa (1920–1992), a situation that was not to change until the 1970s. With regard to the rise of native Japanese popular cultural forms, Tsurumi argues that national feeling had to be channelled away from 'the national flag, the Imperial Edicts, and compulsory military training' and that in the 'post-Occupation period, especially after Japan had entered its period of swift economic growth, the television broadcasting of a song contest by NHK Television at the close of the year seems to have become a major national symbol'.[107] So, it could be argued, was manga.

In addition to being academically and artistically gifted, Tezuka was also a talented musician, playing both the piano and the accordion, and with a considerable knowledge of classical music. He graduated from his medical studies in 1952, the year his *Tetsuwan Atomu* manga debuted. In that same year he moved to Tokyo and began working for large-circulation children's magazines. He lived in a 'rundown apartment building... called Tokiwasō, [which] became a magnet for young artists who idolized Tezuka'.[108] In *Tetsuwan Atomu*, the character of Astro Boy resembles Ambassador Atom in that he is created as a robot double of Dr Tenma's dead son, and is abandoned by Dr Tenma when his mechanical body fails

---

106. Inuhiko Yomota, 'Stigmata in Tezuka Osamu's Works', *Mechademia* 3 (2008): 103.

107. Tsurumi, *A Cultural History of Postwar Japan*, 64.

108. Schodt, *Dreamland Japan*, 236.

to grow, and his inadequacy as a substitute child is exposed. But his character has been developed considerably, and Tezuka envisaged his as a schoolboy (aged somewhere around ten to twelve) who fights for justice and peace, which made him an ideal companion with which real Japanese school children could explore ideas about the future.[109] The manga was serialized in *Shōnen* from April 1952, contemporaneous with the end of the American occupation of Japan. In 1952 Tezuka set *Tetsuwan Atomu* fifty years into the future. Astro Boy has jets in his arms and legs which make him able to fly, he can speak sixty languages, hear and see with far greater capability than ordinary humans, and his brain is a computer while his atomic reactor is located in his chest, where his heart would have been were he human. Astro Boy's quest for personhood as a thinking, feeling machine meant that Tezuka's 'stories did not always have happy endings and...incorporated emotions such as sadness, grief, anger and hate'.[110] Further, the manga explicitly treated themes of discrimination, which reflected Tezuka's experiences of the American occupation, but this was extended to include discrimination by humans against robots, against humans by robots, and all kinds of racism.[111] The manga of *Tetsuwan Atomu* posited that robots in the twenty-first century had been created as slaves and began to develop emotions and to demand to be treated as persons, rebelling against the Laws of Robotics that segregated them from humans. The benevolent Dr Elefun, who rescued Astro Boy, restored his dignity and created a family for him.[112] This is a prescient anticipation of the themes of Ridley Scott's *Blade Runner* (1982), but directed at children rather than adults. This film is an adaptation of Philip K. Dick's celebrated science-fiction novel *Do Androids Dream of Electric Sheep?* (1968) in which replicants (genetically engineered adult humans) fight for the right to live longer than their allocated four years, and to be free rather than enslaved.

Tezuka's art style in *Astro Boy* owed a great deal to Max Fleischer (1883–1972) and Walt Disney. His love of Disney had led him to illustrate Japanese versions of *Bambi* and *Pinocchio*, and the biographical *The Story of Walt Disney*. Frederik Schodt notes that Astro Boy looks similar to the American toy, the Kewpie doll (generally understood to be female), and also mentions that Tezuka admitted the influence of Paul Terry's Mighty Mouse, which first appeared in 1942. Both Mighty Mouse and Astro Boy fly with one fisted arm extended in front. What is particularly

---

109. Schodt, *Astro Boy Essays*, 33.
110. Somerville, 'Japanese *Manga*', 39.
111. Schodt, *Astro Boy Essays*, 121-25.
112. Helen McCarthy, *500 Manga Heroes and Villains* (London: Collins and Brown, 2006), 22-23.

interesting in view of the transition between manga and anime discussed in the next section is that even when working in the 'static' form of manga, Tezuka explicitly used filmic techniques to create particularly effective manga. He has stated:

> I felt that existing comics were limiting. Most were drawn as if seated in an audience viewing from a stage… This made it impossible to create dramatic or psychological effects, so I began to use cinematic techniques… I experimented with close-ups and different angles and instead of using only one frame for an action scene or the climax (as was customary), I made a point of depicting a movement or a facial expression with many frames, even many pages. The result was a super-long comic that ran to 500, 600, even 1,000 pages.[113]

Tezuka also used other film-production techniques in his manga. Natsu Onoda Power draws attention to his 'star system' (where recurring characters appear in multiple manga, like the popular actors and actresses of Hollywood), and the way he often placed himself as a character in the comics (like Alfred Hitchcock's cameo appearances in his films).[114]

Though at first the Disney-influenced style of *Tetsuwan Atomu* was regarded as too Western, it actually became enormously popular, and has in fact become the default style for all those manga artists who acknowledge Tezuka's influence.[115] It is also worth noting that the influence of the Takarazuka Theatre can also be felt in *Tetsuwan Atomu*; Tezuka has said that he intended Astro Boy to be a beautiful female robot, but made him male as the manga was to be published in a boys' magazine. Astro Boy is definitely androgynous in appearance, and in fact he resembles Sapphire from *Ribon no Kishi* as well as the Kewpie doll.[116]

Tezuka's portrayal of advanced robotics was influenced by the technological ambitions of post-war Japan. Many Japanese had blamed their failure in World War II on inadequate technological development. In the immediate post-war years Japan was poor and Tezuka treated patients with malnutrition when he worked as a medical intern. Anne Allison, in her study of Japanese toys, observes that in the immediate post-war period Japanese robots and space toys made for the export market were often made of recycled tin cans.[117] Toys, manga, anime and film are all examples of what Joseph Nye called 'soft power', the means of extending

---

113. Tezuka, quoted in Jamieson, 'Orient Excess', 13.
114. Power, *God of Comics*, 83-87.
115. Schodt, *Astro Boy Essays*, 49.
116. Schodt, *Dreamland Japan*, 236.
117. Anne Allison, *Millennial Monsters: Japanese Toys and the Global Imagination* (Berkeley, Los Angeles and London: University of California Press, 2006), xv.

the cultural penetration of things Japanese into the West.[118] However, there is a great difference between the emotionally complex and morally informed Astro Boy, whom Tezuka conceived of as a 'type of twenty-first century "reverse Pinocchio," a nearly perfect robot who strove to become more human, and hence more flawed...and also to be an interface between two different cultures – that of man and machine'[119] and the dystopian vision of *Godzilla* (*Gojira*), in Ishirō Honda's 1954 film. Godzilla is conceived of as a monster created by nuclear detonations (recalling the injuries and disfigurements of the Hiroshima and Nagasaki bombings). Bearing a name that combines the Japanese terms for 'whale' and 'gorilla', Godzilla has the appearance of a mutant dinosaur, and in the early films is a threat to Japan.

Nothing could be further from the cosy, domestic world of 1950s American popular culture, of *Leave it to Beaver* (1957), *Lassie* (1954) and the *Patty Duke Show* (1963), than the complex, vitalist worldview of interdependent natural and mechanical beings proposed by artists such as Tezuka and Honda. The worldview was dependent on Shintō, but incorporated a newer common set of values suited to technological modernity, which Robert Kisala describes as seeing the

> world...as an interconnected whole, and activity on one level will affect other levels. Therefore, a transformation on the most immediate level of the inner self will have repercussions within one's family, the surrounding society and eventually on the universe as a whole. Consequently, emphasis is placed on individual self-cultivation, centering on the virtues of thankfulness, sincerity and harmony.[120]

The extreme emphasis on technology found in Japanese culture has fuelled the aesthetic of techno-animism, in which all objects are deemed to be persons and alive, whether natural or manufactured, which is heavily dependent on the *kami*-filled, divinely animated universe of Shintō. Allison calls this 'techno-animism' and argues that in *Astro Boy* the boundaries between organic and mechanical life are haywire; both landscape and body have become subordinated to machines:

> this is mecha animated by Shinto, Japan's religion of animism in which everything is endowed with a spirit and spirituality imbues the whole universe from boulders to ants... [R]oboticization has seeped into the

---

118. Joseph Nye, *Soft Power: The Means to Success in World Politics* (New York: Public Affairs, 2004).
119. Schodt, *Astro Boy Essays*, 107.
120. Kisala, quoted in Stephen Covell, 'Religious Culture', in Yoshio Sugimoto (ed.), *The Cambridge Companion to Modern Japanese Culture* (Melbourne: Cambridge University Press, 2009), 163.

very fabric of life itself here, expressed as a universal principle where the fusing of the natural and mechanic is akin to a spiritual truth.[121]

This distinctively Japanese vision of modernity is summed up in the person of Osamu Tezuka, who studied the religions of the world, but remained primarily a believer in science and the ethical application of reason. He once observed that all religions were man-made, not derived 'from any fundamental principles of the universe… [but] are a product of the constantly renewing culture of the time. And older beliefs will therefore always come into conflict with an ever-changing culture, giving rise to yet another kind of world'.[122] In another interview in 1988, the year before he died, he stated that his manga and anime had certain constant themes; the celebration of life, the rejection of war and nuclear power, the protection of the natural world, and 'to think about what it means to be human'.[123] These ideals are identical to the religious transformation of twentieth-century Japan from a nation of traditional Buddhists and Shintōists to one of people who are primarily non-religious and focused on personal growth and happiness (trends that are also pervasive in the West). Stephen Covell has argued that Japanese new religions and 'new new' religions are urban phenomena, centred on a youthful membership, and individualistic in focus. New religions might focus on group counselling and shared experiences, whereas 'new new' religions focus on individual practice and personal transformation. Some have a positive worldview, whereas others (generally new new religions) have a sense of impending doom, which may be the result of nuclear, biological or environmental disaster.[124] The most notorious case of an apocalyptic new religion in recent years is Aum Shinrikyo (Aum Supreme Truth), led by Shōkō Asahara. Aum launched sarin gas attacks on the Tokyo subway in 1995, killing thirteen commuters and injuring nearly one thousand more.[125] It must be stressed that Aum is an exceptional case, and the majority of new religions in Japan (as in the West, where the exceptional cases include Jim Jones's Peoples Temple and Heaven's Gate, both famous for mass suicides in 1978 and 1997 respectively) are peaceful and concerned with personal spiritual development.

---

121. Allison, *Millennial Monsters*, 63.
122. Tezuka, quoted in Allison, *Millennial Monsters*, 142.
123. Allison, *Millennial Monsters*, 144.
124. Covell, 'Religious Culture', 158.
125. Yumiko Iida, 'Between the Technique of Living an Endless Routine and the Madness of Absolute Degree Zero: Japanese Identity and the Crisis of Modernity in the 1990s', *Positions* 8.2 (2000).

The Transition from Manga to Anime

Estimates of the percentage of manga in all magazine and book publications in Japan are claimed to be between thirty and forty per cent. Helen McCarthy argues that 'manga is a huge part of the Japanese publishing industry. At the turn of the millennium there were around a dozen manga weeklies, ten bi-weeklies, and fifteen major monthlies'.[126] In 2006 she estimated that the number of manga artists in Japan was approximately three thousand. Many of these *mangaka* work alone, writing and drawing, then inking and colouring their work (if this latter stage is required), as normal production remains in the black and white format. A successful creator may be in a position to hire an assistant or two, so that he or she can work faster. There are also specialist manga artists that may be called to draw any particular type of image, such as buildings, cars, food, fashion, electrical cables or signage. Unlike their North American colleagues they are less likely to work in production teams that feature a division of labour between such specialized skills as penciller, inker, letter, colourist, writer and artist. *Dōjinshi*, on the other hand, is an area where collaborative teams are more the normal mode of production.

Reflecting Japan's long history of visual art and its graphic applications the best manga contain artwork of the highest quality. There is a stream of low-level work as well, as would be expected because of the large volume required for publication each week, but the quality creations of *mangaka* such as the *dōjinshi* collective CLAMP (which comprises four women, Nanase Okawa, Apapa Mokona, 'Mick' Nekoi and Satsuki Igarashi), Hideshi Hino, Riyoko Ikeda, Shigeri Mizuki, Junko Mizuno, Katsuhiro Ōtomo, Masamune Shirow, Rumiko Takahashi, Jirō Taniguchi, Yoshihiro Tatsumi, Osamu Tezuka and Kazuo Umezu to name just a dozen, reach towards the pinnacle of artistic possibilities in comics production.[127] The strong 'alternative' production stream of manga allows intense and near-unlimited experimentation, and this feeds in to the overall range and quality of the manga published.

Manga is used in Japan today for a variety of purposes, including informational and fictional, practical and entertainment. Even Osamu Tezuka published two sex-education manga in 1970.[128] Adaptation into the manga form results in clearer, more accessible information and increased readership. Russell W. Belk has noted the use of manga in educational contexts, stating that '"manga mania" in Japan has influenced college textbooks to

---

126. McCarthy, *500 Manga Heroes and Villains*, 12, 14.
127. Yang, Gan and Hong, *Eastern Standard Time*, 46–47.
128. Power, *God of Comics*, 105.

adopt the comic format'.[129] In fact, the use of manga as an instructional device is becoming ubiquitous. From images on noodle packets to airline safety sheets for passengers to computer manuals, it is an international language, a language that functions without words. The advertising and marketing industries have adopted this format, and many manga-style characters and graphics have been employed to sell products from cars and ice-cream to shampoo and contraceptives. In the United States, in order to demonstrate to school students between the ages of twelve and fifteen 'the coupled ion-neutral dynamics investigation (Cindi) research mission', NASA requested that the University of Texas design a manga. Its protagonist was Cindi, a female android with two robot dogs who lived with her on a spaceship. This manga is titled *Cindi in Space*.[130]

Because the manga form results in more accessible information and in increased readership, works from the Japanese literary tradition are often adapted as manga. However, manga versions of these do not necessarily follow the original text faithfully, and manga versions of texts have the potential to add a different dimension to the original, to 'digest, embellish, amplify, or rewrite' the story.[131] Transforming a literary work, that is, a written work, into a manga work, that is, a visual work, is a complex process. The range of concerns that manga artists need to address in order to transform literary works into manga include finding the way of visually conveying 'complex emotions and inner musings', also drawing the characters in a way so that their 'peerless beauty or irresistible charm' is conveyed.[132] Furthermore, manga artists are also faced with the challenge of creating interiors as well as the exteriors in the story – elements that are 'not clearly delineated' in its literary original. Manga artists also need to decide which approach to take to the story – 'parody, romance, or whatever' – and the character whose viewpoint will invite reader identification.[133] This shows the complexity of working on literary adaptations which manga artists face. The same challenges face those who adapt manga into the anime form.

Thus, it is useful to regard manga as a medium where characters are created and narratives developed at relatively low cost, which offers the opportunity for particular stories to find an audience. Once a manga

---

129. Russell W. Belk, 'Material Values in the Comics: A Content Analysis of Comic Books Featuring Themes of Wealth', *Journal of Consumer Research* 14.1 (1987): 38.

130. Jan Krikke, 'Computer Graphics Advances the Art of Anime', *IEEE Computer Graphics and Applications* 26.3 (2006): 17.

131. Lynne K. Miyake, 'Graphically Speaking: Manga Versions of *The Tale of Genji*', *Monumenta Nipponica* 63.2 (2008): 359.

132. Miyake, 'Graphically Speaking', 359-60.

133. Miyake, 'Graphically Speaking', 359-60.

has established a fan-base those fans put pressure, through their interest and purchasing power, on the publisher to keep the title in print for as many issues as possible, also with improvements in the quality of printing and paper. As manga stories are serialized, the narrative is released in chapters monthly, bimonthly or even weekly.[134] New fans to the title demand reprints of past volumes that are no longer available and library quality editions for collection rather than the cheaper, lower quality editions that are sent for recycling.[135]

From the initial cheap printing there is an improvement in the quality once a reprint in a library edition format is determined. Library editions, whilst still in paperback, are meant for collection and display and usually have a continuous image displayed across the spines, which becomes visible and complete once all volumes have been collected. The spine design for the library edition of *Ranma 1/2*, for example, shows the father character having metamorphosed into his panda form, carrying out a range of martial arts moves. When all of the volumes are stacked, vertically, in order, a clear static but animated sequence of choreography is displayed.[136]

The manga form has featured many memorable characters that have resonated with local and international audiences to a considerable degree, and which are developed to appeal to specific markets. Tamra Orr, when discussing specific genres, lists the following popular types of manga: *kodomo* (*kodomo muke*) manga for small children; *shōnen* manga for teenage boys, 'dealing with action, battle, sports, science fiction, and fantasy'; *shōjo* manga for teenage girls, 'dealing with romance, comedy, and drama'; *seijin* manga which is directed at an adult male readership, 'dealing with business, crime, political drama, history, and military adventures'; *redikomi* manga 'for adult women, dealing with work, family, and romance'; *gekiga* manga, which treats darker, adult-oriented topics; *dōjinshi* manga, which is produced by fans and amateur cartoonists; and *yonkoma* manga, which is 'traditional four-panel comic strips like those found in daily newspapers'.[137]

The main characters in such titles as *Akira*, *Bleach*, *Dragon Ball*, *Fruits Basket*, *Inuyasha*, *Naruto*, *One Piece*, *Ranma 1/2* and *Slam Dunk*, to name but a few, have their appealing attributes and distinctive character traits, which are directed at specific audiences. Wacky, humorous, mischievous,

---

134. Power, *God of Comics*, 103.
135. Paul Gravett, *Manga: Sixty Years of Japanese Comics* (London: Laurence King Publishing, 2004).
136. Bryan D. Fagan and Jody Condit Fagan, *Comic Book Collections for Libraries* (Santa Barbara, CA: ABC-CLIO, 2011).
137. Tamra Orr, *Manga Artists* (New York: Rosen, 2009), 8.

charming, magical, daring and fearless, are just some of the personality traits demonstrated by this collection of characters. Evidence of the appeal of these characters can be found in their fans' cosplay activities (costume role-playing, dressing up as characters), and their purchase of related merchandise such as t-shirts, posters and miniaturized figures and models along with collections of their complete published manga volumes.[138] These manga are therefore eminently suitable for adaptation into anime. However, it has been argued that the transnational market success of anime is facilitated by 'its softened Japanese presence',[139] which is apparent in 'manga and anime's lack of a clearly identifiable "Japaneseness" in terms of national, racial, or ethnic markers'. The term, *mu-kokuseki* (literally, 'the absence of nationality'), is used by Japanese commentators to describe this process of removing Japanese cultural markers from manga, anime, and computer game characters.[140]

There is an extensive range of graphic and illustrative styles employed in manga, and the graphic techniques include everything from traditional brush calligraphy to current digital pen styles. An examination of the visual styles present in manga finds quotations from the entire history of Japanese art.[141] Although there is a dominant cartoon style that is prevalent in mainstream manga production, and instructional texts such as Christopher Hart's *Manga Mania: How To Draw Japanese Comics* (2001) and *Manga Mania Shoujo: How to Draw the Charming and Romantic Characters of Japanese Comics* (2004) perpetuate this style (which certainly lacks overt 'Japaneseness'), there is overall an extremely disparate palette of graphic styles. Whereas the instructional texts teach the basics of the dominant manga style, such as boys' and girls' appearance, clothing, action poses, dynamic moves, fantasy realms and martial arts moves and weapons, Sugano Yoshinori explicitly argues that the manga form does not require precision in terms of the representation. Rather, the most significant issue in the context of manga drawing is succeeding in successfully expressing meaning to the readers.[142] Historically, in manga

---

138. Craig Norris and Jason Bainbridge, 'Selling *Otaku*? Mapping the Relationship between Industry and Fandom in the Australian Cosplay Scene', *Intersections: Gender and Sexuality in Asia and the Pacific* 20 (2009), at http://intersections.anu.edu.au/issue20/norris_bainbridge.htm (accessed 29 December 2011).

139. Norris, 'Manga, Anime and Visual Art Culture', 238.

140. Ross Mouer and Craig Norris, 'Exporting Japan's Culture: From Management Style to Manga', in Yoshio Sugimoto (ed.), *The Cambridge Companion to Modern Japanese Culture* (Melbourne: Cambridge University Press, 2009), 361-62.

141. Amano Masanao (ed.), *Manga Design* (Köln, London, Los Angeles, Madrid, Paris and Tokyo: Taschen, 2004).

142. Sugano Yoshinori, 'Manga and Non-Photorealistic Rendering', *ACM SIGGRAPH Computer Graphics* 33.1 (1999): 66.

alternative anthologies such as *Garo*, individual creators who did not conform to the dominant manga style were encouraged, and published. This is appropriate for content that is both alternative and outsider in approach as well as being varied and graphically intense.

The long-form nature of manga, wherein narratives can be developed over two hundred pages in a single issue or even serialized over twenty issues of two hundred pages each, allows for much play with the narrative form and the use of complex visual sequences. These epic narratives provide ample time and space for the telling of detailed stories or the documentation of deep transformations in a character's psyche as well as digressions into details of minor themes and supporting characters. Manga artists have followed Tezuka in employing cinematic techniques:

> the pen-and-ink 'camera' of the manga artist holds on foreground objects (a glass of water, a landscape) as conversation takes place 'off screen'; it can 'pan' across a background, pull in for 'close-ups', achieve rapid-cut 'montages', and otherwise perform acts heretofore limited to film.[143]

Time can be manipulated to an extraordinary level, whether it is the delayed suspense of two warriors confronting each other in a duel and waiting and watching for the first sign of a move from the opponent where a few seconds is stretched out to a few minutes, or whether it is the compressed time of a long journey by car into just a few panels where the two-hour journey can be read in just three or four seconds. As Jeff Yang, Dina Gan and Terry Hong note, 'manga artists have reinvented sequential art along a new and exciting paradigm [and] comics on both sides of the Pacific have never been better'.[144]

The establishment of particular successful genres in manga may lead to an interest in those genres in anime form. A spate of samurai or sports manga may lead to a surge in samurai and sports-related anime productions. A fascination with fantasy or spirit-world-based manga may generate television productions of the same genre. Recently there have been popular manga, both inside and outside of Japan, dealing with the afterlife and the recently deceased. *Bleach* is the story of a young college student who inherits the powers and ability of a soul warrior whose job it is to release the deceased from the earthly plane. *The Kurosagi Corpse Delivery Service* features college students with spiritual skills who pool their talents in dealing with the dead as an attempt to obtain income while they are enrolled in their course of studies.[145] The popularity of

---

143. Yang, Gan and Hong, *Eastern Standard Time*, 47.
144. Yang, Gan and Hong, *Eastern Standard Time*, 47.
145. Jason Thompson, *Manga: The Complete Guide* (New York: Ballantine Books/Del Rey, 2007).

Bleach resulted in its anime production before the manga had run its course. In fact the anime had to be delayed on one occasion while new manga material was created to provide script content for the animated television series. Currently *Bleach* has exceeded more than one hundred volumes of manga and its English translation is around thirty volumes, while *The Kurosagi Corpse Delivery Service* has reached thirteen volumes.

Generally, successful manga has a good chance of being developed into animation production either for television or the cinema, or direct video release in the form of OAV ('Original Anime Video'). Apart from the success of manga, the very nature of its production that permits graphic experimentation on paper at a much lower cost than the equivalent for anime production allows the medium to trial inventive sequences, characters and narrative outcomes in key moments that can then be extended to full action sequence animation in the transition from manga to anime. Manga is consequently perceived as a potential drawing board and blueprint for anime design and development. That creative ideas, visual experimentation, character development and extended narratives can readily and economically be trialled and tested in the manga format rather than the considerably more expensive and more time-consuming animation production is only one aspect of the manga/anime relationship. Another is the establishment of characters and stories and genres and the testing of their popularity with manga fans for the potential popularity that may carry over to anime audiences.[146]

Digital technology is impacting on manga design and production. Whereas the traditional mode of production was ink on paper, it is now possible for paper to be removed entirely from the production process even including publication. Around the turn of the twenty-first century it became fashionable to draw manga with the assistance of computer-generated imagery (CGI) programs. However, traditional methods of drawing remain the most popular, as concerns about the use of CGI in manga creation have been raised. Yoshinori has argued that,

> it is still impossible for a computer to imitate the symbolizing process that is essential for us to 'draw' a picture, and then for others to interpret its meaning... The meaning of drawing *manga* with computers lies not in simulating *manga* but in capturing the symbolic essence of *manga* drawings themselves.[147]

Yet technology has had an impact, in that work can be developed on the computer screen, then carefully rendered there using an electronic stylus

---

146. Mouer and Norris, 'Exporting Japan's Culture', 364.
147. Yoshinori, 'Manga and Non-Photorealistic Rendering', 66.

instead of pencil and pen. Lettering and colouring can be accomplished in digital mode, and then the completed manga may be published on screen, rather than in print, via the Internet or for an electronic reading device.[148] A decade or so ago one very noticeable phenomenon in Tokyo was the large number of Japanese commuters of all ages who openly read manga while travelling on underground trains. This is now a rare sight, as commuters now look at the screens of their mobile phones. Manga on mobile phones is another step in the history of the delivery and reception of comics, and is, according to Kazuaki Nagata, one of the most popular 'trends in hand-held digital books'.[149]

There are still significant differences between comics produced in Japan and in the West, despite a century of fruitful cross-fertilization. Whereas both *mangaka* and the Japanese people view comics that are made in the United States and Europe as 'wordy' or overly 'literary', Western audiences find the numerous wordless panels in manga unusual. This wordless character of some manga is shared by the Western comic genre called 'sourds' (which is, however, not a mainstream genre but rather an *avant-garde* style of comic popular with only a limited audience). The important issue is that reading manga involves reading pictures rather than text, despite the fact that not all manga is wordless.[150] Similarly, Adam Schwartz and Elaine Rubinstein-Avila note that manga plots are frequently 'indirect' and 'nonlinear' and feature complex subplots, and often the identity of the main protagonists is somewhat unclear, although there are exceptions to these principles, for example, *Sailor Moon*.[151] Another difference between manga and comics from the United States and Japan is that issues of gender and sexuality are treated more flexibly and openly in Japan. For example, the *shōnen-ai* ('boys' love comics') subgenre features *bishōnen*, beautiful and sexually appealing young men, and stories that feature frank depictions of homosexual relationships which are very popular in Japan, particularly among female readers.[152]

---

148. Krikke, 'Computer Graphics Advances the Art of Anime', 14-19.

149. Kazuaki Nagata, 'Market for Mobile "Manga" Taking Off', *The Japan Times* (11 July 2008), at http://www.japantimes.co.jp/text/nb20080711a4.html (accessed 30 December 2011).

150. Aarnoud Rommens, 'Manga Story-telling/Showing', *Image [&] Narrative: Online Magazine of the Visual Narrative* 1 (2000), at http://www.imageandnarrative.be/narratology/aarnoudrommens.htm (accessed 29 September 2009).

151. Adam Schwartz and Elaine Rubinstein-Avila, 'Understanding the Manga Hype: Uncovering the Multimodality of Comic-Book Literacies', *Journal of Adolescent & Adult Literacy* 50.1 (2006).

152. Patrick Drazen, *Anime Explosion! The What? Why? And Wow! of Japanese Animation* (Berkeley, CA: Stone Bridge Press, 2003), 91-94; Andrea Wood, '"Straight"

Turning to the transition from manga to anime, one curious development that stands midway between manga and anime in Japanese modern history is an activity, now defunct, known as *kamishibai* ('paper theatre'). Falling somewhere between graphic narrative and theatrical performance, this popular cultural form employed a small, television-sized proscenium-arched box theatre into which painted cards were sequentially inserted. Thus, stories were told through 'hand-painted cardboard story sheets that were presented in sequence while the narrator provided sound effects and the story to accompany them'.[153] In Japan from the 1920s until after World War II watching *kamishibai* was a very popular pastime, with children gathering at street-corner meeting places after school to watch and listen to the story-tellers.[154] The theatre-type box was often mounted on the back of a bicycle, so that the *kamishibai* narrators could easily present their stories at multiple locations to different audiences. Some narrators used sound effects gadgets to enhance the experience, and most advertised their presence through beating a drum.[155] The performance was free, but the narrators earned a living selling sweets to the audience. Like manga the cards were drawn images that were static, and several popular *mangaka*, including Sanpei Shirato (b. 1932) and Shigeru Mizuki (b. 1924), trained as artists of the *kamishibai* story cards.[156] The stories the paper theatre narrators told could be heroic tales of war, romantic tales of love, erotic adventures and social comedies. Paper theatres declined and eventually disappeared, unable to compete with films, television, and confectionary shops. Frederik Schodt notes that 'from the end of the war to the year 1953, when television broadcasts began, it was estimated that 10,000 people made a living as *kami-shibai* narrators and that 5 million people a day watched a show'.[157] However, *kamishibai* remains historically an interesting medium in the space between manga and anime, between theatre and television, and between handmade and electronic technology.

Consideration of the earliest adaptations of manga into anime again directs attention to both Japanese modernity and Osamu Tezuka. Early animated films produced in Japan almost all featured patriotic and

---

Women, Queer Texts: Boy-Love Manga and the Rise of a Global Counterpublic', *Women's Studies Quarterly* 34.1-2 (2006).

153. Grigsby, 'Sailormoon', 64.
154. Eric P. Nash, *Manga Kamishibai: The Art of Japanese Paper Theater* (New York: Abrams ComicArts, 2009).
155. Tsurumi, *A Cultural History of Postwar Japan*, 33.
156. Tsurumi, *A Cultural History of Postwar Japan*, 34-38.
157. Schodt, *Manga! Manga!*, 62.

military motifs, and many were overt propaganda. For example, the first full-length animated feature film, *Momotarō: Umi no Shinpei* (*Momotarō, Sacred Soldiers of the Sea*), used the Peach Boy folktale, discussed in more detail in Chapter 2, to represent a narrative of Japan's triumph over the West, characterized in the film as the *oni* (demons) overcome by the hero Momotarō.[158] This film inspired Tezuka to make his own animations, and in 1958 he produced his first film with Tōei Dōga Studios, *Boku no Songokū* (*Songoku the Monkey*), an adaptation of Wu Cheng-en's epic Buddhist novel *Journey to the West*.[159] This film, based on Tezuka's manga (1952–1959), was a great success but Tezuka was frustrated by not being the creative director of the project, which led to him founding his own animations studio, Tezuka Dōga Gaisha (later Mushi Productions). The late 1950s was a time of change for Tezuka: he got married, completed a doctoral degree, and his manga were no longer so popular, as the darker genre of *gekiga* gained in influence.

Working in animation was a chance for Tezuka to reinvent himself. In 1963 *Tetsuwan Atomu* was transformed 'into Japan's first black-and-white television animation series' and two years later *Jungle Taitei* was the first Japanese television animated series to be produced in colour.[160] Both series were dubbed into English and successfully exported to America, the United Kingdom, Australia and other English-speaking countries, as *Astro Boy* and *Kimba the White Lion*. Tezuka adapted his *shōjo* manga classic *Ribon no Kishi* (literally 'A Knight in Ribbons', but known as *Princess Knight*) in 1967, and also had success with the *Amazing Three* (also known as *Wonder Three*) in 1965–1966. The most important issue with Tezuka's animations, without a doubt, is that he adapted his own manga and thus did not need to alter the style of the aesthetic, the nature of the characters, or the plots of the stories. Tezuka's animations were simply 'moving' versions of his manga. Other animators, such as Mitsuteru Yokoyama (1934–2004) the creator of *Gigantor*, found success in the West in the 1960s. The second wave of anime success in the West came in the late 1970s in the wake of the *Star Wars* films, and featured series such as *Star Blazers* (an adaptation of Reiji Matsumoto's manga, *Uchū Senkan Yamato*). The 1990s saw *Sailor Moon* (1995), a series that combined science fiction, magical fantasy and classic *shōjo* themes, and *Pokémon* (1996), become particular hits, and the success of new anime programmes continues unabated into the twenty-first century.[161]

---

158. Power, *God of Comics*, 130.
159. McCarthy, *500 Manga Heroes and Villains*, 115.
160. Schodt, *Dreamland Japan*, 237.
161. Drazen, *Anime Explosion!*, 8-14.

Ghost in the Shell is an instructive case study which illustrates the adaptation of a manga to the anime format in film. There are two principal reasons for selecting this particular narrative; the manga was much lengthier and more complex than the two-hour film, and the visual style and mood of the manga and the anime are radically different. Generally speaking, a manga has the potential to represent a basic storyboard for the production of an animated film. Whereas manga offers the freedom of panel design, shape and ratio on the page layout, anime is restricted to same-size frames, usually of a widescreen 2:1 ratio. Anime also, by necessity, lacks manga's capability of displaying juxtaposed panels, as anime usually only displays one frame at a time, not juxtaposed but with one frame following another. Masamune Shirow, a high-school art teacher, began creating manga in the 1980s as part of the *dōjinshi* scene, and the science-fiction epic *Appleseed* (1985), his professional debut, won the 1986 Seiun Award for Best Manga. He is best-known for *Kōkaku Kidōtai* (*Mobile Armoured Riot Police*), which Shirow released in 1989 and which was translated into English in 1995, the same year Oshii adapted it as *Ghost in the Shell*.

Schodt says of Shirow that his 'manga are characterized by their high tech themes and pseudo-realistic "mecha"; an information-dense visual and narrative structure; and an entertaining, often tongue-in-cheek approach that never lets anything get too serious. Most of his works are science fiction, with alluring female police officer protagonists'.[162] Interestingly, the reclusive Shirow shares with Osamu Tezuka a fascination with insects, and like Tezuka's use of Christian imagery, his manga *Orion* (1991) fuses Shintō, Buddhism and Daoism. Like Tezuka, too, he is not personally religious, stating rather that 'the religious approach in my work is probably closest to animism. When I say "religion," I don't mean something controlled by some omnipotent "God"; I just mean "gods" in the sense of Nature'.[163] His vision and graphic style, which is overtly hard-science oriented and technological, with a tough cyber-punk aesthetic, have become extremely popular with manga fans, chiefly outside of Japan, and Schodt claims he is the only *mangaka* to have had all his works translated into English.

Yet, Shirow's gritty visual style and tongue-in-cheek tone was not replicated by Mamoru Oshii. The graphic style of the anime is clearly different from the manga and Oshii has not attempted to make his anime look as if Shirow had designed and illustrated it.[164] Until *Ghost in*

---

162. Frederik L. Schodt, *An Interview with Masamune Shirow* (1998), at http://www.jai2.com/MSivu.htm (accessed 31 December 2011).

163. Shirow, quoted in Schodt, *An Interview with Masamune Shirow*.

164. Giorgio Hadi Curti, 'The Ghost in the City and a Landscape of Life: A Reading

the Shell, anime films tended to have limited budgets. Oshii's film was made specifically with a Western audience in mind, and the budget was comparatively large, 'with foreign capital provided by the London and Chicago-based company, Manga Entertainment, a subsidiary of the giant Island International'.[165] With a soundtrack by Irish rock band U2, a moody philosophical tone, and a sleek computer-generated visual style, *Ghost in the Shell* was Mamoru Oshii's film, even though it was based on Masamune Shirow's manga. The plot of this dystopian film, set in 2029, has Major Motoko Kusanagi, a cyborg officer in Tokyo's Section 9 security police, hunting the Puppet Master (the Puppeteer in the manga), a hacker of minds and implanter of fake memories. Kusanagi doubts her own selfhood as her body parts have gradually been replaced by mechanical substitutes; as Susan Napier says, she ruminates 'about whether she has a "ghost" (essentially a soul or mind)'.[166] As she pursues the Puppet Master she realizes he is a computer programme that has become sentient; when they meet he persuades her to fuse with him to become a new kind of electronic person. She decides to abandon embodiment to meet the Puppet Master's challenge, 'your effort to remain what you are is what limits you'.[167] One important change between the manga and the anime is that the principal character, Kusanagi, is more composed and chilled in the film, compared with the edgy and uncontrolled personality revealed in the manga. The manga, in fact, works on a complicated multi-level narrative that includes notes and asides from Shirow on why he made certain decisions about the characters and the narrative.[168] By contrast, the anime has been stripped of these and simplified for the film audience, perhaps permitting a more pensive mood to the film that assists in comprehending the philosophical questions that Oshii exploits.[169] For a fan of this title, the manga reading experience of it is clearly different from the experience of viewing the anime.

Oshii's *Ghost in the Shell* has been criticized for being too derivative of two classic Western treatments of the cyborg/cyberpunk genre, Ridley Scott's *Blade Runner* (1982) and William Gibson's groundbreaking science fiction, including *Neuromancer* (1983) and *Virtual Light* (1993). However,

---

of Difference in Shirow and Oshii's *Ghost in the Shell*', *Environment and Planning D: Society and Space* 26 (2008).

165. Schodt, *An Interview with Masamune Shirow*.

166. Susan Napier, 'The Problem of Existence in Japanese Animation', *Proceedings of the American Philosophical Society* 149.1 (2005): 77.

167. Penicka-Smith, 'Cyborg Songs for an Existential Crisis', 263.

168. Orr, *Manga Artists*, 37.

169. Angus McBlane, 'Just a Ghost in a Shell?', in Josef Steiff and Tristan D. Tamplin (eds), *Anime and Philosophy: Wide-Eyed Wonder* (Chicago and La Salle, IL: Open Court, 2010), 37-38.

Giorgio Curti argues that it is both philosophically profound and completely unique, in that it:

> subverts accepted cultural conceptions...by confronting traditionally held dichotomies – mind and body, part and whole, vibrant and static, animate and inanimate, organic and inorganic/artificial, vital and inactive, idea and material – the film frees the landscape, the cityscape, the environment, and ultimately the world from their perceived role as passive subjects as it calls for deeper understandings of the embodied affectual relations of the ghost in the city and a landscape of life.[170]

What Curti is saying, in a slightly opaque way, is precisely what Osamu Tezuka constantly asserted in his work (and what could be argued to be the fundamental doctrine of Shintō); everything is alive (including cityscapes, machines, and the entirety of what constitutes the world), possesses personhood, and demands affective and relational responses. This draws viewers' attention to the fact that the plot of *Ghost in the Shell* is also a complex love story; scholars have often commented that it is clear that Kusanagi's partner agent Batō loves her, though this love is unstated, and their discussions of selfhood, and of the fact that Section 9 effectively owns them, so that if either wished to resign they would have to return their cyborg bodies and become (probably) non-existent, are poignant and intense. But her eventual merger with the Puppet Master is also obliquely a love story, accompanied as it is by a traditional Japanese song of purification and protection before weddings. The lyrics, in ancient Japanese, include the lines: 'Proposing marriage, the god shall descend / The night clears away and the chimera bird will sing / The distant god may give us the precious blessing'.[171] When Kusanagi wakes at the film's conclusion, Batō having found her a new body, she is no longer herself, but a new being, caused by her willing fusion with the disembodied person of the Puppet Master, who is, Sarah Penicka-Smith argues, the god 'proposing marriage'.[172] In the final scene Kusanagi prepares to 'take up life...as a disembodied data stream', and Batō is 'left to wonder when, how, and in what form she may ever reappear to him'.[173]

Contemporary Religion, Spirituality and Popular Culture

This final section discusses changes in the religious and spiritual landscape of both Japan and the West from the late nineteenth century to

---

170. Curti, 'The Ghost in the City', 104.
171. Penicka-Smith, 'Cyborg Songs', 264-65.
172. Penicka-Smith, 'Cyborg Songs', 265.
173. Sharalyn Orbaugh, 'Emotional Infectivity: Cyborg Affect and the Limits of the Human', *Mechademia* 3 (2008): 155.

the early twenty-first century that are broadly parallel, and how these changes have resulted in the imbrication of new spiritualities and popular culture in both the East and West. The development of secularization, individualism and consumer culture in industrial modernity from the late nineteenth century to the present directly affected the varieties of religion that exist today. Peter Berger defined secularization as 'the process whereby sectors of society and culture are removed from the domination of religious institutions and symbols'.[174] Secularization has resulted in the decline of institutional religion, and the growth of many new religions that catered to people for whom the shift from understanding the self as part of a community to valuing the self as an individual was fundamental. Industrial modernity, in turn, gave rise to consumer capitalism, and Colin Campbell argues that modern life is characterized by 'a longing to experience in reality those pleasures created and enjoyed in imagination, a longing which results in the ceaseless consumption of novelty'.[175] These social shifts result in the fact that in the twenty-first century, individuals' consumption of spiritualities, technology, forms of entertainment, and popular culture in general (fashion, music and so on) is an integrated activity that contributes to the self-identity of those who participate. Further, new religions and spiritualities may be based upon novels, films and other popular cultural phenomena, particularly those in the science fiction or fantasy genres.[176] One final element to be noted is the porous and interrelated nature of 'global' culture; Colin Campbell has argued that since the late nineteenth century the West has steadily abandoned its traditional worldview and adopted Eastern notions, a process that he calls the 'Easternisation of the West'.[177] As this chapter has demonstrated, a parallel 'Westernisation of the East' process has impacted Japan since the mid-nineteenth century.[178]

---

174. Peter Berger, *The Social Reality of Religion* (London: Faber and Faber, 1969 [1967]), 107.

175. Colin Campbell, *The Romantic Ethic and the Spirit of Modern Consumerism* (York: Alcuin Academic, 2005), 205.

176. Carole M. Cusack, *Invented Religions: Imagination, Fiction and Faith* (Farnham and Burlington, VT: Ashgate, 2010).

177. Colin Campbell, 'The Easternisation of the West', in Bryan Wilson and Jamie Cresswell (eds), *New Religious Movements: Challenge and Response* (London and New York: Routledge, 1999).

178. Some material featured in the section 'Contemporary Religion, Spirituality and Popular Culture' has been published in the following articles and books: Carole M. Cusack, 'Konkokyo (Golden Light Teachings) and Modernity: A Test of the Faivre-Hanegraaff Six-Point Typology of Western Esotericism', *Australian Religion Studies Review* 20.3 (2007): 317-33; Carole M. Cusack, *Invented Religions: Imagination, Fiction*

There is a broad consensus that after 1800 there are three historical periods when new religions were either founded or enthusiastically promoted in Japan. These are 'around the beginning of the Meiji era (1868)... the beginning of the Showa era (1926), and...after the end of the Second World War (1945)'.[179] In the nineteenth century several important new religions were founded, including Kurozumikyō (Teachings of Kurozumi, founded by Munetada Kurozumi in 1814); Tenrikyō (Divine Wisdom Teachings, founded by Miki Nakayama in 1838); Ōmotokyo (Great Origin Teachings, founded by Nao Deguchi in 1892); and Konkōkyō, founded by Konkō Daijin, formerly Bunjirō Kawate, in 1859. These early *shin shūkyō* were severely restricted by the Meiji government. The restoration of Shintō, the denigration of Buddhism and countering the growing influence of the West were three of the highest priorities of the Meiji Restoration of imperial power.[180]

Thus the nineteenth century was one of parallel trends between Japan and the West, in that new religions began forming in America and Europe as the process of secularization weakened institutional Christianity. These included the Church of Jesus Christ of Latter-day Saints, founded by Joseph Smith in 1830; Spiritualism, which emerged in America with the mediumistic activities of the Fox sisters in the 1850s; and the Theosophical Society, founded by the Russian medium Madame Helena Petrovna Blavatsky and the American Civil War veteran Colonel Henry Steel Olcott in 1875. Theosophy was the most important of these new religions, as it offered a synthesis of Eastern and Western religion, which was claimed to be compatible with science; a claim that was similar to that of the Buddhist scholar and ex-monk Enryō Inoue, discussed earlier in this chapter, that Buddhism was a 'philosophy' compatible with modernity and science.[181] This was a key issue of the day as scientific advances such as Darwin's theory of evolution and Charles Lyell's geological calculation of the age of the earth had challenged the biblical account of creation since the mid-nineteenth century.[182] In Japan, embracing Western modernity similarly required a new narrative that integrated science with religious concerns.

---

and Faith (Farnham and Burlington, VT: Ashgate, 2010); and Carole M. Cusack, 'The Western Reception of Buddhism: Celebrity and Popular Cultural Media as Agents of Familiarisation', *Australian Religion Studies Review* 24.3 (2011): 297-316.

179. Henry van Straelen, 'The Japanese New Religions', *Numen* 9.3 (1962): 229-30.

180. Daniel C. Holtom, *The National Faith of Japan: A Study in Modern Shinto* (London: Paul, Trench, Trubner, 1938), 53-58.

181. Snodgrass, *Presenting Japanese Buddhism to the West*, 137.

182. Elisabeth Jay, *Faith and Doubt in Victorian Britain* (Houndsmills: Macmillan Education, 1986), 107.

Blavatsky and Olcott subsequently became professed Buddhists on 25 May 1880 in the southern port of Galle, Sri Lanka (then Ceylon) becoming the first 'white champions' of Buddhism.[183] Thirteen years later the Chicago Exposition of 1893 was held to commemorate the four hundredth anniversary of Christopher Columbus's discovery of the American continent in 1492. The World's Parliament of Religions, which ran from 11-27 September, as part of the Chicago Exposition, was an overwhelmingly Christian event, and some religions were simply excluded (e.g., Mormons, Native Americans, Sikhs, and others). Yet the Chairman of the Parliament, Reverend Doctor John Henry Barrows, had secured strong representation from Judaism, Protestant, Catholic and Orthodox Christianity, new religions including Theosophy and Christian Science, Hinduism (including P. C. Majumdar of the Brahmo Samaj, and Swami Vivekananda, later the founder of the Ramakrishna Math), and Buddhism. Minor delegations from Islam, Shintō, Daoism, Confucianism and Jainism also participated.

The Buddhist delegation at the Parliament emerged (with Vivekananda) as one of the more influential groups, chiefly due to the enthusiastic reception given to the charismatic Sri Lankan preacher Anagarika Dharmapala (1864–1933). Dharmapala gave the concluding speech at the opening ceremony; and threw down the gauntlet to the organizers by arguing that the Parliament was merely a postscript to the great congress presided over by the Buddhist emperor Ashoka in Paliputra in 242 BCE. By the time of the World's Parliament of Religions Dharmapala was a figure on the global stage. Other Buddhists at the Parliament were also well received; Charles Prebish notes that by the third day 'nearly all of the Japanese delegation had been introduced, including members of the Jodo Shinshu, Nichiren, Tendai, Shingon, and Zen traditions... in this latter group was Sōen Shaku, a disciple of Imakita Kōsen of [the] Engaku Temple'.[184] Anagarika Dharmapala, Sōen Shaku and Swami Vivekananda were all very positively received at the World's Parliament, which created anxiety for its Christian organizers, who regarded religions other than Christianity as marginal and unimportant.

Judith Snodgrass has established the ways in which the Buddhists, particularly the Japanese delegation, argued that Buddhism was the 'other' of Christianity, offering an ethically excellent faith that was also highly compatible with science.[185] Kōsen Imakita, Sōen Shaku's teacher, a zealous modernizer, had been a key supporter of Emperor Meiji, and had

---

183. Snodgrass, *Presenting Japanese Buddhism to the West*, 159.

184. Charles Prebish, *Luminous Passage: The Practice and Study of Buddhism in America* (Berkeley and Los Angeles, CA: University of California Press, 1999), 6.

185. Snodgrass, *Presenting Japanese Buddhism to the West*, 5.

served in the Japanese Ministry of Doctrine in the 1870s. For the purpose of this chapter, it is sufficient to note that in the relatively liberal environment of the Chicago World's Parliament of Religion, Japanese Buddhists were an unexpected (at least to the organizers) success, through linking Buddhism to the crucial issue of the day, which was the compatibility of the various religions with science and technological modernity. After the positive reception of the Buddhists at the Parliament, Buddhist sympathizers such as Paul Carus (editor of the *Monist* magazine and owner of Open Court Publishing) initiated programmes to disseminate Buddhism among Westerners, through personal relationships with both the high-profile Dharmapala, and, especially, Sōen Shaku.[186] Sōen refused Carus's invitation to remain in the United States after the Parliament, but he sent his disciple and English translator Daisetz Teitarō Suzuki (1870–1966) to the United States in 1897. He returned to Japan in 1909, but maintained contacts with the West, marrying Theosophist Beatrice Lane in 1911, and teaching at Columbia University from 1955 to 1957. From the 1890s to his death in 1966, Suzuki exercised a great influence on American Buddhism through his translations of important texts, his original writings, and his lectures. Many prominent individuals felt his influence, amongst these 'Alan Watts, Erich Fromm, Philip Kapleau, John Cage, Thomas Merton, Carl Jung, Jack Kerouac, Allen Ginsberg, Gary Snyder, to name just a few'.[187] Suzuki gained fame as a teacher of Zen Buddhism and his students became prominent in a range of professions (psychology, literature, popular and classical music, among others), extending the popular American understanding of Buddhism and furthering the process of familiarization of this 'alien' religion.

The mid-twentieth century was crucial in both Japan and the West, in that World War II created a significant break in traditional social structures that enabled creativity and innovation to flourish. In the West the 1950s were an important incubator of religious trends that came to fullness in the 1960s. New religions were founded, and the themes of science fiction and popular culture came to the fore. Robert Wise's 1951 film *The Day the Earth Stood Still* (scripted by Edmund H. North, with a score by composer Bernard Herrmann, who composed music for many films by Alfred Hitchcock) portrayed an alien messiah, Klaatu, whose spaceship lands in Washington. His mission is to inform humanity that violence, and the threat of nuclear war in particular, is alarming the peaceful citizens of other planets. New religions focused on alien contacts were founded in the 1950s, including the Aetherius Society, which was founded by George

---

186. Prebish, *Luminous Passage*, 6.
187. Ellen Goldberg, 'The Re-orientation of Buddhism in North America', *Method and Theory in the Study of Religion* 11 (1999): 346.

King (1919–1997) in England in 1955, the Church of Scientology, which was founded by L. Ron Hubbard (1911–1986) in 1954, and the Summit Lighthouse, which was founded by Mark L. Prophet in 1958. These religions continued the 'Easternisation' theme noted by Colin Campbell; although they used tropes such as the messiah from the Judeo-Christian tradition, they also drew upon Hindu and Buddhist notions, such as *karma* and reincarnation.

In Japan there has long been a theory that a number of Japanese *shin shūkyō* (most notably Tenrikyō) were deeply influenced by Christianity, despite the fact that there is only tenuous evidence to support such a claim. Groups of 'secret Christians' (*kakure Kirishitan*) numbering almost fifty thousand were discovered when Japan opened up to foreign influences in 1865.[188] Thomsen confidently asserted that both the nineteenth-century new religion founders, Miki Nakayama of Tenrikyō, and Konkō Daijin of Konkōkyō, acquired their teachings 'through contact with some of the Catholic *kakure Kirishitan*'.[189] Despite these enthusiastic affirmations of a connection between early *shin shūkyō* and *kakure Kirishitan*, no solid evidence to support this contention has been found, though Jeffrey Kamstra argued that Christian books were imported into Japan from China and that, as 'all foreign religions that had been accepted into Japan had undergone a centuries-long incubation in China',[190] this meant that Japanese intellectuals were more receptive to monotheistic notions from Christian sources translated into Chinese. Thus he asserted that Christian influences can be identified in the works of eighteenth- and nineteenth-century Shintō reformers such as Toshiaki Honda and Atsutane Hirata.

The influence of Christianity on Japanese new religions remains unproven, but in the twentieth century a multitude of new religions were founded in Japan. That these new religions participate in the process of 'Westernisation' is certainly true. The Japanese *shin shūkyō* include two new religions based on the *Lotus Sutra*, Risshō Kōsei Kai (founded 1938) and Sōka Gakkai (founded 1937); Denshin-kyō (Religion of the Electricity God), dedicated to the worship of its eponymous deity and Thomas Alva Edison; and P.L. Kyōdan, derided as the *gorufu shūkyō* ('golf religion'). Harry Thomsen notes that after World War II Shintō suffered a loss of face due to the surrender of the Emperor to the Allies, and as neither

---

188. H. Neill McFarland, *Rush Hour of the Gods* (New York: Harper Collins, 1970 [1967]), 32.
189. Thomsen, *The New Religions of Japan*, 75.
190. Jeffrey Kamstra, 'Japanese Monotheisms and New Religions', in Peter B. Clarke and Jeffrey Somers (eds), *Japanese New Religions in the West* (Sandgate, Kent: Japan Library, 1994), 108.

Buddhism nor Christianity were vital and viable religious options, a period of religious fertility resulted in the formation of many new religions.[191] Thomsen singled out eight characteristics of the 'new religions'. First, all have a large headquarters as a focal point; second, all have easy entry, understandable teachings, and are simple to follow; third, they are all optimistic; fourth, they all have charismatic leaders; fifth, they desire to realize the perfected world in the here and now (hence the this-worldly emphasis on spiritual healing); sixth, they are individualistic; seventh, they preach that religion is inseparable from life. Eighth, and finally, they teach that all religions are relative.[192]

This sketch of Japanese new religions is highly congruent with the schema that Yves Lambert has developed to account for the interactions of modernity and religion. He argued that the impact of modernity creates four possible future scenarios: 'decline, adaptation or reinterpretation, conservation, and innovation';[193] and he noted that those relevant to the growth of new religions, reinterpretation and innovation, tended to exhibit certain characteristics. These are this-worldliness, self-spirituality, immanent divinity, dehierarchization, parascientific or science fiction-based beliefs, loose organizational structure, and 'pluralism, relativism, probabilism, and pragmatism'.[194] In the twenty-first century Japan manifests all the symptoms of capitalist modernity that are perceptible in the West. Japan has very high levels of life expectancy, coupled with extremely low birth rates, and almost no immigration. The population has remained virtually static at 127 million since 2000.[195] Further, participation in organized religion is at a record low, and individual choice in life has resulted in a society in which fewer people marry or have children, or otherwise meet familial and societal expectations, preferring to pursue personal goals.[196] This is compatible with the shift in values that posits personal fulfilment and authenticity of experience. Helen Hardacre has argued that:

> new religions took the position that people are basically the same, face the same problems, and can solve them in the same way. This meant that they glossed over society's internal cleavages of class and gender

---

191. Thomsen, *The New Religions of Japan*, 18.
192. Thomsen, *The New Religions of Japan*, 24.
193. Yves Lambert, 'Religion in Modernity as a New Axial Age: Secularization or New Religious Forms?', *Sociology of Religion* 60.3 (1999): 311.
194. Lambert, 'Religion in Modernity as a New Axial Age', 323.
195. Samuel Coleman, *Family Planning in Japanese Culture: Traditional Birth Control in a Modern Culture* (Princeton, NJ: Princeton University Press, 1992).
196. Matthews Masayuki Hamabato, *Crested Kimono: Power and Love in the Japanese Business Family* (Ithaca, NY: Cornell University Press, 1990).

as if these were irrelevant to an understanding of the human condition. Their focus upon affairs crossing class and gender lines decreed a principle of equality among believers, weak status distinctions between leaders and followers, and a de-emphasis on the pollution notions which in the established religions barred women from full participation.[197]

These trends are paralleled in the laicized new religions of the West, which emerged after the collapse of traditional authority in the wake of two World Wars, the Cold War, the counter-culture of the 1960s, and the rise of what has come to be known as the 'Baby Boomers' and the subsequent 'Me Generation'.

The 1960s and 1970s were decades in which the influence of institutional Christianity declined rapidly and new religious movements, many of which were of Eastern origin, became established in Western countries. People turned to 'alternative' faiths, lifestyles and political orientations, and mass campaigns were mounted for equal rights for women, blacks, gays and lesbians. Buddhism, UFO religions, neo-Hindu guru-based religions, and a range of previously fringe phenomena, experienced a mainstreaming in the 1960s, and the West moved away from its traditional values (monotheism, human lordship over the natural environment, and a belief in one lifetime) and adopted an Eastern paradigm (pantheism and deep ecology, the human potential movement, and reincarnation).[198] The other significant adaptation that religion underwent in the 1960s and 1970s was democratization: for example, monastic forms of Buddhism from Asia were laicized in the West. Traditional attitudes to women, and hierarchical relationships between teachers and students, were eroded to render Eastern religions congruent with popular, topical Western values such as democracy and gender equality. The prominence of sexual imagery and the popular notion of fulfilment through sexual relationships, as well as the normalization of drugs and alcohol, profoundly influenced the teachings of new religions that reshaped to meet the spiritual needs of modern individualists.

In keeping with the consumerist ethos of the 1960s and 1970s when fashions changed rapidly due to the availability of cheap, mass-produced clothes, personal identity began to be linked to brands, such as Levi's and Coca-Cola. There was a profoundly romantic streak running through the counterculture of the 1960s, which manifested in apparently contradictory phenomena such as the desire to retreat from industrialized, mechanized modern society and go back to the 'land', the embracing of new technologies and science-fiction scenarios, passionate political activism,

---

197. Helen Hardacre, 'Creating State Shintō: The Great Promulgation Campaign and the New Religions', *Journal of Japanese Studies* 12.1 (1986): 55.
198. Campbell, 'Easternisation of the West', 35-49.

and the quest for mystical experiences. Radically de-traditionalized people in both Japan and the West turned to popular culture and consumerism as sources of meaning and identity in the post-religion world. Cult television series such as *Star Trek* attracted a community of fans who re-enacted scenes from episodes, learned Klingon, and attended science-fiction conventions costumed as the characters.[199] Scholars of religion have observed that contemporary spiritualities draw upon a wide range of practices, experiences and texts in new religious and spiritual forms, including science fiction, comic-book superheroes, and rock stars such as Elvis Presley. Nearly twenty years ago, Michael Jindra argued that fandom and fan behaviours were essentially religious in nature.[200] The *otaku* subculture of manga and anime fans in Japan is similarly tribal and ritualistic, and the texts of manga and anime treat the perennial questions of the meaning of life, the future of the universe, and the fraught relationship of humans and technology in a theological fashion.

When the New Age movement gained momentum in the 1980s it became clear that self-transformation had become the fundamental religious process for modern individuals; religious and spiritual insights melded with the psychological narrative of realizing one's true self as the primary aim of human development, and consumerism became a major part of identity-formation. The locus of authority had shifted from the public sphere, where it had been embodied in institutions, to the private sphere, where it was to be found within the self, which is a theme pursued with philosophical profundity and popular cultural appeal in Oshii's *Ghost in the Shell*.[201] Experience as a touchstone of the real became important as faith in science and Enlightenment rationalism faded. Modern individuals in developed societies such as Japan and the United States choose their own religious and spiritual identity from the vast array of symbols and myths (including popular cultural forms) in a process that sociologists call *bricolage*.[202]

Advances in communications technologies have also affected religious and spiritual communities and behaviours. The Internet was developed in a military context by the United States in the late 1950s and 1960s, but began to expand after the invention of the World Wide Web in 1989,

---

199. Jeff Greenwald, *Future Perfect: How Star Trek Conquered Planet Earth* (New York and London: Penguin Books, 1998).

200. Michael Jindra, '*Star Trek* Fandom as a Religious Phenomenon', *Sociology of Religion* 55.1 (1994): 27-51.

201. Napier, 'The Problem of Existence', 72-79.

202. Stephen D. O'Leary, 'Cyberspace as Sacred Space: Communicating Religion on Computer Networks', in Lorne L. Dawson and Douglas E. Cowan (eds), *Religion Online: Finding Faith on the Internet* (New York and London: Routledge, 2004), 45.

and is now a global informational and entertainment tool. This sketch of the history of the Internet exhibits instructive parallels to anime in Japan, which was originally developed as a medium of military propaganda, but later became a global entertainment form. There was significant overlap between the gaming subculture, anarchist musicians and artists, computer programmers, underground religions and spiritualities, and indeed all groups with strong 'geek' or *otaku* profiles. In the early twenty-first century 'seekers' frequently search the Internet for subjects that intrigue them, follow this up by buying and reading books and attending seminars, without ever needing to join a formal organization. It has been argued that online fandom involves 'subversive consumerism that allows fans to actively participate in their own entertainment media and create a cultural space that more actively serves their interests'.[203] This links online fandom with the cutting-edge *dōjinshi* culture in manga production, and also to the laicized 'do it yourself' ethic of contemporary spirituality.

Although film and television had impacted on religion and spirituality in the second half of the twentieth century, the Internet differed in crucial ways:

> (1) the Internet is an interactive and not simply a broadcast medium; (2) the Internet is truly multimedial; (3) the Internet employs hypertextuality; (4) anyone can launch themselves onto the World Wide Web with relative ease and little expense; (5) the Internet is global in its reach. With a comparatively small investment in time, money, and knowledge, Internet users can make their religious views known, at least potentially, to millions of others throughout the world.[204]

The Internet makes it possible to distribute information on new spiritual concepts and products with extraordinary rapidity, and to create links between people in cyberspace, rather than building a traditional community based on real-life interactions. Further, it has transformed how people interact with texts, including books and films, manga and anime, and create communities based around those texts. Religions based on films and novels, such as Matrixism (based on the 1999 film and its sequels by Lana and Andy Wachowski) and the Church of all Worlds (based on Robert A. Heinlein's 1961 science-fiction novel *Stranger in a Strange Land*) have flourished on the Internet.[205]

---

203. Kathryn Dunlap and Carissa Wolf, 'Fans Behaving Badly: Anime Metafandom, Brutal Criticism, and the Intellectual Fan', *Mechademia* 5 (2010): 270.
204. Lorne L. Dawson and Douglas E. Cowan, 'Introduction', in Lorne L. Dawson and Douglas E. Cowan (eds), *Religion Online: Finding Faith on the Internet* (New York and London: Routledge, 2004), 10.
205. Cusack, *Invented Religions*, 53-82.

In a fascinating parallel to *Ghost in the Shell*, discussed in the previous section, *The Matrix* (1999) is a film that interrogates a philosophical question. Neo (Keanu Reeves), a bored computer hacker, meets Morpheus (Laurence Fishburne), a mysterious character who has the key to 'the Matrix'. Morpheus offers Neo a choice of two pills, a red that will reveal the Matrix and the true nature of reality, and a blue that will permit him to return to his life unchanged. He takes the red pill and discovers that his 'life' was an illusion; that actually his body exists in a dystopic future where:

> machines have taken control of the whole planet and have enslaved the vast majority of human beings. The planet's resources have been depleted and a dense layer of smoke prevents these machines from using solar power. For this reason, human beings are kept alive so their human body can be used as a source of energy. Through a complex process, all human beings are born, live and die in a type of capsule that keeps them constantly dreaming about the twentieth century... These dreams – i.e. the Matrix, this desert of the real – are generated and controlled by these artificial intelligences.[206]

The Matrix investigates the nature of reality, and, like *Ghost in the Shell*'s interrogation of the nature of the self, it is steeped in religious references. Neo is the One, a messianic figure who is resurrected from the dead (a Christian motif, as is the name of the rebels' chief female member Trinity, with the betrayer Cypher resembling Judas Iscariot), and the stripping of illusion to reveal reality connects with Buddhist and Gnostic notions of the illusory nature (*maya*) of everyday life and the physical world.

Thus, in the early twenty-first century, both Japan and the West are societies in which institutional religion has lost power, but where the sacred has been relocated to the self and the range of symbols and narratives that each individual draws upon to establish meaning. The contemporary imbrication of humans with communications technologies and other mechanical enhancements of the 'natural' resonates powerfully with the genres of science fiction and futurological fantasy that dominate the manga and anime production of Japanese and Western artists alike. This book argues that the 'techno-animism' identified by Anne Allison, the worldview of 'mecha animated by Shinto, Japan's religion of animism in which everything is endowed with a spirit and spirituality imbues the whole universe'[207] that can be observed in *Astro Boy* and countless subsequent manga and anime, is a religio-spiritual worldview

---

206. Adam Possamai, *Religion and Popular Culture: A Hyper-Real Testament* (Brussels: Peter Lang, 2005), 105-106.
207. Allison, *Millennial Monsters*, 63.

that is a unique product of Japanese modernity. However, this worldview in which the borders between organic life and machines are decisively blurred has gradually been adopted by the West, as Eastern religions, cultural forms, and religions have gradually become mainstream throughout the twentieth century.

This has implications for both traditional religion and for emergent forms of belief and behaviour that are quasi-religious or religio-spiritual, such as fandom subculture and Internet communities dedicated to popular cultural forms or fiction-based new religions. Stephen Covell has observed that 'Japanese youth, though interested in subjects such as spirits and ghosts, do not seek traditional relationships with religious institutions, but rather, as witnessed by the rise of the [so-called] new new religions, [seek] personal, introspective religious experiences'.[208] In the West, those who participate in new and alternative religions do so in a very different spirit to those who participate in traditional (Christian) religion. The criterion of truth is eclipsed in new religions; members are more likely to ask 'does it work?' than 'is it true?' Their definition of what works is flexible and pragmatic, and as 'seekers', they will move on to another practice or teaching should their current group cease to 'work' for them. In both East and West, the self is the primary site of spiritual work, and consumer behaviours, sexuality, peer-group friendships, digital communication technologies, and a range of other formerly profane, everyday activities and commodities have taken on the lineaments of sacredness. Thus, profane narratives of entertainment (manga and anime) are saturated with religio-spiritual motifs, and the practices of everyday life (fandom, friendship, and watching film and television) are sacred activities. When asked about the presence of religious themes in his anime, Masamune Shirow responded:

> I do think that science and technology are becoming more and more like 'magic'. In other words, the experts know what's going on, but the average person doesn't have a clue... Most people just use computers because they're convenient; they can't explain the principles involved, so they in effect treat the computers like magic. This doesn't mean computers are actually magic. The worlds of science and magic are obviously separate; but in terms of our consciousness and the way we perceive things, they are converging. That may be why, in my work, it may seem

---

208. Stephen Grover Covell, *Japanese Temple Buddhism: Worldliness in a Religion of Renunciation* (Honolulu: University of Hawai'i Press, 2005), 188; and 'The Price of Naming the Dead: Posthumous Precept Names and Critiques of Contemporary Japanese Buddhism', in Jacqueline Stone and Mariko Namba Walters (eds), *Death and the Afterlife in Japanese Buddhism* (Honolulu: University of Hawai'i Press, 2009), 319.

as though I'm trying to integrate sci-tech and religion, because both do seem to be converging.[209]

This perceptive statement encapsulates the aim of this study, which is to interrogate the symbiotic relationship of religion and the spiritual with anime (and the related art form of manga), focusing on the way magic and the supernatural are fused with science and science fiction, to produce a unique cultural product. Tradition, in the form of Shintō and Buddhism, is brought into a relationship with the contemporary, in the form of technology and the hard sciences, in a techno-animistic worldview. This worldview was originally unique to Japan, but has been enthusiastically adopted by the West in recent decades, as it too becomes enchanted by the magic of cyberspace and spiritually nourished by the narratives of cyborg personhood and digital immortality.

Conclusion

This chapter has argued that the artistic forms of modern manga[210] and anime are the culmination of approximately a millennium of Japanese art styles, both religious and secular, which established a sequential, visual means of communicating stories and social commentary. In the mid-nineteenth century Japan's cultural isolation was ended by the intervention of America and Commodore Perry's mission, and rapid modernization and Westernization followed the Meiji Restoration of 1868.[211] This gave Japanese cartoonists familiarity with Western comic-book styles, which became particularly important in the twentieth century with the emergence of the 'classic' manga style of Osamu Tezuka, which owed much to Walt Disney and his fellow European and American cartoon artists. However, it has also been contended that, although the visual forms of manga and anime evidence Western influence, the content reflects explicitly Japanese concerns, including the animistic view of the world promoted in Shintō, the indigenous religion of Japan, and the Buddhist understanding of the self as fragmented and evanescent, continuingly being renegotiated. Further, dark themes of the threat to humanity and nature posed by technology reflect the Japanese experience of the atomic bombs being dropped on Hiroshima and Nagasaki. The contemporary manga and anime scene was examined, and the process of transforming manga into anime was sketched, using Mamoru Oshii's film adaptation of Masamune

---

209. Schodt, *An Interview with Masamune Shirow*.
210. Some material featured in Chapter 1, 3 and 4 has been published in Katharine Buljan, 'Animated Film: Genres and Audiences – Western and Japanese Animated Films', *Lumina: Australian Journal of Screen Arts and Business* 4 (2010): 193-208.
211. Kuroda, 'Shinto in the History of Japanese Religions', 1-21.

Shirow's *Ghost in the Shell* (1995) as an example. Finally, the conditions of contemporary twenty-first-century religion and spirituality were related to popular culture and consumerism and it was argued that as the West 'Easternises' the East is engaged in a parallel process of 'Westernisation'.[212] Finally, the popular cultural media of manga and anime are argued to be sites of contemporary spiritual significance.

---

212. Campbell, 'Easternisation of the West'.

Onoe Baiko as Spirit of Cherry Tree by Kunisada/Toyokuni lll Utagawa (Japan, 1786–1865), made circa 1830. Print (colour woodcut), 37.5 × 26.3 cm. Art Gallery of New South Wales (Gift of Dr Roderick Bain, 1997). Photo: AGNSW. In Japan's history there are many instances of religious/spiritual content in art, and with its direct reference to Shintō Kunisada's work, this is an example of it. Kunisada was one of the best known *ukiyo-e* artists of his time.

Chapter 2

The New Life of Old Beliefs: Religious and Spiritual Concepts in Anime

Introduction

The religious and spiritual content of anime is one of its remarkable qualities, as in the West it is not common for popular cultural forms to be so saturated with the religious and the spiritual. This chapter has four distinct sections. First, it discusses the role and function of religion in Japanese society, and analyses the complex historical dynamic existing between Shintō and Buddhism, giving greater attention to Shintō as the religious tradition that has contributed most substantially to anime. Second, it considers the Western conceptual categories of animism and anthropomorphism as tools of analysis in the identification of religious and spiritual motifs in anime. The third section examines human to animal and animal to human metamorphosis in Japanese folklore, and the role of magical animals in general and their treatment in anime. The final section identifies supernatural themes and motifs in anime (for example types of spirit beings, animal transformations, and issues of life, death and afterlife) and traces their connections with Shintō, Buddhism, and to a lesser extent, the minority traditions of Christianity and new religions (*shin shūkyō*) in Japan.

Religious Traditions in Japan

Contemporary Japanese society is highly advanced in terms of science and technology. While these forms of advancement may often be closely associated with alienation from religion, Japan has successfully managed to balance the tension between participation in technological modernity and traditional religious and spiritual forms.[1] More precisely, although deeply committed to science and technology, Japan's relationship with religion remains a vivid one. This is seen, for instance, in the presence of numerous Shintō shrines and Buddhist temples throughout the country,

---

1. Kasulis, *Shinto*, 170.

and the popularity of the colourful religious ceremonies that mark both the human life-cycle and the phases of the year. Shintō is often understood to be the indigenous religion of Japan, and Buddhism to be a religion imported from India by way of China from the sixth century CE onwards. The reality is more complex and the interplay between Shintō and Buddhism more intimate and interesting as a result.[2] Current scholarship suggests that 'Shintō' came into existence as a separate religion in reaction to Buddhism, because prior to the introduction of Buddhist and Confucian concepts by the Chinese Japan was a non-literate society, and even the term 'Shintō' is a translation of the Chinese *Shen Dao* or 'way of the gods'. The earliest Shintō scriptures include the *Kojiki* (Records of Ancient Matters), which was written in 712 CE and contains annalistic records until 628 CE; the *Nihongi* or *Nihon Shoki* (Chronicles of Japan), which was written in Chinese in 720 CE; the *Kujiki* (Chronicle of Old Events), arguably from the eighth century; the *Kogoshūi* (Gleanings from Ancient Stories); and the *Engi Shiki* (Detailed Laws of the Engi period), which was written in 927 CE. These texts were committed to writing after Chinese Buddhism became established in Japan.[3]

The establishment of Buddhism in Japan also involved the importation of the Chinese religio-cultural systems of Daoism and Confucianism.[4] Some scholars contest whether Daoism and Confucianism are truly 'religions', as the earliest Daoist texts (such as the *Dao De Jing* and the *Chuang Tzu*, dating from the fourth to the second centuries BCE, the 'Warring States' period) could be interpreted as political manuals or philosophical treatises, and the teachings of Confucius are often interpreted as a moral code.[5] However, the current academic consensus is that Daoism (at least since the recognition of the Tianshi or 'Celestial Masters' sect in 215 CE) and Confucianism (even prior to the formal establishment of a cult of Confucius in the seventh century CE) are undeniably religions, invoking transcendent concepts and offering religious compensators.[6] After the introduction of Buddhism to Japan there is evidence to suggest that Daoism was identified with Shintō (which is logical in that *Shen Dao* was the Chinese term for Daoism). Kuroda has argued that many of the

---

2. Kuroda, 'Shinto in the History of Japanese Religions', 1-3.
3. Sokyo Ono, *Shinto: The Kami Way* (Rutland, VT: Tuttle, 1976), 5.
4. William K. Bunce (ed.), *Religions in Japan: Buddhism, Shinto, Christianity*, rev. edn (Rutland, VT: Tuttle, 1967), 104.
5. Herbert Fingarette, *Confucius: The Secular as Sacred* (San Francisco, CA: Harper and Row, 1972).
6. Isabelle Robinet, *Taoism: Growth of a Religion*, trans. Phyllis Brooks (Stanford, CA: Stanford University Press, 1997), 2; Nicholas F. Gier, *Spiritual Titanism: Indian, Chinese and Western Perspectives* (Albany, NY: State University of New York Press, 2000), 179; Fingarette, *Confucius*, 78.

traditional elements of Shintō were in fact imported from Daoism. These include reverence for swords and mirrors as symbols of the divine, the term *tenno* (Chinese 'lord of the universe') for the Emperor, a range of linguistic terms associated with the architecture of shrines and palaces, and the concept of immortality.[7] Confucian ethics permeated Japanese society, with the hierarchical model of relationships (emperor/subject, husband/wife, parents/children, teacher/pupil and elder brother/younger brother) and the need for balance and harmony in society (which also reflects the *yin-yang* principle of Daoism) being especially influential.

The influence of Buddhism in Japan was even more profound, affecting government and daily life, and aesthetics and art forms. Distinctively Japanese forms of Buddhism developed, most prominently Shingon, founded by Kūkai (774–835 CE); True Pure Land, founded by Shinran (1173–1262 CE); and the sect founded by and named after Nichiren (1222–1282 CE). From the eighth to the eleventh century Shintō and Buddhism grew closer, with the concept of *shinbutsu shūgō*, a coalescence of the two, emerging. This doctrine sought ways to relate the *kami* to the *buddhas* and *bodhisattvas*. Kuroda notes the following new interpretations that became popular:

> 1) the *kami* realize that they themselves are trapped in this world of *samsara* and transmigration and they also seek liberation through the Buddhist teachings; 2) the *kami* are benevolent deities who protect Buddhism; 3) the *kami* are transformations of the Buddhas manifested in Japan to save all sentient beings (*honji suijaku*); and 4) the *kami* are the pure spirits of the Buddhas (*hongaku*). Among new religious forms were the *jinguji* (a combination shrine and temple) and Sogyo Hachiman (the *kami* Hachiman in the guise of a Buddhist monk).[8]

Finally, the foundation of Ryōbu Shintō, a deliberate fusion of Shintō and Shingon, emerged by the end of the Kamakura period, in the fourteenth century. Until the Meiji Restoration of 1868, Buddhism was the dominant faith, though it co-existed with Shintō.[9] Many modern Japanese subscribe to the popular phrase 'born Shintō, die Buddhist'. This is at least partly because, as Thomas Kasulis notes, that:

> most Japanese seldom reflect on Shinto as a 'religion' in which they consciously participate. For them, being Shinto is neither a set of beliefs formalized into a creed nor an identifiable act of faith. Its festivals and annual celebrations are things Japanese do because it is traditional.[10]

---

7. Kuroda, 'Shinto in the History of Japanese Religions', 6.
8. Kuroda, 'Shinto in the History of Japanese Religions', 9.
9. Charles W. Iglehart, 'Current Religious Trends in Japan', *Journal of Bible and Religion* 15.2 (1947): 81.
10. Kasulis, *Shinto*, 1.

Japan's population is approximately 127.3 million, and both Christianity and new religious movements in Japan offer a stark contrast to the symbiotic relationship of Shintō and Buddhism. The Jesuit Francis Xavier arrived in Japan in 1549 and Christianity was readily accepted initially. By 1600 there were approximately three hundred thousand Japanese *kirishitan*. However, in 1587 the military ruler Hideyoshi Toyotomi (1536–98 CE) passed an edict that prohibited the spread of Christianity and ordered all priests to leave the country.[11] After 1603, when Ieyasu Tokugawa assumed the shogunate, Christianity was gradually outlawed and Christians went underground. The Meiji Restoration of 1867–1868 disestablished Buddhism and reinstated Shintō as the official religion of Japan, and permitted Christian missionaries into Japan again. They found tens of thousands of *kakure kirishitan* (hidden Christians) who had kept the faith. In the twenty-first century Christians constitute between 0.5 and 1 per cent of the population. Monotheistic Christianity demands exclusive allegiance, and it suffers in Japan from being perceived as a foreign religion. The other minority religious influence in Japan is that of the 'new religions' or *shin shūkyō*, the oldest of which date from the early to mid-nineteenth century (for example, Tenrikyō, Ōmotokyo, Kurozumikyō and Konkōkyō). The Meiji government outlawed the majority of new religions and they remained illegal until religious freedom was proclaimed after World War II ended.[12] Harry Thomsen argues that all *shin shūkyō* share eight core characteristics: a charismatic leader, a desire for this-worldly salvation, large central headquarters, simple doctrines, festivals, individualism, the belief that religion is inseparable from life, and the conviction that all religions are relative, all are paths to the truth.[13] In terms of contemporary Western religion, *shin shūkyō* are broadly comparable to the New Age movement or to Pentecostal churches, emphasizing personal well-being, affluence and affective power over intellectual dogma, tradition or disciplined self-denial.

Defining Shintō is rather more difficult than might be initially supposed. Shintō does not have scriptures in the way that world religions including Christianity, Judaism and Islam do, and it is derived not from an individual founder but from deep-rooted cultural traditions focused on the appreciation of nature and its aesthetics.[14] Shintō is generally translated 'the way of the gods' or 'the way of the *kami* (spirit beings)', and there are thousands of these spirit beings, representing aspects of the earth such as the wind, forests, mountains and rocks. Each community

---

11. Kitagawa, 'Some Remarks on Shintō', 238.
12. Van Straelen, 'The Japanese New Religions', 231.
13. Thomsen, *The New Religions of Japan*, 22-24.
14. Kitagawa, 'Some Remarks on Shintō', 228.

has its own *kami* peculiar to that area and the type of industry undertaken. The people of the mountains venerate mountain *kami* called *yama-no-kami*, while rice farmers worship the paddy-field *kami*, *ta-no-kami*, and those living by the sea worship the sea *kami*, *umi-no-kami*. The term *kami* can also be applied to plants, animals and landforms. It refers to the vital force or essence that resides in everything. The influence of this aspect of the *kami* can be seen in the traditions of *origami* (paper folding) and the traditional garb, the *kimono*, where fabric or paper is folded to avoid cutting, as this would destroy the object's divine essence. Thus, as Kitagawa observes, the fundamental affirmation of the *kami* is 'focused on the sacrality of the total cosmos... [taking] for granted the common *kami* (sacred) nature shared by all beings within the world of nature'.[15]

Kami are the essential reason for classification of Shintō as animistic. While many objects and persons are understood dwelling places of *kami*,[16] it is important to note that not everything is regarded as *kami*.[17] Norinaga Motoöri, one of the greatest eighteenth-century Japanese scholars, writes of *kami* that 'anything whatsoever which was outside the ordinary, which possessed superior power or which was awe-inspiring was called *kami*'.[18] Even 'evil' and 'mysterious things' were referred to as *kami*, according to Motoöri, and this is because what was important was their 'power to inspire' rather than their ethical status.[19] Interestingly, it is believed that *kami* can also make errors as humans do.[20] Although the term *kami* refers primarily to the spirits from the supernatural realm, the dead were also called *kami*. One of the translations of the term *kami* is 'the upper ones' or 'the powers above'.[21] This refers to the three-tier conception of the world, with the divine realm above, the human realm at the centre, and the realm of the dead below that is evidenced in Shintō mythology.

The word *kami* was used in earlier times for anything that appeared 'superior, mysterious, fearful, powerful, or incomprehensible' and it

---

15. Kitagawa, 'Some Remarks on Shintō', 233.
16. Albert C. Moore, *Iconography of Religions: An Introduction* (Philadelphia, PA: Fortress Press, 1977), 182.
17. Ono, *Shinto*, 6-7.
18. Norinaga Motoöri, quoted in Holtom, *The National Faith of Japan*, 23.
19. Norinaga Motoöri, quoted in Holtom, *The National Faith of Japan*, 23.
20. Kada No Azumamaro (1669–1736) quoted in Peter Nosco, *Remembering Paradise: Nativism and Nostalgia in Eighteenth-Century Japan* (Cambridge, MA: Harvard University Press 1990), 84.
21. James Thayer Addison, 'Religious Life in Japan', *Harvard Theological Review* 18.4 (1925): 329.

included not only animate but also inanimate entities.[22] These undertones and qualities are regularly found in anime and manga protagonists who possess supernatural attributes. It is interesting to note that in the past, humanity and the *kami* were on terms of close connection and the interconnectedness of everything was emphasized over differentiation: 'fear was almost totally absent. The idea of the soul and the distinctions between life and death – body and spirit – were extremely vague'.[23] As the word 'gods' is usually used in explaining Shintō's *kami*, this might from a Western (Judeo-Christian) perspective lead to association of *kami* with the immortality and omnipotence of the monotheistic deity. However, *kami* are in no way omnipotent, and they frequently are not immortal, either.[24] According to Shintō, human beings are not the only creatures susceptible to the 'natural law'; the deities are too.[25] Similarly, anime and manga characters with supernatural attributes, although powerful and often stronger than human beings, are not necessarily portrayed as perfect and invincible, but also have weaknesses and vulnerability. For example, Bokko, the female of the three extraterrestrial agents of Osamu Tezuka's 1965–1966 anime *The Amazing Three* (known as *Wonder Three* in Japan) chooses to become a mortal girl at the end of the series, as she has fallen in love with Shinichi, the human youth who has assisted the Three in their mission.[26] This involves the voluntary abandonment of her superhuman powers and her acceptance of aging and death. Closely aligned to Bokko's choice is the nature of divinity in Shintō, which differs radically from its Judeo-Christian counterpart. H. Byron Earhart notes that in Japan 'mortals and gods alike share in the beauty of nature',[27] and divinities interact with mortals and creatively engage with 'the objective world of experience',[28] whereas the Judeo-Christian God as creator remains outside of the physical world, which is His creation.

Shintō is also regarded as a type of ancestor worship, and *kami* take the form of imperial ancestors that were members of noble families and national heroes. This ties in with Bokko's sacrifice of her powers to become human and experience love, referred to above, in that the

---

22. Bunce, *Religions in Japan*, 100.
23. Bunce, *Religions in Japan*, 100.
24. Malcolm D. Kennedy, *A Short History of Japan* (New York: New American Library, 1964), 22.
25. Genchi Katō, *A Study of Shintō: The Religion of the Japanese Nation* (Tokyo: Meiji Japan Society, 1926), 85.
26. Drazen, *Anime Explosion!*, 7.
27. H. Byron Earhart, *Japanese Religion: Unity and Diversity*, 4th edn (Victoria, Australia and Belmont, CA: Thomson/Wadsworth, 2004), 7.
28. Joseph W. T. Mason, *The Meaning of Shinto: The Primaeval Foundation of Creative Spirit in Modern Japan* (New York: E. P. Dutton, 1935), 115.

imperial family of Japan are understood to be the direct descendants of the greatest *kami*, the sun-goddess Amaterasu, who embraced mortality so that they could rule Japan. The *Kojiki* and *Nihongi* preserve Shintō creation mythology though they claim 'to be histories'.[29] According to these texts, the universe began with the primordial creative couple, Izanagi-no-Mikoto and his sister-wife Izanami-no-Mikoto ('He Who Invites' and 'She Who Invites'). They descended from the Plain of High Heaven, and Izanami gave birth first to the islands of Japan, and then to many *kami*, the most important of which was the sun-goddess Amaterasu Omikami. Amaterasu's grandson Ninigi-no-Mikoto was sent to rule over Japan, with the three divine treasures Amaterasu gave him: a sword, a mirror, and a string of jewels.[30] He married the daughter of Mount Fuji, and his son Jimmu became the first Emperor of Japan. The imperial family are, therefore, direct descendants of the goddess, and the emperor is regarded as a god on earth. The imperial family is immensely important to Shintō, with several major national shrines being given over entirely to the Imperial cult, such as the Ise Grand Shrine in Mie prefecture, dedicated to Amaterasu. Indeed, the Japanese flag is the rising sun, and the Japanese name for their country is Nippon, which means 'sun origin', directly referencing Amaterasu.

There is a notable connection between the Japanese mythology and cosmology with anime as their stories frequently feature supernatural beings, miraculous creative powers, and magical talismans. Shintō's central mythology grants *kami*, humans and nature the same shared ancestry and Herbert describes the relationship between human beings and *kami* in terms of a 'spiritual coalescence'.[31] Anime and manga characters such as schoolboys and schoolgirls and so on, although appearing as ordinary humans, frequently possess supernatural powers. This may reflect the Shintō belief in the continuity between the humanity and divinity. Various doctrines of Shintō appear to form the framework of anime in both direct and indirect ways. Visual representations of the close connection of supernatural elements with the physical reality, often encountered in anime, function as a modern adumbration of the ancient Japanese worldview. This cosmic picture had 'no concept of a supernatural world totally distinct from the existing life'.[32] In

---

29. Lafcadio Hearn, *Japan's Religions; Shinto and Buddhism*, ed. K. Kato (New Hyde Park, NY: University Books, 1966), 229.
30. Ono, *Shinto*, 5.
31. Jean Herbert, *Shintô: At the Fountain-Head of Japan* (London: Allen and Unwin, 1967), 21-23.
32. A. Orloff Matsunaga, 'The Land of Natural Affirmation, Pre-Buddhist Japan', *Monumenta Nipponica* 21.1-2 (1966): 203.

contemporary Japan this view is reflected in traditional Shintō, in Buddhist sects such as Zen which strongly value the environment and the contribution of aesthetics to the spiritual, and in the new religions and the 'new new' religions (*shin shin shūkyō*). New religions in Japan usually have a broadly Shintō foundation, and a common thread is the teaching that humans can be living *kami*, a view that closely relates the spiritual to the everyday. Ian Reader argues that adherents of new religions are actively interested in personal encounters with the miraculous and a religiously dynamic life. Just as anime reflects both Japanese and American aesthetics, and the samurai films of Akira Kurosawa were a Japanese re-imagining of the classic Westerns of American directors such as John Ford, modern Japanese religion shares themes and motifs with the New Age in Western countries: there is 'a healthy publishing industry focusing on such issues as spirit possession, UFOs, the myths of Mu and Atlantis, and other such phenomena that appear to be a mixture of "new age" concepts and extremely traditional Japanese folkloric ones'.[33]

A related phenomenon of great interest to both Eastern and Western contemporary religion, which forms part of ancient Japanese tradition, is shamanism. Shamans were believed to have the ability to communicate with the spirit world and harness powers possessed by divine creatures. They did this through practices including 'sorcery, divination, and lustration'.[34] Female shamans in Japan were called *mikos* and they occupied a special place in the religious history of Japan. The Shintō *miko*, as Carmen Blacker observes, was Japan's earliest shaman and was religiously prominent from the late prehistoric era. Interestingly, *mikos* not only worked at the court for the Emperor, 'transmitting the admonitions and instructions of deities to the Emperor himself', but they also acted as mediums between the villagers and their *kami*.[35] This indicates how Japanese cultural heritage abounds with the presence of beings with supernatural powers, be they humans such as *mikos* and male ascetics, as well as the greater and lesser *kami*.[36] Within anime there are female characters that are inspired by *mikos*, that is, human mediums who have the power to see and communicate with the spirit world, such as Rei Hino, Sailor Mars in *Sailor Moon*, and Sakura ('cherry blossom'), the school nurse in the *Urusei Yatsura* manga and anime series. Rei is occasionally seen wearing the white blouse and baggy red *hakama* of the traditional

---

33. Ian Reader, *Religion in Contemporary Japan* (Honolulu: University of Hawai'i Press, 1991), 234.
34. Bunce, *Religions in Japan*, 2.
35. Carmen Blacker, *The Catalpa Bow: A Study of Shamanistic Practices in Japan* (London: Allen and Unwin, 1975), 104.
36. Kasulis, *Shinto*, 77.

miko (a colour scheme that matches her Sailor Mars outfit) and her role at the shrine ties her more firmly to Japanese tradition than any of the other girls in the series. Her exorcism abilities are also part of her Sailor Mars routine. She uses '*ofuda* – little talisman scripts with *kami* names on them, with an incantation *akuryo taisan!* (evil spirits of the dead, depart!) – as her weapon'.[37]

The most significant example of the *miko* as a character in anime is the 2004 twelve-episode series *Kannazuki no Miko (Priestesses of the Godless Month)*, which has the alternative English title *Destiny of the Shrine Maiden*. In this anime, shy Himeko Kurusugawa and popular Chikane Himemiya attend school together. After a lunar eclipse the villain Yamata no Orochi (an eight-headed and eight-tailed serpent) awakens on the first day of October, the 'godless month', which is also Himeko's and Chikane's shared sixteenth birthday. The girls are the reincarnations of the Solar and Lunar *Miko*, and must summon Ame no Murakumo, the deity of swords, whom it is prophesied will defeat the eight Orochi (in the anime the Orochi's eight heads become eight specific evil entities). A major focus is the erotic relationship (*yuri*) between Himeko and Chikane, and at the series' end, after Chikane has sacrificed herself for Himeko, she is reincarnated (in a Buddhist touch) and reunited with Himeko in her next life.[38]

A further connection between this anime and Shintō is that Yamata no Orochi features in the major cycle of myths surrounding the *kami* of the waters, Susanoo no Mikoto, the powerful yet morally ambiguous brother of Amaterasu. Banished from Heaven for offending his sister, Susanoo descended to earth and met two earthly *kami* in the Izumo region, who were lamenting the fate of their daughter, Kushinadahime (Princess of the Rice Field). They told Susanoo that she was their eighth daughter and that the other seven had been devoured by Yamata no Orochi, and that the time approached to hand over Kushinadahime, too.[39] Susanoo requested the girl's hand in marriage to which her parents agreed, and they then assisted him in preparing to combat the serpent *kami*. They set up eight tubs of rice wine and 'when the serpent actually appeared, each head drank one tub of rice wine. It became drunk and fell asleep.

---

37. Drazen, *Anime Explosion!*, 165-66.
38. Crusader, 'Kannazuki no Miko (Redux): The Greatest Love Story Ever Told in Mecha', *That Anime Blog* (2008), at http://www.thatanimeblog.com/index.php/2008/07/kannazuki-no-miko-redux-the-greatest-love-story-ever-told-in-mecha (accessed 3 October 2010).
39. Juliet Piggott, *Japanese Mythology* (London, New York, Sydney and Toronto: Paul Hamlyn, 1969), 16.

Susa-no-o drew his sword [and] chopped the serpent into pieces'.[40] From the tail of the vanquished serpent Susanoo took the legendary sword Kusanagi no Tsurugi, which is one of the three sacred Imperial Regalia of Japan (with the mirror Yata no Kagami and the jewel Yasakani no Magatama).

Interestingly, in the *Kojiki*, there is mention of the 'Ten Sacred Auspicious Treasures' that are considered to have supernatural powers. These treasures fall into four groups: 'the mirrors, the sword, the jewels, and the scarfs'.[41] It cannot be claimed that the Ten Sacred Auspicious Treasures directly inspired the frequent appearance of objects with magical powers in anime, but the general Japanese belief that some objects do possess supernatural powers might demonstrate the continuity from mythology to anime. Talismans appear to be particularly popular objects for help and protection in Japan. Within Shintō 'shaking or jingling talismans or other objects is supposed to have a magical virtue'.[42] In addition, students in Japan rely on the god of wisdom Jurojin 'to guide them in examinations. Jurojin is one of the Shichi Fukujin (Seven Gods of Good Luck) whose amulets and talismans are highly sought after in secular Japan's common pursuit of supernatural intervention in life's happenings'.[43] Within the genre of anime, talismans are a common feature. In Naoko Takeuchi's *Sailor Moon*, developed first as a manga in 1992 and in anime form shortly after, five schoolgirls in Japan are the reincarnated Sailor Soldiers of the Moon Kingdom. Talismans feature in the schoolgirls' recognition of their true identity and mission. As Navok and Rudranath state, 'a klutzy girl named Usagi Tsukino…runs into a talking cat named Luna… [and] she too becomes a sailor soldier, Sailor Moon, through the help of a magical brooch'.[44]

While magic is closely associated with the supernatural and it often appears in anime, the Shintō view of magic is somewhat inconsistent. Aston notes that Shintō 'lends its sanction to some practices of this kind by affirming that they were taught or practiced by Gods, or by deifying the objects used in them. But there are others which it condemns' if these magical practices are used for evil or hostile reasons.[45] Osamu Tezuka's

---

40. Cornelius Ouwehand, 'Some Notes on the God Susa-no-o', *Monumenta Nipponica* 14.3-4 (1959): 388.

41. Katō, *A Study of Shintō*, 21-22.

42. William George Aston, *Shinto: The Way of the Gods* (Bristol and Tokyo: Ganesha Publishing and Oxford University Press, 1997 [1905]), 335.

43. Raymond Lamont-Brown, 'Japan's New Spirituality', *Contemporary Review* 275.1603 (1999): 70.

44. Jay Navok and Sushil K. Rudranath, *Warriors of Legend: Reflections of Japan in Sailor Moon*, 2nd edn (North Charleston, SC: BookSurge, LLC, 2005), 24.

45. Aston, *Shinto*, 337.

1967 *shōjo* anime classic *Ribon no Kishi* (literally 'A Knight in Ribbons', but known as *Princess Knight*, serialized from 1953 to 1956 in the girls' magazine *Shōjo Club*), explores this dualistic approach to magic through the character of Heckett, the daughter of Satan. *Princess Knight* has a medieval fairytale setting in which Princess Sapphire of Silverland, who was born with two hearts (a male and a female), has to pretend to be a man as her parents need an heir for their kingdom. While having adventures as a knight, she falls in love with Prince Frank of the neighbouring kingdom, Goldland, and he with her, though he is unaware of her true identity. The influence of Christianity is apparent in the Western medieval setting, the guardian angel assigned to Sapphire (variously called Tink, Chink, or Choppy), and the presence of Satan as the most powerful villain in the series. Satan has enormous magical powers, which he uses for evil. Yet his teenage daughter Heckett, a witch (her name is derived from Hekate, the Ancient Greek goddess of sorcery), reveals to Sapphire that she yearns to be good, and she uses her magical powers to protect Sapphire and thwart her father's plans. One particular power Heckett has is the ability to transform herself into a number of different animal forms.[46]

It is interesting to note that while on one hand anime is full of supernatural elements and Shintō seems to represent its main source of inspiration, on the other hand anime also frequently features the realities of life, in other words, it often portrays the mundane realities of life. Arguably, this realistic element of the stories may also reflect the influence of Shintō which does not sharply divide the sacred and the secular in the way that Christianity does, rather advocating a '"realistic" affirmation of life and values in this world, accepting life and death, good and evil, as inevitable parts of the world we live in'.[47] In relation to the term 'religion' Jason Ānanda Josephson notes that, in the mid-nineteenth century when this term was introduced to Japan, Japanese translators could not determine its equal in the Japanese language, and were puzzled as to its meaning. He elaborates that 'there was no indigenous word that referred to something as broad as "religion," nor a systematic way to distinguish between "religion" as members of a larger generic category'.[48] This argument applies to many cultures apart from that of Japan, and has led to a widespread scholarly belief that 'religion' is a Western construction

---

46. Rebecca Suter, 'From *Jusuheru* to *Jannu*: Girl Knights and Christian Witches in the Work of Miuchi Suzue', *Mechademia* 4 (2009): 241-56.
47. Tsunetsugu Muraoka, paraphrased in Earhart, *Japanese Religion*, 38.
48. Jason Ānanda Josephson, 'When Buddhism Became a "Religion" – Religion and Superstition in the Writings of Inoue Enryō', *Japanese Journal of Religious Studies* 33.1 (2006): 144.

that derives from Christianity and is not an exact fit for the traditions of other peoples. Thomas P. Kasulis has noted that many Japanese who are deeply involved in the festivals and observances of Shintō will nevertheless say that they have no 'religion' (*shūkyō*) because the term is both alien and generally understood prescriptively.[49] What they are doing is simply living. Thus the mixture of pragmatic realism and spiritual magic that is characteristic of anime reflects the union of the sacred and the secular in Shintō.

The spiritual beliefs of the Japanese people, already present in their religions prior to the production of anime, have provided a vital source of inspiration for various aspects of anime, including its graphic and narrative forms. In terms of these religious traditions, Shintō is clearly dominant, followed by Buddhism, Christianity, and other religions that are present in Japan. It is important to note that it is not the intention here to develop a sociological discussion about why the religions that are present in Japan are also present in anime, or to explain the dominance of Shintō motifs and themes. Rather, the focus is on a selection of elements from a set of religions present in Japan that can be identified in anime. It is unsurprising that religions such as Shintō and Buddhism would feature more prominently, as anime is a Japanese creation and the socio-cultural mix of Japan provides the major, though not the sole, source of inspiration for anime artists. Cultural products inevitably reflect the host culture in which they are developed, regardless of whether they stand in opposition to that culture or valorize it. Some of the elements from Shintō that are reflected in anime and are considered in this chapter include animism, metamorphosis, the supernatural including ghosts and spirit beings, the spirit world, objects of power, and sexual ambiguity and androgyny. This chapter also examines how Buddhist notions of immortality and reincarnation are visually represented and treated in a selection of anime. The notion of apocalypse and post-apocalypse are some of the Christian elements that appear in certain anime, such as *Neon Genesis Evangelion* and *Trinity Blood* (in which a boy Pope leads humanity against post-apocalyptic vampires).[50] As detailed knowledge of Christian theology is not part of Japanese culture, these anime do not literally employ the Christian apocalypse; rather, they use the idea of world destruction and the nature of human life after it.

---

49. Kasulis, *Shinto*, 69.
50. Adam Barkman, 'Did Santa Die on the Cross?', in Josef Steiff and Tristan D. Tamplin (eds), *Anime and Philosophy: Wide-Eyed Wonder* (Chicago and La Salle, IL: Open Court, 2010), 111-15.

Animism and Anthropomorphism: Categories for Analysing Anime

Shintō is often classified as an animistic religion, and animism is a useful category to employ in the analysis of anime and certain other aspects of Japanese culture and aesthetics. Animism as an analytical tool was developed in the late nineteenth century by the founding father of anthropology Edward Burnett Tylor in *Primitive Culture* (1871). Animism, as Taylor describes it, is the view that entities that are usually considered to be soulless and without the trace of life (such as thunder, stones, and so on) are not soulless and inanimate but that they too have soul and life in them. Tylor further observes that animism is:

> the belief in the animation of all nature, rising at its highest pitch to personification...a belief in personal souls animating what we call inanimate bodies, a theory of transmigration of souls as well in life as after death, a sense of crowds of spiritual beings, sometimes flitting through the air, but sometimes also inhabiting trees and rocks and waterfalls, and lending their personality to such material objects.[51]

In the broadest sense, animism, according to Tylor, is the thesis that individual life force is present in the entities from the natural world which are usually considered lacking it. There is not an entity which does not possess a life force in itself, Tylor argued when speaking about the highest form of animism; if an entity exists, whatever that entity may be, it does possess a life form, a 'spirit' and 'psychological being' that is not very different from 'that of humans and animals'.[52] The belief in the personal spirit leaving the corpse after death is epitomised in the expression 'being "beside oneself"'.[53] This expression is the literal meaning of 'ecstasy', derived from the Greek *extasis*. Tylor 'described the phenomenon of a ghost soul, able to enter into, possess, and act in animals, plants, and objects (e.g., weapons, clothing, food)'.[54] The animistic worldview, widely spread in early human culture, was the seed, Tylor believed, from which would later grow the phenomenon called religion.[55] One of the important postulates of the animistic worldview is the idea that the 'souls' are endowed with the ability to change the place of dwelling in a sense that their rebirth can be actualized in either a living creature other than human, a material entity or another human

---

51. Edward B. Tylor, *Primitive Culture: Researches into the Development of Mythology, Philosophy, Religion, Art and Custom*, vols. 1 and 2 (New York: Gordon Press, 1974 [1871]), 60.
52. Michael Hill, *Slave to the Rhythm: Animation at the Service of the Popular Music Industry*, unpublished MA thesis (Sydney: University of Technology, 1995), 7.
53. Hill, *Slave to the Rhythm*, 7.
54. Hill, *Slave to the Rhythm*, 7.
55. Tylor, *Primitive Culture*, 83.

being. An animal soul can also move into the human body. When this is actualized an individual inherits that animal's character trait, for example, 'a person becomes cunning like a fox' or the human undergoes therianthropic transformation,[56] as in the myth of Diana and Actaeon from Ovid's *Metamorphoses*.

Tylor's notion of animism had a lineage in the philosophy of religion, and thus was not new. The term had been coined as *animismus* by the German scientist Georg Ernst Stahl around 1720, and the Scottish Enlightenment philosopher David Hume's *Natural History of Religion* (1757) was one of the earliest significant sources on animism, though he did not use the English term. Hume explained religion in terms of humanity's tendency to posit 'invisible intelligent powers' and this is linked to animism due to humanity's 'universal tendency' to project human nature onto the surrounding objects and entities, conceiving 'all beings like themselves' and to 'transfer to every object those qualities... of which they are intimately conscious'.[57] It is immediately clear that Hume's formulation links animism to anthropomorphism, discussed below, in that while the elements of the natural world possess spirit or an animating principle, for Hume the crucial issue is that these invisible powers are modelled on humanity itself. It is interesting to note that while Charles Hanly observes how the Renaissance represents a turning point which designated a progression from 'animistic' to 'scientific thinking',[58] this appears to be exclusively a Western transition. Japan is indifferent to this shift, as these two ways of thought seem to coexist there without mutual negation. Bearing this in mind, it is logical to accept that anime in which technology is an important part of the story, such as science-fiction anime, also involves animism.

It is valuable to note that since Tylor proposed his theory on animism it has been 'revised little if at all'.[59] Tylor establishes two 'dogmas' of animism where the 'surviving souls of the dead' is the focus of the first one, while various other types of spirit beings, including deities, are the focus of the second. The spirit world of these beings, however, is not separated from a material reality and its inhabitants. These otherworldly creatures are involved in various ways in the lives of human beings and belief in them necessarily involves humans in religious prac-

---

56. Hill, *Slave to the Rhythm*, 7.
57. David Hume, *A Dissertation on the Passions and the Natural History of Religions*, ed. T. L. Beauchamp (Oxford: Clarendon Press, 2006 [1757]), 40.
58. Charles Hanly, 'Pragmatism, Tradition, and Truth', *American Imago* 63.3 (2006): 268.
59. Nurit Bird-David, '"Animism" Revisited: Personhood, Environment, and Relational Epistemology', *Current Anthropology* 40 (1999): S67.

tice. Tylor succinctly explains that 'animism, in its full development, includes the belief in souls and in a future state, in controlling deities and subordinate spirits, these doctrines practically resulting in some kind of active worship'.[60]

Reflecting on this notion in 1918, the founder of psychoanalysis, Sigmund Freud, endorsed the Tylorian theory of animism with scarcely any changes. The focus of his essay 'Animism, Magic and the Omnipotence of Thought' was to explain the way that early humans observed sleep and dreaming and linked these to death, which appeared similar, and formed the idea of a soul or animating part of the human person that was separate from the body and did not die. Freud perceived the connection between animism and anthropomorphism, commenting that 'animatism', the doctrine of the 'universality of life' and the term 'manism' were similarly applicable.[61] In Shintō, having a soul is not a privilege exclusive to humans. More precisely, animals as well as inanimate objects also 'have souls'.[62] In the West a general view would be that objects are simply objects, whereas in Japan objects are not seen as mere 'things' that are consumed and consequently thrown away. Thus problems arise for people in terms of what to do with their used objects. Instead of simply discarding items such as dolls which their owners no longer wish to keep, there are special memorial services organized where the ritual performed is believed to enable the dolls to reach enlightenment or 'Buddhahood'.[63] The most important recent reformulation of animism, by the English scholar Graham Harvey, shifts the emphasis from determining what is or is not 'alive' (possessing a spirit) to an orientation focused on interpersonal relationships, between human and non-human persons. He argues that animists 'recognise that the world is full of persons...and...life is always lived in relationship with others'.[64] This attitude is far more prevalent in contemporary Japan. As Anne Allison notes, 'an animist sensibility percolates the postmodern landscape of Japan today in ways that do not occur in the United States', and that this sensibility is nourished by both folklore and religion.[65]

The belief in animism in Japan runs deep and extends to the personhood of natural phenomena, veneration of the ancestors, and spirits

---

60. Edward B. Tylor, *Primitive Culture: Researches into the Development of Mythology, Philosophy, Religion, Language, and Art, and Custom*, vol. 1, 4th edn (London: John Murray, 1903 [1871]), 427.
61. Sigmund Freud, *Totem and Taboo* (London: Routledge, 2003 [1950]), 75–91.
62. Reader, *Religion in Contemporary Japan*, 45.
63. Reader, *Religion in Contemporary Japan*, 46.
64. Graham Harvey, *Animism: Respecting the Living World* (Kent Town, SA and London: Wakefield Press and C. Hurst and Co., 2005), xi.
65. Allison, *Millennial Monsters*, 12.

animating modern technological objects. The advent of technology in the nineteenth century, in the wake of Commodore Matthew C. Perry's 1853 mission opening Japan to the West and the rapid industrialization under the Meiji government did not cause a rift with the old tradition of Shintō, so although twenty-first century Japan is highly developed in terms of technology 'there still seems to be a place for communication with the intangible *kami* that, in Shintō belief, permeate all of life'.[66] In anime inanimate entities are often endowed with life, and these entities are both natural and mechanical. The first of Osamu Tezuka's anime to gain a Western audience, 1963's *Tetsuwan Atomu* ('Iron-Arm Atom', usually called *Astro Boy* in English) featured a child-robot created by scientist Dr Tenma to replace his dead son Tobio. Rejected by Dr Tenma because he was not truly human, Astro Boy is rescued by the benevolent Dr Elefun and dedicates himself to fighting crime. Interestingly, Dr Tenma is constantly shown to be wrong about his creation, as throughout the series Astro's emotional life is explored in detail, and he is shown to be kind and loving, brave and loyal, capable of joy and suffering.[67] In short, machines feel and are animate, are just like people, and are loved and mourned, like the dolls mentioned above.

As previously noted, Shintō's nature worship has also been described as 'a way of life'.[68] Shintō is deeply imbricated with the lived reality of the Japanese. Japanese tradition focuses on balance, equilibrium and the attainment of union between humanity and the environment, and this union is seen as vital.[69] A close relationship with Shintō is reflected in anime as its various aspects are often embedded in their stories and in the beliefs and philosophies of their characters. Amongst these, perhaps the most frequently encountered one is animism. Animistic references are rife in anime, and may play an integral part of the story such as in Hayao Miyazaki's films *My Neighbour Totoro* (1988), *Princess Mononoke* (1997) and *Spirited Away* (2001), among others, which celebrate the role and power of nature gods present in the wild forest and view human life as steeped in magic, metamorphosis and spirituality. However, in terms of the presence of 'religion' in his work, Miyazaki appears to give contradictory statements. In relation to this George J. Tanabe notes that Jolyon

---

66. Mary Pat Fisher, *Religions Today: An Introduction* (London: Routledge, 2002), 134.
67. Claudia Dreifus, 'A Passion to Build a Better Robot, One with Social Skills and a Smile', *New York Times* (10 June 2003), at http://www.philosophicalturn.net/intro/Consciousness/Emotional_Robots.pdf (accessed 5 October 2010).
68. Bunce, *Religions in Japan*, 98.
69. Tetsunori Koizumi, 'Traditional Japanese Religion and the Notion of Economic Man', *Journal of Cultural Economics* 1.2 (1977).

2 The New Life of Old Beliefs

Baraka Thomas has argued that *shūkyō asobi*, 'religious play', is at work in the film, conflating religion and entertainment. However, Miyazaki:

> denies any connection between his work and religion, and says that his *anime* productions are just for entertainment. At other times, Miyazaki admits his use of spiritual themes, even if he dissociates their connection with particular religious traditions. Thomas uses his idea of *shūkyō asobi* to account for Miyazaki's sliding scale in which religion and entertainment can intertwine. Thomas argues that religion and entertainment conflate, and that any separation between the two is artificial and ultimately impossible.[70]

It is, however, possible to read Miyazaki's ambivalence towards religion to be the result of his experience of World War II, as his family owned an aeronautics firm that manufactured parts for the Japanese airforce.[71] As noted in Chapter 1, the role played by Shintō and Japanese nationalism during the War creates a problematic legacy for manga and anime artists. Yet the fusion of religion and entertainment posited by Jolyon Baraka Thomas is at the core of the argument of this book. Modern people watch anime and read manga, use their mobile phones and computers to communicate, go to the gym and shop for identity-conferring consumer goods, and find spiritual meaning in all these activities.

Another notion that frequently appears in anime is anthropomorphism, and indeed Miyazaki's *My Neighbour Totoro* attributes human-like characteristics to animal creatures, just as *Astro Boy* attributes them to machines.[72] In simple terms, anthropomorphism refers to an animal or object that displays human characteristics or behaviour. It could be argued that anthropomorphism in anime derives from two major religious sources: Buddhist teachings and Japanese animal scrolls. In his research into primal cultures Tylor elucidated the idea of anthropomorphism and described it as 'a sub-category of animism'.[73] Endowment of entities other than human beings with the characteristics of the latter is called anthropomorphism,[74] and it has its roots in Greek terms, '*anthrōpos*

---

70. George J. Tanabe Jr, 'Playing with Religion', *Nova Religio: The Journal of Alternative and Emergent Religions* 10.3 (2007): 98.
71. Helen McCarthy, *Hayao Miyazaki: Master of Japanese Animation. Films, Themes, Artistry* (Berkeley, CA: Stone Bridge Press, 1999), 26.
72. Colin Odell and Michel le Blanc, *Studio Ghibli: The Films of Hayao Miyazaki and Isao Takahata* (London: Kamera Books, 2009), 78.
73. Hill, *Slave to the Rhythm*, 12.
74. Anon, 'Anthropomorphism, n.'; 'Metamorphosis, n.'; 'Androgyny, n.', *Oxford English Dictionary* (Oxford: Oxford University Press, n.d.), at http://www.oed.com (accessed 3 October 2010).

"human being" ... [and] *morphē* "form"'.⁷⁵ Anthropomorphism finds its application in many fields and one of this is architecture where the house, with its doors and windows, is made in such a way 'to be read as [human] faces'.⁷⁶ Mickey Mouse, Donald Duck and Goofy are some of many Disney's animal characters, which, apart from being dressed in the garments of humans are also endowed with behaviour, reasoning, feeling, and ability of speech as human beings. Michael Hill notes that, '[i]nanimate objects, as well as coming to life, often have human features, as do landscapes'.⁷⁷ It is interesting to note that, while anthropomorphism has old roots, in contemporary times this ancient notion has become appreciated by the scientific community in the fields of computing and robotics. The reason for this lies in the fact that they believe that anthropomorphism 'appears to be the most efficient and most spontaneous register through which humans establish – consciously or not – a strong relationship with artifacts or other non-human living beings'.⁷⁸

Aston claims that Shintō is an anthropomorphic religion because 'its deities are for the most part personified powers, elements and objects of nature'.⁷⁹ Amaterasu Omikami, the sun-goddess, presides over other gods and goddesses that include the 'Moon-God, the God of Growth, the Food-Goddess, Gods of Fire, Wind, Water, Earth, Seas, Mountains, Rivers, Thunder, Trees, and Islands'.⁸⁰ Animal symbolism is particularly important in Shintō anthropomorphism and its manifestation in the anime. Religion and art abounded with 'animal symbols' long before the use of these in animations.⁸¹ A retrospective view of world cultures discloses many deities whose appearance was a mix of human and animal, such as Egyptian Hathor, Amon and Thoth, and the Indian Ganesha, an elephant-headed deity. In order to seduce a woman to whom he is attracted, the chief god in Greek mythology, Zeus, would metamorphose into an animal (swan, bull or eagle). Egyptians and the seventeenth-century Algonquin Indians shared a belief that the sun and the moon were siblings (brother and sister) with the difference that to Egyptians they were also spouses (Osiris and Isis).⁸² To modern people personifications in mythology are

---

75. Anon, 'Anthropomorphous', *Oxford Dictionaries* (n.d.), at http://oxforddictionaries.com/definition/english/anthropomorphous (accessed 27 December 2012).
76. Hill, *Slave to the Rhythm*, 12.
77. Hill, *Slave to the Rhythm*, 12.
78. Denis Vidal, 'Anthropomorphism or Sub-anthropomorphism? An Anthropological Approach to Gods and Robots', *Journal of the Royal Anthropological Institute* (New Series) 13.4 (2007): 919.
79. William George Aston, 'Japanese Myth', *Folklore* 10.3 (1899): 315.
80. Aston, 'Japanese Myth', 315.
81. Hill, *Slave to the Rhythm*, 12.
82. Tylor, *Primitive Culture* (1974 [1871]), 26.

often understood metaphorically, which is in a sharp contrast to early human cultures where 'metaphor was replaced by animism and anthropomorphism. The stars really were dancing men who had climbed a very tall tree which had been cut down, leaving them stranded in the sky'.[83]

Another example of anthropomorphism can be traced back to the ancient Japanese belief that objects such as 'musical instruments, kitchen utensils, religious paraphernalia, clothing, armor, and so on' after having been disposed of may may become alive, and then 'commit all sorts of pranks, some mischievous, others hostile' as well as take revenge on their former owners.[84] For example, Hildburgh observes that brooms and similar objects believed also to be the dwelling place of spirits 'receive generally kindly and respectful treatment, and even, in some cases, devotion'.[85] It is likely that the attribution of inhabiting spirits to brooms has to do with their function in cleaning, which extends to the belief that brooms are 'efficacious in the clearing away or the rendering powerless of spectral or of psychical impurities'.[86]

This attitude prevails in contemporary Japanese religious ceremonies regarding dolls and other items to be disposed of, and in manga where machines are the emotional and moral equivalent of human persons. The plot of Mamoru Oshii's *Ghost in the Shell 2: Innocence* (2004) concerns gynoids, sex-toy androids, who are killing their male owners, apparently due to defective programming. Batō, a detective from Division Nine, witnesses one of these 'dolls' commit suicide by tearing apart her own mechanical body after pleading with him '*tasukete, tasukete*' (help me, help me). As he investigates Batō discovers that the company manufacturing the gynoids 'has been using trafficked children in an illegal procedure called "ghost-dubbing", transferring their "ghosts" to gynoids to animate them… [which] endow[s] androids with a crude version of a ghost, or soul'.[87]

Anthropomorphism is also detected in clay figures that date from ancient Japan[88] which most likely represent its earliest expressions. Interestingly, while Japanese history records the belief in anthropomorphism, on the other hand, there was also the belief in theriomorphic transformation. More precisely, the Japanese also believed that 'Buddha

---

83. Hill, *Slave to the Rhythm*, 12.
84. Elizabeth Lillehoj, 'Man-made Objects as Demons in Japanese Scrolls', *Asian Folklore Studies* 54.1 (1995): 8.
85. Walter L. Hildburgh, 'Some Magical Applications of Brooms in Japan', *Folklore* 30.3 (1919): 189.
86. Hildburgh, 'Some Magical Applications of Brooms in Japan', 171.
87. Orbaugh, 'Emotional Infectivity', 156.
88. Johannes Maringer, 'Clay Figurines of the Jomon Period: A Contribution to the History of Ancient Religion in Japan', *History of Religions* 14.2 (1974): 128.

and the gods might take the form of an animal to save a person in trouble'.[89] In Buddhist teachings, animals often symbolize the embodiment of Buddha's 'superlative qualities'.[90] Anthropomorphism is further encountered in the folk performance *Shishi odori*, in which is incorporated 'the anthropomorphic behaviour of a deer that mediate[s] the real and the spiritual worlds'.[91]

Hill writes that this 'aspect of anthropomorphism' results in 'the mixing of the objective and the subjective'.[92] Claude Lévi-Strauss noted this occurrence while discussing the harmonious relation between sentiment and knowledge in the case of a zoologist who gave a name, Flippy, to a dolphin, while also calling it *tursiops truncatus*.[93] The presence of anthropomorphism was also reflected in *The Trials of Life*, a television series where scientists give human names to the animals they researched; a killer whale is called Bernard, a female elephant is called Tulip, and the scientist also discusses Tulip's choice of a partner from the group. People assigning a name, designated for humans, to their vehicles, cats and dogs, and also to their homes is a frequent occurrence. Hurricanes and cyclones are regularly given human names by meteorologists. Hill observes that:

> There is a further connection with nature in the early musical cartoons through the use of animal characters and animal symbolism, with the animal characters representing humans. This is extended with the common use of the fable form of storytelling, often used in animation, in which animal characters, representing humans, play out some moral tale for the edification of the humans.[94]

Prehistoric times abound with the examples of humans adorned with the features of an animal (feather, for instance) transforming, symbolically speaking, into it during rituals, as in the case of the famed 'Dancing Sorcerer' painting in the cave of Les Trois Frères.[95] There was also a practice in which, to ensure a successful hunt, the images of animals were painted on the walls of caves and attacked with a weapons. In Jung's

---

89. Robert Smith, 'On Certain Tales of the *Konjaku Monogatari* as Reflections of Japanese Folk Religion', *Asian Folklore Studies* 25 (1966): 232.

90. Tony Page, *Buddhism and Animals: A Buddhist Vision of Humanity's Rightful Relationship with the Animal Kingdom* (London: UKAVIS, 1999), 87.

91. Christopher S. Thompson, 'The Ochiai Deer Dance: A Traditional Dance in a Modern World', *Journal of Popular Culture* 38.1 (2004): 131.

92. Hill, *Slave to the Rhythm*, 13.

93. Claude Lévi-Strauss, *The Savage Mind* (London: Weidenfeld and Nicholson, 1966), 38.

94. Hill, *Slave to the Rhythm*, 13.

95. Herbert Kühn, *The Rock Pictures of Europe*, trans. Alan Houghton Brodrick (London: Sidgwick and Jackson, 1956).

psychoanalytic approach, the image of an animal is associated with both the instinctual aspect of the human psyche and human beings' link with the natural world.[96]

Closely linked to anthropomorphism is the ancient idea of metamorphosis. It was a key theme in Classical Greek and Roman mythology, and gave its name to the poet Ovid's most important work. Since the inception of the medium of animation, this idea was enthusiastically adopted and became so important that, in the context of animation studies, it is known as an 'animation concept'. Metamorphosis is defined as '1. a. The action or process of changing in form, shape, or substance; *esp.* transformation by supernatural means'.[97] Greek and Roman writers found metamorphosis intriguing and attempted to offer explanations of it. While the works of two ancient Greek writers, Heraclitus and Palaephatus, contain 'transformation stories' these 'were seen as misunderstandings of everyday events, or as springing from metaphors or exaggerations'.[98] Yet there is also another dimension to the metamorphosis stories; metamorphic stories that feature in the poetry of Homer have been viewed 'as examples of philosophical allegory' and as expressing intellectual arguments.[99] Contemporary students of metamorphoses hold that such stories are products of human imagination, but ancient thinkers held them to be genuine occurrences that required explanation. Significantly, Marion Gymnich and Alexandre Segão Costa note that cultures throughout the world in their 'collective memory' contain 'the motif of human-animal transformation', and writers such as William Shakespeare, Gerard Manley Hopkins, Franz Kafka, Geoffrey Chaucer, Richard Flanagan and Michel Faber, all dealt in their work with the theme of this type of transformation.[100] These examples are all from the Western tradition, but a majority of world cultures have stories about human into animal transformations and vice versa. The biological reality of transformations experienced by animals, such as snakes sloughing off their skins and the development of butterflies, gave humans a rich store of images for reflecting on change and transformation.

The idea of metamorphosis or transformation of a human being after his or her death was also present in ancient Japanese beliefs. Mary

---

96. Carl Gustav Jung, *Four Archetypes* (London: Routledge, 2006 [1969]).
97. Anon, 'Anthropomorphism, n.'; 'Metamorphosis, n.'; 'Androgyny, n.'.
98. Paul M. C. Forbes Irving, *Metamorphosis in Greek Myths* (Oxford: Clarendon Press, 1990), 1.
99. Irving, *Metamorphosis in Greek Myths*, 1.
100. Marion Gymnich and Alexandro S. Costa, 'Of Humans, Pigs, Fish, and Apes: The Literary Motif of Human-Animal Metamorphosis and its Multiple Functions in Contemporary Fiction', *L'Esprit Créateur* 46.2 (2006): 70.

Picone notes that in Japan the decomposition of the corpse was a particularly powerful process, believed 'to parallel the life cycle of certain beings, such as snakes and insects'.[101] Death offers one of the most powerful examples of transformation, as the untended corpse will putrefy, becoming liquid and stinking where when living it was solid and wholesome. The three-tier cosmos of Shintō mythology has been mentioned above; the realm of the dead, Yomi-no-Kuni, meaning the 'land of eternal night', is a filthy and gloomy realm, situated in a remote place beneath the earth. The Shintō idea of purity and impurity is chiefly conceived of as physical, and death is regarded as pollution. At the Great Shrine of Ise, the chief shrine of the imperial cult in Japan, it is forbidden even to mention the words 'death' or 'grave'. After giving birth to the fire deity Kagutsuchi, Izanami died and went to Yomi.[102] Her brother-husband Izanagi ventured to Yomi to seek her. When they met she told him that she had eaten the food of the dead and would have to consult the *kami* of the dead as to whether she might return to the world of the living. She requested that Izanagi wait in the darkness for her.

The *Nihon Shoki* (*Nihongi*) contains an extensive account of this tale. Myths where living beings seek the resurrection of the dead usually result in the lesson that once one is dead, life is gone forever. This example is no exception:

> Izanami tarried so long within that he became impatient. Then, taking the wooden comb that he wore in the left bunch of his hair, he broke off a tooth from one end of the comb and lighted it, and went in to look for Izanami-no-Mikoto. But he saw her lying swollen and festering among worms; and eight kinds of Thunder-Gods sat on her... And Izanagi, being overawed by the sight, would have fled away, but Izanami rose up, crying: 'Thou hast put me to shame! Why didst thou not observe that which I charged thee?... Thou hast seen my nakedness; now I will see thine!' And she bade the Ugly Females of Yomi to follow after him and slay him; and the eight Thunder-Gods also pursued him, and Izanami herself pursued him.[103]

Having been in contact with the corruption of death, Izanagi must bathe in the sea to regain a state of ritual purity. This myth reveals why reincarnation is so popular in anime. One of the main reasons why Japanese people say they are 'born Shintō, die Buddhist' is that while Shintō welcomes newborn babies into the shrine community, and through

---

101. Mary Picone, 'Lineaments of Ungratified Desire: Rebirth in Snake Form in Japanese Popular Religion', *RES: Anthropology and Aesthetics* 5 (1983): 105.

102. Piggott, *Japanese Mythology*, 15.

103. Hearn, *Japan's Religions*, 231-32.

ceremony they become a 'child of the *kami*', when the person dies a Buddhist ritual is performed.

It is interesting to note that prior to the arrival of Buddhism in Japan, as Ensho Ashikaga observes, there was no strict separation of the realm of the living from that of the dead. Early Japanese apparently held the view that those who died went to 'dark country from a light country', passing through the 'gloomy gate of death'.[104] Yet after death there is nothing for the devout save the grim underworld of Yomi, where there is neither reward nor punishment, just the misery of prolonged existence. This was the Yomi of the Izanagi and Izanami mythos, which was recorded in the *Kojiki*. The introduction of Buddhism to Japan resulted in a completely different view of the afterlife, in which 'the existence of the world after death consisted of the "six places," one of which was the hell of hunger'.[105] However, Buddhism offers a more positive vision of the afterlife through reincarnation, and the ultimate goal of achieving enlightenment through Buddhahood or attaining bliss in the Pure Land of the West. Of particular interest with regard to anime, where humans merge with machinery to become cyborgs, robots are endowed with feelings, and consciousness is able to be continued after the death of the mortal body through computer circuitry, is the Japanese custom of conducting memorial ceremonies to grant release to unquiet spirits, particularly those who have died unmarried. Klaus Antoni explains that if a person died from unnatural causes and prematurely, particularly if they were 'young and unmarried', they would not achieve Buddhahood after death, but would transform into 'wandering spirits'.[106] These wandering spirits are not benign towards the human beings that are still alive but are dangerous to them. Thus, doll spouses are provided for these unfulfilled dead (who include young men killed in war and members of both sexes who have died in childhood), and through ritual they are rendered complete by means of symbolic marriage, and enabled to enter Buddhahood.[107]

Although metamorphosis is an ancient concept and animation is a modern visual medium, they are complementary phenomena. Metamorphosis is the complete change of form from one condition to another, radically different condition. In the context of animation 'plasticity of

---

104. Daiei Kaneko in, Ensho Ashikaga, 'The Festival for the Spirits of the Dead in Japan', *Western Folklore* 9.3 (1950): 224.
105. Ashikaga, 'The Festival for the Spirits of the Dead in Japan', 224.
106. Klaus Antoni, '*Yasukuni-Jinja* and Folk Religion: The Problem of Vengeful Spirits', *Asian Folklore Studies* 47.1 (1988): 130.
107. Ellen Schattschneider, 'Family Resemblances: Memorial Images and the Face of Kinship', *Japanese Journal of Religious Studies* 31.1 (2004): 143.

form' is an element that is crucially important.[108] Andrew Darley notes that it was Sergei Eisenstein (1898–1948) who coined the term 'plasmatic', referring to 'dynamic flexibility (metamorphosis, elasticity)', and in Eisenstein's view this was intrinsically characteristic of 'the imagery of drawn animation'.[109] Eisenstein's 'liberation of forms from the laws of logic'[110] refers to the line in animated films and its unconstrained ability of malleability; because of this, an item in an animated film 'is not limited by its own form'. Because metamorphosis is regularly used in animation making, malleable items in animated films 'are capable of assuming any form', which they frequently do.[111] The cast and props in animated films can comfortably do things that are behind the realm of the possible, such as those described in *Alice in Wonderland* by Lewis Carroll; an elephant finds no problem in squeezing through the needle's eye in animated films. These actions represent a type of 'reaction' to the world that is constrained by the law of physics and logic. Events in animated films have connection with those in dreams, a realm where everything is possible. Hill observes that, '[th]e practice of metamorphosis in animation allows the expression of this plasticity in animation as well as the practice of an animate design disintegrating or being destroyed then reassembling itself and reverting back to its original shape'.[112] Disney's animations were inspired by the artists Ludwig Richter and Wilhelm Busch, whose work embraced the expression of metamorphosis on a frequent basis.[113] While Richter made 'illustrated animal characters with an earthy rural humour and a refined naturalism', Busch's cast of *Max und Moritz* were 'illustrated with lyrical, flowing lines like corkscrew effects'.[114] The Disney cartoons subsequently influenced the manga and anime creations of Osamu Tezuka (1928–1989), but it can also be argued that metamorphosis is naturally present in anime by virtue of Shintō and Buddhist beliefs.

The blending of masculine and feminine is another popular motif in anime. Whether it is the suggested androgynous qualities of some of Osamu Tezuka's leading characters (particularly Princess Sapphire in *Ribon no Kishi*) or the more blatant play with gender transformation in

---

108. Hill, *Slave to the Rhythm*, 16.

109. Andrew Darley, 'Bones of Contention: Thoughts on the Study of Animation', *Animation: An Interdisciplinary Journal* 2.1 (2007): 74.

110. Sergei M. Eisenstein, *Eisenstein on Disney*, ed. J. Leyda (London: Methuen, 1988), 22.

111. Hill, *Slave to the Rhythm*, 16.

112. Hill, *Slave to the Rhythm*, 16.

113. Rebecca-Anne Do Rozario, 'Reanimating the Animated: Disney's Theatrical Productions', *Drama Review* 48.1 (2004): 164.

114. Hill, *Slave to the Rhythm*, 16.

Takahashi's *Ranma 1/2* (in which the sixteen-year-old boy Ranma Saotome is cursed by turning into a girl when he is splashed by cold water, though hot water will return him to being male), this motif has attracted a significant amount of attention and strongly appeals to both Japanese and Western audiences. Androgyny refers to the 'union of [the] sexes in one individual; hermaphroditism',[115] and in contemporary Japan, Erica Stevens Abbitt notes that it 'plays a central role in at least two aspects of Japanese contemporary culture' – one of these being fashion, 'where Japan has achieved international prominence in a new form of androgynous chic', the other being manga (and by extension anime), which features 'sexually ambivalent heroes exploring dangerous worlds'.[116]

When considering androgyny in Japanese mass media, Jennifer Robertson notes that:

> [s]ince the mid-1980s the English loanword *androjenii* (androgyny) has appeared frequently in the Japanese mass media and elsewhere in reference to clothing fashions, including 'cross-dressing', an expression most often used in reference to men's clothing adapted by and for women... Since *androjenii* is a transliteration, the term is often simultaneously defined in Japanese as either *ryōsei* (both sexes/genders) or *chūsei* (between sexes/genders).[117]

Androgyny, broadly interpreted to embrace all blurring of gender boundaries,[118] has a place in both Shintō and Buddhism. Some *kami* have changed sex over time; Tetsuo Yamaori observes that Inari Ōkami, the *kami* of rice, agriculture, fertility and worldly success, was originally of 'feminine character' and worshipped as a maternal deity; 'from the latter part of the ancient period to the medieval period' this kami had 'the character of an aged man (*okina*)'.[119]

Androgyny was also present in traditional modes of entertainment in Japan. *Kabuki* theatre, for example, was founded in the seventeenth century by a priestess named Okuni, who 'performed a mixture of Buddhist rites and erotic comedy wearing Portuguese pants and a Christian cross'.[120] However, later females were forbidden to perform and male

---

115. Anon, 'Anthropomorphism, n.'; 'Metamorphosis, n.'; 'Androgyny, n.'.
116. Erica Stevens Abbitt, 'Androgyny and Otherness: Exploring the West through the Japanese Performative Body', *Asian Theatre Journal* 18.2 (2001): 250-51.
117. Jennifer Robertson, 'The Politics of Androgyny in Japan: Sexuality and Subversion in the Theatre and Beyond', *American Ethnologist* 19.3 (1992): 420.
118. Rebecca Beyman and Jürgen W. Kremer, 'The Spirit of Integration: Mythic Androgyns and the Significance of Shamanic Trance', *Revision* 26.1 (2003): 41.
119. Tetsuo Yamaori, *Wandering Spirits and Temporary Corpses: Studies in the History of Japanese Religious Tradition*, ed. and trans. Dennis Hirota (Kyoto: International Research Center for Japanese Studies, 2004), 13.
120. Abbitt, 'Androgyny and Otherness', 250.

performers played both male and female roles. These performers were called *onnagata* and 'due in no small part to the slippage between their biological gender and the roles they enacted' they became highly popular.[121] Karen Nakamura and Hisako Matsuo argue that these gender blurrings, and in particular what they call 'female masculinity', exist in the Takarazuka Theatre, in *shōjo* (young girl) culture, and in manga and anime. The Takarazuka Theatre, founded in 1913, is the reverse of the situation in *kabuki*. This theatre is an all-female troupe, in which some women play *musume-yaku* ('the role of a woman') and some women play *otoko-yaku* ('the role of a man'). These actors are immensely popular and have legions of devoted fans. Those women who play men are often 'portrayed in the context of an "ideal male" image... They are outstandingly handsome, pure, kind, emotional, charming, funny, romantic and intelligent – that is, the complete antithesis of the salaryman'.[122] Nakamura and Matsuo link the Takarazuka Theatre to the birth of *shōjo* culture, as Osamu Tezuka's Sapphire, the heroine of *Ribon no Kishi* ('Princess Knight'), was both the original *shōjo* heroine and the first 'female masculine' manga and anime character.[123] This was no accident as Osamu Tezuka grew up in Takarazuka City (Hyōgo Prefecture) and attended many theatre performances with his mother, who was a fan. Frederik Schodt notes that Tezuka 'had Takarazuka stars among his neighbors, and after the War he drew cartoons for several Takarazuka Revue fan publications'.[124] Later *shōjo* heroines, particularly Hayao Miyazaki's Nausicaä from *Nausicaä of the Valley of the Wind* (1984), reiterate the tropes of female masculinity established by Sapphire: liminal, young, female, not yet adult, strong, capable and independent, courageous and moral. For the argument of this chapter, it is suggested that specific blurring of gender boundaries and androgyny in all its forms can be understood as a sub-category of metamorphosis and transformation.

Little has been said thus far about the Buddhist contribution to Japanese anime. However, in discussing metamorphosis, it becomes necessary to consider the Buddhist understanding of reality. Siddhartha Gautama, known as the Buddha ('enlightened one'), taught a doctrine of impermanence, which radically challenges any notion of a permanent, stable world. All is in flux, all is subject to change, including the

---

121. Abbitt, 'Androgyny and Otherness', 250.
122. Karen Nakamura and Hisako Matsuo, 'Female Masculinity and Fantasy Spaces: Transcending Genders in the Takarazuka Theatre and Japanese Popular Culture', in James E. Roberson and Nobue Suzuki (eds), *Men and Masculinities in Contemporary Japan: Dislocating the Salaryman Doxa* (London and New York: RoutledgeCurzon, 2003), 63.
123. Nakamura and Matsuo, 'Female Masculinity and Fantasy Spaces', 72.
124. Schodt, *Dreamland Japan*, 255.

idea that there is a permanent 'self'. Although there is a great difference between the Shintō and Buddhist attitudes to death, noted above, as Rajyashree Pandey notes:

> in Buddhism the body itself comes to serve as a pedagogical truth of the doctrine of impermanence… Part of the training of a Buddhist monk involved spending time at the charnel fields in order to observe in minute detail and meditate on the putrefaction of the human body. The purpose of this training was to recognise the true nature of the body and the self and to rid oneself of attachment and desire… Indeed if the self is problematised then the disintegration of the self takes on a radically different meaning and becomes the means for the attainment of enlightenment and liberation.[125]

This is particularly relevant when considering Mamoru Oshii's cyberpunk anime *Ghost in the Shell* (1995). This film was discussed in some detail in Chapter 1. Here it is only necessary to note that the film is:

> very optimistic about the future of human and technological 'symbiosis', with no real nature-guilt involved at all – rather a vindication of technology as humanity's vehicle to realize its future potential fully. There is a scene near the end of *Ghost in the Shell* where gunfire destroys all the indications of evolutionary pre-historical (that is, natural) stages on the wall of a museum, leaving only the reference to humanity (hominid) intact. This is a graphic way of saying that humanity's natural past is now obsolete, and the fusion between humans and machines is the next important stage in evolution.[126]

This film also plays with the notion of the 'internet as a "utopian" space devoid of race, gender, age or infirmity',[127] but the idea of fusing your individual person into a network of electronic impulses also fits very well with the Buddhist notion of *nirvana*, the extinction of the illusion of personhood in the oceanic bliss of the monistic unity of all.

Animal Transformations in Japanese Folklore and Anime

As noted in Chapter 1, *Chōjū Giga* are important Japanese animal scrolls, the creation of which is attributed to the Buddhist priest Kakuyū, more commonly known as Toba. These scrolls are held in the Kōzanji (Kōzan-ji) Temple in Toganoo, a Kyōto suburb situated in the mountains.

---

125. Rajyashree Pandey, 'The Medieval in Manga', *Postcolonial Studies* 3.1 (2000): 28-30.
126. Marco Olivier, 'Nihilism in Japanese Anime', *South African Journal of Art* 22.3 (2007): 67.
127. Carlo Silvio, 'Refiguring the Radical Cyborg in Mamoru Oshii's *Ghost in the Shell*', *Science Fiction Studies* 26 (1999): 54.

According to legend, there were originally five scrolls, of which only four are extant.[128] Close inspection of the drawing techniques in the scrolls has suggested that they were neither created by the same person nor at the same century. The earliest two scrolls are believed to date from the twelfth century, while the other two date from the thirteenth century. There is also an assumption that these scrolls were not executed by the 'Imperial Court' artists, but rather by 'priest-painters': '[the] illustrations are related to Buddhist iconographical drawings, and many of the games and sports, as well as the human figures and animal caricatures, can be directly associated with priests and Buddhist monasteries'.[129] The first of the scrolls, which is also the most widely known one, depicts animals in human situations exhibiting human behaviour in the manner of caricature. This scroll also includes the image of a monkey dressed as a monk who worships a 'frog Buddha'.[130]

Taihei Imamura interestingly observes that it is from the 'use of imaginative power' of the picture scrolls of medieval Japan that those who create Japanese animation today can learn a great deal. He explains that the 'scrolls came out of a backward and stagnated feudal Japan; under such oppression people generally find release in their imaginations rather than in reality'.[131] In other words, the escape into the imaginative world of picture scrolls was proportional to the degree of the repression that people in those times in Japan experienced. Yet, although some of the scrolls are highly imaginative, they do not necessarily represent escape from the reality, but on the contrary, they can also depict everyday life, much in the way anime combines mystical views with the quotidian. Amongst the picture scrolls that are outstanding in terms of creativity are '*Choju Giga Zukan* (picture scroll of birds and beasts), *Gaki-Zoshi* (storybook of famished devils), and *Hyakki-Yako-Zu-emaki* (picture scroll of pandemonium)'.[132] According to Imamura's interpretation, the images of animals dressed as and behaving as humans in *Chōjū Giga Zukan* scrolls depict 'the corrupt living conditions of the aristocracy and clergy in the end of the Heian era, a thousand years ago'. Another scroll, *Gaki-Zoshi*, shows the images of devils who symbolically represent the

---

128. Tsugio Miya, 'Chōjū Giga, Scroll of Frolicking Animals', in Shin'ichi Tani (ed.), *Japanese Scroll Paintings Chōjyū Giga* (Tokyo: Kadokawa Shoten, 1976), 1.

129. Miya, 'Chōjū Giga, Scroll of Frolicking Animals', 3.

130. K. Ueno, 'Explanation of Plates', in Shin'ichi Tani (ed.), *Japanese Scroll Paintings Chōjyū Giga*, 4.

131. Taihei Imamura, 'Japanese Art and the Animated Cartoon', *Quarterly of Film and Television* 7.3 (1953): 221.

132. Imamura, 'Japanese Art and the Animated Cartoon', 221.

vices. Similarly, through the images of anthropomorphized animals, the *Hyakki-Yako-Zu-Emaki* scroll depicts the 'feudalistic monarch's self-satisfaction, his retainers' ignorance, and their corrupt living conditions'.[133]

Inspired by the fables, a rich array of anthropomorphic animal characters are seen in numerous pioneering animated films. Human culture abounds with the use of fables and it is likely that the seed of fables is found in the early cultural heritage of humanity where the humans in those times lived in intimate connection with the animal world 'and from whose observations of animal behaviour similarities with human behaviour were deduced'.[134] Fable had a significant role in England during the eighteenth century where it was used not only to teach young members of the society of the approved behaviour within the society but also as a political satire. With mainly anthropomorphic animals as protagonists, legends and myths provided the main source of inspiration for fables. Jean de La Fontaine, a poet and fabulist, translated Phaedrus's and Aesop's fables, according them a proper place in the context of literary tradition.[135] Fables were indirectly applicable to human beings as they featured anthropomorphic animal characters. The readers had different opinions on these stories; that is, there were those who were open to this idea allowing 'the inherent communication process to work on themselves', while others 'rejected this application on an anthropomorphic interpretation alone', and did not find these stories neither amusing nor a wise choice.[136] The disguised teaching content of animal character fables was more readily accepted by readers than if it was expressed by human characters. The anthropomorphic animal characters in fables are frequently depicted as endowed with an ability to reason that was superior to those of their human counterparts; these characters (humans) had also been depicted as the ones who had lost their contact with the natural world. Cartesian perception which equates mindless machines and animals was thus not in harmony with this.[137]

Gods, inanimate entities, and humans also featured as the protagonists of fables, most likely to facilitate the readers' empathy. The acceptance of the anthropomorphic animal characters contributed to the fable's status as a 'memorable' piece of work, due to the audience becoming active participants, symbolically speaking, rather than just being passive listeners or readers. The listeners or readers of fables had also

---

133. Imamura, 'Japanese Art and the Animated Cartoon', 222.
134. Hill, *Slave to the Rhythm*, 14.
135. Anne Lynn Birberick, *Reading Undercover: Audience and Authority in Jean de La Fontaine* (Cranbury, NJ: Associated Universities Press, 1998).
136. Hill, *Slave to the Rhythm*, 14.
137. Anita Avramides, 'Descartes and Other Minds', *Teorema* XVI.I (1996): 33.

the task of abstracting the moral message from its content. The audience who first heard the song 'Who's Afraid of the Big Bad Wolf?' in the Disney animated film *Three Little Pigs* (1933) understood that this song contained a message relevant to the Depression era; thus, this audience were not just amused by the three anthropomorphic pigs in the film.[138]

Literary tradition, world mythologies and religious and also arts (both graphic and visual) are other fields that abound with examples of anthropomorphism. Apart from the *Chōjū Giga*, Japanese scrolls from the twelfth century featuring anthropomorphic animal characters satirizing humans, Japan also holds in its cultural heritage three other scrolls called the Hungry Ghost Scrolls, the Hell Scrolls and the Disease Scrolls which also satirize humans and their condition. Giuseppe Arcimboldo, painter, and J. J. Grandville, caricaturist and illustrator, both played with a combination of animal and human forms in their respective works; Arcimboldo used items from the natural world (grapes, pears, eggplants, birds and so on) in creating portraits of human faces suggesting the human's close and organic link with the natural world, while Grandville's work, featuring humans with the heads of the animals, was satirical in nature.[139] Apart from Arcimboldo and Grandville, there are also Norman Lindsay, Griset, Beatrix Potter, Landseer, Dorothy Wall, May Gibbs and Edward Lear, artists whose work also features anthropomorphic characters.[140] A reactionary attitude towards the views of Kant, Voltaire and Enlightenment whose stress was on empiricism and rationalism has been present in the works from the fabulist La Fontaine (in the seventeenth century) through the work of Hans Christian Anderson (in the eighteenth century), and Lewis Carroll (in the nineteenth century) to the creations of Walt Disney; all of them had a thread woven through their works that deals with the re-establishment of the close connection with the natural world.

In animation 'images fully metamorphose onscreen as space, objects and figures both emerge and dissolve'.[141] Technical developments also affected the capacity of animation to engage the viewer. For example, Patricia Vettel Tom argues that the introduction of sound in animation had an effect on the role of metamorphosis in animation. This was because before there was sound, metamorphosis was crucially important 'in forwarding the plot'. However, when sound started to be used in

---

138. Hill, *Slave to the Rhythm*, 15.

139. Thomas DaCosta Kaufmann, *Arcimboldo: Visual Jokes, Natural History, and Still-Life Painting* (Chicago, IL: University of Chicago Press, 2009).

140. Hill, *Slave to the Rhythm*, 15.

141. Aylish Wood, 'Re-Animating Space', *Animation: An Interdisciplinary Journal* 1.133 (2006): 139.

animation as a story device, metamorphosis ceased to be indispensable for the development of story.¹⁴² This raises the question of what might qualify as the first anime in Japan, and how its effectiveness might be affected by the fact that the audience already knew the story? While the first animated film made in Japan was in fact a propaganda film commissioned by the Imperial Navy, Japan's first colour animated feature film was *Panda and the White Serpent*.¹⁴³ This story is based on the Chinese legend, known from at least the sixteenth century, which claimed that a snake demon was imprisoned beneath Thunder Peak Pagoda, on West Lake in Huangzhou. This tale appears in Feng Menglong's collection of forty stories, *Jingshi tongyan* ('Stories to Caution the World') from 1624.¹⁴⁴ The tale concerns Xu Xian, a young pharmacist, who meets Lady Bai (Lady White) and her maid Little Blue in the rain. He lends them his umbrella and Lady Bai suggests they get married when he calls on her to collect it. He demurs on account of his lowly status, and she gives him a silver ingot that a local official, Mr Li, recognizes as stolen. When he tries to arrest Lady Bai she vanishes; Xu is banished to Suzhou. Lady Bai visits him and he agrees to marry her. The local Daoist priest warns Xu that he is bewitched but is defeated by Lady Bai. Xu and Lady Bai marry, but he is again banished, this time to Zhenjiang, when she is again detected with stolen goods. Lady Bai and Little Blue again escape punishment by disappearing. They rejoin Xu in Zhenjiang where he is working for a pharmacist called Li. Li attempts to rape Lady Bai and discovers her alone in the form of a giant snake; she is a serpent demon. Xu leaves his employ and sets up his own business. The Daoist monk Fahai warns him about Lady Bai. Later when Xu, Lady Bai and Little Blue have returned to Huangzhou and Xu has become frightened of his demonic wife, Fahai helps Xu trap them (as a snake and a blue carp), and confines them to a sealed jug that he buries at Thunder Peak Monastery. Xu becomes a Buddhist monk and constructs Thunder Peak Pagoda on top of the buried jug.¹⁴⁵ The story reached Japan in the eighteenth century. The 1958 animated film directed by Taiji Yabushita takes some liberties with the plot; for example Xu Xian and Lady Bai are deeply in love, and Fahai is a fanatical monk determined to separate them at any cost. Xu has two cute pandas

---

142. Patricia Vettel Tom, 'Felix the Cat as Modern Trickster', *American Art* 10.1 (1996): 86.

143. Fred Patten, 'An Animation Industry Begins', in Jerry Beck (ed.), *Animation Art: From Pencil to Pixel, the History of Cartoon, Anime & CGI* (New York: Harper Design International, 2004), 197.

144. Wilt L. Idema, *The White Snake and Her Son: A Translation of the Precious Scroll of Thunder Peak* (Indianapolis, IN: Hackett, 2009), xii.

145. Idema, *The White Snake and Her Son*, xiii.

as pets, Panda and Mimi, and they help to reunite the lovers. To ensure a happy ending, Lady Bai gives up her supernatural power to convince Xu of her love.[146] The film was well-received at the 1959 Venice Children's Film Festival, but was a box-office failure in the United States when it was released in 1961.

In the context of anime dealing with both erotic passion and metamorphosis, the Japanese term *hentai* (which is commonly applied to pornography) can also mean 'metamorphosis' as 'in the change from caterpillar to butterfly or in a chemical reaction'.[147] However, as Mariana Ortega-Brena explains, while '*hentai* literally means "changed or strange figure"...in Japan it usually refers to sexual material "of an extreme, 'abnormal' or 'perverse' kind"...'.[148] Within the cultural context of Japan, however, such 'perversions' are often less shocking than they would be in the West. Christianity has acted as a check on sexuality in Western culture; both Shintō and Buddhism in Japan show a healthy appreciation of the variety of sexual desires and activities. It is also interesting to consider how the particular manga and anime subcategory 'tentacle *hentai*' realizes in cartoon form the content of Hokusai's celebrated early nineteenth-century image, *Awabi Fisherwoman and Octopus*, which was mentioned in Chapter 1.

Writing about the Alice character in Walt Disney's *Alice in Wonderland* and the transformation of her body from very large to very small, as well as her swimming in her own tears after this change, Sergei Eisenstein asked, 'is there a borrowing here by Disney? Or is this image of elasticity of shapes generally widespread?'[149] In other words, would this type of visual transformation appeal across cultures? Eisenstein also recalls the more eerie example of 'the many-metred arms of *geishas* reaching out after frightened customers through the gratings of Yoshiwara's teahouses' found in the Japanese etchings from the eighteenth century.[150] In Japanese tradition anthropomorphism, metamorphosis and animism often combine in complex and bewildering forms, such as the beings that appear in medieval visual representations of hell, such as the Kumano Mandala, which

---

146. Jerry Beck, *The Animated Movie Guide* (Chicago, IL: A Capella Books, 2005), 190.
147. Mark McLelland, 'A Short History of "*Hentai*"', *Intersections: Gender, History and Culture in the Asian Context* 12 (2006), at http://intersections.anu.edu.au/issue12/mclelland.html (accessed 14 October 2010).
148. A. N. Nelson and S. Nakao paraphrased and Mark McLelland quoted in Mariana Ortega-Brena, 'Peek-a-boo I See You: Watching Japanese Hard-core Animation', *Sexuality & Culture* 13.1 (2008): 19.
149. Eisenstein, *Eisenstein on Disney*, 12.
150. Eisenstein, *Eisenstein on Disney*, 12.

shows a 'human-headed ox and horse',[151] yet there are Western Christian examples from a similar historical period which provide similarly exhilarating viewing; the remarkable triptych 'The Garden of Earthly Delights' by Hieronymus Bosch (c. 1450–1516), with its mixture of heavenly, earthly and hellish symbolism, features weird creatures including the Tree Man, mermaids, a griffin and a unicorn, and a vast array of peculiar conjunctions of human, animal and food elements.[152]

Metamorphosis not only appears in anime in terms of physical transformation, but it also appears in the Japanese cultural heritage where examples of character transformation, in contrast to purely physical transformation, can be found. One of these examples is the *kappa*. In relation to its drastic character metamorphosis Michael Dylan Foster explained that 'the *kappa* is a mischievous water goblin of Japanese folklore… Through folklorism, artists, writers, cartoonists, and commercial interests have transformed the *kappa* from a malicious and unpleasant water deity into a harmless and lovable mascot'.[153] During the Edo and Meiji eras, the *kappa* was understood as a 'grotesque and potentially deadly creature, one with some very odd and unpleasant habits' and it was only recently that the *kappa* metamorphosed into 'a cute, harmless creature'.[154] *Kappa*, and other grotesque creatures such as *tengu*, named after the Chinese dog-demon Tiangou (which began as avian beings and later developed into dog-shaped *yōkai* [monster-spirits]), were sometimes venerated as benevolent *kami*. In terms of popular media, these spirit beings are frequently found in horror manga and video games.[155] The most famous example of a *kappa* appearing in anime is *Kappa Mikey*, an American series created by Nickelodeon in 2006, proof of the cross-fertilization that occurs between West and East. Billed as 'the only anime series to be entirely created and produced in the U.S.', *Kappa Mikey* is a 'show within a show' in which Mikey Simon from Cleveland joins the cast of *LilyMu*, a struggling anime series, and becomes its rising star.[156]

---

151. R. Keller Kimbrough, 'Preaching the Animal Real in Late Medieval Japan', *Asian Folklore Studies* 65.2 (2006): 188.

152. Peter Glum, 'Divine Judgement in Bosch's Garden of Earthly Delights', *Art Bulletin* 58.1 (1976): 45-54.

153. Michael D. Foster, 'The Metamorphosis of the *Kappa*: Transformation of Folklore to Folklorism in Japan', *Asian Folklore Studies* 57 (1998): 1.

154. Foster, 'The Metamorphosis of the *Kappa*', 2-3.

155. Martin Picard, 'Haunting Backgrounds: Transnationality and Intermediality in Japanese Survival Horror Video Games', in Bernard Perron (ed.), *Horror Video Games: Essays on the Fusion of Fear and Play* (Jefferson, NC: McFarland, 2009), 104.

156. Sarah Baisley, 'U.S. Born and Raised Anime Series *Kappa Mikey* Takes to Worldwide Waves', *Animation World Network* (2006), at http://www.vfxworld.com/

Japanese animators may or may not have been inspired by the idea of metamorphosis from North American cartoons. However, Shintō and Japanese folk heritage are potential sources of inspiration when it comes to metamorphosis, and it is undeniable that the two cultures did very different things with animal metamorphosis. Emiko Ohnuki-Tierney notes that when comparing the animal characters in Japanese folktales and their Western counterparts, the fairytales of the Brothers Grimm and others, in Japanese tales animals often metamorphose into human characters, which is very rare in Western stories. She claims that 'this contrast implies that in the West, the demarcation line between humans and animals must be kept sharp, so that lowly animals may not be transformed into humans'.[157] This is because in the Western tradition the Christian God stands outside the universe, which he created; in Japan, the Shintō *kami* and both society and the universe are interpellated. She further explains that forty-two Japanese tales belonging to the 'pre-Early Modern' period feature human-into-animal metamorphosis, while ninety-two tales, from the same period, feature animal-into-human transformation. Human-into-monkey metamorphosis occurs only in three tales out of the forty-two human-into-animal tales and these metamorphoses are seen as 'a form of punishment' for humans. Monkey-into-human and human-into-monkey metamorphoses occurred more often in the early tales, as monkeys were viewed as mediators of the divine and humans, whereas in the later tales 'the monkey becomes a scapegoat figure'.[158] This more positive vision of monkeys is apparent in the 1950s' Osamu Tezuka manga adaptation of the popular Chinese Monkey King legend (from the classic novel *Journey to the West* by Wu Cheng-en)[159] and the Japanese television series *Saiyūki* (*Monkey* or *Monkey Magic* in English), shot in China in 1978–1979, with Japanese actors dubbed into English. The series ran for fifty-two episodes and was a cult hit in New Zealand, Australia and the United Kingdom. *Journey to the West* is based on the story of a real monk, Xuanzang, who travelled to India (like the priest Tripitaka and his companions, Monkey, Sandy and Pigsy, in the series) in 629 CE to collect Buddhist scriptures and take them back to China. The immense popularity of *Monkey* continues, with

---

news/television/us-born-raised-anime-series-kappa-mikey-takes-worldwide-waves (accessed 12 January 2013).

157. Emiko Ohnuki-Tierney, *The Monkey as Mirror: Symbolic Transformations in Japanese History and Ritual* (Princeton, NJ: Princeton University Press, 1987), 32.

158. Ohnuki-Tierney, *The Monkey as Mirror*, 33.

159. Fred Patten, 'A Capsule History of Anime', *Animation World Magazine* 1.5 (1996), 3 at http://www.awn.com/mag/issue1.5/toc1.5.html (accessed 15 October 2010).

English rock musician Damon Albarn's (formerly of Blur) opera based on the series.[160]

Monkeys are not the only supernatural or transformative animals in Japanese folklore. Foxes, badgers, cats and dogs all have complexes of beliefs surrounding them, some benevolent and some malevolent. These animals are all able to metamorphose into other forms, the term for which is *bakeru* (which implies fraud or deception) or *bakemono*, which could mean ghost or apparition, but 'is principally the "thing", *mono*, into which a fox, badger, or cat has transformed itself'.[161] During the period of the Han Dynasty (202 BCE to 221 CE) Chinese literature contains stories about supernatural trickster foxes, although, as U. A. Casal observes, the earliest written evidence for these beliefs in Japan is the *Genji Monogatari* ('Tale of Genji') from the eleventh century. The author adds that:

> a somewhat more definite reference to this type of magic foxes – some demonically powerful *reiko*, ghost-fox, or some almost as dangerous *koryō* haunting fox – appears in a slightly later story-book, the *Uji-shūi Monogatari*, also of the 11th century.[162]

A range of powers are attributed to supernatural foxes (*kitsune*); the most dangerous are able to assume human form and speak and be in every way like a human being, which makes them capable of bewitching humans through erotic power. Foxes and badgers, in particular, were believed to possess powers because they lived in burrows, in holes in the earth. Pure white fox spirits are also closely associated with Inari, one of the principal Shintō *kami*. Inari is the patron deity of agricultural fertility, rice, blacksmithing, industry and worldly success, as well as of foxes.[163] Inari is variously envisaged as a young woman, an old man, and an androgynous figure; no one form is fixed or authoritative, as was noted above. Karen A. Smyers argues that for Inari worshippers there is substantial personalization of the deity, and the fox guardian spirit is often understood as a symbol of individuality and nonconformity.[164]

---

160. Tom Geoghegan, 'What Was *Monkey Magic* All About?' *BBC News Magazine* (2008), at http://news.bbc.co.uk/1/hi/magazine/7520243.stm (accessed 15 October 2010).

161. U. A. Casal, 'The Goblin Fox and Badger and Other Witch Animals of Japan', *Folklore Studies* 18 (1959): 6.

162. Casal, 'The Goblin Fox', 1-2.

163. Morris E. Opler and Robert Seido Hashima, 'The Rice Goddess and the Fox in Japanese Religion and Folk Practice', *American Anthropologist* (New Series) 48.1 (1946): 43-53.

164. Karen A. Smyers, ' "My Own Inari": Personalization of the Deity in Inari Worship', *Japanese Journal of Religious Studies* 23.1-2 (1996): 85-116.

Masashi Kishimoto (b. 1974) created the manga series *Naruto*, which has run from 1999 to the present and was televised as an anime in 2002, with the sequel *Naruto: Shippuden* premiering in 2007. In the story Naruto Uzumaki is a teenage *ninja* who aspires to become a *hokage*, the most revered and powerful *ninja* in his village, Konohakagure ('village hidden in the leaves'). Naruto has within him an extremely powerful fox spirit which possesses nine tails, 'keen intelligence and cunning, [a] malicious, mischievous [and] manipulative nature [and] is a golden brown colour'.[165] Being possessed by this fox spirit is a burden to Naruto; it makes him an outcast and he experiences discrimination because of it. Yet in the series he perseveres in his quest to be the most noble of ninjas, and develops friendships that connect across barriers and break down prejudices. Masashi Kishimoto acknowledges the profound influence that Shintō mythology and folklore have on his work, along with two other influences, his upbringing in the relatively sparsely populated Okayama Prefecture, and the work of Akira Toriyama, the creator of the *Dragonball* series.[166]

The range of beliefs about badgers is rather greater than that concerning foxes. The raccoon-dog or *tanuki* can transform itself into a male who seduces females, but a badger can also transform into 'a beautiful maiden' whose purpose is to entrap unsuspecting males through her amorous charms. Casal further notes that 'the victim is generally induced to sleep in "her" embrace, [and] his disgust is all the greater when he awakens from the phantom in the morning, and finds himself bedded on rotting leaves in a desolate spot'.[167] Badgers can also create mirages while sitting in trees, so that those who travel along the road become confused, and they can also take on the form of government tax collectors with the intention of troubling the people.

Curiously, given their propensity to amorousness and greed in folklore, badgers also frequently shape-change into well-fed, plump Buddhist monks. In this guise they are 'often found sitting on a cushion, beating the Buddhist wooden drum known as a *mokugyō*'.[168] Badgers are frequently associated with Buddhist temples and funerary rituals. Violet Harada records a number of tales in which badgers engage in haunting; for example, the story of a military man sheltering overnight

---

165. Penny Pinkerton, 'Themes in *Naruto* Manga and Anime are Lessons in Japanese Culture', *Examiner.Com* (2010), at http://www.examiner.com/anime-in-national/themes-naruto-manga-and-anime-are-lessons-japanese-culture (accessed 16 October 2010).
166. Pinkerton, 'Themes in *Naruto* Manga and Anime'.
167. Casal, 'The Goblin Fox', 51.
168. Casal, 'The Goblin Fox', 52.

in a temple who is visited by a monstrous being that he fights and kills. When daylight comes he finds the corpse of a badger on the ground nearby. Another such story involves the badger taking on the form of a *bodhisattva* to deceive pious monks.[169] Cat spirits are believed to take on human form to cast spells over humans, often causing calamity and occasionally death. This may seem puzzling to anime fans, familiar with the benevolent, smiling Catbus of Hayao Miyazaki's film *My Neighbour Totoro* (1988), who resembles the Cheshire Cat of Lewis Carroll's *Alice in Wonderland*. Some critics have compared Catbus to the Japanese cat spirit (*bake neko*) that is usually regarded as a monster, 'because of his big eyes that see through the dark and his big mouth that lets out a horrifying noise'. Rieko Okuhara argues that 'fans find Catbus adorable and enjoy the humor in the way he runs on narrow electric cables and jumps over trees', and that his role in assisting eleven-year-old Satsuki find her lost four-year-old sister Mei is entirely benevolent.[170] Dog spirits are generally regarded as benevolent protectors of the home, though William Fairchild noted that in Kōchi Prefecture it was customary, when walking past a house known to be inhabited by dog spirits, 'to pin a needle on the clothing over the breast to prevent possession'.[171] This may be because aged dogs were believed to have accrued great wisdom, and to be willing to reveal secrets. This superstition was often invoked in order to euthanase old dogs.

Matthias Eder notes that while tales involving marriages between humans and animals are found in all parts of the world, there is an important difference between generic tales of this type and Japanese examples. He observes in Japanese folklore 'the animal [marriage partner] is and remains an animal', and is not a bewitched human being. In Japanese tales, usually when the bride is a fish, cat, clam, snake, or 'the maid from the Dragon-palace', the marriage will be happy. However, if the groom is a monkey, horse, snake, demon or dog the marriage is viewed as unlucky and the human partner can only be released through strong magical aid.[172] The story of Xu Xian and his marriage to the serpent-woman Lady Bai, filmed as *Panda and the White Snake* (1958), discussed above, reflects these principles broadly. When Lady Bai is in the company of Xu Xian

---

169. Violet Harada, 'The Badger in Japanese Folklore', *Asian Folklore Studies* 35.1 (1976): 4.

170. Rieko Okuhara, 'Walking Along with Nature: A Psychological Interpretation of *My Neighbour Totoro*', *The Looking Glass: New Perspectives on Children's Literature* 10.2 (2006), at http://www.lib.latrobe.edu.au/ojs/index.php/tlg/article/view/104/100 (accessed 15 October 2010).

171. William P. Fairchild, 'Shamanism in Japan', *Folklore Studies* 21 (1962): 35.

172. Matthias Eder, 'Reality in Japanese Folktales', *Asian Folklore Studies* 28.1 (1969): 23.

she appears as a woman, but when she is alone she reverts to her serpent form, which is how the pharmacist Li discovers her identity (as he was spying on her in order to rape her). In the Chinese story, the magical aid Xu Xian receives to escape the marriage is from the virtuous Daoist monk Fahai; in the animated film Lady Bai's love is proved to be true, and she gives up her snake demon powers to be with Xian (demonstrating Eder's point that snake brides may be regarded positively).

Regardless of the precise nature of the influences, once anime production got underway its creators' acceptance of both Shintō ideas and North American cartoons infused the resultant work with a quality unlike any other animation being produced. This developed and evolved over time and helped give anime its unique characteristics that led to its appeal to audiences outside Japan who had never seen anything quite like it. Whereas the animated product widely seen in the West was either directed at children or in short 'art film' form at film festivals for adults, anime ran the whole gamut of genres, ages and appeal. There was something for almost everyone.

Supernatural Themes and the Anime Genre

One particular genre of anime in which all of the aspects of animism, anthropomorphism and metamorphosis have found a home is the supernatural genre. *Yōkai* (apparitions, ghosts, supernatural beings and monsters) are a recurring convention of the supernatural genre of anime, and this genre draws heavily on traditional Japanese folk tales for its characters and stories. The modern Japanese term *yōkai*, as Foster explains, is 'variously translated as monster, spirit, goblin, ghost, demon, phantom, spectre, fantastic being, lower-order deity, or, more amorphously, as any unexplainable experience or numinous occurrence'. He elaborates:

> In the 1980s and 1990s, *yōkai* continued to gather momentum in both academic and popular media. The phrase *yōkai boom* is now so commonly used as to be a cliché. One element of this putative boom, however, is the continued production of new *yōkai*. The excitement inspired by *Kuchi-sake-onna*, for example, was complemented by a slew of other monstrous rumors – such as that of the *jinmenken* (human-faced dog) that became a short-lived media sensation in 1989, and Toire-no-Hanako-san (Hanako of the Toilet), a ghostly young girl haunting elementary school bathrooms. For children, the schoolhouse was a particularly fertile spawning ground for frightening, *yōkai*-infested stories.[173]

---

173. Michael D. Foster, *Pandemonium and Parade: Japanese Monsters and the Culture of Yōkai* (Berkeley, Los Angeles and London: University of California Press, 2009), 205.

The appeal of such stories is not restricted to Japan, although manifestations in the West are likely to be culture specific. One fascinating example mentioned by Foster is Hanako of the Toilet, an urban legend about the ghost of a schoolgirl who committed suicide in a toilet cubicle that is dated to the 1980s, though there is speculation that the legend may have existed since the 1950s, since an earlier explanation claimed that she had been killed by an American air raid during World War II.[174] Hanako of the Toilet is a malevolent presence, with her fringed bob and red pleated school skirt; she will harm those who summon her. The Western equivalent, Moaning Myrtle, the schoolgirl ghost of the Hogwarts toilets in J. K. Rowling's *Harry Potter* series of novels, is a more benevolent character. Myrtle was killed in 1943 by a basilisk at the orders of Tom Riddle (who later metamorphoses into the villainous Lord Voldemort). However, both murdered female child toilet ghosts attest to the power of liminal spaces as locations for supernatural experiences.[175]

In addition to appearing in urban myths and contemporary popular cultural forms, Laurence C. Bush observes that a a myriad supernatural beings are depicted in the visual arts of Japan. The majority of Japanese books that deal with supernatural themes are lavishly illustrated, including Michiko Iwasaka and Barre Toelken's *Ghosts and the Japanese*, Stephen Addiss's *Japanese Ghosts and Demons: Art of the Supernatural*, and *Japanese Grotesqueries* by Nikolas Kiej'e.[176] Concerning the earliest presence of 'supernatural elements' in Japanese tales, Wayne Pounds argues that this happened in the ninth century in the *Nihon ryōiki*. A second early source of these tales is a twelfth-century 'compilation of stories used by Buddhist priests' called the *Konjaku Monogatari*.[177] E. Dale Saunders has observed that Japanese myths and folktales lack coherence: stories are 'episodic rather than epic... [and] form a miscellaneous body... rather than a co-ordinated system of legends'.[178] This indeterminacy is actually a strength for the creators of manga and anime, who make eclectic and adventurous use of the multitude of supernatural beings found in Japanese art, myth and folklore. This section analyses a number of

---

174. Diane E. Goldstein, Sylvia Ann Grider and Jeannie Banks Thomas, *Haunting Experiences: Ghosts in Contemporary Folklore* (Logan, UT: Utah State University Press, 2007), 36-38.

175. Alice Mills, 'Harry Potter and the Terrors of the Toilet', *Children's Literature in Education* 37.1 (2006).

176. Laurence C. Bush, *Asian Horror Encyclopedia: Asian Horror Culture in Literature, Manga and Folklore* (San Jose, CA: Writers Club Press, 2001), 14.

177. W. Pounds, 'Enchi Fumiko and the Hidden Energy of the Supernatural', *Journal of the Association of Teachers of Japanese* 24.2 (1990): 168.

178. E. Dale Saunders, 'Japanese Mythology', in Samuel Noah Kramer (ed.), *Mythologies of the Ancient World* (Garden City, NY: Anchor Books/Doubleday, 1961), 413.

these figures and identifies their supernatural characteristics and links to religious tradition, as well as their appearance in anime. In describing the *baku*, Bush translates the term as 'eater of dreams' and explains that when Japanese peasants had bad dreams, they would 'ask the *baku* to eat up their bad dreams to prevent them from coming true or harming them'.[179] *Baku* are creatures made up of parts of various animals including horse, cockerel and lion. The anime film *Urusei Yatsura 2: The Beautiful Dreamer* (1984) features a *baku* and, as Bush notes, it 'plays a significant role'.[180]

Beautiful Dreamer, directed by Mamoru Oshii, is the second film in the series *Urusei Yatsura* ('Those Obnoxious Aliens') of six feature films. The films are based on a manga series by Rumiko Takahashi (b. 1957) that ran for nine years from 1978 to 1987 in the *Shōnen Sandee* ('Boys' Sunday').[181] *Urusei Yatsura* is a comic tale that mixes high-school romance with space opera in inventive and witty ways. The central character is Ataru Moroboshi, an inept and lecherous high-school boy. The story begins with Ataru having to battle Lum, the daughter of the alien commander of an army that has come to invade and destroy the earth. To encourage him, his girlfriend Shinobu says they can marry if he wins the contest. He defeats Lum by removing her tiger-skin bikini top, forcing her to use her hands to cover her breasts rather than to attack him. Unfortunately, Lum falls head over heels in love with Ataru and misinterprets his announcement that he can get married as a proposal, which she accepts.[182] Lum is immensely sexually attractive, with abundant viridian hair (through which peep two small horns) and enormous eyes, and she is very powerful (she can 'zap' people with an electric charge). She becomes Ataru's fiancée, moving in with his family and attending Tomobiki High School. Ataru continues to chase every girl he meets, constantly being zapped by the jealous Lum, who despite her powers is not very intelligent.

This part of the chapter concerns the range of supernatural agents in Japanese folklore and how these agents are portrayed in anime. *Urusei Yatsura* is a particularly rich anime stream to be mined for these motifs and will be discussed in detail. With reference to the *baku*, noted above, *Beautiful Dreamer* meditates on the philosophical question of how do we know when we are awake and when we are dreaming? The plot concerns the town of Tomobiki apparently decaying and collapsing, and the denouement explains that Tomobiki has (in *Groundhog Day* fashion) been

---

179. Bush, *Asian Horror Encyclopedia*, 20.
180. Bush, *Asian Horror Encyclopedia*, 20.
181. Reider, 'Transformation of the Oni', 149.
182. Annalee Newitz, 'Magical Girls and Atomic Bomb Sperm', *Film Quarterly* 49.1 (1995): 4.

2 The New Life of Old Beliefs

constantly re-living the day before the High School Festival, due to the power of Lum's dream (to live happily with Ataru and his family and to have fun with her schoolfriends) that is being used by the dream demon Mujaki (whose name literally means 'guileless'), in his fight to control reality. Ataru has to battle Mujaki to escape the dream (which Mujaki claims will inevitably become a nightmare) and avoid being devoured by him, as he is a *baku*. Although the film mixes aliens and high-school comedy romance, Japanese folktales are woven through the plot.

Because anime is a medium in which anything is possible it is a natural environment in which to introduce the non-natural, the supernatural and the fantastic. Yet, even the outlandish elements of *Urusei Yatsura* can be located in traditional Japanese folklore. The next category of supernatural beings to be considered is the *oni*. Over the centuries this term has evolved in meaning; the tenth-century Chinese–Japanese dictionary *Wamiōshō* says that *oni* means 'the spirits of dead men [that] refuse to reveal their form'. Aston thought that meant that *oni* were originally similar to ghosts, but by the time of Norinaga Motoöri (1730–1801), *oni* referred to demons or devils.[183] These demons (or goblins) are 'evil, monstrous supernatural creatures malevolent to living beings',[184] and were depicted with strange-coloured skin (yellow, red, black or blue) and a horn or horns on their heads. They have wide mouths and 'canine teeth', and are shapeshifters that can take on human shape, 'but their typically gruesome appearance often reflects their evil dispositions'.[185] They are usually male, clad in tiger skins, believed to indulge in cannibalism, and are most frequently associated with the natural phenomenon of lightning.

Turning once more to *Urusei Yatsura*, in modern Japanese stories *oni* are often represented as lonely and misunderstood and when *Urusei Yatsura* debuted, *oni* became cute and sexy. The alien tribe to which Lum belongs is called the Oni, and her customary costume is a tiger-skin bikini and knee boots (she also appears in school uniform and jeans and a t-shirt throughout the series). She has blue-green hair, unobtrusive small horns, sexy canine teeth, and her mouth becomes enlarged when she becomes jealous of Ataru's lecherous appreciation of other girls. The 'zapping' she uses to re-focus his attention on her alone is, in fact, lightning. Reider further enumerates Lum's *oni* qualities as follows:

> although Lum herself does not transform into any non-recognizable creature, her former fiancé, Rei, who is so taken with Lum that he comes

---

183. Aston, 'Japanese Myth', 321-22.
184. Noriko T. Reider, '*Onmyōji* Sex, Pathos, and the Grotesquery in Yumemakura Baku's *Oni*', *Asian Folklore Studies* 66 (2007): 107.
185. Reider, '*Onmyōji* Sex, Pathos', 110.

after her from his home planet, transforms into a huge tiger/ox-like monster when he gets excited. Ordinarily, Rei is an *oni* with an incredibly good-looking human appearance (complete with two horns and tiger skin outfit). Since Lum's *oni* folks originally arrived on earth with the intention of invading the planet, they are obviously antiestablishment.[186]

Further, Lum attracts other aliens to Tomobiki, which is destabilizing and dangerous. Three of her female friends appear regularly in the series: Benten (named after Benzaiten, the only female member of the Shichifukujin, the Seven Lucky Gods, and the Shintō goddess of knowledge, art and beauty); Oyuki, the Princess of the frozen realm of Neptune, who is one of the most powerful characters because of the strength of her wrath when roused; and her childhood companion, the redheaded Ran, who also is a student at Tomobiki High School. Ran appears sweet but is able to suck the life out of people by kissing them (like a succubus). Noriko Reider's other, very interesting, contention about Lum as *oni* has to do with the Japanese attribution of the term *oni* to their wartime enemies, the Allied forces.[187] Lum came to earth as an invader (and for comic effect her surname is 'Invader' in the anime, and her parents are referred to as 'Mr and Mrs Invader'). She and her family are clearly not Japanese; Mr Invader can speak Japanese, but Mrs Invader speaks only Oni, which in Takahashi's manga is represented by *mah-jongg* tiles in her speech bubbles. It is therefore worth considering the traditional Japanese attitude to strangers and outsiders.

Teigo Yoshida argues that villagers in Japan were mistrustful of strangers and believed they had 'mystical evil qualities', and notes that in villages in northeastern Japan strangers could not become residents unless they formed 'fictive kinship relations with one of the prominent families of the village'.[188] Through becoming engaged to Ataru and moving into the house of Mr and Mrs Moroboshi, Lum becomes kin to the residents of Tomobiki. Reflecting further on villagers and attitudes to strangers, Yoshida observes that the Japanese attitude towards the European foreigners in the sixteenth CE and subsequent centuries was tinged with anxiety about strangers. Foreigners were perceived to have supernatural powers and to be 'mystically dangerous'. Yoshida mentions that one of these 'supernatural abilities' was 'the power to find miraculous stones which could bestow longevity and even eternal life'.[189] Lum certainly endangers the community of Tomobiki throughout the series;

---

186. Reider, 'Transformation of the Oni', 107, 150.
187. Reider, 'Transformation of the Oni', 147-48.
188. Teigo Yoshida, 'The Stranger as God: The Place of the Outsider in Japanese Folk Religion', *Ethnology* 20.2 (1981): 88.
189. Yoshida, 'The Stranger as God', 88.

her zapping constantly reduces classrooms to ruins and her presence on earth attracts other alien threats. Yet ultimately she is benign; she has a devoted following among the boys of the school, including Shutaro Mendou, the son of a wealthy industrialist, and the four 'nerds' (*otaku*), Megane, Perm, Kakugari and Chibi (who are nameless in the manga but are recurring characters in the anime), known collectively as the Stormtroopers.

Further insights into Lum can be gathered from considering the folktale of Tarō Urashima, which underlies much of the plot of *Urusei Yatsura 2: Beautiful Dreamer* (which is itself an elaboration of a television anime episode). In the previous section reference was made in passing to the 'maid from the Dragon Palace'. In the folktale, Tarō Urashima, a young fisherman, spared the life of a small turtle, returning it to the sea. The next day a huge turtle told him that he had saved the life of Otohime, the Princess of the Dragon Palace. The turtle took Tarō Urashima to the palace on the sea-bed, where he met the Emperor and the Princess and feasted with them. After a period of time he became homesick and asked to return to see his parents. The Princess agreed, giving him a lacquer box that she warned him not to open. She turned into a turtle and carried him to the surface. He found that centuries had passed and strangers inhabited his village. While waiting for the turtle on the shore he opened the box: 'the waft of smoke that billowed out was delayed time. Within seconds Urashima's body aged, his skin shriveled, his hair turned white, and he died'.[190] This folktale underlies much of *Beautiful Dreamer*, in which there are lengthy debates about the nature of time: Mujaki the dream demon's dream realm is underwater; one by one the citizens of Tomobiki disappear, leaving only Ataru's 'gang' of schoolfriends (those who are core to Lum's dream of a happy life); and when Mendou and Sakura take action they discover that Tomobiki is whirling through space on the back of a giant turtle. W. Michael Kelsey has emphasized that water deities and underwater realms are closely linked to death and the dead in Japanese folk religion.[191] At the close of the film it is implied that despite his constant girl-chasing, Ataru loves Lum, and although loving the Princess resulted in Tarō Urashima losing his community, she did seek to preserve his life and he died only because he disobeyed her command. Lum awakens from her dream and Mujaki is vanquished; Ataru does not lose anything, but gains the knowledge that he loves Lum. In a variant version of the folktale, the fisherman saves a bream and is carried on the back of

---

190. Ben-Ami Shillony, 'The Princess of the Dragon Palace: A New Shinto Sect is Born', *Monumenta Nipponica* 39.2 (1984): 178.

191. W. Michael Kelsey, 'The Raging Deity in Japanese Mythology', *Asian Folklore Studies* 40.2 (1981): 223.

a jellyfish. However, after the banquet in the Dragon King's underwater palace, the fisherman is rewarded with a magic ear and returns to the surface, where the ear enables him to understand the conversation of birds and cure a nobleman's sick daughter, whom he then marries.[192]

The most popular of all Japanese fairytales, the story of Momotarō is also referenced throughout the television series *Urusei Yatsura*. This story tells of a childless elderly woman who was washing clothes in the river; a large peach floats by, and she took it home. When it was cut in half there was an infant boy inside, and the woman's husband called him Momotarō, 'Peach Boy'. He grew rapidly and became very strong. Reider retells the tale:

> at that time, *oni* from a distant island frequented the capital, looting treasures and abducting people. The young Momotarō decides to confront and subjugate the *oni*. His elderly parents provide him with dumplings for food. En route, Momotarō meets a dog, monkey, and a pheasant which all became his vassals in exchange for his remarkably delicious dumplings. Momotarō and his three vassals go to the *oni's* island, defeat the *oni*, and take back all the treasures of the island with them.[193]

During World War II Momotarō became a nationalist figurehead in Japan, with the demons he defeated being cast as the Allies, chiefly America and the United Kingdom. In the short, animated film *Momotarō Sea Eagles* (1943) Hawai'i is presented as the demons' island, and the *oni* 'are characterized by their external appearance (a horn on their head) and an incomprehensible language (English)'.[194]

Throughout all versions of *Urusai Yatsura*, Lum's alienness is emphasized by the fact that she always calls Ataru by the English endearment 'Darling'. However, because *oni* are no longer feared and terrifying, Momotarō becomes a figure of fun (in one episode of the television series Ataru's gang run into him, and he is entirely different to his folktale reputation, being wimpy and totally unsuccessful in hunting down *oni*). His story is also adapted to the lives of other characters. For example, Lum's baby cousin Ten (who has a single horn, breathes fire and wears a tigerskin nappy) came to Tomobiki in a spaceship encased in a giant peach, and on another occasion Ataru's gang find a giant peach floating in the river. When opened it is found to contain Sakuranbou, Sakura's wandering monk uncle, who is usually known as Cherry (from *Sakuranbou*,

---

192. Alsace Yen, 'Thematic Patterns in Japanese Folktales: A Search for Meanings', *Asian Folklore Studies* 33.2 (1974): 13-14.
193. Reider, 'Transformation of the Oni', 148.
194. Klaus Antoni, 'Momotarō (The Peach Boy) and the Spirit of Japan: Concerning the Function of a Fairy Tale in Japanese Nationalism of the Early Showa Age', *Asian Folklore Studies* 50.1 (1991): 179.

which in *kanji* can literally mean either 'cherry' or 'deranged monk'). With regard to the domestication of the *oni* in *Urusei Yatsura*, it could be argued that Ataru's persistent running away from Lum is a sign of the sexual fear of foreigners or aliens. Because *Urusei Yatsura* is a high-school comedy-romance all the relationships are not depicted as explicitly sexual and the series participates in that curious amalgam of the exotic and the everyday, discussed above as quintessentially Shintō. Yet Newitz's contention that the message about sexuality found within the *mecha* subgenre, and particularly the OVA (original video animation) *The Overfiend*, is one of fear of 'multicultural sexuality'[195] strikes a chord. This is because:

> all 'others' are monsters and all monsters are out to destroy human society... While multiculturalism is at odds with Japanese monoculturalism, it is more importantly connected to the United States, which invaded and occupied Japan for decades after violently defeating them in World War II.[196]

The school setting of *Urusei Yatsura* owes much to American high-school films of the 1950s and television programmes such as *The Patty Duke Show*, and the light comedic mood means that the full negative implications of Newitz's contention never emerge. However, Lum does speak English, and is much more 'Western' in appearance than Japanese. She is an invading alien who first fights Ataru, then entraps him into an engagement, and who disciplines him with violence (her lightning 'zap') when he strays. Lum's electric power does mean that Ataru has to wear a rubber suit whenever he is pictured in bed with her, indicating the danger of involvement with *oni*.[197]

The next type of supernatural being to be considered is the guardian spirit, of which there are several manifestations. Carmen Blacker notes that medieval texts concerning Japanese holy men often mention 'a class of spirits or deities called *gohō*, protectors of the Law'.[198] The term *gohō* within Mahayana Buddhism frequently designates figures in the Mahayana pantheon of *buddhas* and *bodhisattvas* who defend the law of the Buddha from enemies during the last days of earth, before the coming of Maitreya, the future Buddha. These figures include the Hindu gods Brahma and Indra, 'and the well-known figures of the Four Deva Kings and the Twelve Generals, whose terrific aspect was intended to cow the opponents of Buddhism, [who] are all described as *gohō-zenshin*,

---

195. Newitz, 'Magical Girls', 9.
196. Newitz, 'Magical Girls', 9.
197. Drazen, *Anime Explosion!*, 63-64.
198. Carmen Blacker, 'The Divine Boy in Japanese Buddhism', *Asian Folklore Studies* 22 (1963): 77.

beneficial deities protecting the Law'.[199] She also notes that an anonymous 'divine boy' also features in the Middle Ages as a guardian spirit; he is called *gohō-dōji*, and particularly protects saintly monks and priests. These 'divine boys' may act as assistants to the holy men, and in some cases the boys are identified as prominent characters from the supernatural pantheon, 'such as the Eight Boys attendant on the deity Fudō Myōō'.[200]

When considering the Japanese view of the relationship between children and the spiritual realm, Irene H. Lin observes that the Japanese believed children were 'close to the gods and the demons' and that only when young girls reached thirteen years and young boys fifteen years were they considered adults and reached full status as human beings. Lin explains that:

> since children were not of the world or of society, they were placed or displaced into the margins or boundaries of the Buddhist and social world. This capacity for traversing borders as boundary beings led to a number of protective threshold deities manifesting in the form of children in Japanese religion.[201]

When considering the power of the child in anime, it is overwhelmingly clear that anime heroes and heroines are either children or adolescent at the oldest. The robot hero Astro Boy is a child of approximately ten; the alien child heroes *Space Ace*, who was discovered by the benevolent scientist Dr Tatsunoko and his daughter Asari ('Ginger' in the English version) within a radioactive pearl found in a giant clam (in the monochrome anime screened 1965–1966), and *Prince Planet*, the hero from the Universal Peace Corps of Planet Radion (screened in 1965–1966), were also pre-adolescent children. The pilots of *Neon Genesis Evangelion* (discussed below) are all fourteen year olds. The high-school kids of *Urusei Yatsura* are at the upper end of the age group where supernaturally-tinged intervention in their lives is likely. The fact that they are all, despite their passionate emotional and sexual yearnings, celibate, also reinforces their childlike magical powers and supernatural sensitivities.

With reference to the aesthetic conventions of visual representations of ghosts and demons, Theodore Bowie notes that in the Yamato-e School (from the fifteenth century onwards), these figure appear 'very early in the scrolls' of this school. He notes that from the thirteenth century, *Gaki Zoshi or* 'Hungry Demons' paintings depict skeletons that

---

199. Blacker, 'The Divine Boy in Japanese Buddhism', 77.
200. Blacker, 'The Divine Boy in Japanese Buddhism', 77.
201. Irene H. Lin, 'Child Guardian Spirits (*Gohō Dōji*) in the Medieval Japanese Imaginaire', *Pacific World: Journal of the Institute of Buddhist Studies*, Third Series 6 (2004): 155.

are exsiccated yet 'the external organs are still present'. Bowie further notes that it is possible that Japanese contact with Europeans transmitted awareness of scientific research which triggered Japanese 'interest in human dissection' because skeletons were hardly ever depicted before the end of the eighteenth century.[202] When pondering Japanese ancestor worship and the general Western fear of ghosts, Nobushige Hozumi notes that for the Japanese it is 'nearer the truth to say that it was the *love of ghosts* which gave rise to the custom of ancestor-worship'.[203] The inhabitants of the spirit world can visit and occupy environments in anime productions, as can mortals who strive to be gods in their manipulation and control of technology and its power over the populace. One example of this is the Puppet Master, a sentient computer programme in Mamoru Oshii's *Ghost in the Shell* (1995), who exists in cyberspace as an electronic sequence and yet lives.

Another important motif in both mythology and folklore is abduction by a supernatural being. According to Birgit Staemmler, the Japanese term *kamikakushi* means 'being hidden by a deity'.[204] She adds that 'spirited away' is a approximate good English translation of the concept. This term reflects folklore about supernatural beings that seize humans in a 'sudden and mysterious disappearance'.[205] Carmen Blacker has researched child abductions and argues that the victims are generally male and if they are not found quickly the family are likely to resort to a *miko* to seek the restoration of their son. Blacker's research suggests that the agents of such kidnappings are generally *tengu* (dog-spirits), who disguise themselves as *yamabushi*, or mountain ascetics of the Shugendō movement of popular piety.[206] Hayao Miyazaki's anime feature film *Spirited Away* has contributed to the restoration of popularity of this motif.

Miyazaki's *Spirited Away* (2001) is the story of a ten-year-old girl, Chihiro, whose parents are turned into pigs when they visit an abandoned amusement park en route to their new home. This negative transformation is seen to be the result of their materialistic, selfish lifestyle, and their lack of respect for the Shintō shrines they pass. Chihiro is initially a whining and unattractive child, but through enduring ordeals and doing hard work she grows into a competent, responsible and mature moral

---

202. Theodore R. Bowie, 'A Note on the Skeleton in Japanese Art', *Art Journal* 21.1 (1961): 16.
203. Nobushige Hozumi, *Ancestor-Worship and Japanese Law* (Charleston, SC: BiblioBazaar, 2008), 19.
204. Birgit Staemmler, 'Virtual *Kamikakushi*: An Element of Folk Belief in Changing Times and Media', *Japanese Journal of Religious Studies* 32.2 (2005): 342.
205. Staemmler, 'Virtual *Kamikakushi*', 342.
206. Carmen Blacker, 'Supernatural Abductions in Japanese Folklore', *Asian Folklore Studies* 26.2 (1967): 116.

agent.²⁰⁷ Chihiro, aided by Haku (a boy who turns out to be a dragon), gets a job in a bathhouse run by Yubaba, a witch who enslaves people by stealing their names. Yubaba renames Chihiro 'Sen'. Sen is given the foulest jobs, and successfully cleans a polluted water-spirit, who in gratitude gives her a dumpling. She feeds half of the dumpling to a monster called No-Face after he has devoured the bathhouse attendants; he then regurgitates them. When Haku is wounded she feeds him the other half and he coughs up a slug, which Sen kills, and a seal. Sen takes the seal and Yubaba's baby son who has been turned into a mouse to Yubaba's sister, the witch Zeniba (who is responsible for turning the baby into a mouse). Zeniba, a benign character, says Sen's love has broken the spell; No-Face begins to learn to behave morally and assists Zeniba in making a hair-tie talisman for Sen to wear. Haku comes to take her back to Yubaba to liberate her parents, and she helps him remember that he was a river-spirit and his name is Kohaku. At the bathhouse, Yubaba is grateful for her restored son, and tells Sen she will save her parents if she can recognize them among the herd of pigs. She correctly says they are not there; all the pigs are restored to their original forms and Chihiro gets her name back. Haku/Kohaku accompanies her to the gate of the spirit world where she is reunited with her parents, and the family proceeds to its new home.

Shintō themes are very apparent in *Spirited Away*, with the presence of the *kami* of rivers and other natural phenomena, witches and the spirit world being the most obvious instance, and the focus on the need to be cleansed of pollution through bathing in purifying waters being another. Miyazaki has stated that the bathhouse location is inspired by 'the solstice rituals when villagers call forth all the local *kami* and invite them to bathe in their baths'.²⁰⁸ Susan Napier has argued that the film shows modern Japan as liminal, no longer strongly connected to the past and facing an uncertain future. She claims that:

> the repressed past returns in the form of a fantastic array of spirits who occupy the bathhouse, an institution that has largely disappeared, except for the occasional hot spring visit, from the lives of most contemporary Japanese... The bathhouse spirits and their environs are no longer part of the 'real world' in which the young protagonist Chihiro

---

207. Susan Jolliffe Napier, 'Matter Out of Place: Carnival, Containment and Cultural Recovery in Miyazaki's *Spirited Away*', *Journal of Japanese Studies* 32.2 (2006): 298-300.

208. James W. Boyd and Tetsuya Nishimura, 'Shinto Perspectives in Miyazaki's Anime Film "Spirited Away"', *Journal of Religion and Film* 8.2 (2004), at http://www.unomaha.edu/jrf/Vol8No2/boydShinto.htm (accessed 10 December 2010).

2 The New Life of Old Beliefs

initially appears but, to the Japanese viewer, their visual manifestations and functions evoke images from Japanese folklore.[209]

Boyd and Nishimura draw attention to the fact that Yubaba and Zeniba are identical twin sisters, and argue that they:

> represent a Shinto ethical outlook that views events in one's life as either reducing (polluting) or promoting (purifying) one's ability to participate fully in the life energy that permeates all of Great Nature... Miyazaki is reaffirming aspects of the Japanese tradition preserved in Shinto thought and practice that can serve as transformative sources of confidence and renewal for both young and old.[210]

The terrible effects of industrial pollution on the natural world are also graphically illustrated in *Spirited Away*, and the film views consumer capitalism as a form of passive nihilism.[211] Chihiro's cleansing of the river spirit is also interesting because for the Japanese, wild nature can be fearsome, and it is constantly necessary to tame and shape nature; 'true and ideal nature thus only becomes apparent when all offensive elements are removed'.[212] The *kami*-filled quality of nature is one of the ways in which Japanese culture makes nature 'pure', in that *kami* are beings, and people can therefore establish relationships with nature more successfully.

Christianity, as previously noted, has been a minority religion in Japan since the mid-sixteenth century. Despite the small numbers of Japanese Christians, Christian motifs are quite widely known in Japanese culture, and some new religions (*shin shūkyō*) also have included Christian elements in their doctrines. One example is Sukyo Mahikari, which was founded by Yoshikazu Okada in 1959.[213] Mahikari teaches that the islands of Japan were part of the lost continent of Mu, and that Japan has the most advanced civilization on earth. All the great religious leaders of the world received their spiritual training in Japan, and Christianity in particular is given a Japanese focus. Okada often referred to the Takenouchi documents, which were allegedly discovered at the start of the twentieth century, and which 'prove' that Jesus died and was buried in Japan. For Mahikari members:

---

209. Napier, 'Matter Out of Place', 292.
210. Boyd and Nishimura, 'Shinto Perspectives'.
211. Olivier, 'Nihilism in Japanese Anime', 56-59.
212. Arne Kalland, 'Holism and Sustainability: Lessons from Japan', *Worldviews* 6.2 (2002): 149.
213. Richard Anderson, 'Vengeful Ancestors and Anima Spirits: Personal Narratives of the Supernatural in a Japanese New Religion', *Folklore* 54.2 (1995): 116.

> Jesus was born in 37 B.C. and proceeded to travel through China and India on his way to Japan, where he arrived when he was 18. After acquiring magical Shinto powers, he left Japan and practiced his powers in many countries before arriving in Judea. There his performance of miracles caused him to be sentenced to death by the Romans who controlled the country. But Jesus' brother, Isukiri, allowed himself to be crucified in place of Jesus. Later when he was 36, Jesus began a four-year odyssey back to Japan, which took him through Europe, Africa, Asia, and the Americas. Once back in Japan, he married a Japanese, had children, and lived to be over 100 years old.[214]

Mahikari has certain popular cultural features, and its central beliefs include healing through performing *okiyome* (radiating the 'true light' of Su no kamisama, the deity of the religion) and post-mortem spiritual training in the astral world. Spirits who cling to this world are called possessing or attaching spirits, and ancestor veneration by Mahikari members is believed to assist the spirits of the departed to be reborn in this world and make further spiritual progress. Adam Barkman argues that anime that features Christian doctrines and practices exhibits a similar pluralist understanding to new religions like Mahikari: 'particular doctrines are seen as largely unimportant, whereas a general spiritual mood – a mood often created by blending many different religions together – is all-important'.[215]

In line with its historical reception in Japan, Christianity is usually depicted as an evil, alien religion. For example, *Angel Sanctuary* and *Chrno Crusade* depict the Christian God as apathetic or actually evil, and *Ninja Resurrection* is the tale of a would-be Christian messiah who 'becomes the incarnation of Satan'.[216] Laurence C. Bush further observes that when Japanese anime and manga artists use Christian symbolism in their work it is because these symbols 'represent the exotic occult' and the anime *Neon Genesis Evangelion* (*NGE*) is a prime example which features numerous Christian elements, 'angels, crosses and even the Spear of Longinus'.[217] *Neon Genesis Evangelion* (which literally means 'new beginning gospel') is set in 2015, and is based on a manga by Yoshiyuki Sadamoto that debuted in 1995. The anime consisted of twenty-six television episodes that screened in 1995–1996, and three films were later released to bring the series to a more satisfying conclusion. The plot concerns the second attack on earth by Angels in 2015. In 2000, the Angels had attacked and destroyed half the Earth's population, in an event known

---

214. William Sanborn Pfeiffer, 'Mahikari: New Religion and Japanese Popular Culture', *Journal of Popular Culture* 34.2 (2000): 163-64.
215. Barkman, 'Anime, Manga and Christianity', 27.
216. Barkman, 'Anime, Manga and Christianity', 31.
217. Bush, *Asian Horror Encyclopedia*, 31-32.

as the Second Impact. In response, the United Nations established the military organization, NERV, which developed giant mechas called Evangelions (EVAs) as weapons against the Angels' return. The main protagonist, Shinji Ikari, the Third Child, is one of a group of fourteen-year-olds who are the pilots of the EVAs. His mother Yui is dead and his father Gendo Ikari has rejected him. Shinji is the ward of Misato Katsuragi, the Head of Operations at NERV. As the plot progresses it becomes clear that the Angels are not what they seem, and the sinister outcome (the Third Impact) will realize the Human Instrumentality Project, in which all people will lose their individual existence and merge into a single soul.

The series is filled with violent battles and death, and the young pilots suffer mental distress and anguish over their role in the conflict. Barkman argues that:

> a loose interpretation of the Christian apocalypse as is found in the book of Revelation, can (though it doesn't have to) be seen as an allegory for the hostile, alien, Christian West invading Japan. Moreover, since the whole concept of global destruction is an idea that Japan got from the Christian West, it makes sense that when the Americans dropped the two atomic bombs on Japan during the Second World War, a number of Japanese understood this in apocalyptic terms. Of course, since most Japanese weren't Christians, they didn't literally see World War II as Armageddon, but certainly the biblical ethos was in the air and acted as a source of dark inspiration for many future anime and manga artists.[218]

The eighteen Angels of *Neon Genesis Evangelion* are ambivalent beings, in that they are largely presented as monstrous creatures that attack Earth violently, and destroy the EVAs and their pilots, but they are also divine beings who may occupy human bodies. Christophe Thouny argues that ultimately the difference between the Angels and the child pilots of the EVAs turns out to be one of degree rather than of kind. The Angels are merged organic and mechanical beings, and one of the revelations at the end of the series is that 'the soul of each pilot's mother has been transplanted in their respective EVAs' making the EVA more than purely mechanical.[219]

Further, the original Angels, Adam and Lilith, are the source of the other sixteen, and cells taken from Adam are the raw material for later Evangelions, except for Unit 01 which was taken from Lilith. Rei Ayanami, the First Child and pilot of Unit 00, is discovered to be a vessel for the Angel Lilith and fuses with her to become a powerful divine being during the progress of the Human Instrumentality Project. As Thouny

---

218. Barkman, 'Anime, Manga and Christianity', 34.
219. Christophe Thouny, 'Waiting for the Messiah: The Becoming-Myth of *Evangelion* and *Densha otoko*', *Mechademia* 4 (2009): 117.

remarks, 'humanity is the last generation of Angels, the end product of a long line of genetic experiments starting with Adam and Lilith. The line is definitively blurred between the pilot and the robot; they are cousins, different and not so different'.[220] It must be noted that *Neon Genesis Evangelion* uses Christian tropes, but in fact its use is generally superficial, and its understanding of the apocalypse being realized through the fusion of all individuals into a single soul resembles certain types of Buddhism more profoundly. Drazen argues that the 'mythic foundation of the series remains totally Japanese'.[221] The First Impact splits an entity into the White and the Black Moon, 'respectively the source of the Angels and the source of human life on Earth. The White Moon was buried in Antarctica until the Second Impact liberated it. The Black Moon was buried under the Izu Peninsula'.[222] This cosmogony derives from the Japanese perspective of the primordial cosmic 'stuff', which is separated into light and heavy (the heavens and the sea, with the sky in between), which is found in the *Kojiki* and other early texts.

Additionally, the three main characters, Shinji, Rei and Asuka, could be seen to correspond to the offspring of the primordial *kami* Izanami and Izanagi: Susanoo, Amaterasu and Tsukiyomi. Japan has accepted the material culture of Christianity, ever since the arrival of the first missionaries. It became popular among aristocrats to flaunt rosary beads, and wear gaudy crucifixes, even though they knew little of the faith. The tendency still exists today with the popularity of Christian weddings in a country where approximately 1 per cent of the population identify as Christian. However, Drazen cautions that the generally sinister portrayal of Christianity in anime, including *Neon Genesis Evangelion*, is because Christianity is understood to be a belief system that contains a plausible threat of global annihilation, something that Shintō and Buddhism do not. He concludes that Christianity 'thus serves the Japanese the way Islam or voodoo serves the pop culture of the West: as a fantasyland onto which we can project our fears and suspicious [sic], claiming that this arcane and alien faith is capable of almost anything'.[223]

Conclusion

This chapter has introduced the religions of Japan, Shintō, Buddhism, Christianity and new religious movements. The greatest emphasis has been given to Shintō, as its *kami* (divine spirits) and supernatural beings

---

220. Thouny, 'Waiting for the Messiah', 117.
221. Drazen, *Anime Explosion!*, 305.
222. Drazen, *Anime Explosion!*, 298.
223. Drazen, *Anime Explosion!*, 307.

are most often referenced in manga and anime, and its determined lack of a distinction between the sacred and the profane informs the curious mixture of the mundane and the fantastic found in the works of great anime creators such as Osamu Tezuka, Mamoru Oshii and Hayao Miyazaki. Motifs and themes from Buddhism, Christianity and new religions have been identified and discussed in less detail. The chapter also focused on animism and anthropomorphism as methodological lenses through which to understand the use of supernatural motifs in manga and anime. These lenses were then utilized to examine animal transformations in religion, folklore and anime. Finally, a range of supernatural beings from religion and folklore were described and their roles identified in contemporary anime productions.

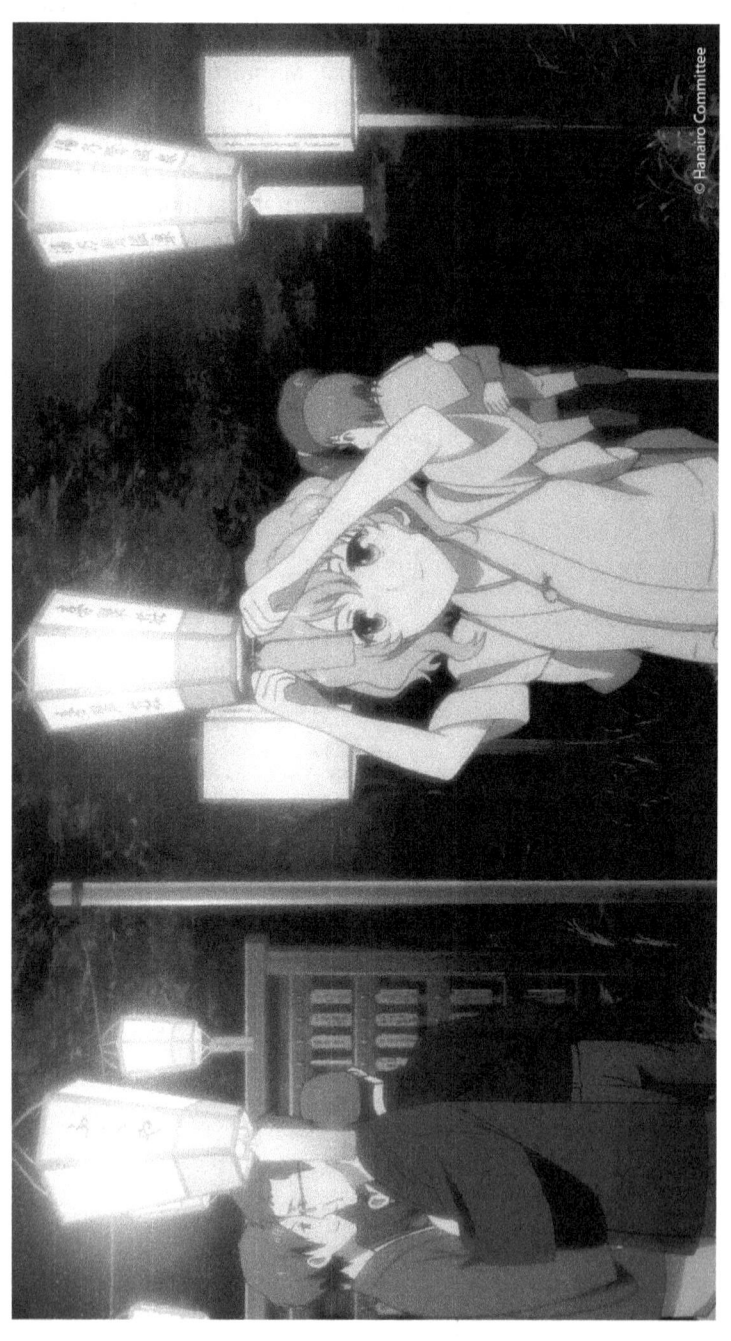

Reproduction copy in black and white of a still from the anime series *Hanasaku Iroha – Blossoms for Tomorrow* showing the main character Ohana Matsumae attaching her wish to the *bonbori* light. This series was directed by Masahiro Ando, written by Mari Okada, and produced by P. A. Works. Image kindly supplied by Pony Canyon Inc. Image ©Hanairo Committee.

Chapter 3

From Realistic to Supernatural: Genres in Anime

Introduction

Anime is particularly distinguishable from its Western counterpart, animated cartoons, in one significant way: the wide spectrum of genres found within it. The sources that gave rise to this generic richness include manga and its artistic predecessors, and Japanese literary tradition. This chapter has four sections. First, it discusses the notion of genre, and argues that the rich variety of genres in anime gave rise to generic hybridity, which over time became a frequent feature of anime, having the potential to attract diverse audiences. These generic hybrids often include supernatural subgenre. The second section analyses the female characters in a number of generic hybrids, which also contain supernatural subgenre, and argues that the portrayal of their power is more influenced by Western Pagan ideas about the sacredness of the Earth and Gaia as goddess, rather than that of the Shintō sun-goddess Amaterasu. Third, it investigates a number of anime belonging to a subgenre with realistic subject matter – that of tragedy – and highlights elements of the supernatural subgenre that are also present in it. As 'tragedy often ultimately celebrates the dignity of the human spirit in confronting [and]...overwhelming misfortune',[1] this section argues that the supernatural elements function as a metaphor for either the celebration of the human spirit despite the calamities, or a metaphor for the resilience and strength of the human spirit, or as symbols that have soteriological meaning, or as symbols of personal transformation. The fourth section examines the child/young adult characters in works by Hayao Miyazaki, Mamoru Oshii, Tatsuya Ishihara and Katsuhiro Ōtomo. World 'mythologies' and 'religions' abound with examples of 'the child

---

1. Ross C. Murfin and Supryia M. Ray, *The Bedford Glossary of Critical and Literary Terms*, 2nd edn (Basingstoke: Palgrave Macmillan, 2003), 484.

motif',[2] and this section argues that the child characters in Miyazaki's and Oshii's works share a limited similarity with the idea of the 'divine child' in the sense that they act as key mediators between the supernatural and natural worlds. This section also focuses on young adult characters in the works of Ishihara and Ōtomo, discussing the way in which their god-like powers are portrayed. The aim of this chapter is to demonstrate a number of facets of the supernatural subgenre of anime, and to note their spiritual significance.

The Rise of Generic Hybridity in Anime

The analysis of genre means entering into an ever-changing and slippery terrain. An attempt to reach a clear and final definition of the term will inevitably result in an imperfect statement. One of the principal reasons for this is the inherently evolving nature of genre. Because of this, viewing genres as 'processes that are ongoing'[3] rather than as stable and unalterable entities is an appropriate strategy. Another difficulty that arises in the discussion of genre is the lack of clear indicators regarding the confines of a single genre. Having said this, the distinguishing line between individual genres is visible to a certain degree; however, the deeper the level of genre investigation is, the more blurred, deceptive, elusive, and even invisible the line that separates them becomes. Yet, genre has been an important analytical instrument in the context of literary tradition and continues to be so in anime, despite methodological obstacles. Genre has enabled appreciation and discussion about literature in a 'most reasoned way',[4] which is also applicable to anime. Discussing genre in terms of its elements or building blocks is the method adopted in this chapter. However, any analysis of genre first requires the consideration of a number of broad genre-related issues.

While the term 'genre' is frequently encountered in film discourses, its origins lie in literary criticism,[5] a fact that is often insufficiently recognized in anime scholarship. Discussion about genres in anime here borrows from both film theory and literary criticism. One of the basic interpretations of the term 'genre' is that it refers to '[a] particular

---

2. Wallace B. Clift, 'Child', in Mircea Eliade (ed.), *The Encyclopedia of Religion*, vol. 3 (New York: MacMillan, 1987), 243.
3. Barry Keith Grant, *Film Genre: From Iconography to Ideology* (London and New York: Wallflower, 2007), 34.
4. Adena Rosmarin, *The Power of Genre* (Minneapolis, MN: University of Minnesota Press, 1985), 39.
5. Andrew Tudor, 'Genre', in Barry Keith Grant (ed.), *Film Genre: Theory and Criticism* (Metuchen, NJ: Scarecrow Press, 1977), 16.

style or category of works' which has 'a particular form, style, or purpose' with specific reference to literature.⁶ Yet the same model is also applicable to anime. This basic definition indicates that works, which share some similarities, fall within the same genre.

David Fishelov argues, with reference to literature, that there are no cultural and language confines when it comes to genre,⁷ in the sense that a particular audience can relate to works that belong to a language and culture other than their own. However, the validity of this contention is only partial, as there are also aspects of the works which will be undetected by that audience, not because of the subtlety of those aspects but because of factors such as the different socio-cultural backgrounds of the audience (unless an audience has a certain level of familiarity with the socio-cultural and linguistic context from which the work originated). One significant example of this in anime is the sixty-nine-episode series *Yakitate!! Japan* (in English, *Freshly Baked!! Japan*). Yasunao Aoki directed this comedy series, which ran from 2004 to 2006 and was based on a manga by Takashi Hashiguchi. In this anime, the boy Azuma Kazuma ardently wishes to invent a type of bread that will be the pride and joy of Japan. Although not very intelligent, he possesses 'solar hands' which facilitate fermentation, a process necessary to produce good quality bread. In the episode 'Maharajah! The Day Mount Fuji Fell!', Azuma mishears the word 'croissant' for 'Kurowa-san', as they sound the same, which has a comic effect for the Western audience and it does not require an intimate knowledge and familiarity with Japanese culture in order to be understood, but this cannot be said for all comic effects in this anime.

Gilles Poitras claims that there are three types of humour in anime and one of them 'is so culturally based that it requires an insider's knowledge',⁸ reinforcing the argument that Fishelov's point about genres not being limited by cultural and linguistic confines is flawed. With regard to two other types of humour, Poitras explains that, '[s]ome of the humor in anime is simply slapstick or situational, and much of this translates quite well... [s]ome humor does not translate well. With puns and other verbal humor this is to be expected; translators try to substitute other jokes, explain the puns in linear notes, or just ignore them'.⁹ This indicates that

---

6. John A. Simpson and Edmund S. C. Weiner (eds), *The Oxford English Dictionary*, 2nd edn, vol. 6 (Oxford: Clarendon Press; Oxford; New York: Oxford University Press, 1989), 446.

7. David Fishelov, *Metaphors of Genre: The Role of Analogies in Genre Theory* (University Park, PA: Pennsylvania State University Press, 1993), 16.

8. Gilles Poitras, *Anime Essentials: Every Thing a Fan Needs to Know* (Berkeley, CA: Stone Bridge Press, 2001), 41.

9. Poitras, *Anime Essentials*, 41.

there are genres that are more prone to encountering difficulty when it comes to conveying their content to a foreign audience.

The significance of an individual director's contribution to a particular 'generic tradition' is acknowledged, yet it must be agreed that contribution does not *make* that tradition but remains a 'part' of it.[10] The validity of this contention is confirmed by consideration of Osamu Tezuka, discussed in Chapter 1. His *Astro Boy* is one of the most significant contributions to the science-fiction genre anime, not only because it was one of its earliest examples, but also because its influence was far-reaching. Anime directors succeeding Tezuka, such as Mamoru Oshii, took humanoid robots endowed with human personalities to a new level, consequently carrying and building on a tradition in which Tezuka left a deep and lasting mark. This genre, arguably, 'is the major genre in anime'.[11]

In scholarly writings, genres are often examined in terms of so-called 'genre elements', and this chapter adopts this approach. Items including 'setting', 'iconography', 'narrative', 'types of characters' and 'style'[12] are usually referred to as the elements of genre in genre scholarship. Setting not only describes physical geography but also temporal periods. The term 'iconography' is borrowed from art criticism and in the context of the moving image, it 'refers to objects, or sounds, which are associated with a genre'; whether iconography in a film context also includes other things apart from 'objects and sounds' is open to debate.[13] Narrative is made up of 'events' (or sets of linked events), and they include both 'actions' and 'happenings'.[14] The axis of the work is 'the narrative question' that is solved at the end; this question is also a driving force in engaging and maintaining the spectators' attention.[15] Many anime genres that also contain many conventions of supernatural subgenre are often similar in terms of the narrative questions on which they converge. Furthermore, different kinds of characters inhabit different genres; for example, aliens are characteristic of the science-fiction genre and zombies of the horror genre. Not only the type of being, but also their personalities and design are taken into consideration when analysing character type. A genre's name may also derive from the character type, as in the

---

10. Fishelov, *Metaphors of Genre*, 15.
11. Poitras, *Anime Essentials*, 34.
12. Nick Lacey, *Narrative and Genre: Key Concepts in Media Studies* (Basingstoke: Macmillan, 2000), 136.
13. Lacey, *Narrative and Genre*, 139.
14. William H. Phillips, *Film: An Introduction*, 3rd edn (New York: Bedford and St Martins, 2005), 637.
15. Jane Stadler, *Screen Media: Analysing Film and Television* (Crows Nest, NSW: Allen and Unwin, 2009), 344.

case of the *mahō shōjo* (magical girl) genre, in which the lead character is a girl who possesses magical powers.[16]

Genres have typical 'styles',[17] which may refer to the visual style of the work. While different genres are characterized by different visual styles, many contemporary mainstream anime, despite their genres, are executed using a two-dimensional animation technique; also, the backgrounds in many productions appear to be frequently executed using a three-dimensional animation technique. Anime creators do not seem to use pixilation or cut-outs, both two-dimensional techniques, but rather, techniques that are often digitally assisted but create the look of a hand-drawn two-dimensional animation. While the technique used does have an impact on a visual style of anime, that visual style is shaped accordingly to reflect the work's genre(s), and two anime examples which clearly demonstrate this are *High School of the Dead* (2010) and *Kaleido Star*. Tetsurō Araki directed the former series. Its colour palette accentuates the sense of horror. This choice by the director suggests that this is a horror/high school/zombies generic hybrid, executed using two-dimensional animation technique. While the same animation technique appears to be used in the making of *Kaleido Star*, its choice of a vivid and brightly coloured palette suggests a different generic hybrid. *Kaleido Star* is a series directed by Jun'ichi Satō that premiered in 2003. It concerns a Japanese girl, Sora, who travels to America wishing to perform in the Kaleido circus, an ambition she had held for many years. This is a supernatural/drama generic hybrid. Although the same animation technique is used for different genres, the way it is used (that is, the director's creative choices) is what determines the realization of a visual style characteristic for that particular genre. Thus, despite the fact that each animation technique has its own aesthetic, which impacts upon the work, it cannot be said that one animation technique is more suited than the other to a particular genre.[18]

Some of the genres found in anime include fantasy, supernatural, comedy, black comedy, tragedy, drama, *kodomo* (*kodomo muke*) (children's genre), romance, *mahō shōjo* (magical girl genre), high school, experimental, art, martial arts, political, horror, *yaoi* (boys' love genre), *yuri* (girls' love genre), *hentai* (pornography), *ecchi* (erotica), science fiction, *mecha* (piloted robots), cyberpunk, crime, sport, *samurai*, literary adaptations, and action/adventure. This rich, yet not comprehensive, list of

---

16. Buljan, 'Animated Film', 203.
17. Lacey, *Narrative and Genre*, 141.
18. Some of the material featured in the 'Introduction' and the section 'The Rise of Generic Hybridity in Anime' has been published in Buljan, 'Animated Film', 193-208.

genres is characteristic of contemporary anime. Not all of these genres have existed since the origins of anime production. Their number has risen over several decades and, as is argued in this section, this has provided a basis for the formation of many generic hybrids. This is not to say that generic hybridity is an exclusive characteristic of contemporary anime. There are generic hybrids in early anime production too, but their number is significantly fewer than in contemporary anime. To demonstrate this it is necessary to document the gradual emergence of certain anime genres from the origins of the art form onward.

Modern scholarship suggests that the birth of animation as an artistic medium was around the end of the nineteenth century, frequently linked to Charles-Émile Reynaud's invention of Théâtre Optique ('Optical Theatre'). The history of anime begins between 1910 and 1915, slightly later than its Western counterpart. It was the imported American and French animations that impressed artists in Japan in the early years of the twentieth century, and these artists then began working on the nation's first anime in imitation of Western examples.[19] It is not surprising that early anime did not feature an abundance of genres, as they were produced in a time of familiarization and experimentation with the new medium, simultaneously testing its limits and potential. Ōten Shimokawa made the first anime in 1916, which was followed by his *Mukuzō Imokawa, The Concierge* (1917), which was a mere five minutes in length. Jun'ichi Kōuchi's *Hanahekonai's New Sword* (1917), also known as *The Fine Sword*, appeared the same year as Seitarō Kitayama's *The Battle of the Monkey and the Crab*. Both of these were anime shorts and the latter was 'the earliest animated adaptation of an Asiatic folk tale'; Kitayama's 1918 *Tarō the Sentry: Submarine* had the same sources of inspiration, and it 'updated the folk-tale hero Momotarō, the Peach Boy, into a juvenile modern sailor, patrolling the harbor in his toy submarine'.[20] Taking into consideration their sources of inspiration, *The Battle of the Monkey and the Crab* and *Tarō the Sentry: Submarine* are the earliest examples of the fantasy genre in anime. Concerning other anime genres, Kōuchi made the earliest anime that deals with politics, *The Spotlight is on Shinpei Gotō* (1924); following the Great Kanto earthquake 'Shinpei Goto was the minister in charge of Tokyo's reconstruction'.[21] Also in 1924, Kitayama Eiga Seisakujo (Kitayama Movie Factory), the studio established by Kitayama, made an anime inspired by Aesop's fable of *The Tortoise and the Hare*, which thus

---

19. Fred Patten, 'Early Asian Animation', in Jerry Beck (ed.), *Animation Art: From Pencil to Pixel, the History of Cartoon, Anime & CGI* (New York: Harper Design International, 2004), 30.
20. Patten, 'Early Asian Animation', 30.
21. Patten, 'Early Asian Animation', 30.

became one of the earliest recorded Western influenced anime in the fantasy genre.

One of the earliest productions of the erotic anime genre is *Cooling Off on the Boat* (1929) by Hakusan Kimura, an early contributor to this genre. This work was a narrative based on an 1878 image of a courtesan on a ship, and resulted in Kimura's arrest, due to its erotic nature. Yasuji Murata created works which 'ranged from folk tales...to funny animal sports comedies'.[22] Murata's works in the latter genre are *The Animals' Olympics* (1928) and *My Baseball* (1930). Both these films were influenced by American cartoons of the second decade of the twentieth century. The 1930s saw the emergence of yet another genre, war propaganda, although the production of works based on folktales continued (and, in some cases, most clearly with the tale of Momotarō, the 'peach boy', discussed in Chapter 2, these two types of anime were combined). War propaganda anime from this period include Murata's *Aerial Momotarō* (1931), Mitsuyo Seo's *Sankichi the Monkey: Air Defense Military Exercise* (1933), a hybrid of military propaganda and 'funny-animal comedy', and the overtly antagonistic to the West *Black Cat Hooray!* (1934), directed by Takao Nakano. In *Black Cat Hooray!* 'a party of dolls in Japanese costumes and traditional Japanese toys are attacked by vicious bandits who are rat parodies of Mickey Mouse and snake parodies of American or British sailors. Momotarō and other Japanese folk heroes save the day'.[23] In Murata's anime series with army-related content titled *Norakuro* (1933–1934), translated in English as *Black Dog*, the influence of Western animation is evident. This story in which 'the loyal doggy joins the army'[24] is representative of the change that took place in that decade towards a modern, fast-paced humour.

In the second half of the 1930s anime production included adult comedies such as Kenzō Masaoka's *The World of Power and Women* (1933), 'folk tales and funny animal animation, and militaristic comedies'.[25] The setting for the adult comedy genre was often the medieval past of samurai warriors and legendary heroes, for example Mitsuyo Seo's *Love in the Genroku Era: Sankichi and Osayo* (1934). Children's anime were generally based on folklore, funny animals and Western stories. The production of propaganda dominated the period of the Second World War, an example of which is Masaoka's *The Spider and the Tulip* (1942). With regard to Western influence on the fantasy genre in the late 1950s

---

22. Patten, 'Early Asian Animation', 31.
23. Fred Patten, 'The Slide Toward War', in Beck (ed.), *Animation Art*, 53.
24. Jonathan Clements and Helen McCarthy, *The Anime Encyclopedia: A Guide to Japanese Animation Since 1917*, rev. edn (Berkeley, CA: Stone Bridge Press, 2006), 457.
25. Fred Patten, 'The War Clouds Thicken', in Beck (ed.), *Animation Art*, 53, 76.

and early 1960s, the Tōei Dōga anime studio made three anime which 'followed the Disney feature formula of being (or looking like) adaptations of ancient Chinese or Japanese folk tales, with lots of fantasy and magic, and cute funny-animal companions frolicking around the humans'.[26] These films are *Panda and the Magic Serpent* (1958), *Magic Boy* (1959), and *Alakazam the Great* (1960). Fantasy-genre feature-length productions by Tōei Dōga in the 1960s continued to be based on Japanese legends, such as *The Little Prince and the Eight-Headed Dragon* (1963). This anime is an an action-adventure tale and is based on the 'Japanese myth of a young god/prince named Susanoo, who embarks on an adventurous journey to the Underworld to find his dead mother Izanami'.[27] This myth was discussed in Chapter 2.

After experiencing lack of financial success with their exported works inspired by Eastern myths and legends, Tōei Dōga began making anime based on European sources for export, an example of which is *The Little Norse Prince* (1968). Thus, there is a shift recorded in the source of inspiration for Tōei Dōga's fantasy-genre works in this period.[28] As Tōei Dōga turned to European sources as the basis for its exported works, the studio continued to make anime for the Japanese national audience, based on sci-fi manga. The 1960s was an important decade in which several anime genres blossomed. The anime series *Iron Man #28* (1963) was the earliest example of the 'giant robots' subgenre,[29] and the *Eightman* series (1963) was an early representative of 'the transformation genre'.[30] This decade also saw the emergence of the 'magical girl' genre, when *Sally the Little Witch* debuted in 1966.[31] In 1968 the horror genre was inaugurated by the release of the series *GeGeGe no Kitarō*, an early generic hybrid, as it contained comedic elements. Concerning other genres in this decade, '*Sasuke* and *The Detective Stories of Sabu and Ichi* (1968), [were] the first two significant series in the sixteenth-nineteenth century "samurai-ninja" historical-adventure genre', and *Mrs Sazae* (1969) tapped into the housewives' market.[32]

At the end of the 1960s the earliest examples of sport-genre anime appeared; *Attack No. 1* (1969) was about a girls' volleyball team; and *Tomorrow's Joe* (1970) concerned boys' boxing. Thus, the spectrum of anime

---

26. Fred Patten, 'An Animation Industry Begins', in Beck (ed.), *Animation Art*, 196.
27. Fred Patten, 'An Explosion of Anime', in Beck (ed.), *Animation Art*, 236-37.
28. McCarthy, *Hayao Miyazaki*, 217.
29. Napier, *Anime from Akira to Princess Mononoke*, 87.
30. Manabu Yuasa, 'Japanese TV Animation in the Early Years: Animation and Animated Humans', *Kaboom! Explosive Animation from America and Japan* (Sydney: Museum of Contemporary Art, 1994), 63.
31. Patten, 'An Explosion of Anime', 236.
32. Patten, 'An Explosion of Anime', 237.

3 From Realistic to Supernatural

genres has been continuously expanding. The 1970s saw the proliferation of animation for television in Japan and '[t]he most significant advance in TV animation was the upgrading of its target audience from children to adolescents and young adults'.[33] This shift automatically implies genre multiplication and diversity of audience. With regard to character types (an element of genre), young heroes/saviours are found in many contemporary anime, but in 1972 Gō Nagai produced *Mazinger Z*, the earliest example of an anime featuring a giant mechanical being. This was the first instance of the *mecha* genre. Yoshiyuki Tomino's 1979 *Mobile Suit Gundam* is significant in that it 'recast the giant robots from unique superhero suits to more realistic futuristic military combat vehicles, and the adversaries from humans versus demonic aliens to warring human space nations'.[34] From 1981 the *Urusei Yatsura* anime (discussed in Chapter 2) ushered in the high-school fantasy genre. In the 1980s, an emergent genre was the 'World War Two drama emphasizing Japan's suffering civilians, seen through children's eyes', and examples of this include *Barefoot Gen* (1983), *Kayoko's Diary* (1991) and *Rail of the Star* (1993). *Barefoot Gen* was 'a semi-autobiographical account of the 1945 nuclear bombing of Hiroshima by cartoonist Keiji Nakazawa'.[35] These productions classified as belonging to World War II drama inevitably also contain elements of the genre of tragedy.

During the last decade of the twentieth century, animation became a global popular cultural phenomenon. With regard to narrative and character type, which are particular elements of genre, the studio Madhouse, through 'its distinctive character designer/director Yoshiaki Kawajiri, established a trademark style of adult situations featuring characters who are sophisticated, sensual and dangerous' in the 1990s.[36] The 1990s was also the decade in which Mamoru Oshii, Satoshi Kon, Rintaro (b. Shigeyuki Hayashi) and Hayao Miyazaki came to prominence as feature-film directors. With regard to original video animation (OVA), the *Record of Lodoss War* (1990) was among the most important works, introducing the sword and sorcery style of fantasy, set in the European Middle Ages. In the 2000s, two anime series for television, *Noir* and *Witch Hunter Robin*, both contained important Western influences. The former series features young, female, hired assassins and resembles Luc Besson's *La Femme Nikita* (1990), while the latter concerns 'an agency assigned to hunt "witches" (people with psychic abilities such as teleportation and telepathy) who use their powers in criminal ways – a cross between a

---

33. Fred Patten, 'Sci-Fi & Puppets', in Beck (ed.), *Animation Art*, 260.
34. Patten, 'Sci-Fi & Puppets', 260.
35. Fred Patten, 'Growth in All Directions', in Beck (ed.), *Animation Art*, 295.
36. Fred Patten, 'Anime in the 1990s', in Beck (ed.), *Animation Art*, 330.

police-procedural series and *The X-Files*'.[37] In spite of (or perhaps because of) the Western influences, both of these series, released in 2001 and 2002 respectively, achieved widespread popularity.

As noted, with each decade starting from the 1910s new genres appeared in anime. The above section discussed the emergences of genres including fantasy, political, comedy, war propaganda, science fiction, supernatural, samurai, sport, erotic, anime noir, World War II drama, and semi-autobiography, indicating that anime storytellers have tried to accommodate the interests of their audience, which includes children, young adults, mature adults, housewives, those with an interest in porn, and even those for whom bread-making holds an interest, as in the comedy anime *Yakitate!! Japan*, discussed above.

Thus, since its inception in the early years of the twentieth century anime has been gradually enriched by a variety of genres. Particular subgenres have also emerged over time, for example, the *mecha* subgenre of science fiction. This subgenre is characterized by machines 'that are often, but not always, giant robots'. The original conception of such robots was that they were 'radio controlled, but in the 1970s anime introduced pilots riding inside the machine',[38] which demonstrates the evolving nature of this subgenre. Science fiction has a variety of subgenres, including:

> vigilante teams (*Bubblegum Crisis* 1987–1991), special agents (*Dirty Pair*, 1985), and war-story adventures (*GunBuster*, 1988–1989)...bounty hunters on the frontier (*Cowboy Bebop*, 1998), and massive political epics on a grand scale (*Legend of the Galactic Heroes*, or *Ginga Eiyū Densetsu*, 1988–95).[39]

The fact that this abundance of genres has become characteristic of contemporary anime indicates that anime storytellers have taken full advantage of the potential for this multiplication of genres, and fracturing into subgenres. Sources including Japanese literary tradition, manga and its predecessors, and to a lesser degree Western cultural referents, had an impact on anime genre formation. The great number of genres and subgenres was, and still is, an excellent basis for the formation of generic hybrids. Generic hybrids did feature in earlier anime productions, for example, the above-mentioned *The Animals' Olympics* (1928). However, their number has risen significantly over time. The next section will discuss the notion of generic hybridity and how it relates to specific anime storytellers.

---

37. Fred Patten, 'Small-Screen Success', in Beck (ed.), *Animation Art*, 368.
38. Poitras, *Anime Essentials*, 35.
39. Poitras, *Anime Essentials*, 36.

In genre scholarship the term 'hybridity' designates the appearance of plural genres in a single work. A number of factors appear to have exercised an influence on anime creators' approaches to their work, in terms of combining the elements of diverse genres and consequently creating generic hybrids. First, the basic assumption appears to be that the anime storytellers have taken the medium of animation seriously, much more seriously than the majority of their Western counterparts, in the sense of recognizing its potential as a medium for attracting a diverse audience. Generic diversity within the art-form attracts different audiences, but having generic hybrids means that a single work has the potential to attract multiple demographics as an audience group. Factors that have facilitated the creation of new generic hybrids include the transition of anime from shorts to feature-length films, and the creation of anime series. Second, anime storytellers have also realized that generic hybrids are one of the tools for enriching the diegetic world of their work. The diegetic world is the world lived in and experienced by the story's characters,[40] while the non-diegetic parts of anime are those parts of which the audience is aware, but not the characters. For instance, the anime *Akira* directed by Katsuhiro Ōtomo (1988) features scenes of Tetsuo Shima and his friends riding motorbikes. The audience hears two sounds, one of the motorbikes and the other of background music. In this case, the sound of motorbikes is diegetic sound, as the characters hear this sound, but since the characters do not hear the sound of the background music, which is heard by the audience, that sound is non-diegetic sound. The richness of the diegetic world of anime, enabled by generic hybridity, has the potential to be more appealing to audiences.

As noted above, the rise of genres within anime appears to be particularly strong through the 1960s, the 1980s and the 1990s; also the first decade of the twenty-first century features a greater richness and a higher emergence of generic hybrids. Examples of generic hybrids from the 1990s and 2000s include, but are not exhausted by, drama/comedy/acrobatics/supernatural (*Kaleido Star* series, 2003), action/*mecha*/crime (*Burst Angel* series, 2004), *mecha*/science (*Argentosoma* series, 2000), historical/comedy/martial arts (*Musashi: The Dream of the Last Samurai*, 2009), and supernatural/action/drama/ecology (*Arjuna* series, 2001). The existing genres provided a large pool of settings (in terms of place and time), iconography, type of characters, and visual style. The adventurous use of narrative, and the mixing of these elements of genre in new ways, gave rise (and continues to do so) to the creation of new generic hybrids. Yet many generic hybrids in anime also derive from manga upon which they are based. Examples of generic hybrids that are derived from manga include

---

40. Stadler, *Screen Media*, 337.

martial arts/comedy/supernatural/romance hybrid (*Ranma 1/2*, 1989–1992 anime series; 1987–1996 manga), sport/drama/high school (*The Prince of Tennis*, 2004 anime series; 1999–2008 manga), high school/action/martial arts/drama/comedy (*Gokusen*, 1989–1992 anime series; 2000–2007 manga), drama/supernatural/recently departed/action (*Bleach*, 2004–2012 anime series; manga series 2001– continuing), and horror/drama/high school/tragedy (*Highschool of the Dead*, 2010 anime series; manga series 2006– continuing).

There are certain anime genre(s) that target particular audiences. The Japanese term *shōnen* translates as '[a] young man' or 'youth',[41] thus *shōnen* anime targets a youthful male audience. Similarly, the Japanese term *shōjo* has several translations, such as 'girl', 'virgin', '[a]n unmarried woman,' while *shōjo* translates as '[a] little girl'.[42] Consequently *shōjo* anime targets a youthful female audience. However, with anime's potential to generate new generic hybrids with target audiences that are more diverse than those of the current examples, it becomes arguable whether the *shōnen* and *shōjo* anime classifications will eventually become obsolete. The variety of generic hybrids in contemporary anime now appears to be standard, rather than exceptional.

The supernatural subgenre is present in many anime generic hybrids. This subgenre is closely related to others, including science fiction and fantasy. Some of the sources of inspiration for the supernatural subgenre in anime are world religions, mythologies, and the spiritual and cultural heritage of legends and folklore. As noted in Chapter 2, this is the subgenre where the richness of the Shintō tradition shines through, and it can be argued that the supernatural subgenre is inextricably linked to religion and spirituality. The frequency of the supernatural subgenre in generic hybrids suggests that it is among the most popular in anime. The number of elements of this subgenre featuring in diverse anime contexts will be discussed in the remainder of this chapter.

As noted above, it is problematic to attempt to elucidate genre in terms of its boundaries. In has been demonstrated that the abundance of genres that characterize contemporary anime is the result of a gradual process occurring from the second decade of the twentieth century onwards. Subgenres of some of these genres also appeared, equipping the anime storytellers with a myriad of different types of stories, characters, settings, narratives, visual styles and themes, which enabled them to pick and choose, and combine these elements of various genres in many different ways, creating appealing works belonging to a range

---

41. Fred Brinkley, *Brinkley's Japanese-English Dictionary*, vol. 2 (Cambridge: W. Heffer and Sons, 1963), 1324.

42. Brinkley, *Brinkley's Japanese-English Dictionary*, 1318.

of generic hybrids. Consequently, generic hybridity became the norm in contemporary anime, which attracted diverse audiences. This section has further highlighted that many generic hybrids contain elements of the supernatural subgenre, seemingly one of the most popular in anime. The following section analyses a range of anime contexts featuring generic hybrids containing this subgenre.

Western Pagan Ideas in the Supernatural Subgenre of Anime

The frequent appearance of the elements of the supernatural subgenre in numerous anime suggests that it is one of the most popular subgenres. The term 'supernatural' refers to an event, entity, action, happening or phenomenon, which springs from 'a higher realm...than that of nature'.[43] Thus, the supernatural subgenre in anime frequently borrows from world religions and mythologies, and a number of instances of this phenomenon were considered in some detail in Chapter 2. In scholarly writings the supernatural is often understood as a subgenre of fantasy, which is the view adopted here. Poitras claims that 'fantasy' and 'supernatural' content in anime inspired by sources from the West does not have a long history.[44] Yet, as noted, the Japanese animation studio Tōei Dōga began making anime based on European folktales for viewers outside Japan when their 1960s works inspired by traditional Eastern culture underperformed financially.[45] This fact qualifies the validity of Poitras's contention (taking into consideration that folk tales often contain elements of supernatural and fantasy).

The feature film *Nausicaä of the Valley of the Wind* (1984) belongs to the supernatural subgenre and the fantasy genre, and contains Japanese, but also Western influences; this anime is a newer example in which the fantasy and supernatural content is inspired to a certain extent by Western religious heritage. This section analyses the protagonist Nausicaä, and argues that the concept of power attributed to this type of female character is more influenced by Western Pagan ideas about the sacredness of the Earth, rather than by the culturally appropriate rolemodel, the Japanese sun-goddess Amaterasu. One distinct feature of many anime is the high level of frequency of the female characters appearing in lead roles; this feature sets it apart from its Western counterpart. This is not a characteristic of merely one, but of many, anime genres ranging

---

43. John A. Simpson and Edmund S. C. Weiner (eds), *The Oxford English Dictionary*, 2nd edn, vol. 17 (Oxford: Clarendon Press; Oxford; New York: Oxford University Press, 1989), 233.
44. Poitras, *Anime Essentials*, 39.
45. Patten, 'An Explosion of Anime', 236.

from comedy, high school, *mecha*, science fiction, and the action genre. Thus, they even appear in genres where fighting and killing play an important part in the plot, and in which the lead role would be usually assigned to a male protagonist. Many of the female characters in anime often have particular powers. The theme of ecological catastrophe is encountered in various genres and the power of the female leads that use them to resolve that problem is often closely associated with the belief about the sacredness of the Earth, the main feature of modern Western Paganism and eco-spirituality. The character of Nausicaä is the best example, though the issue of the power of Princess Mononoke's character from the Miyazaki film (1997), which is also an example of the fantasy and supernatural subgenre, in a certain sense is also related to Western Pagan ideas of the sacredness of the Earth.

Nausicaä of the Valley of the Wind (1984) was directed by Hayao Miyazaki and is also based on a manga he created. This anime concerns the human population living in the Valley of the Wind situated close to the Sea of Decay. Much of the Earth has been rendered uninhabitable in a 'global bio-nuclear war that kill[ed] most of humanity and radically alter[ed] the earth's eco-system'.[46] The Valley of the Wind is a post-apocalyptic community that lives in peace with nature, both the jungle and the mutated insect population that lives in it. The plot turns on the rediscovery of a living weapon in the kingdom of Pejite, and the warlike Tolmekian princess Kushana's invasion of Pejite to secure the weapon. On the return journey, her airship crashes in the Valley of the Wind, and in the subsequent fighting Nausicaä's father is killed. Nausicaä, who will play a crucial role in positively transforming the relation between humans and nature, seeks 'an end to war and suffering through a deeper understanding of the [natural] world...and a harmonious relationship between humanity and the jungle's insects'.[47] It can be argued that the powers given to Nausicaä's character are more in line with Western Pagan ideas about the sacred Earth and the goddess Gaia, than with the Japanese goddess Amaterasu, as she befriends animals with whom she can communicate, and understands the natural environment as kin to human beings, rather than conquered and exploited.

The name of the heroine in this anime appears also in Homer's *Odyssey*, and Miyazaki's Nausicaä, like the character in the *Odyssey*, is a princess. Miyazaki's Nausicaä is depicted as a strong, courageous, intelligent, kind and determined young woman who has a special talent for

---

46. Daniel Haas, 'Why Nice Princesses Don't Always Finish Last', in Josef Steiff and Tristan D. Tamplin (eds), *Anime and Philosophy: Wide-Eyed Wonder* (Chicago and La Salle, IL: Open Court, 2010), 121.
47. Haas, 'Why Nice Princesses Don't Always Finish Last', 126.

communicating with *Ohmus*, the gigantic insects that inhabit the Sea of Decay.⁴⁸ *Ohmus* are hostile towards humans because of their carelessness towards, and disrespect of, the Earth. Nausicaä's grandmother explains that, '[t]he *Ohmus*' rage is the fury of the Earth itself'. Nausicaä's role and fate have been foreshadowed in an earlier scene in which her grandmother narrates the legend about a saviour who will deliver the people from their difficult situation. This legend is presented visually on a tapestry, and according to it, a person who is dressed 'in blue robes' will come 'onto a golden field, to join bonds with the great earth'. Nausicaä completes her grandmother's sentence adding, 'and guide the people to the pure land'. This legend is realized in Nausicaä at the climax of the story. At that point, she is injured and apparently killed by an enraged running herd of *Ohmus* after she saved a baby *Ohmu*; but there is a twist in the plot. The *Ohmus* calm down and lift Nausicaä upwards, healing her simultaneously with their feelers. This sight, watched by the people, is parallel to the legend depicted on the tapestry. Surrounded by light, Nausicaä gets up and begins walking, held beneath by *Ohmus*'s feelers. This scene was described by one of the children to Nausicaä's blind grandmother: 'The princess is wearing strange blue clothes. It's like she's walking through golden fields'; the scene is identical to the one on the tapestry described earlier.

Miyazaki was inspired to create this particular manga and anime when he became aware of 'the pollution with mercury of Minamata Bay, as a result of which the fish stocks – left untouched as they would evidently be inedible – adjusted to the uncongenial environment by learning how to absorb the poison and indefatigably continued to reproduce'.⁴⁹ Central to this film is the issue of ecological responsibility and of human interrelatedness with nature. Despite the existence of powerful female *kami* in Shintō and the important bodhisattva Kannon (the goddess of mercy) in Japanese Buddhism, the modern Western Pagan goddess Gaia is the most relevant divine figure for *Nausicaä of the Valley of the Wind*. Her name derives from Greek mythology in which she was the 'personification of Mother Earth'.⁵⁰ Pagan scholar Graham Harvey explains that, 'ecology is of the essence of Paganism as a spirituality of Nature'⁵¹ and

---

48. Ian DeWeese Boyd, '*Shōjo* Savior: Princess Nausicaä, Ecological Pacifism, and the Green Gospel', *Journal of Religion and Popular Culture* 21.2 (2009), at www.usask.ca/relst/jrpc/pdfs/art21(2)-ShōjoSavior.pdf (accessed 10 December 2010).

49. Dani Cavallaro, *The Cinema of Mamoru Oshii: Fantasy, Technology and Politics* (Jefferson, NC and London: McFarland, 2006), 48.

50. Kees Zoeteman, *Gaiasophy: The Wisdom of the Living Earth. An Approach to Ecology*, trans. Tony Langham and Plym Peters (Hudson, NY: Lindisfarne Press, 1991), 157.

51. Graham Harvey, 'The Roots of Pagan Ecology', *Religion Today* 9.3 (1994): 40.

Nausicaä's character is closely linked to ecological problems and the restoration of nature in the film. Modern Paganism is eclectic and diverse, but all Pagans 'hold one belief or philosophy in common, and that is that Mother Earth is a sacred entity which must be cared for'.[52] Thus, the sacredness of the Earth is central to modern Paganism; and the mission of Nausicaä is to (re)awaken awareness of the sacredness of the Earth in other human characters in the story. She is the only one with the power to do so, and in this context her special ability to communicate with the animal world plays a crucial role.

Human dominion over nature is not acceptable in the Pagan tradition. Consequently this tradition cultivates the awareness of the importance of nature preservation. One of the 'primary roots of Pagan Ecology [is] the widely-held perception that the Earth is endangered by human activities'.[53] It is exactly this issue of lack of respect towards nature, which consequently leads to its abuse by humans, that is the cause of the ecological catastrophe in this anime. The drama of the film comes from Nausicaä's conflict with the martial leader Kushana, princess of the Tolmekian Empire. Both women want to rid the world of toxicity and restore the environment, but their methods separate them. Nausicaä seeks answers from nature and the environmental sciences. Kushana's solution is violent obliteration, and the wrongful nature of her solution is clear from the fact that the insects who save and resurrect Nausicaä have attacked Kushana's body, as a result of which she is part-machine. It can be argued that Nausicaä's character acts as a means of reconciliation between humans and nature, and her special powers facilitate the healing of the Earth's wounds. Harvey observes, with regard to the interdependence of all things, that, '[t]he second root of Pagan ecology is summed up in the phrase, "Everything that lives is Holy"'.[54] The Pagan worldview is one in which the distinction between human and non-human life is blurred and all life is worthy of respect. This is reflected in Nausicaä's character, as her deep understanding of, and respect for, the natural world and its inhabitants set her apart from the other human characters. This is demonstrated, for example, in her spending time in the Sea of Decay. Nausicaä's character and her powers are analogous with Western Pagan ideas about the feminine divine, rather than Shintō's Amaterasu.

---

52. Amy Simes, 'Children of the Gods: The Quest for Wholeness in Contemporary Paganism', in Alaine M. Low and Soraya Tremayne (eds), *Women as Sacred Custodians of the Earth? Women, Spirituality and the Environment* (New York: Berghahn Books, 2001), 220.
53. Harvey, 'The Roots of Pagan Ecology', 40.
54. Harvey, 'The Roots of Pagan Ecology', 40.

Amaterasu is the daughter of Izanagi and Izanami, the primordial deities in Japanese mythology, discussed in Chapter 2. Because of her exceptional beauty Amaterasu resides in Heaven. The *Nihongi*, an early repository of Japanese mythology and legends, says of her, '[s]o beautiful was she that Izanagi and Izanami declared: "She ought not to be kept long in this land, but we ought of our own accord to send her at once to Heaven, and entrust to her the affairs of Heaven" (*Nihongi* 1.2.18)'.[55] Amaterasu's brother Susanoo was given dominion over the Earth. On one occasion, upset by the behaviour of her brother, Amaterasu 'withdrew into the Rock-Cave of Heaven, fastened the door, and refused to come out'.[56] This deprived the Earth of sunlight, and only through the combined efforts of the gods did she emerge, allowing the light to shine over the Earth again. These important features of Amaterasu suggest that she is linked to the heavenly realm than to nature and the Earth. The Japanese animistic understanding of the physical world, that rocks, mountains, waterfalls and other natural phenomena are inhabited by *kami*, is generally compatible with Western Pagan conceptions of living nature. The point being made is simply that Nausicaä, who is preoccupied with the healing of the Earth and preservation of its sacredness, and whose powers serve this purpose, mirrors Pagan ideas about sacred nature and Gaia as Earth Goddess, rather than the mythology of the Japanese Amaterasu. There are other important characteristics of Amaterasu which will be discussed below, which also support the argument that Nausicaä's character and powers are not closely associated with indigenous models of the divine feminine, but that Miyazaki was inspired by Western Pagan conceptions of nature.

With regard to Miyazaki's later film *Princess Mononoke* (1997), the power of its titular character in a certain and limited sense (and much less than the character of Nausicaä) mirrors Pagan ideas about the sacredness of the Earth. The plot has similarities to that of *Nausicaä of the Valley of the Wind*, in that it concerns the damaged relation between humans and the Earth, due to the former's disrespect and carelessness towards the latter. There is also a significant conflict between two powerful female characters, one of whom respects the Earth while the other does not. Princess Mononoke strongly disapproves of humans' exploitation of the riches of the Earth and fights against it. Her appreciation of the Earth appears to be derived from her experience of growing up in her adoptive family of wolves. The initial balance between humans and Earth is described in the narrator's words at the start of the film.

---

55. Bettina Liebowitz Knapp, *Women in Myth* (Albany, NY: State University of New York Press, 1997), 151.

56. Knapp, *Women in Myth*, 162.

> In ancient times, the land lay covered in forests, where from ages long past, dwelt the spirits of the gods. Back then, man and beast lived in harmony, but as time went by, most of the great forests were destroyed. Those that remained were guarded by gigantic beasts...who owed their allegiance to the Great Forest Spirit, for those were the days of gods and demons.

The balance between the humans and Earth has been damaged. Princess Mononoke's enemy Lady Eboshi sets out with a group of men to kill the Great Forest Spirit (in an action reminiscent of the Babylonian *Epic of Gilgamesh*, when Gilgamesh and Enkidu kill the spirit of the cedar forests, Humbaba, and subsequently incur the wrath of the gods). They behead the Great Forest Spirit, but Princess Mononoke (together with Prince Ashitaka), succeed in restoring his head, after which the regeneration of the Earth occurs. Princess Mononoke's character, like that of Nausicaä, closely reflects Pagan ideas about the sacredness of the Earth, deep respect and awareness of its needs, and concern to protect it and safeguard its well-being. Yet Lady Eboshi has a 'softer side', as Jolyon Baraka Thomas argues, because she 'has provided sanctuary for former prostitutes and people suffering from Hansen's disease [leprosy]'.[57]

However, unlike Nausicaä, Princess Mononoke does not have a close relationship with humans. Rather, she is hostile towards them because of their disrespectful treatment of the Earth, and she has a special ability to communicate with the inhabitants of the forest. Princess Mononoke, too, lacks a connection to Amaterasu, because the central tenet of Paganism (deep respect for the Earth) does not feature in the mythology of Amaterasu. Amaterasu is closely linked to Japan; as Lotte Motz argues, she 'guided and directed the conquest of Japan from her heavenly abode'.[58] This goddess is also the ancestress of the imperial family, as her 'grandson descended from heaven, and his grandson in turn became the first emperor of Japan, ascending the throne in 660 B.C.E.'.[59] This geographical specificity and concern for a particular race and place find no parallel in either Nausicaä's or Princess Mononoke's stories. Their concern is for nature and the Earth as a totality, and for the benefit of all living beings. Furthermore, three *kami* symbols associated with Amaterasu (the sword, the mirror and the jewel) were given to Ninigi, Amaterasu's grandson, as 'the emblems of his royal office, descended to earth'.[60] Neither Nausicaä nor Princess Mononoke is associated with these sacred items, and in fact

---

57. Thomas, *Drawing on Tradition*, 116.
58. Lotte Motz, *The Faces of the Goddess* (New York: Oxford University Press, 1997), 176.
59. Knapp, *Women in Myth*, 141.
60. Motz, *The Faces of the Goddess*, 171.

specifically Japanese and Shintō references are absent from these two Miyazaki films.

In summary, the two female protagonists Nausicaä and Princess Mononoke reveal the influence of Western Pagan ideas about nature and the earth-goddess Gaia, rather than the Japanese female divinity, Amaterasu, the sun-goddess. Both Nausicaä and Princess Mononoke are closely linked to the healing of the Earth's wounds, understood to be environmental devastation inflicted by human abuse of natural resources, and both are devoted to peace between all living creatures and the restoration and protection of the sacredness of nature.

The Supernatural in Anime with Realistic Subject Matter

The supernatural, as noted above, is one of the most frequent subgenres in anime and many anime generic hybrids often contain elements of this subgenre. Interestingly, subgenres with realistic subject matter, such as tragedy, may contain elements of the supernatural subgenre. The anime considered in this section are *Grave of the Fireflies*, *Les Misérables: Shōjo Cosette*, *Tokyo Godfathers* and *Blossoms for Tomorrow*. There are no heroes and heroines with magical powers in these stories. Human characters and the circumstances in which they live are portrayed quite realistically, and the first two above-mentioned anime are dramas belonging to the tragedy subgenre. *Tokyo Godfathers* and *Blossoms for Tomorrow* also belong to the genre of drama. Yet, in each of the four examples there are unexpected supernatural elements present. This section argues that, although the supernatural elements are a minor feature in these anime, they function as a metaphor for either the celebration of the human spirit despite tragedy (in *Grave of the Fireflies*), or as a metaphor for resilience and strength of human spirit (in *Les Misérables: Shōjo Cosette*), or as a symbol that contains soteriological meaning (in *Tokyo Godfathers*), or as a symbol of personal transformation (in *Blossoms for Tomorrow*).

The presence of supernatural elements in the subgenre of tragedy is not a contemporary phenomenon, let alone a phenomenon exclusive to anime. With regard to ghosts, Adrian Poole observes that, '[i]n the first surviving complete tragedy that has come down to us, Aeschylus' *Persians* (472 BC), the ghost of the dead King Darius rises from his tomb'.[61] Thus, the supernatural in tragedy dates back more than two millennia. In terms of generic classification, tragedy is categorized as a subgenre of drama. In general, tragedy is perceived as 'serious' and is linked to

---

61. Adrian Poole, *Tragedy: A Very Short Introduction* (Oxford and New York: Oxford University Press, 2005), 33.

'sorrow'.[62] One characteristic of this subgenre is that its stories often involve death and anguish. Tragic stories, 'often begin happily, but that initial happiness is abruptly shattered by some unexpected occurrence; catastrophic consequences for the protagonist (and often for other individuals in tragic works) result from some error in judgment...made by the protagonist'.[63] Another important characteristic of tragedy is that, '[d]espite the cataclysmic events that befall tragic protagonists, tragedy often ultimately celebrates the dignity of the human spirit in confronting such overwhelming misfortune and in accepting the consequences of actions'.[64] These characteristics of tragedy will be discussed with reference to *Grave of the Fireflies* and *Les Misérables: Shōjo Cosette*, with particular emphasis on the function of supernatural elements in these productions.

Grave of the Fireflies was directed by Isao Takahata and released in 1988. As noted earlier, in the 1980s a new genre appeared in anime – the World War II drama – in which the horrors of war were presented from a child's perspective. The film *Grave of the Fireflies* tells of the tragic fate of the orphaned brother and sister, Seita and Setsuko, in Japan during World War II. Their father, a member of the Japanese Navy, dies when his ship is sunk. Seita and Setsuko's mother falls ill and during the Allied bombardment of Kōbe she, too, is killed. Their aunt becomes the children's guardian; but after an argument with her, Seita decides to leave home with Setsuko. It is then that their desperate struggle for survival begins. They manage to find a shelter for themselves, and fourteen-year-old Seita, the older brother, provides food and water by stealing from the houses of people fleeing the bombs. Yet Seita and Setsuko suffer malnutrition, and on her deathbed Setsuko hallucinates, offering Seita a 'rice ball' that she made out of mud. Soon after Setsuko's death, Seita also dies. This film is an adaptation of Akiyuki Nosaka's 'semi-autobiographical' novel of the same name.[65] Nosaka 'says in interviews that he wrote the story as a personal apology to his two sisters who died of malnutrition during World War II... His reaction is classic survivor's guilt, but he is also fully aware that his own immaturity was a factor in his [younger] sister's death'.[66] The physical setting and the backgrounds in this anime are inspired by the works of artist Hiroshige Utagawa (1797–1858) and the artistic style

---

62. Carl H. Klaus et al. (eds), *Elements of Literature: Essay, Fiction, Poetry, Drama, Film*, 4th edn (New York: Oxford University Press, 1991), 787.
63. Murfin and Ray, *The Bedford Glossary*, 484.
64. Murfin and Ray, *The Bedford Glossary*, 484.
65. Odell and le Blanc, *Studio Ghibli*, 73.
66. Hal Shipman, 'Grave of the Child Hero', in Josef Steiff and Tristan D. Tamplin (eds), *Anime and Philosophy: Wide-Eyed Wonder* (Chicago and La Salle, IL: Open Court, 2010), 201.

of Georges Prosper Remi, known as Hergé, who made *The Adventures of Tintin* comics.[67]

Grave of the Fireflies contains the classic elements of the tragedy subgenre. First, from Seita's recollections it is clear that prior to the tragedy his was a happy family, in which he and his sister felt secure and protected by their parents. This situation suddenly changed due to the loss of their parents in a short period of time. Seita's surprise at the news of his father's ship sinking demonstrates that he trusted his father's reassurance that the Japanese Navy was so strong that nothing could harm it. Second, Seita's decision to leave his aunt's house not knowing that this would have fatal consequences, not only for himself but also for his little sister, is a classic tragic error of judgment (Greek *hamartia*, literally 'to miss the mark'). Seita's wrong decision was underpinned by a 'tragic flaw', characteristic of tragedy genre protagonists. This flaw is '[a] character trait in a tragic hero or heroine that brings about his or her downfall. Traits like arrogance or *hubris* (excessive pride) are common tragic flaws'.[68] Seita's flaw is his pride, which did not allow him to reconcile and return to his aunt after their disagreement, despite receiving advice from adults to do so. Akiyuki Nosaka describes the story as 'a double-suicide story', and Isao Takahata shares this view, finding it similar to 'double-suicide plays' by Monzaemon Chikamatsu.[69] Furthermore, in the story there is the use of the term *yokoana*, which has several meanings, one of which is 'tombs' in archaic Japan.[70] Seita's and Setsuko's shelter resembles a cavern, and by extension a grave or tomb (which will be their ultimate destination). If the classification of *Grave of the Fireflies* as a 'double-suicide story' seems harsh, it is nevertheless undeniable. Seita receives advice from a number of adults to return to his aunt's house (for example, the farmer from whom he requests food recommends that he apologize to his family and return to the house, in order to receive rationed food), and when he takes Setsuko to the doctor, he is unable to comprehend that malnutrition cannot be reversed by the 'quick fix' of medicine. The tragic weight of *Grave of the Fireflies* is particularly poignant because in anime the resilient child-protagonist who

---

67. Roger Ebert, 'Grave of the Fireflies (1988)', *Chicago Sun-Times* (2000), at http://rogerebert.suntimes.com/apps/pbcs.dll/article?AID=/20000319/REVIEWS08/3190301/1023 (accessed 10 May 2012).

68. Murfin and Ray, *The Bedford Glossary*, 486.

69. Anon, 'The Animerica Interview: Takahata and Nosaka – Two Grave Voices in Animation', *Animerica: Anime and Manga Monthly* 2.11 (1994): 7. Originally published in *ANIMAGE Magazine* (1987).

70. Fukushima, cited in Dani Cavallaro, *Anime and the Art of Adaptation: Eight Famous Works from Page to Screen* (Jefferson, NC: McFarland, 2010), 29.

triumphs over challenging circumstances is such a familiar and ever-present character type.

However, the director breaks the conventions of tragedy, not only by introducing the spirits of Seita and Setsuko into the story, but also by portraying them as content in the afterlife. The film opens with a scene in which the candy tin that is Setsuko's cremation urn 'spills open, [and] the *rei* (spirit) of Setsuko rises out of cremated remains and the *rei* of Seita steps out of the train station'.[71] Seita's spirit narrates his own tragic fate, 'September 21, 1945… That was the night I died'. Yet, Seita's and Setsuko's spirits as supernatural elements in this film, it can be argued, function as a metaphor for the celebration of the human spirit. With regard to the supernatural when it appears in a 'realistic story' Dana Del George writes:

> [w]hether the supernatural is considered real or imagined, it is useful to think of it as an environment, comingled with the natural environment, though usually inaccessible to the physical senses. As an environment, dealt with as meaning, it has values and provokes responses that the natural can never have or do. Thus, the representation of the supernatural in a realistic story will add levels of meaning to the narrative.[72]

This can be applied to *Grave of the Fireflies*, so that the supernatural appearance of Seita's and Setsuko's contented-looking ghosts at the conclusion of the film conveys the celebration of the human spirit, despite the calamities that befell the children in their brief and tragic lives. The spirits of Seita and Setsuko are together at the end of the film; and their appearance contains a Shintō reference. With regard to the visual style used to portray these spirits, Fukushima writes, '[t]he spirit world is washed in light red visually separating it from the world of the living. This color surprisingly evokes neither anger nor anxiety, but rather warmth and serenity'.[73] This is correct, as Seita and Setsuko are shown together and content after their short and suffering-filled lives, which affirms contemporary notions that the afterlife is a place of spiritual reassurance and gentle calm.

One motif that also brings a breath of the otherworldly to the story, and which in an indirect way supports the notion of the spirit world as a metaphor for the triumphant human spirit, is the appearance of the fireflies. The firefly 'has strong mythological and literary significance in

---

71. Shipman, 'Grave of the Child Hero', 197-98.
72. Dana Del George, *The Supernatural in Short Fiction of the Americas: The Other World in the New World* (Westport, CN: Greenwood Press, 2001), 3.
73. Dennis H. Fukushima Jr, 'The Lost Fireflies', *Fukushima Review* (n.d.), at http://www.willamette.edu/~rloftus/jfilm/hotarurev.html (accessed 10 May 2012).

Japanese history'.[74] A Japanese legend tells of a lunar princess who grew up on Earth. Saddened by the fact that on her twentieth birthday she has to leave Earth and her beloved prince, she wept, and '[a]s her magical tears approached the ground, they began to glow bright green and turned into fireflies'.[75] It can be contended that this myth is analogous with Seita's and Setsuko's longing never to be parted from each other (due to appearance of the fireflies in the story). As the motif of fireflies appears again after their deaths, together with their spirits, the meaning is changed and intensified at that point, to support the metaphorical function of the supernatural elements (that is, the children's spirits) serving to celebrate the human spirit in the face of tragedy.

The second anime that will be discussed in this section is *Les Misérables: Shōjo Cosette*. This series, based on the 1862 work by French author Victor Hugo, was directed by Hiroaki Sakurai and released in 2007. The story concerns a mother and daughter, Fantine and Cosette, who are seeking a better life. On their way to Paris they stop in a little country town, where Fantine is persuaded by a family of restaurant owners to leave her daughter with them while she looks for work in the city. She does not want to be parted from Cosette, but views it as the best option for their situation.[76] As soon as Fantine leaves, Cosette is forced into work that is brutally hard for her age. Fantine is unaware of Cosette's mistreatment, and tragically dies before she can see her daughter again. Jean Valjean, a reformed criminal who has become a rich man, and in whose factory Fantine worked before her death, then raises Cosette as his own daughter. Valjean changes his name a number of times in an attempt to hide his past. Although the subject matter is realistic, there are some elements of the supernatural, with a metaphorical function, in the story.

Les Misérables: Shōjo Cosette follows, to a certain extent, the established pattern of the tragedy subgenre, discussed above. The setting (an element of genre) is nineteenth-century France, which, as seen in the story, was a very difficult era for single mothers, who were discriminated against in terms of employment. Similarly, children suffered, as there were no laws to protect them against exploitation. In a similar way to Seita from *Grave of the Fireflies*, Fantine also makes a serious 'error in judgment' (*hamartia*), by leaving Cosette with an unknown family, which consequently leads to her abuse. Unlike Seita, however, Fantine's

---

74. Ronald E. Yates, *The Kikkoman Chronicles: A Global Company with a Japanese Soul* (New York: McGraw-Hill, 1998), 158.

75. Christopher Dewdney, *Acquainted with the Night: Excursions through the World after Dark* (London: Bloomsbury, 2010).

76. Victor Hugo, *Les Misérables*, trans. Lee Fahnestock and Norman MacAfee (New York: Signet Classics, 1987), 145-53.

character is not depicted as having a particular tragic flaw.[77] Weaving a number of supernatural elements into this realistic and tragic story may seem an interruption, and disharmonious with the flow of the plot, but it adds a special level of meaning and intimacy concerning the relationship between the three principal characters, Fantine, Cosette and Valjean. An example of the supernatural in this anime is that while Fantine is in Montreuil-sur-Mer and Cosette is in Montfermeil, on a few occasions they seem to have heard each other's voices telepathically calling to each other. Furthermore, in episode 52 *The Silver Candlesticks*, when Valjean is about to die, the spirit of the late Bishop Myriel (who helped him to abandon his criminal past), appears with the spirit of the late Fantine. Seeing them, Valjean knows that his end is near. While not seeing their spirits, Cosette, who was with Valjean, hears her late mother's voice. It can be argued that the presence of these supernatural elements demonstrates that this anime breaks the convention of the drama/tragedy generic hybrid and that the supernatural elements function as a metaphor for the resilience and strength of the human spirit in the face of calamity and death. Fantine and Cosette's ability to hear each other's voices shows that neither distance nor overwhelmingly difficult circumstances could completely separate one from the other, or break their spirits. Their bond is further confirmed when Cosette hears her mother's voice after her death. Consequently, this supernatural element has a metaphorical meaning in sense of the strength and resilience of the human spirit, which does not succumb to tragedy.

The genre of drama refers to works that 'treat some important (non-trivial) issue or difficulty'.[78] Drama, as commonly understood, 'denotes conflict, contradiction, confrontation, defiance'.[79] Drama is the dominant genre in *Tokyo Godfathers* (2003), though there are also elements of tragedy. Drama also dominates in the anime series *Blossoms for Tomorrow*. It can be argued that the supernatural elements in *Tokyo Godfathers* function symbolically and with soteriological meaning, while in *Blossoms for Tomorrow* the supernatural functions as a symbol of personal transformation.

Tokyo Godfathers, directed by Satoshi Kon, concerns three homeless people who find a baby in a pile of rubbish on Christmas Eve.[80] They are

---

77. Lambert M. Surhone, Mariam T. Tennoe and Susan F. Henssonow, *World Masterpiece Theatre: Anime* (Saarbrücken: Betascript, 2010).
78. Murfin and Ray, *The Bedford Glossary*, 120.
79. Keith Sanger, *The Language of Drama* (London and New York: Routledge, 2000), 6.
80. Alexander Zahlten, 'Tokyo Godfathers', in John Berra (ed.), *Directory of World Cinema: Japan* (Bristol: Intellect Books, 2010), 82.

very different personalities: Miyuki is a young girl who has run away from home; Hana is a middle-aged transvestite gay man; and Gin is an alcoholic. Hana gives the baby the name 'Kiyoko', which has spiritual connotations. He explains to Gin and Miyuki that the name derives from '*kiyo*, "pure," on this purest of nights'. Kiyoko, coincidentally, is also the name of Gin's daughter. Though the anime features a subplot in which a woman, Sachiko Nishizawa, falsely claims to be the baby's mother, at the conclusion the child is reunited with her biological parents. Interestingly, Peter B. Kyne's novel inspired the film *Three Godfathers* (1948) directed by John Ford, and Ford's film similarly inspired this anime. Jerry Beck notes that, '*Tokyo Godfathers* is Kon's first feature to swing all the way from straight drama and tragedy through gentle humor to blatant comedy, emphasized by a visual shift from realistic character design to an exaggerated super-deformed grotesqueness'.[81] These observations assist to clarify the type of generic hybrid that is *Tokyo Godfathers*.

As a drama, *Tokyo Godfathers* deals with a serious issue, homelessness. Conflict, one of the crucial elements of drama, is also significant in this anime; for example, Hana became homeless due to conflicts at work. Yet, within this quite realistic story, Kon masterfully integrates elements of the supernatural, the symbolic meaning of which will be analysed below. One supernatural element is seen in a scene in which Sachiko Nishizawa is about to jump with the baby Kiyuko off a building. Hana manages to catch the baby as she falls, although the banner that supported them begins to give way. Yet, contrary to expectations, defying the laws of physics, Hana and Kiyoko land safely on the ground through the mysterious assistance of a seemingly divine agency. It can be argued that in this broadly realistic anime, supernatural elements function as symbols with soteriological meaning. But it is valuable to first discuss the characters and their relationship to the spiritual. The appearance of the sacred in the physical reality is termed a 'hierophany' by Mircea Eliade. Eliade argues that '[t]he sacred always manifests itself as a reality of a wholly different order from "natural" realities'.[82] The director, Kon, weaves these two realities together in a masterful way; of the three main characters, Hana is the most attuned to and understanding of that other 'sacred' reality. In this anime Kon uses the characters of Gin and Hana to represent two different 'takes' on religion. Gin is a non-believer, which is clear from the comments he makes about the sermon he hears with the others at the soup kitchen on Christmas Eve. Hana, on the other hand, on numerous occasions throughout the story,

---

81. Beck, *The Animated Movie Guide*, 284.
82. Mircea Eliade, *The Sacred and the Profane: The Nature of Religion* (New York: Harcourt Brace Jovanovich, 1987 [1959]), 10.

is demonstrated to be a spiritual person. Eliade notes that, 'for [the] religious man the supernatural is indissolubly connected with the natural',[83] a notion that is apparent in Hana's character. For example, Hana is convinced that divine working is behind the arrival of a baby in their lives; Hana exclaims at one point, "I knew it! Kiyoko really is the messenger of God!' It is perhaps not surprising that Kon chooses Hana, rather than Gin or Miyuki, to jump from a high building to save the baby, because Hana is more receptive towards the supernatural and its miraculous possibilities. After the rescue, all three are at the hospital, where they are visited by the baby's parents, who ask them to be her godfathers. Finally, they have been given a very special recognition. Thus, this miraculous event is a turning point in the plot, because it symbolizes a significant change in the lives of the three that presumably follows. Homelessness and separation from society marked them at the start of the anime; the role of godfathers signifies their re-integration into society.

Christian references play an important role in this anime. Some of these are explicit, while others are more implicitly presented in the story. One of the explicit Christian references is in the anime's title, in which the word 'godfathers' (which should be 'godparents' as one of the characters is a female) refers to the individual who holds the child during baptism and whose role is to provide spiritual guidance to that child. One example of an implicit Christian reference is the number of key characters, three. This number holds a special meaning in a Christian context in the sense that it can signify the Holy Trinity, the three kings who visited the infant Jesus with gifts, and the three days between Jesus' death and resurrection. Furthermore, the story opens at a soup kitchen on Christmas Eve, with a group of children performing on stage the story of the nativity and the three kings from the *New Testament* and singing the Christmas carol *Silent Night*; this is followed by a priest's sermon about Jesus. Adam Barkman has noted that Catholic imagery is more often used in anime than Protestant types of Christianity, and *Tokyo Godfathers* is suffused with angel imagery and miracles.[84]

The miraculous is a particularly powerful theme towards the end of the story. This 'divine agency' is an important point in the context of Christianity, where '[d]ivine agency is not understood as unintentional behaviour; it is necessarily intentional action'.[85] The saving of the lives of Hana and the baby Kiyoko, preventing potential tragedy, was followed by a dramatic reversal in the lives of all three key characters. Christoph Schwöbel

---

83. Eliade, *The Sacred and the Profane*, 117-18.
84. Barkman, 'Did Santa Die on the Cross?', 115-17.
85. Christoph Schwöbel, 'Divine Agency and Providence', *Modern Theology* 3.3 (1987): 227.

observes that, '[b]eing finite...human agents are limited in their intentions, as well as in their actions. Our lack of knowledge of the context of our actions may cloud our intentions and limit our possible courses of action'.[86] This general human characteristic applies to the three central characters, since for a considerable amount of the story none are empowered, or perhaps they fear to act in a way that would change their lives for the better. Of these three key characters, Hana is particularly important for the religio-spiritual aspects of the story through her wish to keep the baby, naming her Kiyoko, while Gin and Miyuki want to hand her over to the police.

Kiyoko can be understood in a certain sense as a saviour who entered the lives of three people who had lost their way. On one level, divine intervention acted as a medium for saving the lives of Hana and Kiyoko, but on another level it may be interpreted as soteriological, that is the salvation of the souls of the principal characters, since this event enabled the invitation to godfatherhood, requiring that they be responsible for the spiritual growth of a child. This also implies that they will take care of their own spiritual growth. The three homeless people have unselfishly fostered the baby, and Hana was even prepared to die for her. At the commencement of the story, the priest explained, 'The Lord Jesus was laid in a manger...to bring salvation to the souls of those...with no place of their own'; this line has importance as it foreshadowed the events that followed in this anime. If Kon had not introduced any supernatural elements, then Hana and Kiyoko would not have been saved, and logically there would be no offer to become godfathers, and no soteriological elements within the story.

The fourth work discussed in this section is the anime series *Hanasaku Iroha* (2011, English: *Blossoms for Tomorrow*), directed by Masahiro Ando. It concerns a young girl, Ohana Matsumae, who is sent by her mother Satsuki Matsumae – who has formed a new relationship – to live with her grandmother, Sui Shijima. Ohana has to work hard at her grandmother's tavern, the Kissuiso Inn. The grandmother is aloof, and the atmosphere at the inn is gloomy. Yet by the end of the series she has managed to build a close relationship with her grandmother. In this realistic and dramatic story about a young girl who needed to mature quickly, there are elements of a supernatural subgenre the meaning of which will be discussed subsequently. Similarly to *Tokyo Godfathers*, this anime is a drama in a sense that it deals with realistic, serious and difficult subject matter; young Ohana is at an age when she needs a parental presence, yet there is no mention of her father and her mother's selfishness places her own interests first. Some of the spiritual or supernatural

---

86. Schwöbel, 'Divine Agency and Providence', 228.

references are seen in two episodes, 'Grey Heron Rhapsody' and 'A Tearful Chef Romance', in which Ohana converses with two different characters about the Bonbori festival, a festival of lanterns which runs from 6-9 August.[87] Yet, in this series and also according to Elaine Gerbert, as seen below, Bonbori is held in October. In a scene in the former episode, Nako Oshimizu, an employee at the Kissuiso Inn, explains to Ohana that during the festival in question people 'illuminate a path' with *bonbori* for the gods who are returning from Izumo, so that they do not lose their way. Izumo is the place where many of Susanoo no Mikoto's adventures occurred, while the Izumo Taisha shrine is devoted to his son.[88] Surprisingly, there is no direct reference to this shrine in the anime. Mythology states that the eight million *kami* from all over Japan come together in Izumo in October of every year,[89] which is the same month mentioned in *Blossoms for Tomorrow* (thus, this is most likely the event to which Nako refers). The gathering of the *kami* in Izumo signifies the honouring of Amaterasu's emerging from the cave upon hearing the laughter of the gods,[90] a myth that was discussed in Chapter 2. Interestingly, '[t]he Earth-gods who every year took part in this commemorial resurrection were said to bring back with them a divine blessing on their return home',[91] which is reflected in this anime in the fulfilment of Ohana's wishes. In the episode 'A Tearful Chef Romance', Ohana discusses the Bonbori festival with her uncle Enishi Shijima, who explains to her the meaning of the festival wish card by saying, '[i]f you write your wish on it and tie it to the *bonbori*, a god will use it to illuminate his path home back to Izumo, and in return, he'll grant you your wish'. It can be argued that these spiritual or supernatural elements function as a metaphor for personal transformation. This is due to the fact that when Ohana's grandmother found out about her granddaughter's wish written on her *bonbori* wish card (that she wants to become like her, 'I want to be Sui Shijima-Ohana'), a substantial transformation occurred in her, and as a consequence a good relationship was established between grandmother and granddaughter. This example of writing a wish on a card in the hope that it will somehow be realized by means of a divine

---

87. Rex Shelley, Teo Chuu Yong and Russell Mok, *Japan* (Singapore: Times Books International, 1990), 113.
88. Helen B. Chapin, ' The Gion Shrine and the Gion Festival', *Journal of the American Oriental Society* 54.3 (1934): 284.
89. Elaine Gerbert, 'Laughing Priests in the Atsuta Shrine Festival', in Hans Geybels and Walter Van Herck (eds), *Humour and Religion: Challenges and Ambiguities* (London and New York: Continuum, 2011), 56.
90. Halldor Stefansson, 'Earth-Gods in Morimachi', *Annals of Human Sciences* 6 (1985): 35.
91. Stefansson, 'Earth-Gods in Morimachi', 35.

3 *From Realistic to Supernatural* 145

intervention, reflects a long-standing Japanese tradition and also demonstrates how the spiritual is tightly interwoven with the everyday in Japan. There are other references to the supernatural or the spiritual in this series, the most important one in the context of the argument of this chapter being the appearance of a child goddess accompanied by a fox. The above-mentioned conversation between Nako and Ohana occurs near a small shrine to which Nako takes Ohana, and later, as will be seen, this place plays an important role in the fulfilment of Ohana's wish. During their conversation, Nako tells Ohana that she is a frequent visitor to that shrine where she prays to a child goddess 'who tamed a fox'. On either side of this little shrine is a statue of a fox, suggesting that this could be a reference to the Inari shrine. It is perhaps not surprising that Inari devotion was chosen to feature in this anime, as Morris E. Opler and Robert Seido Hashima explain, '[t]he shrines to Inari are about the most numerous in Japan and every village has one'. Interestingly, the fox is particularly associated with the cult, and '[i]nvariably you find foxes carved out of stone set before large Inari shrines, on both sides of the shrine, as guards. Often they have the right paw lifted in a sort of beckoning gesture'.[92] This point is also reflected in the anime in a scene where the shrine featured is adorned with the two statues of foxes yet both their paws are on the ground. Inari is a bringer of sustenance and patron of business; another reason why she and her shrine feature in this anime is perhaps because Ohana's wish is to be like her grandmother, who is a businesswoman (the owner of the inn).[93]

The shrine, the multitude of *bonbori* with wish cards, and the little goddess accompanied by the fox about which Nako spoke to Ohana, appear in Ohana's thoughts during the aforementioned conversation between Ohana and her uncle. In this vision, the hand of the little goddess was seeing reaching for the *bonbori* wish cards, presumably reading what would later be Ohana's wish, among the wishes of others. This vision foreshadowed Ohana's writing the wish on a *bonbori* card, through which medium the divine intervention will be effected. In the episode titled 'Slight Fever', the third appearance of the little goddess accompanied by the fox underlines the significant role they play for Ohana.

In this anime the director could have used many different means to bridge the emotional distance that exists between Ohana and her grandmother, but instead spiritual or supernatural references were chosen for this. As noted previously, in Japan everyday life is suffused with spiritual aspects, and in this anime it is implied that divine intervention, most likely by the child goddess accompanied by the fox, ultimately enabled

---

92. Opler and Hashima, 'The Rice Goddess and the Fox', 45.
93. Opler and Hashima, 'The Rice Goddess and the Fox', 45.

the transformation of Ohana's relationship with her grandmother. Thus, Ohana's dream of a child goddess with a fox was not merely an omen of good things to come, although there is no visible magical working in this story as there is in Tokyo Godfathers. The transformation of Ohana's grandmother is seen at the end of the story when Ohana departs; her grandmother closes the inn and gives Ohana the inn's logbook, with the promise that she will wait for her, a gesture unthinkable earlier in the story.

This section has argued that in anime there is a range of metaphorical functions of the supernatural combined with realistic subject matter (tragedy and drama genres). It has been demonstrated that this function can be in terms of a metaphor for the celebration of the human spirit in the face of tragedy and the grief it brings (as in Grave of the Fireflies), and also as a metaphor for the resilience and strength of the human spirit (as in Les Misérables: Shōjo Cosette). It has also been argued that in the drama genre the supernatural can be understood as a symbol that carries a soteriological meaning in the context of characters' lives when circumstances seem against them (as seen in Tokyo Godfathers). It has been further argued that the supernatural or spiritual elements in the context of the dramatic genre can also function as a metaphor for personal transformation (as seen in Blossoms for Tomorrow). This demonstrates that there are a variety of elements of the supernatural genre in anime that has realistic subject matter, and that many concern the lives and personalities of the human characters.

The Child/Young Adult Protagonist and the Supernatural

In Chapter 2 the special powers possessed by children and young adolescents were canvassed in the context of popular folktales and myths such as that of the 'peach boy' Momotarō, and the protagonists of manga and anime films and series, such as Hayao Miyazaki's Spirited Away (2001), Osamu Tezuka's Astro Boy from the 1960s, and Hideaki Anno's Neon Genesis Evangelion (1995–1996). The popular belief that children are 'close to gods and demons' was noted, as was the fact that this manifested in 'protective threshold deities manifesting in the form of children in Japanese religion'.[94] The children and young adults who populate anime in great numbers are often related to these mythological beings, exhibiting courage, protective qualities and the ability to traverse both the supernatural and the physical worlds. This section discusses the motif of the 'divine child' in a range of anime productions, including the comic, dramatic, tragic and action genres.

---

94. Lin, 'Child Guardian Spirits (Gohō Dōji)', 155.

3 From Realistic to Supernatural 147

Hayao Miyazaki and Mamoru Oshii are amongst the most popular anime directors in the West. They have their own signature anime styles and both are often referred to as *auteurs*. Their works differ greatly in many respects, including theme, narrative structure and visual style, yet child or young adult characters and the supernatural subgenre are prominent in the works of both. As noted, the supernatural subgenre in anime often borrows from world religions and mythologies. Miyazaki's work borrows predominantly from Shintō and Western sources whereas Oshii's work depends upon a slightly broader range of religious traditions. These include Christianity (*Angel's Egg*), Indian religions (*The Sky Crawlers*), and certain elements from Confucianism, Judaism, and Shintō, which may be identified in *Ghost in the Shell 2: Innocence* (along with Christian elements). This section examines works featuring child characters within a supernatural context: these are Miyazaki's *Ponyo* (2008), Oshii's *Angel's Egg* (1985), and *My Neighbour Totoro* by Miyazaki. It is argued that the child characters in these three works share a similarity with the mythological 'divine child', who is a mediator between the supernatural and physical worlds. Thomas Armstrong writes that 'profound and even ultimate levels of reality are accessible to the youngest living human',[95] which suggests that children are particularly open and receptive to the realms beyond the physical. In addition to Miyazaki's and Oshii's films, the anime series *The Melancholy of Haruhi Suzumiya* (directed by Tatsuya Ishihara) will be analysed in terms of certain Sufi views. It will be argued that the relation Haruhi's character has with physical reality accords with the Sufi view that physical reality exists in the mind of God. This is expressed by the thirteenth-century Sufi poet Jalāl ad-Dīn Muhammad Rūmī, 'I have lived on the lip of insanity, wanting to know reasons, knocking on a door. It opens. I've been knocking from the inside'.[96] Finally, this section also considers the motif of a young adult character contesting the negative portrayal of his god-like powers in Katsuhiro Ōtomo's film *Akira* (1988). It will be argued that this negative portrayal is partially due to the disassociation of the awakening of godlike powers from spiritual awakening.

Miyazaki's *Ponyo* concerns the friendship between a five-year-old boy, Sōsuke, and a little supernatural sea creature he names 'Ponyo'. Ponyo's wizard father desperately tries to break up their friendship, believing that Ponyo's feelings for a human boy could cause chaos in the universe, but Ponyo's mother, the Goddess of Mercy, tells him that if

---

95. Thomas Armstrong, *The Radiant Child* (Wheaton, IL: Theosophical Publishing House, 1985), 13.
96. Coleman Barks, *A Year with Rumi: Daily Readings* (New York: Harper Collins, 2006), 352.

Sōsuke's devotion is pure and true, she will permanently transform into a human girl and the universe will remain in harmony. The anime ends with Ponyo becoming human and renouncing her supernatural powers (rather in the fashion of Bokko from Osamu Tezuka's *The Amazing Three*, discussed in Chapter 2).

The story is set in a small coastal town where Sōsuke lives with his parents. His mother Lisa is a nursing-home worker, and his father Kōichi, who is absent for most of the film, is a ship captain. Sōsuke's freeing of a little sea creature imprisoned in a glass jar early in the film foreshadows the relation of the two worlds in this anime, the human world and the supernatural world. The supernatural world in *Ponyo* is informed by a combination of Japanese mythology, Shintō, Buddhism, and also Western tales. The motifs of the underwater castle (the dwelling of Ponyo's father Fujimoto), shape-shifting ability (Ponyo turns into a human girl), and the relation between human and non-human creatures (Ponyo possesses supernatural powers and has the face of a human girl) are found in Japanese religion and mythology. *The Little Mermaid* by Hans Christian Andersen (a Western fairytale) and the myth of Tarō Urashima, discussed in Chapter 2, underpin the story in important ways.[97] *Ponyo*'s story parallels the Japanese myth of Tarō Urashima, in that the human male protagonist saves the magical sea creature. Tarō Urashima saves a turtle, which turns out to be Princess Otohime, daughter of Ryūjin, the Emperor of the Sea.[98] Buddhism is reflected in the name of Ponyo's mother, Goddess of Mercy, which is the title of the Chinese *bodhisattva* of infinite compassion, Guanyin (Japanese Kannon). Ponyo's birth name is 'Brunhilde' which is the name of a Valkyrie (warrior maiden) in Norse mythology (another Western influence). Ponyo uses her supernatural powers to maintain her friendship with Sōsuke, who is equally enthusiastic to stay in contact. On one occasion her powers create a tsunami, recalling the Japanese myth about the giant catfish Namazu that causes earthquakes 'when it swims through the bowels of the world'.[99] Both Namazu and Ponyo are sea creatures constrained against their wills in watery environs (Ponyo by her controlling father), and both have the power to create an imbalance in nature of great proportions (earthquake, tsunami), but there are no other similarities between them.

Sōsuke is a happy child who enjoys Ponyo's company. He is not shocked or fearful when Ponyo transforms his toy boat into one large

---

97. Caroline McKenzie, 'Ponyo', *Reverse Shot – Reviews* (2009), at http://www.reverseshot.com/reviews/entry/376/ponyo, accessed 10 May 2012.
98. Michael Ashkenazi, *Handbook of Japanese Mythology* (Oxford and New York: Oxford University Press, 2003), 281-82.
99. Ashkenazi, *Handbook of Japanese Mythology*, 220.

enough for both of them to sail in. Sōsuke's relationship with Ponyo can be described in three stages: first he saves Ponyo; second he becomes her friend; and third, he commits to loving her. All of these reflect his positive relation to Ponyo and the supernatural world. Sōsuke does not find the supernatural realm strange, but rather is open to, understanding of, and accepting of it. He welcomes Ponyo's friendship, which confirms his positive and open attitude towards the supernatural in general. Sōsuke can be understood, in certain limited ways, to be the 'divine child', who acts as a mediator between the supernatural and the physical worlds. The archetypal psychologist Carl Gustav Jung (1875–1961), here summarized by Donald Kalsched, argued that:

> [t]he *child motif*...is almost always associated with something miraculous or divine – the wonder-child whose origins are extraordinary (virgin birth) and whose deeds are somehow associated with redemption of the darkness and recovery of the light... It links up the real and imaginal worlds and holds the promise that the imperishable numinous world might find life in this world. It is for this reason that the child is mythology's almost universal answer to the question 'Does God manifest himself in history?' As Moses, as Christ, as Bhudda [sic], as Krishna, the answer is always the divine child.[100]

Sōsuke possesses these qualities, in that he plays a central role in bringing together the physical and supernatural worlds. While some examples of the 'divine child' have magical origins, others (such as the biblical infant Moses, discovered by Pharaoh's daughter in the bulrushes at the edge of the Nile) do not. Sōsuke has human parents and his birth is not magical. In *Ponyo* Miyazaki integrates the supernatural and the real, the physical and the spiritual worlds, in a typically Shintō fashion. As noted in Chapter 2, visual representations of the closeness of supernatural reality with the physical world, often encountered in anime, function as modern instantiations of the ancient Japanese cosmic picture. This worldview had 'no concept of a supernatural world totally distinct from the existing life',[101] something that is quite different to the Judeo-Christian world picture.

Mamoru Oshii's *Angel's Egg* differs substantially from *Ponyo*, yet shares with it the child protagonist who mediates between the supernatural and physical worlds, like the 'divine child'. *Angel's Egg*, one of Oshii's earlier animated works, is the story of a young girl who must protect a large egg. A mysterious young man follows her and eventually catches her off-guard, breaking the egg, to her horror. The impact of this work, which has minimal dialogue as its narrative is mainly conveyed through

---

100. Donald Kalsched, *The Inner World of Trauma: Archetypal Defenses of the Personal Spirit* (London and New York: Routledge, 1996), 203.
101. Orloff Matsunaga, 'The Land of Natural Affirmation', 203.

the characters' actions and types of setting, is surreal.[102] The story contains Christian symbolism, which features in four scenes in particular. The first of these is a scene in which a group of men with fishing rods apparently chase the fish. The young girl protagonist explains to the mysterious young man who has been following her that these men are trying to catch the fish, '[e]ven though there aren't any fish anywhere'. In the second scene the shadows of large fishes that appear to be swimming through the streets of a desolate city are seen, with the men hunting them. These scenes could be interpreted as referencing the Christian fish symbol (*ichthus*), and referring to the absence of faith. The third scene depicts the girl at a fountain. This in itself has no particular religious, or more precisely Christian, connotation; but the fountain resembles Rome's Fountain of the Four Rivers, situated at the centre of Piazza Navona, in walking distance of Saint Peter's Basilica. This fountain features the sculptures of four male figures representing gods, created by the sculptor Gian Lorenzo Bernini. The girl is alone at the fountain in the darkness, which intensifies the above-mentioned sense of the absence of faith.

The fourth scene featuring Judeo-Christian material directly references Noah and the flood from the book of Genesis. The mysterious young man quotes from the Bible to the girl:

> I will blot out man whom I have created from the face of the ground, man and beast and creeping things and birds of the air, for I am sorry that I have made them. I will send rain upon the earth forty days and forty nights, and every living thing that I have made I will blot out from the face of the ground. And after seven days the waters of the flood came upon the earth. On that day all the fountains of the great deep burst forth, and the windows of the heavens were opened. And rain fell upon the earth forty days and forty nights. The ark floated on the face of the waters, and all flesh dies that moved upon the earth. Birds, cattle, beasts, all swarming creatures that swarm upon the earth, and every man. Only Noah was left, and those that were with him in the ark. Then he sent forth a dove from him, to see if the waters had subsided from the face of the ground. Then he waited another seven days, and sent forth the dove, and she did not return to him any more.

Like many Judeo-Christian references in anime this dramatic speech is not a direct quotation from Genesis, chapters 6–8, in which the story of Noah is contained. Having captured the girl's attention, the young man speaks of the bird, which Noah sent to search for dry ground, and poses the question, 'Maybe the bird never existed at all?' After a pause, the girl responds, 'It exists'. The young man's exposition of the story of Noah

---

102. Clements and McCarthy, *The Anime Encyclopedia*, 20.

and the flood, and his expression of doubt about the existence of the bird represents the forces of unbelief and absence of faith that buffet the young girl's efforts to preserve the egg, and to hold onto what she believes to be the truth.

The way in which the Christian symbolism combines with the use of a predominantly dark colour palette, the desolate setting, and the sense of emptiness created by the absence of people all contribute to the sombre mood of *Angel's Egg*, which suggests the loss of faith in religion. The absence of religious faith can be associated with non-acceptance of the supernatural, or at least the rejection of some of its aspects. For the sake of the argument the word 'supernatural' will be used instead of the word 'faith'. Amid the sombre scenes stands a small, fragile girl carrying a large egg, which she is seeking to protect. In Christian symbolism, as George Wells Ferguson writes, '[t]he egg is the symbol of hope and resurrection. This meaning is derived from the manner in which the small chick breaks from the egg at its birth'.[103] Furthermore, taking into account the previous discussion of this anime, it can be argued that the egg also symbolizes the acceptance of the supernatural. The young, mysterious man who follows the girl does not want to acknowledge the supernatural, which is evidenced by the scene in which the girl tells him about the bird contained in the egg. She says, 'I can hear the sound of wings. It must be dreaming of flying in the sky', to which he replies, 'That's just the sound of the wind outside'. She is the sole protector of this unborn bird, and thus shares a limited role with the 'divine child', acting as a mediator who works to connect the supernatural and physical worlds. Unlike Sōsuke's character from *Ponyo*, nothing is known of the parents of the young girl in *Angel's Egg*. However, since the title is *Angel's Egg*, it can be assumed that the young girl is indeed an angel, thus her roots are perhaps divine. Thus, this supposedly divine origin is one characteristic that her character shares with some examples of divine child motifs from religions and mythologies.

Hayao Miyazaki's *My Neighbor Totoro* (1988) is the third anime discussed in this chapter that features a child character who mediates between the supernatural and natural worlds. Hal Shipman classifies this film as 'an exploration of the Japanese concept of the spirit world'.[104] This supernatural/fantasy/drama generic hybrid is the tale of two young sisters, Satsuki and Mei, who move with their father to a country house while waiting for the recovery of their mother, who is in hospital. In their new environment, the sisters are able to interact with a range of supernatural

---

103. George Wells Ferguson, *Signs and Symbols in Christian Art* (Oxford: Oxford University Press, 1961 [1954]), 18.
104. Shipman, 'Grave of the Child Hero', 200.

creatures that no adult can see; importantly, they do not express any fear or surprise on seeing them. In the house they see little supernatural creatures that they call *makkuro-kurosuke*. An elderly lady from the neighbourhood says these creatures are called *susuwatari*; she tells the girls that in her youth she also possessed the ability to see *susuwatari*, which reinforces the connection between childhood and the supernatural (as adults have lost the liminal power that children possess). The creature with whom they establish a special bond is their 'neighbour' (a warm and kindly designator) Totoro. Satsuki and Mei are analogous with the 'divine child' motif, as they can access not only the natural realm but also the supernatural world. Similar to the young boy Sōsuke, from Miyazaki's *Ponyo*, both Satsuki and Mei display an attitude of openness, receptivity and curiosity towards the inhabitants of the magical world they discover.

This is particularly true of younger four-year-old Mei, who happily follows the little supernatural creatures whenever she sees them, and even falls asleep on the large belly of Totoro. The supernatural creatures are protective of the girls, as can be seen when Mei becomes lost on her way to visit her mother in the hospital. The people of the local village search for her unsuccessfully, even assuming that she may have drowned after finding a child's shoe in the water. Fortunately, Totoro calls the Catbus, and they find the lost Mei and take the girls to the hospital where they see their mother and father in conversation. The Catbus is one of the more monstrous supernatural beings, described by Shana Heinricy as a 'weird, contorted, hollowed-out Cat-body that people can ride inside of. Creepy',[105] but the girls instinctively know that the Catbus, like Totoro, is good and benevolent. Interestingly, Brian Eggert explains that, 'Miyazaki based Mei and Satsuki on himself, with Mei representing his age when he realized his own mother was ill and hospitalized with spinal tuberculosis, and Satsuki as his age when he began to grow up because of the ordeal'.[106] Many of the protagonists in Miyazaki's works are very young, ranging from small children to young adults. Although, as Eggert previously noted, Miyazaki's horrific personal experience provided a basis for the characters in this anime, the story has a positive tone, due, to a large degree, to the appearance of the good-natured, lovable, furry, supernatural creatures.

---

105. Shana Heinricy, 'Take a Ride on the Catbus', in Josef Steiff and Tristan D. Tamplin (eds), *Anime and Philosophy: Wide-Eyed Wonder* (Chicago and La Salle, IL: Open Court, 2010), 3.

106. Brian Eggert, 'My Neighbour Totoro (1988)', *Deep Focus Review* (2010), at http://www.deepfocusreview.com/reviews/myneighbortotoro.asp (accessed 24 August 2012).

With regard to Totoro's character, Eggert notes that he does not stem directly from Shintō sources, for 'Miyazaki invented the concept of forest spirits called "Totoro" for the film, combining imagery associated with bears and owls for the final design'.[107] Yet the Totoro character is broadly in harmony with Shintō animal guardian spirits, discussed in Chapter 2, and the director's imaginative amalgamations of different creatures recall the importance of metamorphosis and hybridity in both the animistic Shintō universe and the artistic medium of anime. Mark I. West describes Totoro as 'a loveable and protective monster',[108] yet, to call him a 'monster' seems an exaggeration. Totoro's character design is quite cute, not eerie, and not intimidating despite his large size, which in the eyes of small children might seem even larger. Eggert rightly observes of the supernatural elements in the film that, '[t]hough the idea of ghosts and spirits fill the dialogue, their presence never feels menacing in any way'.[109] While many of the story's happenings involving the supernatural creatures take place during the night, Eggert insightfully argues that in this anime 'Miyazaki avoids any hint of a Dark vs. Light dichotomy. Nighttime does not mean scary and evil. There is no malevolence in this film'.[110] Eggert's observation grasps the essence of the supernatural content in Miyazaki's *My Neighbor Totoro*. Similarly to *Ponyo*, Miyazaki breaks the generic convention of the supernatural subgenre, which associates night with frightening supernatural occurrences or creatures. By portraying the supernatural in a positive, not intimidating light, and in a not uncanny but friendly way, the film enables the two little sisters (and, by extension, child viewers) to feel comfortable and establish a friendly relationship with Totoro and his companions. Totoro even gives them a gift of nicely wrapped tree seeds. Perhaps the supernatural world of Totoro manifested to the children in order to render less painful their experience of having their mother in hospital. Their father is not surprised when his daughters tell him about these supernatural creatures. Roger Ebert says of the father that he 'is reasonable, insightful and tactful, accepts stories of strange creatures, trusts his girls, [and] listens to explanations with an open mind'.[111] Thus,

---

107. Eggert, 'My Neighbour Totoro (1988)'.
108. Mark I. West, 'Invasion of the Japanese Monsters: A Home-Front Report', in Mark I. West (ed.), *The Japanification of Children's Popular Culture: From Godzilla to Miyazaki* (Lanham, MD: Scarecrow Press, 2009), 18.
109. Eggert, 'My Neighbour Totoro (1988)'.
110. Eggert, 'My Neighbour Totoro (1988)'.
111. Roger Ebert, 'My Neighbor Totoro (1993)', *Chicago Sun-Times* (2001), at http://rogerebert.suntimes.com/apps/pbcs.dll/article?AID=/20011223/REVIEWS08/112230301/1023 (accessed 23 August 2012).

the children in this anime (similarly to the child protagonist of *Ponyo*) act as mediators of the supernatural world for their respective parents.

The next young anime protagonist examined is Haruhi Suzumiya from the anime series *The Melancholy of Haruhi Suzumiya* (2006, directed by Tatsuya Ishihara). The specific supernatural aspects of Haruhi's character have a resemblance to the Sufi view that all physical reality exists in the mind of God. Previously the motif of a child as mediator between the supernatural and real world was posited, but here the young adult protagonist (although having a close link with both of these worlds) is entirely unaware of her immense supernatural powers. This anime series concerns an eccentric high-school student with a passion for paranormal phenomena called Haruhi Suzumiya who, when she becomes bored, threatens, unknowingly, to destroy the whole world. She establishes the SOS Brigade, which stands for 'Save the world by Overloading it with fun with Haruhi Suzumiya's Brigade', at school. Haruhi does not know that those she brought into her club, though appearing to be human, are not. Rather, bookish Yuki Nagato is an artificial human from outer space with the power to alter her environment at will, timid Mikuru Asahina is a time traveller, and Itsuki Koizumi is an 'esper' (one possessed of extra-sensory perception). All three have been sent to observe Haruhi and prevent her realizing her extraordinary, apocalyptic powers. The only 'ordinary human' member of her club is Kyon, for whom she later develops feelings. The series is a fantasy mixing comedy, drama and high- school romance with space opera in clever and witty ways, recalling Rumiko Takahashi's *Urusei Yatsura* manga series (1978–1987), discussed in Chapter 2. In fact, the plot of 'Endless Eight', as discussed by Jonathan Evans, closely resembles the plot of *Urusei Yatsura 2: Beautiful Dreamer*, directed by Mamoru Oshii (1984). In that film the town of Tomobiki is apparently decaying, which is because (in *Groundhog Day* fashion) Tomobiki has been constantly re-living the day before the high-school festival, due to the power of the *oni* (demon/extra-terrestrial) heroine Lum's dream (to live happily with her teenage boyfriend Ataru and his family, and to have fun with her schoolfriends). This seemingly harmless dream has been used by the dream demon Mujaki to control reality and Ataru has to battle Mujaki to escape the dream, and restore Tomobiki. Evans notes that 'Endless Eight' is:

> the story of Haruhi and the SOS Brigade's summer vacation, which sees them go to the public pool, work part-time jobs, go to a Bon festival, catch cicadas, etc. Kyon, the narrator, begins to experience déjà vu, before finding out that he and the other characters have been experiencing the same two-week period, with variations, for 15,498 cycles... Haruhi Suzumiya is causing a time-loop as she feels something is missing from their summer... Kyon eventually breaks the loop by saying that

he needs to finish his homework..., identifying the one thing Haruhi cannot think of to complete her summer.[112]

The resemblances are obvious: the continual repetition of a period in the high-school calendar (the day before the high-school festival, and the summer vacation) due to the mental state of the female protagonist (Lum's dream, or rather wish-fulfilment, and Haruhi's feeling that something is 'missing' from the school holidays), and the breaking of the 'spell' by the human love object (Ataru battling the demon Mujaki, and Kyon focusing on homework, which proves to be a real-world restorative). One further similarity is that extra-terrestrial Lum, like melancholic Haruhi, attracts aliens and other non-humans to Tomobiki, which is destabilizing and dangerous.

Haruhi's ability to destroy the world just by entering a particular state of mind, boredom, indicates that she possesses divine attributes, but without knowing it. It may be that this divine or supernatural characteristic is one of the reasons she prefers the company of non-humans to humans. Early in the series she tells her classmates, 'I have no interest in ordinary humans. If there are any aliens, time travellers, sliders, or espers here...come join me'. This statement suggests that her boredom is caused by 'ordinary' humans, and having to live in a world in which the supernatural is not acknowledged.

It is worth noting that there is a close link between boredom or melancholy and the supernatural in many religions and historical periods. Julia Kristeva notes that 'medieval monks did promote sadness: as mystical *ascesis* (*acedia*) it became essential as a means toward paradoxical knowledge of divine truth'.[113] Martin Lings, speaking of Sufism, the mystical tradition of Islam, states that 'in that the path's Ultimate End, the Supreme Self may be said to include everything subjectively...the sacred books give us to know that in the supra-formal freedom of the worlds of the Spirit, object and subject are not separated by the same barriers as they are in the rigid domain of forms'.[114] Thus, at least to some degree, Haruhi's character has basis in religious tradition(s). In the series Itsuki Koizumi (the esper) tells Kyon that the world they live in might perhaps be the one created by Haruhi, and in deference to her abilities, even refers to her as a 'god'. Thus Itsuki explains that Haruhi's boredom can

---

112. Jonathan Evans, 'The Repetition of Haruhi Suzumiya', *The Comics Grid: Journal of Comics Scholarship* (2012), at http://www.comicsgrid.com (accessed 18 November 2012).

113. Julia Kristeva, *Black Sun: Depression and Melancholia*, trans. Leon S. Roudiez (New York: Columbia University Press, 1989), 8.

114. Martin Lings, 'Sufi Answers to Questions on Ultimate Reality', *Studies in Comparative Religion* 13.3-4 (1979): 9.

destroy the present world in order to create a new one ('If this world loses the favor of God...it could simply be destroyed and recreated at whim'). Haruhi's supernatural ability to change the world via her state of mind is a crucial aspect of this story. As seen from the above, Haruhi is not easily classified as a typical *mahō shōjo* subgenre belle. Further, while the relation between the supernatural and real worlds in Miyazaki's *Ponyo* and *My Neighbor Totoro* are maintained in a harmonious balance, this anime is a very different story.

While the title is rendered in English as 'The Melancholy of Haruhi Suzumiya', Haruhi is not a typical melancholic. According to Sigmund Freud, melancholics can be suicidal, which Haruhi certainly is not. From Freud's perspective melancholy is also closely related 'to the real loss of a loved object',[115] which is irrelevant to Haruhi's character. Yet disappointment can give rise to melancholy, and Haruhi tells Kyon about an event that caused her to be disappointed with her own life. A baseball game she attends with her family triggers reflections on how many people there are in the world who do many things, which undermines Haruhi's self-image as 'special', that is, she realises how insignificant her life is ('Not only was I just one little person in that sea of people in that stadium but that sea of people was merely a drop in the ocean'). Thus, melancholy descends on her as she becomes aware that many have the same 'ordinary' experiences as she ('Once I realized this I suddenly found that my surroundings were beginning to lose their color'). She subsequently resolved to lead an interesting life, which explains why she has no interest in 'ordinary' humans. When Haruhi becomes melancholic her state of mind creates 'closed spaces', which are situated in the physical world but invisible to humans. The closed spaces also function to confine giant ghostly destructive figures to prevent them annihilating the real world. If not for her boredom, Haruhi's supernatural powers would have probably never have been realized. Akin to the protagonists from *Ponyo* and *My Neighbor Totoro*, Haruhi does have an inclination towards the supernatural, but it is questionable what she would have done if she had been aware of her powers.

The view that Haruhi's character has some analogy with Sufi ideas about world/physical reality existing in the mind of God is also supported by a conversation between Kyon and Itsuki Koizumi, who says:

> Perhaps this world is but a dream a certain being is seeing. That is what the higher-ups in the 'Agency' [an esper organization] believe.

---

115. Sigmund Freud, 'Mourning and Melancholia', in James Strachey (gen. ed. and trans.), Angela Richards (ed.), *On Metapsychology, The Theory of Psychoanalysis: Beyond the Pleasure Principle, the Ego and the Id, and Other Works* (Harmondsworth, Middlesex: Penguin Books, 1984 [1917]), 259.

3 From Realistic to Supernatural

> And because it is just a dream creating and altering this world we call reality is but child's play for that being. And we know the name of the being who is capable of such acts [Haruhi]... Humans have defined such a being as God.

Yet, the analogy with Sufi view is applicable only to a certain degree, because Haruhi does not possess an awareness of the relation between reality/the world and her mind, and also because she is surrounded by individuals who are trying to prevent the destruction of the current physical reality by Haruhi's boredom. Thus Dana Del George's comment concerning the imbrication of the natural and the supernatural is particularly relevant:

> [i]n his 1931 volume *The Natural and the Supernatural*, philosopher John Wood Oman describes the supernatural as an 'environment' in which we live, analogous to the natural, and 'so constantly interwoven [with the natural] that nothing may be wholly natural or wholly supernatural' ... Oman writes, 'We may be living by this higher environment as fishes in the water live by air, and be equally ignorant of the fact: and the reason may be lack of interest, not of capacity'...[116]

This section will conclude with the discussion of a young adult character, Tetsuo Shima, who falls victim to his god-like, supernatural powers in Katsuhiro Ōtomo's cyberpunk anime *Akira* (1989). *Akira* is set in Neo-Tokyo after World War III. This conflict broke out in 1988 when Akira, Number 28 in a group of children with 'immense psychic powers', lost control and destroyed most of Tokyo. His remains were then 'cytogenetically entombed for later scientists to research'.[117] Three of the original children, Number 25 (Kiyoko), Number 26 (Takashi) and Number 27 (Masaru), are still alive in 2019 (though they look like aged children, with white hair and wrinkles), when a chance encounter between Tetsuo Shima, a teenage biker gang member, and Takashi releases Tetsuo's own powers. He is ignorant of the full extent of his powers and has no ability to control them, though his gang leader Shotaro Kaneda tries to curtail him. Despite 'some experiments and drugs provided by the government, his power goes out of control, threatening to totally destroy Neo-Tokyo'.[118] Kiyoko, Takashi and Masaru intervene, and Akira is summoned when Tetsuo triggers a second apocalyptic event. The anime ends with a close-up shot of an eye and the voice-over, 'I am...Tetsuo'.

---

116. Del George, *The Supernatural*, 3.
117. Andrew Wells Garnar, 'It's the End of the Species as We Know It, and I Feel Anxious', in Josef Steiff and Tristan D. Tamplin (eds), *Anime and Philosophy: Wide-Eyed Wonder* (Chicago and La Salle, IL: Open Court, 2010), 294.
118. Garnar, 'It's the End of the Species as We Know It', 294-95.

This anime is a generic hybrid in which elements of the supernatural subgenre occupy an important place. Religious notions that appear include a reference to Akira as 'Lord', 'Messiah' or 'absolute energy', reference to Tetsuo's powers as 'power of God', and the occurrence of apocalyptic events. Concerning the term 'apocalypse' Susan J. Napier explains that, '[t]he most common understanding of apocalypse is as something on the order of global destruction. But its original meaning is actually "revelation" or "uncovering," as of secrets or the fundamental nature of things'.[119] Napier adds that in *Akira* 'the anticipation of the revelation of "secrets" or "mysteries" is an important narrative technique'.[120] The triggers of apocalyptic events in *Akira* are found in 'technological and psychic forces'.[121] Depending on the perspective employed, the apocalypse may be interpreted as the ultimate price paid for the government's ambition to resolve the mystery, and control the god-like powers the psychic children possessed.

In certain anime discussed in this section, the supernatural opens up positive opportunities to its young protagonists, but in *Akira* it represents a threat to Tetsuo, as he is not ready for it. Tetsuo's awakening powers brought him to the attention of a government project (which investigated Akira in the past, with the three other children, Kiyoko, Takashi and Masaru) and he was placed under scientific observation and experiments, where his powers were evaluated against those of Akira. The danger posed by researching Tetsuo's powers is clear (the Colonel who is in charge of the project states, 'Maybe we shouldn't touch that power'); nevertheless the government will not hold back (the Colonel says, 'But we *have* to. We have to touch it and *control* it'). This decision has devastating and far-reaching consequences. Tetsuo himself has no understanding of what is happening to him ('Am I dreaming or something?'). As he cannot control his powers, he uses them for destructive purposes, even killing. But Kiyoko tells Shotaro Kaneda that 'We're partly to blame for his [Tetsuo's] actions'. Tetsuo fell victim to his own power ('My power is acting on its own...!'), and as a consequence, he metamorphoses into a gigantic fleshly creature, a highly dramatic supernatural event and a remarkable example of metamorphosis. With regard to Tetsuo's transformation, Susan J. Napier observes that, 'Tetsuo...sometimes resists the transformation but also at times nihilistically glories in it, and ultimately asserts his monstrous new identity unflinchingly at the film's end'.[122] Concerning Tetsuo's character, Napier notes that, 'as

---

119. Napier, *Anime from Akira to Princess Mononoke*, 195-96.
120. Napier, *Anime from Akira to Princess Mononoke*, 196.
121. Napier, *Anime from Akira to Princess Mononoke*, 202.
122. Napier, *Anime from Akira to Princess Mononoke*, 40.

his mutations continue and begin to take over his whole body, Tetsuo's aspect changes from cocky self confidence ("I never knew I could have such power!" he exults at one point) to frenzied desperation'.[123] The metamorphosis of his body, which in the process also caused (against his will) the death of his girlfriend Kaori, was stopped from further development by the resurrection of Akira (summoned by the three numbered children). This resurgence of Akira caused another apocalyptic event, as noted. What can be observed is that rather than being accompanied with a spiritual knowledge, growth, bliss, inner peace and enlightenment, Tetsuo's god-like powers are associated rather with negativity, and became an unbearable burden, which caused not only a negative transformation in him but also negative consequences for everything around him. Neither did he engage in ethical self-questioning regarding his use of these god-like powers. He was endowed with these powers abruptly; there was no gradual, preparatory, spiritual phase in the life of this character that would have prepared him for this gift. Similarly to the Western character of Superman, Tetsuo is also endowed with the ability to fly, and like Superman he at one point also wears a red piece of material like a rope, but he puts his powers to a different use. Tetsuo's powers did not assist him to transcend certain personal issues (for example, he was not able to rise above his sense of inferiority when it comes to his friend Shotaro Kaneda). Furthermore, his character was not portrayed as having a spiritual guide-figure to assist him, but rather as the victim of a scientific project whose purpose was to use him (Doctor Onishi, the chief scientist, was requested to kill him if his powers became too hard to handle). Paradoxically, Tetsuo's awakened god-like powers brought him to a helpless state, becoming their victim.

In summary, this section has discussed five different child/young adult motifs in the generic context where the supernatural dominates. Although *Ponyo* and *Angel's Egg* lie in stark contrast to each other in many respects, both child protagonists reflect a divine child motif as a mediator between the supernatural and the physical, material worlds. *My Neighbor Totoro* also contains the child motif as a mediator between the two worlds. It has been further argued that the character of the young adult protagonist, Haruhi Suzumiya, in *The Melancholy of Haruhi Suzumiya* series, has some analogy with the Sufi view that the physical reality exists in the mind of God. In this section it has also been argued that a young adult character's awakened god-like powers in *Akira* have been negatively portrayed, partially due to the lack of their association with spiritual awakening and enlightenment.

---

123. Napier, *Anime from Akira to Princess Mononoke*, 45.

Conclusion

This chapter has discussed how anime abounds with multiple genres, which over time gave rise to many generic hybrids. Consequently, generic hybridity appears to have become the norm in anime. Generic hybrids have the advantage of attracting particularly diverse audiences, and there is a possibility that the number of generic hybrids in anime will continue to grow. It has been also noted that many generic hybrids often contain elements of the supernatural subgenre, suggesting that it is one of the most popular subgenres in anime. It has been further argued that there is a type of anime female character whose power is more associated with Western Pagan ideas about the sacredness of the Earth rather than with the Japanese sun-goddess Amaterasu.

In anime there are also genres/subgenre that deal with realistic subject matter such as tragedy, and it has been highlighted that elements of the supernatural are also found in this subgenre, where they function as a metaphor for either the celebration of the human spirit despite calamities, or for the resilience and strength of the human spirit, or as a symbol that has soteriological meaning, or a symbol of personal transformation. Finally, Wallace B. Clift writes that 'not surprisingly, the motif of the child is found in religions and mythologies from earliest times and all around the world',[124] and, '[t]he child represents...receptivity';[125] in line with this observation, this chapter has analysed the role of the child protagonist in the work of Miyazaki, Oshii, and others, which are different in many respects. It has been argued that these child/young adult protagonists share certain limited similarities with the 'divine child' in terms of a mediator between the supernatural world and the physical world. This chapter has thus forcefully argued for the vitality of the supernatural subgenre, and the intimate connections that this subgenre has with mythology, religion and spirituality.

---

124. Clift, 'Child', 243.
125. Clift, 'Child', 243.

Sydney cosplayer dressed as Howl from the anime *Howl's Moving Castle* (2004) directed by Hayao Miyazaki. Photographer Ivan Buljan ©, 20 February 2014.

Chapter 4

Power Within:
The Fan's Embrace of Profane and Sacred Worlds in Anime

Introduction

Some anime aficionados can rightly be called 'devotees' as they manifest a deep, almost religious, devotion to anime in various ways. They seek to make personal connections with events and characters of anime stories through visits to anime conventions, the performance activity cosplay ('costume play'), and travel to cities, towns and natural sites in Japan that are featured in anime. It is clear that these fan phenomena are not unique to anime or only observable in Japan, as over the last twenty years there has been a small but growing body of scholarship produced that deals with both Western fan behaviours and the possible religio-spiritual motivations and benefits of these individual and communal activities.[1] This chapter will draw upon these studies, particular those focused on the fan community attached to Gene Roddenberry's cult American television and film series *Star Trek* (debuted 1965), to establish a framework for interpreting anime fandom, in addition to specific studies of anime aficionados.

This chapter is divided into four sections. The first focuses on the devotion of Western anime aficionados to anime. It is argued that Fred Patten's observation that '[e]arly *anime* fandom had a strongly evangelical fervour' remains true in the first quarter of the twenty-first century.[2] Further, a considerable amount of credit for this goes to anime aficionados' creativity and unconventional initiatives in the pursuit of knowledge about and experiences of the anime art form. The second section discusses cosplay, a practice closely associated with anime fans, and argues that this activity may be interpreted as conveying deeper

---

1. See Jennifer E. Porter, 'Pilgrimage and the IDIC Ethic: Exploring *Star Trek* Convention Attendance as Pilgrimage', in Ellen Badone and Sharon D. Roseman (eds), *Intersecting Journeys: The Anthropology of Pilgrimage and Tourism* (Urbana and Chicago, IL: University of Illinois Press, 2004), 160-79; and Cusack, *Invented Religions*, 27, 119, 160.

2. Fred Patten, '*Anime* in the United States', in John A. Lent (ed.), *Animation in Asia and the Pacific* (Eastleigh, UK: John Libbey Publishing, 2001), 60.

meanings than mere entertainment. That is, the act of cosplaying can be seen as symbolic stepping into an alternative reality, the diegetic world of anime narratives, which often have supernatural or otherworldly dimensions. Being attired as a favourite or beloved character thus represents a transformation of the fan from his or her 'profane' self in the real world to a 'sacred' self in the world of anime, which is perceived as richer and more appealing than everyday life. The third section advances a range of reasons why Western audiences find anime intriguing, with a particular focus on anime aficionados' understanding of the spiritual and religious aspect of anime. In this context, Jin Kyu Park's interpretation of the relationship between fans interested in anime and the so-called 'spiritual seekers' in the United States, which suggests that anime's religio-spiritual content is a major part of its attraction, is employed.[3]

It is also posited that the 'free-floating' nature of the religious and spiritual elements borrowed from world religions such as Christianity, which have often been stripped of their original meaning and theological context, opens the possibility for some members of the audience to develop distinctive personal interpretations of those religious elements. Yet, it is noted that religious and spiritual content in anime may also trigger curiosity in viewers, who will seek to familiarize themselves with the religious tradition in question (Shintō, Christianity, Buddhism, and so on). The final part of this chapter considers how certain places in Japan, which are portrayed in anime, have become target destinations for anime aficionados. The sites are often referred to as 'sacred' and aficionados and scholars both refer to this travel as 'anime tourism' or 'anime pilgrimage'.[4] In this context it is argued that these special anime-related journeys function similarly to cosplay performance, in the sense that they can be understood as a desire to participate more fully in anime narratives, a phenomenon that has also been documented with regard to Peter Jackson's *Lord of the Rings* and *The Hobbit* films and specific sites in New Zealand.[5] The purpose of this chapter is to investigate the intense, almost religious, nature of anime aficionados' close relationship to the object of their devotion, anime.

---

3. Park, 'Creating My Own Cultural and Spiritual Bubble', 393-413.
4. Yamamura, 'Anime Pilgrimage and Local Tourism Promotion', 1-9.
5. Toby Manhire, 'Hobbit Tourism Scatters More of Tolkien's Magic across New Zealand', *The Observer* (13 October 2012), at http://www.guardian.co.uk/world/2012/oct/13/hobbit-new-zealand-tourism (accessed 21 December 2012).

A Story of Devotion: Anime and its Western Aficionados

When musing upon the worldwide reception of the anime films *Legend of the White Serpent* (1958) and *Magic Boy* (1959) produced by the influential studio Tōei Dōga, Michael Arnold noted '[t]he title of a 1961 *Asahi Newspaper* article about Toei's international releases eagerly summed up the mood: "Japanese-made cartoon movies making dollars! Cheap, easy to understand...but how long will it last?"' He then wryly observed, '[w]ell, it never stopped'.[6] In the early decades of anime's distribution outside Japan there was a general uncertainty regarding its future, as it was suspected that Westerners regarded anime as a novelty product (much in the way that, prior to the rise to prominence of Bob Marley, the first Third World music superstar in the early 1970s, Jamaican releases had been marketed as 'novelty' songs in the West). Yet over fifty years later, it is impressive to see how anime has become a widely accepted and high-status art export from Japan. What the next fifty years of Japanese anime export to the West may hold can only be speculated upon, as it depends on a multitude of factors, but judging by current levels of interest, anime seems likely to become even more popular as it appears that its momentum has not yet peaked.

This section focuses on the reception of anime in the West. The early period of anime's presence in the West, broadly from the late 1950s to the mid 1970s, was characterized by deep devotion among fans. It is here argued that this intense immersion in the medium continues to characterize anime fandom to the present day. The ways that anime came to the attention of particular Western audiences are often unconventional, involving self-initiatives by anime aficionados. This chapter uses the term 'aficionado' more often than 'fan' (or the Japanese *otaku*, which generally is understood as 'extreme fan' or 'nerd') to refer to those audience members who are passionately enthusiastic about anime. *Aficionado* is used to accentuate their affection for and devotion to anime, and to avoid the often negative or trivializing connotations of 'fan' or *otaku*.

While anime has steadily increased in popularity in the West, this has not been an entirely smooth process. Japanese artists were impressed by French and American animations imported into Japan from approximately 1910 onwards. Reciprocally, the earliest Japanese animation export to the West happened soon after; Seitarō Kitayama's anime *Momotarō* ('Peach Boy') was sent to France in 1917.[7] Thus Japanese artists had

---

6. Michael Arnold, 'Japanese Anime and Animated Cartoons', *Midnight Eye: Visions of Japanese Cinema* (2004), at http://www.midnighteye.com/features/animated_cartoons.html (accessed 16 November 2007).

7. Daisuke Miyao, 'Before Anime: Animation and the Pure Film Movement in Pre-War Japan', *Japan Forum* 14.2 (2002): 191–209.

quickly embraced animation, which was at the time a relatively new artistic medium. While it seems that a large amount of scholarship on anime in the West focuses on anime exports dating from the 1940s onwards, Arnold's genealogy of anime exports to the West traces the story of the Western reception of anime back to 1917. This re-contextualizes Western anime fandom across almost a century, and thus puts the recognition and momentum that it enjoys today into proportion. Laurie Cubbison notes one obstacle to the reception of anime; since anime aficionados in the West are not familiar with the cultural context of Japan their understanding of films and television series 'can never contain the same level of meaning' as it can for Japan audiences who understand the cultural nuances contained therein.[8] For example, in an episode of the series *Urusei Yatsura* there is 'a classroom of sick students...wearing surgical masks', which would be interpreted by some members of the audience in the West as 'a classroom filled with young medical surgeons', due to unfamiliarity with the notion that in Japan those who are feeling unwell put on masks to prevent others from catching cold.[9] However, anime has found large numbers of admirers among Westerners who neither speak Japanese, nor are familiar with the socio-cultural context of Japan.

This indicates that Western audiences find anime easy to relate to; this is not, however, difficult to appreciate, nor is it unique. Early studies of fandom in the United States tended to focus on *Star Trek*, the cult science-fiction television series created in 1965 by Gene Roddenberry. This first incarnation, now called *The Original Series*, consisted of three series, featuring classic characters and actors, including Captain James T. Kirk (William Shatner), Mr Spock (Leonard Nimoy), Lieutenant Uhura (Nichelle Nichols) and Hikaru Sulu (George Takei).[10] This spawned numerous spin-offs, including a 1970s animation series, the critically acclaimed *Star Trek: The Next Generation* (1987), which starred Patrick Stewart as Captain Jean-Luc Picard, and *Star Trek: Voyager*, which featured a female captain, Kathryn Janeway (played by Kate Mulgrew). There are also twelve films, commencing with *Star Trek: The Motion Picture* (1979) through to *Star Trek: Into Darkness* (2013). In the more than two decades between *The Original Series* in 1965 and the reboot in 1987 with *The Next Generation*, the series' cult status among fans grew steadily, due to constant television repeats of the original series, and the inexpensive but popular two-season animation series. Science fiction is a

---

8. Laurie Cubbison, 'Anime Fans, DVDs, and the Authentic Text', *The Velvet Light Trap* 56 (2005): 49.
9. Shinobu Price, 'Cartoons from Another Planet: Japanese Animation as Cross-Cultural Communication', *Journal of American & Comparative Cultures* 24.1-2 (2001): 156.
10. Greenwald, *Future Perfect*.

genre that decisively demonstrates that familiarity with the 'culture' of the ethnic community or nation being portrayed does not have to exist before viewing or reading. This is because such knowledge, initially at least, cannot exist; the peoples and places are fantastic and inventions of the writers' imagination; thus, familiarity with this strange and new universe comes over time and with greater exposure to episodes and related information (novelizations, merchandise, board games, websites, online games, and scholarly and popular publications about the fictional world).

Star Trek fandom is a complex and multi-faceted phenomenon, and is thus appropriate as a comparison to anime aficionado activities and beliefs. For example, there are those who meet 'decked out in regulation...Star Fleet uniforms'[11] and fans in Germany who conduct Qet'lops, festivals that celebrate the military might of the Klingons (an enemy race from the original series who became allies of the Federation in the 1987 reboot, which featured Michael Dorn as the Klingon Lieutenant Worf). Jeff Greenwald has researched these dedicated followers, who learn to speak Klingon, an invented language developed to a level of great complexity, don latex headpieces to give them the distinctive Klingon ridged foreheads, make elaborate costumes, learn swordplay, develop 'real-world' equivalents of Klingon cultural features from the series and films (such as coloured vodka for bloodwine, and Klingon-language recordings of hard-rock songs, including 'Born to be Wild' by Steppenwolf), and even hold Klingon weddings. He wrote:

> [t]here is more drinking, more singing, and drinking again. When darkness falls the warriors reconvene for a Klingon wedding. Qor-Zantai Haqtaj, commanding officer of the Dark Vengeance Fleet, will wed the half-Klingon, half-human B'Elanna Torres. The bride and groom look marvellous. Haqtaj struts among the picnic tables in his armadillo-like jacket, bedecked with medals and pins; B'Elanna (named for the half-Klingon engineer on *Voyager*) adjusts her headpiece and applies dark make-up to her nose. Though the ceremony won't have the blessing of the holy church, it's carried out in reverent Klingon style. Haqtaj literally battles his way to the altar. He's a big man and brooks no nonsense. Thick-suited warriors...[shout], their swords clanking into the dust... They exchange vows and drink together from a silver chalice. Finally the bride and groom snarl at each other and share a savage kiss. Blood (or something close) flows down their chins. They exit the stage amid roars of congratulations.[12]

---

11. Greenwald, *Future Perfect*, 31.
12. Greenwald, *Future Perfect*, 75.

Greenwald's research revealed that being Klingon was far more than entertainment, far more than a hobby, for these dedicated fans. What he observed was an instance of what David Lyon calls 'shopping for a self', the construction of a personal identity from a range of sources, and the subsequent formation of a communal identity that is founded upon elective affinity, rather than ethnicity, religion or family, as would have been the case in the past.[13] As will be demonstrated later, *Star Trek* provides an alternative philosophy, system of ethics, and in some intense cases, religious experience, for deeply devoted aficionados.

Thus the lack of familiarity, at least initially, with Japanese language and culture should not prove an insurmountable obstacle to potential fans of anime. Yet it must be acknowledged that early anime audiences were small; Helen McCarthy documented that anime was not always received positively in Western countries, including certain regions of the United States, as well as France and the United Kingdom.[14] This situation varied over time. For example, in the early 1970s anime whose target audience was teenagers or adults were moved to 'Japanese-language cable channels' because viewing audiences decreased on mainstream American television stations.[15] Interestingly, judging by the great number of anime conventions held in the United States, it seems that the largest number of anime aficionados outside Japan is today found in the United States, which indicates that these early difficulties have been largely overcome, and that Internet-facilitated communication has been crucial in disseminating information.

This process of anime garnering the attention of Western audiences involved some unconventional, self-initiated actions by aficionados. Historically, building a fan-base for anime occurred as a result of a range of disparate factors. For example, Shinobu Price noted that 'these intriguingly different "cartoons"' came to America principally due to the armed services who were based in Japan after World War II.[16] In this early stage fans in the United States circulated copies of anime that had been privately recorded from Japanese-language cable television. They also made contact with anime fans in Japan, from whom they received the Tōei Dōga series *Getter Robo* (1974–1975) and other as yet uncirculated anime,

---

13. David Lyon, *Jesus in Disneyland: Religion in Postmodern Times* (Cambridge: Polity Press, 2002 [2000]), 76.

14. Helen McCarthy, 'The Development of the Japanese Animation Audience in the United Kingdom and France', in John A. Lent (ed.), *Animation in Asia and the Pacific* (Eastleigh, UK: John Libbey Publishing, 2001), 82.

15. Henry Jenkins, 'When Piracy Becomes Promotion: How Unauthorized Copying Made Japanese Animation Profitable in the United States', *Reason* 38.7 (2006): 78.

16. Price, 'Cartoons from Another Planet', 160.

in return for copies of *Star Trek* and certain other cult American television shows.[17] This indicates that anime made early forays into subcultural credibility in the West. By the 1980s, illegal copies of anime were made being accessible by student fans in the United States. In order to inform those interested in 'anime artists, styles, and genres', college students provided viewing sessions on campus.[18] This is another example of casual and spontaneous spreading the word about anime which enhanced its popularity. In the late 1970s and early 1980s science-fiction conventions began to play a greater role in hosting anime screenings in the United States. Customarily, at these events a self-appointed mediator explained to the audience what was happening in the film or series being screened, as they were in Japanese, and dubbed and sub-titled versions were not yet available. Usually, these speakers could not understand Japanese and would indicate to the audience that they had memorized this information 'from another recital of the plot at another screening'.[19]

Thus, thirty to forty years ago anime in the West was not yet seen as a valuable art form (or economic product) that required dedicated conventions or expertly rendered translations, which is in sharp contrast to the present situation. Films and television series were often radically edited and otherwise altered before being screened in Western countries. Brian Ruh has documented the failed reception of the American dubbed and edited *Warriors of the Wind* (1985), which was made from Hayao Miyazaki's *Nausicaä of the Valley of the Wind* (1984), an acknowledged masterpiece discussed in Chapter 3. This version cut approximately twenty minutes from the original in a series of nineteen separate cuts, though the plot was broadly preserved as 'the dub script for *Warriors of the Wind* is often very close to the original Japanese dialogue… it is obvious that the producers of…[the film] worked from a translation of the script'.[20] Such mangling of anime was commonplace before the mid-1980s (and had affected series including *Robotech*, *Voltron*, and *Battle of the Planets*), but the anime fan lobby was gaining strength when *Warriors of the Wind* was released, and these aficionados campaigned powerfully on the principle that Miyazaki was an *auteur*, a superb filmmaker whose work had been desecrated by barbarous and ignorant Americans.

---

17. Jenkins, 'When Piracy Becomes Promotion', 78.
18. Henry Jenkins, 'Pop Cosmopolitanism: Mapping Cultural Flows in an Age of Media Convergence', in Marcelo M. Suárez-Orozco and Desirée Baolian Qin-Hilliard (eds), *Globalization: Culture and Education in the New Millennium* (Berkeley, CA: University of California Press, 2004), 128.
19. Jenkins, 'Pop Cosmopolitanism', 128.
20. Brian Ruh, 'Transforming U.S. Anime in the 1980s: Localisation and Longevity', *Mechademia* 5 (2010): 42.

Further, they insisted on the right of fans to see Miyazaki's artistic productions as he himself intended them. Thus the consequences of this activism included the importation and translation of a wider range of manga and anime products, which intensified the devotion of the aficionados and enabled them to gain greater knowledge of the field, thus creating a market for greater sales and more products.

As a result of the growth in the anime fan-base in the late 1980s, and the increased appreciation of anime as an art form, in 1990 the first important United States anime convention was held over the last weekend in July in Dallas, Texas. The event was called Project A-Kon and was organized by the Earth Defense Command Animation Society, and in addition to anime it included comics and American animated films. In 1991 AnimeCon'91 was held in San Jose, California. This was a convention that featured manga and anime exclusively, and 1,700 visitors attended. The first Anime Expo convention was held in San Jose in 1992, though it subsequently moved to Los Angeles, and a range of smaller conventions emerged from 1993 onwards, including BAKA!-con (Seattle), Anime North (Toronto) and Katsucon (Arlington).[21] Anime conventions thus emerged about twenty years ago in the United States, many decades after the first anime were screened in the West. These conventions were the heirs of the science fiction and fantasy conventions that became popular among certain subcultures (including students, artists and musicians, computer scientists, and fans of speculative fiction) in the 1960s. The hosting of dedicated anime conventions in the 1990s points to the mainstreaming of of this art form and the emergence of a large enough fan-base to support a burgeoning anime industry.

Anime aficionados also played an important role as organizers of anime conventions; for example, in Australia, anime aficionados organized anime events about a decade after their counterparts in America. The first Australian convention dedicated to Japanese popular culture was the Animania Festival held in Sydney in 2002, which has also since been held in Brisbane in 2005 and Melbourne in 2006.[22] There are numerous conventions dedicated to Japanese popular culture in Europe; these include AyaCon in the United Kingdom, Japan Expo in France, and AnimagiC in Germany. Anime aficionados around the world share their passion for anime at these conventions, the increase in which is an indicator of the rising popularity of this art form and the rising numbers of anime aficionados (also confirmed by the growth in scholarly publications on the topic). Yet there are complex factors at play in this apparent

---

21. Patten, '*Anime* in the United States', 63.
22. Anon, 'Animania Festival', *About Animania* (n.d.), at http://animania.net.au/2011/animania (accessed 28 April 2011).

success story that scholars have drawn attention to. Earlier it was suggested that Western aficionados could become immersed in anime, even if they were initially ignorant of the Japanese language and culture, and become knowledgeable about and respectful of Japan. That scenario is possible, but Koichi Iwabuchi has warned that the discourse of 'cool Japan' has to date involved 'superficial and nationalistic observations that people outside Japan are rejoicing in Japanese media culture' which is largely divorced from the facilitation of a 'deeper understanding of the complexity of Japanese society and culture'.[23] He has called for more engagement with questions of global power, economic flows and neoliberal globalism accompanying the seemingly innocent activities of watching and purchasing anime, and participating in fan activities.[24]

This is an intriguing place to shift attention from the consumption of anime as a cultural and artistic product to the question of anime fans' productions of independent versions of anime, which was briefly discussed in Chapter 1. In Japan, the *dōjinshi* phenomenon, in which fans use characters and settings by particular *mangaka* to create new products, has generated some great artists of the manga and anime fields, including Masamune Shirow (b. 1961), the creator of the manga *Ghost in the Shell*. In the West these types of activities exist as well. One particular activity, the subtitling of anime, is referred to as 'fansubbing'. Anime fans began to subtitle and translate anime in an unofficial capacity for the first time at the beginning of the 1990s.[25] Such 'fansubbing' represented an extension of anime aficionados' activities, and a new theatre for creative engagement. Luis Pérez González has claimed that '[f]ansubbing, a new subtitling-based mediation phenomenon postulated by anime fans (and hence amateur subtitlers), was born to provide fellow fans worldwide with the fullest and most authentic experience of anime action and the Japanese culture which embeds it'.[26] This translation activity is not insignificant, and involves considerable generosity which increases community solidarity, as '[s]cripts are posted on internet newsgroups and circulated among clubs and individuals'.[27] There is a complex process underlying this activity, as programmes are specifically written for sundry computer platforms to enable fans to undertake subtitling. Yet,

---

23. Koichi Iwabuchi, 'Undoing Inter-national Fandom in an Age of Brand Nationalism', *Mechademia* 5 (2010): 89.
24. Iwabuchi, 'Undoing Inter-national Fandom', 87-96.
25. Jenkins, 'When Piracy Becomes Promotion', 78.
26. Luis Pérez González, 'Fansubbing Anime: Insights into the "Butterfly Effect" of Globalisation on Audiovisual Translation', *Perspectives: Studies in Translatology* 14.4 (2006): 260.
27. Abé Mark Nornes, 'For an Abusive Subtitling', *Film Quarterly* 52.3 (1999): 31.

despite these aficionados' love of anime, Abé Mark Nornes has termed the subtitles produced in this fashion 'abusive', in the sense that they feature a jumble of fonts, different coloured text, dictionary-style definitions of difficult Japanese words, and an abundance of other features that are unacceptable in professional studio subtitles.[28]

This self-initiated engagement with anime texts reflects a high degree of enthusiasm among anime aficionados, and a willingness to invest substantial amounts of time. Fan distribution of anime and fansubbing of Japanese animations were phenomena that, for some considerable time, Japanese authorities were largely unaware of. This is unsurprising, as it would have been impossible to predict such an enthusiastic reception of anime by Western fans. It is important to note that, while illegal distribution by fans contributed to the increasing popularity of anime, corporations did not understand the full extent of this phenomenon.[29] Yet, fan activities directly contributed to Japanese companies working to provide better and more varied products to non-Japanese anime enthusiasts. Antonia Levi has observed that:

> [u]ntil the mid-1990s, aside from a few edited and dubbed offerings on network television like *Astro Boy* (1963), *Star Blazers* (1979), and *Robotech* (1985), fans were on their own when it came to watching anime or reading manga. Only later, once the fans had shown the way, did Japanese companies like Bandai begin to…market their products in the United States.[30]

This is important, as it would generally be expected that, in order for a product to be successful in a new market, the producers would work with marketing staff to promote it, rather then simply waiting for potential consumers to discover the product independently and begin to promote it themselves. In the context of the consolidation of non-Japanese anime fandom, from around 1995 fansubbing constituted a major communal activity. Thus, fansubbing played an important role in the context of anime's popularity, as through it fans were able to communicate their dissatisfaction with 'anime localization policies' that existed, and alerted the anime studios of the existence of an active, enthusiastic but also demanding and critical audience for their products.[31] Furthermore, although it is not legal, fansubbers have claimed that their activity is

---

28. Nornes, 'For an Abusive Subtitling', 31-32.
29. Sean Leonard, 'Progress against the Law: Anime and Fandom, with the Key to the Globalization of Culture', *International Journal of Cultural Studies* 8.3 (2005): 295.
30. Antonia Levi, 'The Americanization of Anime and Manga: Negotiating Popular Culture', in Steven T. Brown (ed.), *Cinema Anime: Critical Engagements with Japanese Animation* (New York: Palgrave Macmillan, 2006), 46.
31. González, 'Fansubbing Anime', 265.

beneficial in both attracting more audience and raising the monetary gain of those who produced the work.[32]

The active engagement in translation and fansubbing of anime undertaken by aficionados is evidence of both their real devotion to anime, and also to their intense desire to familiarize others with anime and convert them from being non-anime viewers to being anime viewers, a mission that exemplifies what Patten termed 'evangelical fervour'.[33] In terms of fansubbing activity, Ian Condry's contention is that fansubbing has an educational dimension: the 'orientation of fansubs, explaining words... obscure references and jokes, all reflect a desire to teach. Of course, this desire to demonstrate experience also reminds us that fandom is about participation but also about status...communitarian and aesthetic'.[34] Naturally, in practical terms anime acquired popularity in the West through conventional marketing and retail campaigns, and not merely through fan activities. The United States is richly supplied with stores selling videos, DVDs and board and computer games, and there is an extensive array of television channels, and many 'private anime clubs'.[35]

One phenomenon among Western aficionados that points to their profound devotion, and to the popularity of anime (and all related cultural things) to them is the use of the Japanese term *otaku* as a self-designator. As noted in Chapter 1, *otaku* are 'nerds', the most engaged and passionate fans of popular cultural forms including manga and anime. The term was introduced by Akio Nakamori in 1983, in order to 'characterise a very idiosyncratic fan gathering that began to attend the "comic market" in Tokyo',[36] and the academic study of such Japanese fandom is known as 'otakuology'. The term quickly acquired both trivializing and highly negative connotations; Akio Nakamori himself considered *otaku* to refer to 'social rejects' in a harmless sense, but when the serial killer Tsutomu Miyazaki was described in the media as an *otaku* in 1989 (despite the fact that he himself did not know what the word meant), the negative connotations became entrenched.[37] Thus, in 2007 Miyuki Hashimoto, quoting Yoshihiro Yonezawa:

---

32. Jordan S. Hatcher, 'Of Otakus and Fansubs: A Critical Look at Anime Online in Light of Current Issues in Copyright Law', *SCRIPT-ed* 2.4 (2005): 562.

33. Patten, '*Anime* in the United States', 60.

34. Ian Condry, 'Dark Energy: What Fansubs Reveal about the Copyright Wars', *Mechademia* 5 (2010): 203.

35. Elaine Gerbert, 'Images of Japan in the Digital Age', *East Asia: An International Quarterly* 19.1-2 (2001): 108.

36. Miyuki Hashimoto, 'Visual Kei Otaku Identity: An Intercultural Analysis', *Intercultural Communication Studies* 16.1 (2007): 88.

37. Patrick Galbraith and Thomas Lamarre, 'Otakuology: A Dialogue', *Mechademia* 5 (2010): 363.

otaku is a kind of fan of cartoons and comics who are discriminated against by others. They are reclusive, mentally unbalanced and obsessed with details. In addition, they cannot communicate well with others. They...do not care about their clothing and thus are not dressed well. This word became widely used as a result of reports on the Miyazaki murders.[38]

This definition would seem to establish *otaku* as socially inept, generally male, and with borderline psychiatric and psychological problems such as autism and obsessive compulsive disorder, concerned with little apart from collecting examples of their favourite form of popular culture. It is significant that these sorts of people openly challenge Japan's work-oriented, conformist culture, and were thus strongly disapproved of.

Two factors assisted 'to diffuse the media panic about *otaku* as socio-paths that had regained in the late 1980s and early 1990s'; these are the widespread popularity of anime outside Japan and an extraordinary increase of '*otaku*-related commerce' in the late twentieth century.[39] This change in the social perception of *otaku* in Japan is partially the result of the embrace of certain late-modern trends by young Japanese, including widespread rejection or delaying of marriage, and the adoption of self-expression through distinctive types of fashion and the cultivation of subcultural identities. One anime that played a crucial role in signalling that 'the *otaku* market' had to be taken into account was Hideaki Anno's *Neon Genesis Evangelion* (1995–1996). Anno is well-known for both his valorization, and his 'harsh criticism', of both anime and *otaku* culture,[40] but there is no doubt that *Neon Genesis Evangelion* (*NGE*) appealed to the 'cool *otaku*'. Patrick Galbraith has detailed how *NGE* stimulated the mass purchase of anime figurines and other customized merchandise.[41] Fans in different countries have adapted the term *otaku* in various ways: for example, Australian aficionados have a special term for them, *oztaku*, as 'Oz' is an affectionate abbreviation of 'Australia'.[42]

---

38. Yoshihiro Yonezawa quoted by Hashimoto, 'Visual Kei Otaku Identity', 88-89. Hashimoto is referencing Yoshihiro Yonezawa (1953–2006), the famous manga critic and founder of Comiket. See http://www.meiji.ac.jp/manga/english/yonezawa_lib/profile (accessed 21 December 2012). The work referred to is Yoshihiro Yonezawa's commentary on *Basic Knowledge of Modern Words* (1990) (in Japanese).
39. Thomas Lamarre, *The Anime Machine: A Media Theory of Animation* (Minneapolis, MN: University of Minnesota Press, 2009), 152-53.
40. Lamarre, *The Anime Machine*, 153-54.
41. Patrick Galbraith, 'Akihabara: Conditioning a Public "Otaku" Image', *Mechademia* 5 (2010): 215-16.
42. Kede Lawson, 'Aso's "Manga Museum" Plan Cool with Aussies', *Japan Times Online* (*Kyodo News*) (2009), at http://www.japantimes.co.jp/text/nn20090714f2.html (accessed 20 February 2012).

It is unusual that the meaning of a term has changed to such a degree over time. Frederik L. Schodt explained that '[o]*taku* was originally written as *o-taku*...[with] the honorific phonetic character *o-* preceding the Chinese character for "house"...[and] could therefore mean "your house" or "your home"'.[43] It is still used with this meaning in old-fashioned formal Japanese today. In the 1980s the pejorative meanings detailed above accreted to the term *otaku*. Yet, in Japan male aficionados of anime and manga began using the term amongst themselves in the early 1990s; before then the term '*mania*' was used for Japanese anime and manga fans. This word is 'a "Japlish" concoction derived from the English "maniac" (just as the similar "fan" is a contraction of "fanatic")'.[44] The use of *otaku* as a self-designation by Japanese anime fans signalled a cultural shift; *otaku* (like Western nerds) had ceased to be social rejects and had become 'cool' from the 1990s onwards. This changed perception is evident in Tatsuhiko Takimoto's novel *Welcome to the NHK* (2002), which was made into a manga series (2004–2007) written by Takimoto and illustrated by Kendi Oiwa (Kenji Ōiwa). A twenty-four-episode anime series produced by Gonzo was screened in 2006. The plot is semi-autobiographical, and is centred on Tatsuhiro, a twenty-two-year-old *hikikomori* (recluse) who lives alone in a tiny apartment in Tokyo. He is gradually drawn out of his solitude and learns to interact with the world through his relationship with Misaki, a disturbed young girl who self-harms and whose mother has committed suicide.[45] Marc Hairston has explained that:

> [t]he term *hikikomori* is derived from the Japanese words *hiku* (pulling in) and *komoru* (retiring) and refers both to the syndrome and to the person with the syndrome. In most cases these are young males... in their teens or twenties who have developed a psychological fear of social interaction with the outside world and who spend all their time in their room at home. In extreme cases, the *hikikomori* refuses even to interact with other family members. The phenomenon was first reported in the 1990s, and the Japanese Ministry of Health, Labor and Welfare officially recognized the problem in 2001.[46]

The causes of the *hikikomori* phenomenon include bullying in high school, depression and a sense of hopelessness among the young who see no future due to Japan's stagnant economy, and rebellion against social and parental pressures.

---

43. Schodt, *Dreamland Japan*, 43.
44. Schodt, *Dreamland Japan*, 44.
45. Brenner, *Understanding Manga and Anime*, 166, 196.
46. Marc Hairston, 'A Cocoon with a View: *Hikikomori, Otaku*, and *Welcome to the NHK*', *Mechademia* 5 (2010): 311-32.

Concern about, and social criticism of, *hikikomori* has replaced media discourses about the dangers of *otaku* since approximately 2000. The principal drivers of this change are the enormous popularity of anime and manga, and the consequent mainstreaming of fandom. For example, it was noted in Chapter 1 that Tarō Asō, who was briefly Prime Minister of Japan in 2008–2009, happily self-identified as an *otaku* and had established the International Manga Award while Foreign Minister in 2007.[47] Takimoto's *Welcome to the NHK* chronicled this transition in self-aware and humorous ways; Tatsuhiro sleeps a lot, lives off an allowance from his parents, has conversations with electrical appliances, and believes the Japanese television network NHK is at the heart of a conspiracy to turn all Japanese young people into *hikikomori*. After connecting with Misaki, Tatsuhiro meets a new neighbour, Kaoru, and discovers that they used to attend the same school, and he had once tried to protect Kaoru from being bullied. Kaoru is a real *otaku*, and Tatsuhiro's interactions with him send up *otaku* culture mercilessly. Kaoru studied art to 'work in the manga, anime, and game industry' but he has an inflated estimation of his talents and a persistent lack of success, both in career terms and with women. He tells Tatsuhiro 'how much better the imaginary two-dimension anime/manga women are' when they are walking in Akihabara, the shopping district for popular culture fans, and tries to persuade Tatsuhiro to become an *otaku* too.[48] Thus, this popular story that was first published in 2002 sharply demarcates *otaku* (who are the butt of humour, but still attend college, hold down jobs, and have friends) from *hikikomori*, who are also satirized, but are shown to be largely incapable of doing these relatively straightforward things. There are a number of meanings attached to the initials NHK throughout the story, and 'in Misaki's case they stand for Nihon Hikan Kyokai (Japan Pessimists' Association)'.[49] Yet the story ends with Tatsuhiro having escaped his fate as a *hikikomori*, working part-time and tutoring Misaki for her college entrance exams. They have not yet admitted their love for each other, but the friendship and support they have given each other have transformed both their lives, and the world as a consequence.

In Chapter 3 Tatsuya Ishihara's anime series *The Melancholy of Haruhi Suzumiya* (2006) was examined in detail, with a focus on the supernatural and religious content. The teenage protagonist, eccentric Haruhi, is fascinated by the paranormal and possesses the ability to destroy the world,

---

47. Anon, 'Japan Launches International Manga Award – A "Nobel Prize in Manga"', *Icv2* (25 May 2007), at http://www.icv2.com/articles/news/10648.html (accessed 2 November 2013).
48. Hairston, 'A Cocoon with a View', 316-17.
49. Hairston, 'A Cocoon with a View', 321.

if she experiences boredom, *ennui* or melancholy. Her friends therefore have to keep her diverted in order to avert this catastrophe. The overall tone of the series is wittily comic, yet all her friends are strange (in fact, they are not human at all). The only human in the SOS Brigade is the cynical Kyon, who struggles to maintain the façade of normality for Haruhi, and with whom she later falls in love. Despite its humorous elements, *Welcome to the NHK* also gives expression to the depressive and melancholy state of many Japanese young people. In both stories a misfit girl and boy become friends due to shared fringe interests, develop a sense of community among similar oddballs, and finally find love together. It has been suggested that the presence of similar themes – melancholy, disaffected youth, and consumerist motifs – is one reason for the popularity of the works of Haruki Murakami (b. 1949), the best-selling Japanese novelist.[50] The relevance of this type of story arc to anime fandom is obvious; aficionados often openly affirm that they are misfits, and that their particular passion, whether it be anime, science fiction, fantasy literature or model railways, is the only thing that gives meaning to their life and cements their identities. When Jeff Greenwald met Trekkies in Budapest he was told by Emese Felgevi that Hungary was 'a peripheral country' and that the *Star Trek* characters she most identified with were 'outsiders' like the android Data and the shape-shifter Odo, who never really 'belong'.[51]

The fans he interviewed had not seen the television series, which had not been shown in Hungary, and only a limited number of the films had been released. However, via the Internet they were well-informed about *Star Trek*, had gone to great efforts to design a spaceship, the *Arpad* (named after the general who unified Hungary in the ninth century), and expressed the view that the *Star Trek* Fan Club was the focus of their lives. For example, Kata stated '[a] lot of the people in this group were lonely souls before they came to the club... But we are together and we are happy now. We can sow friendship, real friendship. We were looking for it, and we found it here'.[52] Tamas proclaimed, '[a]ll I can say is that Picard is like a father to me, and Riker like a brother. Watching *Star Trek* is like going home',[53] and Zsolt summed up, 'I'm happy that I'm a Trekker. It gives meaning to my life'.[54] All the members reiterated that Hungary was a country that had no local popular culture, was only slowly

---

50. Matthew C. Strecher, 'Magical Realism and the Search for Identity in the Fiction of Murakami Haruki', *Journal of Japanese Studies* 25.2 (1999): 263-98.
51. Greenwald, *Future Perfect*, 91.
52. Greenwald, *Future Perfect*, 94.
53. Greenwald, *Future Perfect*, 93.
54. Greenwald, *Future Perfect*, 95.

recovering from years of Soviet dominance, and that 'Hungarians are very pessimistic'. Zsolt was convinced that '[i]f *Star Trek* ran on Hungarian TV, there would be a possibility, a chance, for optimism'.[55] All these intensely held beliefs, expressed in the context of fandom directed at an American television programme, are relevant to and congruent with the life experiences of anime aficionados.

The popularity of anime proceeded at a different pace in various Western countries. One example of this phenomenon is that despite the dominance of *Astro Boy* in the United States, viewers in the United Kingdom were initially more impressed by *Marine Boy* and certain other anime series.[56] Today the Internet enables anime aficionados to connect with each other more or less instantaneously and to share knowledge of different films and television series, manga adaptations and directors. Prior to the advent of the Internet, contact between early aficionados was sporadic and limited by the available technology, and fan groups in one country may have been unaware of a particular series while being greatly devoted to another that they were viewing at the time. It is worth noting that while the anime following in America 'had been stirring since the late 1970s', anime aficionados in Great Britain started communication both among themselves and also with their counterparts across the Atlantic somewhat later.[57] Anne Cooper-Chen has observed that in Europe '[t]he first generation of European cartoon fans – those born between 1965 and 1970 – watched such TV series as "Heidi of the Alps," "Grandizer" (retitled "Goldorak") and "Candy Candy," which aired first in Spain (1975), next in Italy (1977) and then in France (1978)'.[58] Italy's exposure to anime began with *Legend of the White Serpent* (1958), which was released in 1959 in Italy (and in the United States as *Panda and the Magic Serpent*) and was discussed in detail in Chapter 2. Italy's cinemas screened 'at least' seventeen further anime between the late 1950s and the mid-1970s.[59] Italy was the European country that imported the most anime in these early decades, indicating there was a market for it and possibly an early fan culture (though there is no solid evidence that has survived which scholars might use to reconstruct the characteristics of the Italian anime audience); this contradicts Cooper-Chen's observation that the first anime aficionados in Europe were born between 1965 and

---

55. Greenwald, *Future Perfect*, 94.
56. McCarthy, 'Development of the Japanese Animation Audience', 74.
57. McCarthy, 'Development of the Japanese Animation Audience', 76.
58. Cooper-Chen, *Cartoon Cultures*, 119.
59. Marco Pellitteri et al., *The Dragon and the Dazzle: Models, Strategies, and Identities of Japanese Imagination – A European Perspective*, trans. Roberto Branca (Latina, Italy: Tunué, 2010), 401.

1970. In Italy, even the Vatican expressed an interest in anime. When Osamu Tezuka died in 1989, the anime series based on biblical stories, which the Vatican commissioned from him, was unfinished. However, the project was completed in 1992, eight years after Tezuka received the initial commission.[60]

In Germany anime's rise to market popularity came later; in 1998 *Lady Oscar* and *Sailor Moon* gained a significant audience. While it has been noted that Seitarō Kitayama's anime *Momotarō* was sent to France in 1917, it was not until the 1970s that anime series were televised in that country.[61] As the first motion picture was made in 1895 and the cinema was established rapidly as a dominant popular cultural form, whereas television was not commercially available until the late 1920s and did not become widespread until the 1950s, it can be concluded that it took far longer for anime to reach a television audience, both in Europe and the United States, than it did for anime films to be screened. There is evidence, too, that certain landmark productions had disproportionate influence at crucial times. For example, Robin E. Brenner has claimed that Katsuhiro Ōtomo's film *Akira* (1988), analysed in Chapter 3, was 'the first major arrival of anime in the United States'.[62] Another important 'moment' was the screening of Miyazaki's *Princess Mononoke* (1997) in America in 1999, when there was '[p]ublic recognition of the widespread following of anime'.[63] In the eleven years between the release of *Akira*, a cyberpunk dystopian film, and the rapturous reception that *Princess Mononoke*, an epic high fantasy film, received in 1999, the audience for Japanese animations had mushroomed to a size that made it of interest in economic, as well as cultural, terms. The radically different nature of these two landmark anime represented another significant change: the recognition that anime were marketable to both adults and children,[64] due to the range of genres and subgenres that were examined in Chapter 3. Thus this section has highlighted the different rates of growth in popularity that anime registered in a limited sample of Western countries.

The Internet has played an important role in disseminating knowledge about anime and thus to the community of aficionados. For English speakers, the need for translations of Japanese manga and anime are the two principal obstacles. The Internet acted as a communications medium, supporting the spread of 'Japanese fan forums' and enabling

---

60. Cooper-Chen, *Cartoon Cultures*, 123.
61. McCarthy, 'Development of the Japanese Animation Audience', 80.
62. Brenner, *Understanding Manga and Anime*, 11.
63. Gerbert, 'Images of Japan', 108.
64. Levi, 'Americanization of Anime and Manga', 45.

aficionados to contact each other swiftly and efficiently to share information.[65] In 2007, according to PR Newswire Europe Including UK Disclose, '[t]he [n]ew cutting-edge Japanese animation network, GONG, dedicated to teens and adults...the first international on-demand, on-line [a]nimé channel in Europe and North America' was launched.[66] The founders of GONG, Benoit Runel and André de Semlyen, asserted that anime and manga aficionados are 'a new generation in the new media space' and are eager to embrace online media, as 'traditional' television is not keeping up with new types of audience. In order to expand anime's fame and reach, the plan behind GONG is to use 'broadband internet and mobile distribution' since the target viewer group is predominantly males and females from fifteen to thirty.[67] It is clear that GONG is an original and valuable anime-related initiative, but although contemporary anime fans have the opportunity to view and enjoy anime through a range of new media, the cinema screen has not been surpassed when it comes to an impressive anime experience. It remains to be noted that certain anime possess enduring appeal to audiences: Osamu Tezuka's *Astro Boy* entered the hearts of the audience worldwide in the 1960s, as did a large number of Tōei Dōga's early animated feature films.[68] Yet fifty years after the *Astro Boy* anime series was released, this work retains its power and appeal, demonstrated by the recently released 3D *Astro Boy* animated film (2009). Even people who are largely ignorant of Japanese animation have probably heard of Astro Boy. This familiarity is likely to continue and perhaps grow, considering the extensive information regarding Tezuka, *Astro Boy*, and all things anime on the Internet, just a Google search away.

It has been noted that devotion to anime sometimes motivates aficionados to learn more about the Japanese culture and language. Frequent anime viewing may assist with acquiring knowledge of language, in that it facilitates 'word recognition, listening and pronunciation, and awareness of various Japanese linguistic features'.[69] Thus, anime may play a role in encouraging fans to learn Japanese, though colloquial language is frequently used in anime. Recalling Iwabuchi's caution that much more

---

65. Francesca Coppa, 'A Brief History of Media Fandom', in Karen Hellekson and Kristina Busse (eds), *Fan Fiction and Fan Communities in the Age of the Internet: New Essays* (Jefferson, NC: McFarland, 2006), 56.
66. Anon, 'GONG, the UK Based Japanese Animation Channel Launches in Over 30 Countries', *PR Newswire Europe Including UK Disclose* (New York, 2007).
67. Anon, 'GONG, the UK Based Japanese Animation Channel'.
68. Arnold, 'Japanese Anime'.
69. Natsuki Fukunaga, '"Those Anime Students": Foreign Language Literacy Development through Japanese Popular Culture', *Journal of Adolescent and Adult Literacy* 50.3 (2006): 213.

than anime is needed to increase Western audiences' stock of knowledge regarding Japan, which is fair considering that the majority of anime featured fictional characters living in imaginative worlds, it should be noted that the anime series *Sazae-san* reflects the lifestyle of a typical Tokyo suburban household, in which the characters 'attend Shinto festivals, eat Japanese food, and sleep on futons on tatami floors'.[70] Thus there is definite potential in anime to offer a learning experience for the viewer, something more than just entertainment.

This section has discussed Western anime aficionados and argued that their devotion to Japanese animation has been growing in intensity and frequency since the first animated films were exported from Japan to the West in the wake of World War I, nearly one hundred years ago. It has been argued that, to a considerable degree, the popularity of anime is due to activities initiated by fan networks, which are often creative and unconventional. It has been also noted how anime devotion has the potential to stimulate interest in Japanese culture and language among aficionados. The model of fandom developed around the American cult series *Star Trek* was introduced, and will continue to influence the interpretation of anime aficionado culture in the following sections. Despite a range of obstacles (including the language barrier and a limited familiarity with the Japanese socio-cultural context in which anime originates), the development of anime fandom was not inhibited, and in the first quarter of the twenty-first century, anime enjoys unprecedentedly high levels of popularity.

The Fulfilment of Cosplay

This section is focused on cosplay, a type of performance by anime aficionados. It is argued that this activity can be seen as symbolically stepping into the diegetic world of anime narratives, which frequently feature supernatural elements.[71] First, the origins of cosplay are considered, accompanied by a description of characteristic elements. The beginnings of cosplay lie in aficionados' donning costumes for the event known as the Comic Market or Comiket that originated in Japan in 1975. Initially, aficionados only placed images of the anime characters on their t-shirts, a humble beginning for what is now an elaborate and sophisticated practice. In 1983 a fan attended Comiket costumed as Lum (the alien heroine from Rumiko Takahashi's manga and anime, *Urusei Yatsura* – 'Those Obnoxious Aliens' – discussed in detail in Chapter 2). This is the earliest

---

70. Price, 'Cartoons from Another Planet', 156.
71. Some material featured in the section 'The Fullfilment of Cosplay' has been published in Buljan, 'Animated Film', 193–208.

recorded example of an anime-related outfit among aficionados.[72] Thus, for approximately thirty years anime aficionados have made an art out of donning costumes and acting the part of favourite anime characters. It was Nobuyuki (Nov) Takahashi who coined the term 'cosplay' after he 'was sent to Worldcon in Los Angeles to cover the events for various magazines back in Japan' in 1984.[73] Thus the mutual imbrication of Eastern and Western cultures, which has already been noted in terms of manga and comic books, anime and animation, religious and spiritual developments and much more, is once again in evidence in the use of the term 'cosplay'. In Australia, '[o]ne of the first cosplay conventions' was organized at the Australian Centre for Independent Gaming, Melbourne in 2000.[74] As the first signs of cosplaying in Japan and the United States were recorded in the 1980s, it can be seen that cosplay activity took some time to manifest in Australia.

Once again scholarship concerning *Star Trek* fandom practices is significant for developing a framework through which to view and interpret cosplay as a specific fan culture activity, with a significance that far exceeds the (accurate) description, 'dressing up as popular anime characters'. The sociologist Michael Jindra undertook extensive fieldwork among *Star Trek* fans, referred to as 'Trekkies' or 'Trekkers', and published detailed studies of the beliefs and behaviours of this distinctive community. The *Star Trek* universe is rich and very detailed, as more than seven hundred episodes of the television series have been made, in addition to novelizations, films, board games, online sites, conventions, and associated merchandise.

Jindra contended that *Star Trek* is a popular cultural phenomenon that contemporary Westerners find 'sacred', and that its millions of fans clearly engage in devotional acts. Jindra's research, now nearly twenty years old, details the show's popularity in the early 1990s:

> over $500 million in merchandise sold over the last 25 years…, over 4 million novels sold every year (often bestsellers), dictionaries of ST alien languages, institutes that study them, 'fanzines' numbering in the thousands, hundreds of fan clubs, conventions, on-line computer discussion groups, and tourist sites, plus of course the endless reruns, broadcast in over 100 countries. Captain Kirk and Mr Spock, the two main characters

---

72. Michael Bruno, 'Cosplay: The Illegitimate Child of SF Masquerades', *Glitz and Glitter*, Millennium Costumers Guild (2002), at http://millenniumcg.tripod.com/glitzglitter/1002articles.html (accessed 6 July 2010).

73. Bruno, 'Cosplay'.

74. Larissa Hjorth, 'Game Girl: Re-imagining Japanese Gender and Gaming via Melbourne Female Cosplayers', *Intersections: Gender and Sexuality in Asia and the Pacific* 20 (2009), at http://intersections.anu.edu.au/issue20/hjorth.htm (accessed 1 July 2011).

on the original series (TOS), are household names not only in the United States but in other English-speaking countries, as is the spaceship... 'Enterprise'. Other popular culture fads have come and gone, but ST recently celebrated its twenty-fifth anniversary and shows no sign of letting up.[75]

Jindra's typology of fandom distinguishes 'casual' fans from 'serious' fans, and he has noted that for serious fans *Star Trek* is 'a way of life', a philosophy that informs their values and guides their conduct in the 'real world'.[76] He argues that *Star Trek* is best characterized as a folk philosophy, which is defined as 'beliefs found among ordinary people that do not have any central organization or leadership and that are expressions of deep-set cultural convictions'.[77] Central values include the Prime Directive, which states that there should be no Federation interference in the development of other civilizations, and Infinite Diversity in Infinite Combinations (IDIC), a principle of multi-ethnic, multi-cultural society. The crew of the starship 'Enterprise', led by Captain Kirk, modelled inter-racial and inter-species harmony, which was congruent with the 1960s push for black, gay and women's rights, and the series expresses faith in both science and humanism.

In terms of cosplay behaviours, *Star Trek* conventions ('cons') are central; they feature 'trivia and costume contests, artwork, literature, bridge mock-ups [copies of 'Enterprise' stage sets], and appearances by actors'.[78] Greenwald's account of a Klingon wedding, described above, is a clear example of cosplay that crosses over into significant identity-defining behaviour, in which the adopted Klingon identity has become as important as the participant's 'real-world' identity. In another striking case study, Greenwald interviewed Ralph Roncoli about the re-enactment of a *Star Trek* episode, 'Arena', that was filmed at Vasquez Rocks, near Pasadena. He and his friends decided to re-enact it, although without costumes. Roncoli related the incident as follows:

> [o]ne of the guys had a videotape of the episode copied onto his camcorder...and we all drove up there. Sure enough, there were the rocs, and there was the place where Kirk ran up the cliff. By keeping one eye on the viewfinder and one on the scenery, we could tell within five feet where everything had been shot. So we filmed the same scene, each of

---

75. Jindra, '*Star Trek* Fandom', 28.
76. Michael Jindra, '"*Star Trek* to Me is a Way of Life": Fan Expressions of *Star Trek* Philosophy', in Jennifer E. Porter and Darcee L. McLaren (eds), *Star Trek and Sacred Ground: Explorations of Star Trek, Religion, and American Culture* (Albany, NY: State University of New York Press, 1999), 217.
77. Jindra, '*Star Trek* to Me is a Way of Life', 218.
78. Jindra, '*Star Trek* Fandom', 39.

us taking different parts. Then we edited it all together with sounds and dialogue from the original show.[79]

Greenwald's popular book is filled with examples of such fan devotion, in which being in the place of a beloved character (whether costumed as that character, or re-enacting a story in which the character was featured) is sought as a form of personal fulfilment or a transformation of one's mundane self into a supernatural (or at least extra-terrestrial) superior being. Andreas, one of the Klingons he interviewed, commented that his Klingon identity was 'more than a hobby' but 'not exactly a religion either, but something in between. It shows me how to understand other cultures; how to solve my own problems in a way of peace'.[80] The Klingon female warrior Taj'IH (American medical practitioner Astrid) and her partner Q'Eltor (German Ralf Gebhart) informed Greenwald that they met when Ralf found a photograph of her in warrior garb on a Klingon website, and '[t]he first few times they went out, both wore full Klingon costume'. Thus, when she first saw Ralf *as Ralf*, Astrid 'barely recognised him'.[81] The relationship between these two extreme fans is enriched by their Klingon identification, and enhanced by the elaborate costume play and complex ritual that the German Klingon community affords them, which is evident from the plentiful photographs that illustrate Greenwald's book.

During the act of cosplay, an important ritual for its protagonists is the photographic session. In photographs the cosplayers imitate their chosen character in 'body language and expressions in staged temporary poses'.[82] The standard by which their cosplaying is judged depends on how well they succeed in acting out the character they have chosen. Further, by keeping a track record of their photographic images, anime aficionados can improve their performance through successive cosplaying. Photographers of cosplayers are usually *kameko* (amateurs) or other cosplayers. The term *kameko* is comprised of two words – 'camera' and '*kozō*' – which translates as 'camera boy'. Cosplay performance bears a crucial significance for a large number of anime aficionados, as Michal Daliot-Bul's research, interviewing anime aficionados in a cosplay performance, revealed. She concluded that, '[t]he appeal of cosplaying lies in the personal *transformation* it allows. "Becoming the character I love," "becoming someone else," and "changing my mood" were among the

---

79. Greenwald, *Future Perfect*, 23.
80. Greenwald, *Future Perfect*, 69.
81. Greenwald, *Future Perfect*, 73.
82. Michal Daliot-Bul, '*Asobi* in Action: Contesting the Cultural Meanings and Cultural Boundaries of Play in Tokyo from the 1970s to the Present', *Cultural Studies* 23.3 (2009): 368.

most common replies to "Why do you cosplay?"'.[83] Thus anime aficionados seek 'personal transformation', which the act of cosplaying enables them to achieve.

Craig Norris and Jason Bainbridge insist on the centrality of ritual in cosplay: '[f]rom *Star Trek* fans in replica Starfleet uniforms to rugby league supporters in team jerseys, dressing up is part of the ritual of identification with a particular character, a way of marking out a fan's alignment'.[84] Furthermore, far from merely exhibiting clothes and various embellishments, cosplaying anime and manga fans inhabit 'the role of a character both physically and mentally' in the tradition of acting and stage performance.[85] These scholars come close to advancing the argument of this chapter that through cosplay anime aficionados seek to merge into the alternative reality of anime. As seen in Chapter 3, many anime genres have supernatural elements and anime protagonists often possess supernatural traits. Through cosplaying, aficionados take on the qualities of a character; this indicates that they like that character, but it is the anime world, its events and backstory through which the traits and behaviour of that character are reflected, that the cosplayer desires to be part of.

Consequently, anime aficionados who cosplay are likely to be drawn to supernatural world settings, and desire to experience the spectacular qualities of the dramatic story of which their character is part. The term 'cosplay' is an abbreviation of 'costume' and 'play'; the costumes are a vital part of cosplaying as they assist fans to emulate the anime character. Thus, aficionados often sew their cosplay costumes.[86] While to casual observers the act of cosplay may appear to be mere entertainment, from the perspective of its protagonists this act has a deeper meaning that connects with the experience of *Star Trek* fans, discussed above. It is here argued that cosplaying can be understood as symbolically stepping into the diegetic world of anime, and as a mode of self-transformation for protagonists who seek to enter the supernatural world and to experience the magical powers of their chosen anime character. The sociological model underlying these processes is akin to that which is fundamental to anime pilgrimage, discussed in the final section of this chapter. In both cases, Victor Turner's notion of the journey from the profane to the sacred, through withdrawing from everyday life and entering a liminal state during which personal transformation and

---

83. Daliot-Bul, '*Asobi* in Action', 368.
84. Norris and Bainbridge, 'Selling *Otaku*?'
85. Norris and Bainbridge, 'Selling *Otaku*?'
86. Buljan, 'Animated Film', 205.

sacred status are achieved, provides a powerful interpretive model for the experience.[87]

Finally, cosplay resembles fansubbing in that both fan behaviours involve blurred boundaries between the activities of producers and consumers. The aficionados themselves produce new products (amateur subtitled anime and photographs that are often archived on websites, such as the Klingon site described above, where Ralf first saw Astrid), rather than passively consuming anime, manga or whatever popular cultural form they are attached to. Danielle Kirby has argued that consumption models are a poor fit for individuals or groups where active engagement with cultural products (in her study of the Otherkin, these are narratives) is the norm.[88] Kirby's argument is particularly relevant, in that the Otherkin – a group of individuals who believe that they are not entirely human, but may be part angel, werewolf, elf or orc (to name but a few options), species that are generally sourced from fictional narratives and popular culture – are a primarily online elective community and in their belief that being Otherkin defines their identity, they occupy the same sort of indefinite boundary zone between fandom, spiritual identification and actual religious affiliation that is characteristic of anime aficionados.[89] Another, significant, boundary that cosplay crosses is that of gender. Chapter 2 drew attention to the fluidity of gender identity and its close relationship with the Japanese tradition of animal transformation, the anthropomorphic understanding of machines and features of the landscape (among other things generally believed to be inanimate or to lack the quality of life). Patrick Galbraith's study of Akihabara, the *otaku* retail district of Tokyo, featured a 'young male construction worker who called himself "Haruhi," because he wore the girl's school uniform from the anime *The Melancholy of Haruhi Suzumiya*'.[90] This particular gender-bending *otaku* enjoyed significant media attention, particularly after 'Haruhi and some fifty costumed followers accomplices took over the pedestrian paradise [Chuo Street, the centre of Akihabara] in summer 2007 to perform a street dance which became an international sensation (or at least a meme) on online video sharing sites'.[91] There is a close parallel here with online sites such as *Second Life*, and Massive

---

87. Victor Turner, 'The Centre Out There: Pilgrim's Goal', *History of Religions* 12.3 (1972): 191-92.
88. Danielle Kirby, 'Readers, Believers, Consumers and Audiences: Complicating the Relationship between Consumption and Contemporary Narrative Spiritualities', *Australian Journal of Communication* 39.1 (2012): 119-31.
89. Kirby, 'Readers, Believers, Consumers and Audiences', 124-25.
90. Galbraith, 'Akihabara', 219.
91. Galbraith, 'Akihabara', 219.

Multiplayer Online Role-Playing Games (MMORPGs) including *World of Warcraft*, indeed all online media in which the adoption of an alternative identity separate to the individual's real-world identity allows for the limitations of gender, species, age, race, and other 'real world' qualities to be overcome.

Like the Otherkin, cosplayers take a largely passive text and render it active through entering and transforming it, changing the boundaries between 'the viewer and the viewed' as they become the characters and are immortalized through photography.[92] Eron Rauch and Christopher Bolton, when discussing images taken by cosplay photographers, both amateur and professional, argued that the Internet and digital technology have transformed this fan activity, too:

> [t]en years ago a fan could spend twenty or thirty dollars just to develop a few rolls of film at the grocery store and get a small stack of 4x6-inch prints to share with the local anime club. Today nearly every convention attendee interested in cosplay has some kind of networked digital image-making device (cell phone, camera, camcorder, and so on), and the growth of online forums, communities, networking services, and photo sharing has produced huge sites like cosplay.com, as well as cosplay communities on image-sharing sites like Flickr and deviantArt.[93]

This is of interest, because it suggests that fans that costume themselves to 'become' certain characters (such as Zan, whose portraits of herself as the girls from *Sailor Moon* are justly famous), themselves become 'stars' and acquire their own 'fans' when they post images of themselves online.[94] This adds an extra, and powerful, dimension to cosplay; the self-transformation process does not only involve the possibility of entering the anime world and becoming a supernatural being for a brief period, but also the potential to become a minor celebrity online.

Audiences and the Religio-Spiritual Content of Anime

This section considers attractive qualities in anime that have the potential to cause members of Western audiences to become anime aficionados. Jin Kyu Park has argued that the most significant of these qualities is the religious and spiritual content. This section discusses the relationship of contemporary 'spiritual seekers' and the supernaturally-oriented

---

92. Eron Rauch and Christopher Bolton, 'A Cosplay Photography Sampler', *Mechademia* 5 (2010): 177.
93. Rauch and Bolton, 'A Cosplay Photography Sampler', 178.
94. Zan, 'Zan's Profile', *Cosplay.com* (n.d.), at http://www.cosplay.com/member/1663/costumes (accessed 21 December 2012).

content of anime.⁹⁵ It is argued that some of this content taken from the world religions (including Buddhism, Christianity and Shintō) is largely devoid of its original meaning, making it susceptible to personal interpretation. Yet this diluted religious and spiritual content can still pique the viewers' curiosity, causing them to seek out information about the religion in question.

When considering why anime is attractive to Westerners, it is valuable to realize that many adults who loved *Astro Boy* and other anime series as children later confessed they did not know they were Japanese products. This is because when anime were imported into the United States, '[t]he Japaneseness of these shows was fiercely camouflaged, along with any mature content in order to redirect the appeal to a strictly American, as well as a younger, audience'.⁹⁶ Today it is well known that anime is Japanese and its distinctive style is recognizable, but this was not always the case. When their works enjoyed significant popularity in the West, anime directors had a double reaction to the wide acceptance of their work outside Japan. They were both confused and delighted by the world-wide positive reaction their work received, as they had intended the work only for Japanese audiences. The attraction of non-Japanese viewers to anime thus seems to have been largely accidental.

Scholars have advanced reasons why anime is successful with Western audiences, often as a result of conversations with directors. Minoru Ideta and Rosemary Iwamura interviewed Katsuhiro Ōtomo, who asserted that:

> [i]n America and Europe, there's no animation produced for the late teenage market. That's probably why Japanese animation is so popular now. In America you have that whole superhero thing. In Japan, the heroes are shorter, and wear sailor suits and school uniforms – characters that kids can relate to. It's not too distant from the lives of the people who watch it. That probably accounts for its popularity in the West.⁹⁷

Thus, feeling a close connection or empathy with anime characters is one of the elements that can trigger the Western audience's interest in anime. Additionally, Price has theorized that a 'realistic approach to mature, relatable topics and its sincere depiction of human emotion' are features of anime that audiences in the United States may find likeable.⁹⁸ It seems then that mere entertainment is an insufficient reason to explain Western audiences' fascination with anime. Mamoru Oshii observed, when

---

95. Park, 'Creating My Own Cultural and Spiritual Bubble'.
96. Price, 'Cartoons from Another Planet', 161 and 166.
97. Ōtomo, in Minoru Ideta and Rosemary Iwamura, 'Otomo Interview', *Kaboom! Explosive Animation from America and Japan* (Sydney: Museum of Contemporary Art, 1994), 139.
98. Price, 'Cartoons from Another Planet', 167.

discussing the emotional content of anime, 'Japanese animators are very good at hand-drawing, at depicting emotions with very slight gestures or expressions, that's their greatest strength. Utilizing this skill makes a richer film. So, for me it's not a choice to make animation like this, I can't do anything else'.[99] Thus masterful representation of emotions is another feature of anime that Western audiences may be attracted to.

A significant feature of some anime narratives is that they break with generic conventions; for example, despite the promise of a romance, there may not be a happy ending. Thus, Hayao Miyazaki's *Princess Mononoke* concludes with Mononoke and Ashitaka still apart, despite their mutual liking for each other. The same fate befalls the protagonists in *Escaflowne*, Hitomi Kanzaki (also known as the Goddess of Wings) and Lord Van. Therefore, although the audience may have expected or hoped for a happy ending in the romantic sense, that did not occur. Natsuki Fukunaga's research has demonstrated that aficionados like the 'uniqueness' of this Japanese artistic product, which is so different to its American counterpart.[100] Despite the range of visual styles in anime and the different types of stories delivered, there is something that is distinctive and special about them. Some aficionados are most drawn to the anime aesthetic; Fukunaga also found that 'the distinctive art style of anime, exemplified in drawings of characters with "big eyes"' was a unique selling point with Western audiences.[101] Anime aficionados in the United States have expressed the view that '[anime] provides them with appealing alter ego-like characters to relate to' and this is one of its most compelling qualities.[102] The previous section on cosplay demonstrated the validity of this contention.

Yet there are further reasons why anime intrigues Western audiences. Antonia Levi observed that, 'Japan is not a Judeo-Christian culture. Not in the least. And that means that the Japanese view of truth, the universe, reason, and reality are all very different'.[103] Naturally, this is reflected in anime. As a consequence, what American aficionados find appealing is anime's 'unpredictability, its off-beat weirdness that makes you stop and think about things you never even noticed before'.[104] This insightful comment provoked the speculation that those unfamiliar with

---

99. Oshii, quoted in Catherine Maxwell, 'Interview – Mamoru Oshii', *Omusubi* (Sydney: The Japan Foundation, 2004), 4, at http://www.jpf.org.au/06_newsletter/oshii-ishikawa_interview_omusubi_02.pdf (accessed 24 February 2012).

100. Fukunaga, 'Those Anime Students', 212.

101. Fukunaga, 'Those Anime Students', 212.

102. Price, 'Cartoons from Another Planet', 166.

103. Antonia Levi, *Samurai from Outer Space: Understanding Japanese Animation* (Chicago, IL: Open Court, 1996), 17.

104. Levi, *Samurai from Outer Space*, 17.

Japan are attracted precisely to anime's 'uniquely odd world'. Chapter 2 has analysed the role of religion and mythology in Japanese culture in general and anime in particular, and the lack of familiarity that Western audiences have with the various sects of Japanese Buddhism, Shintō, and the new religions (*shin shūkyō*), substantially contributes to the fascinating strangeness of much anime. This strangeness empowers anime aficionados 'to find a voice within an exciting realm of fantasy, and lets them relate to real life human emotions', and also helps them 'see the world through a stranger's eyes'.[105] Although there are many factors that account for the attractiveness of anime to Western audiences, Jin Kyu Park has identified one feature (the religious and spiritual content in anime) that some aficionados from the United States, or more precisely, those who are 'spiritual seekers' find particularly compelling. It is worth noting that Park does not argue that the religious aspects of anime are paramount, but acknowledges that there are many aspects to why fans like anime. Park is candid that the number of aficionados who are drawn to this aspect of anime is neither large nor 'explicitly articulated'.[106]

This study has explored the links between anime and religion, mythology and spirituality in a number of specific ways. In Chapter 1 the process of modernization experienced by Japan in the nineteenth and twentieth centuries was understood as intimately connected with both the development of anime as an art form, and with religious and cultural changes. Chapter 2 explicitly considered religious elements that appear in a diverse range of anime, and related the presence of religion in this popular cultural form to the Shintō worldview, in which everything is alive and interconnected. In Chapter 3 the focus shifted from formal religion to the looser concept of spirituality, and the focus was on anime that featured supernatural settings, characters or other elements. The theme of self-transformation emerged as particularly important, and has been pursued in this chapter's investigation of fan behaviours.

However, it is undeniable that the representation of some elements from religions (for instance Christianity, Buddhism and Shintō) is largely devoid of the meaning and value that it had in its original context. An example of this is *Princess Knight* ('Ribon no Kishi') by Osamu Tezuka, which is briefly discussed in Chapter 2. This anime has a medieval European setting, in which Princess Sapphire of Silverland lives as a male as her parents need an heir. The influence of Christianity is apparent in the setting, the guardian angel assigned to Sapphire (who is called Tink, Chink or Choppy in the various translations of the anime), and Satan features as the villain of the series. Satan has great powers, which

---

105. Price, 'Cartoons from Another Planet', 166.
106. Park, 'Creating My Own Cultural and Spiritual Bubble', 409.

he uses for evil. Yet his daughter Heckett, a teenage witch, yearns to be good and uses her magic to protect Sapphire and to thwart Satan's plans.[107] While there is the possibility that elements from particular religions may be misunderstood, this is balanced by the fact that anime may trigger curiosity about the original religious context of the narrative element or motif. It is possible that many aficionados first heard about these religious themes due to anime. For example, in the film *Ghost in the Shell II: Innocence*, which was written and directed by Mamoru Oshii, there is a scene in which the protagonist Batō explains the story of the *golem*, and the meaning of the Hebrew words *aemaeth* and *maeth* ('truth' and 'death') associated with it. A *golem* is a man-made animated being, of which the most famous was that created from clay by Rabbi Judah Loew of Prague in the sixteenth century, to protect the Jewish community against accusations of murder.[108] This tale is part of Jewish folklore and as such would be unfamiliar to the majority of viewers. Consequently, *Ghost in the Shell II: Innocence* (2004) may inspire them to learn more about this story and Jewish tradition (this is similar to anime's potential to trigger an interest in learning Japanese, discussed above).

The *Ghost in the Shell* films are examples of anime that contain religious motifs, the most significant of which is the question of the relationship of body and spirit that is explored through the existential quest of the Major Motoko Kusanagi to discover if she is really a person, if she possesses a soul. This famed cyborg heroine also has a name that has a religious meaning:

> *Kusanagi* (Japanese: 'Grass-Mower'), in Japanese mythology, [is] the miraculous sword that the sun goddess Amaterasu gave to her grandson Ninigi when he descended to earth to become ruler of Japan, thus establishing the divine link between the imperial house and the sun. The sword, along with the mirror and jeweled necklace, still forms one of the three Imperial Treasures of Japan. The sword was discovered by the storm god Susanoo in the body of the eight-headed dragon (which he killed) and presented by him to his sister Amaterasu. It derives its name from an incident when the hero Yamato Takeru was attacked by Ainu warriors. They started a grass fire around him, from which he escaped by cutting down the burning brush with the sword.[109]

The myth of Susanoo's combat with the serpent Orochi, and the genealogy of Amaterasu's descendants who rule Japan and the precious regalia

---

107. Suter, 'From *Jusuheru* to *Jannu*', 241-56.
108. Elizabeth R. Baer, *The Golem Redux: From Prague to Post-Holocaust Fiction* (Detroit, MI: Wayne State University Press, 2012).
109. Anon, 'Kusanagi', *Encyclopædia Britannica Online* (2012), at http://www.britannica.com/EBchecked/topic/325455/Kusanagi (accessed 23 February 2012).

that symbolizes their power, was discussed in some detail in Chapter 2. These are a few examples of religious elements that anime aficionados may find intriguing and discover through watching anime. These may then inspire them to seek further knowledge of the religions involved, though it is more likely that, similarly to the *Star Trek* fans discussed above, they may prefer to consider their engagement with anime as a religion substitute, something that creates meaning in their lives and obviates the need for more traditional religious allegiance.

As noted earlier, Park used the phrase 'spiritual seeker' when discussing the religious appeal of anime. Those to whom this phrase is applied say that they are 'spiritual but not religious'.[110] Although there is no commitment to an established religion, these individuals are interested in spirituality, which ties in neatly with Andreas's comment that his Klingon practice is more than a 'hobby' but less than a 'religion'.[111] Spiritual seekers typically cherry-pick the world's spiritual and religious heritage and assemble a personal faith from elements of many traditions.[112] The religious content of anime is attractive because it 'is not limited to symbolic figures derived from religions and myths. The content of most anime not only involves, but is centred around, religious themes and ideas',[113] and directors represent these religious and mythological elements in a range of ways. With regards to the religious and spiritual content in anime and spiritual seekers, Park notes that:

> [t]he younger generations show generally negative responses towards organised religion while still seeking religious meanings in subjective and reflexive ways. Their feeling of 'sick-and-tired-ness' also relates to US pop culture. It appears that the negativity towards both organised religion and US pop culture is prevalent amongst most young people. In this context, young spiritual seekers construct their religious identity in the process of consuming various resources including certain types of cultural products. For the seekers in this study, anime is one of the cultural products that fit their own idea of spirituality.[114]

It is thus demonstrable that there is a close link between the religious and spiritual content of anime and anime aficionados who are on a spiritual quest, although there is potential that only shallow and misinformed ideas will be held by anime aficionados who are 'seekers'. More

---

110. Christian Smith and Melinda Lundquist Denton, *Soul Searching: The Religious and Spiritual Lives of American Teenagers* (Oxford and New York: Oxford University Press, 2005), 73.
111. Greenwald, *Future Perfect*, 69.
112. Smith and Denton, *Soul Searching*, 72-73.
113. Park, 'Creating My Own Cultural and Spiritual Bubble', 397.
114. Park, 'Creating My Own Cultural and Spiritual Bubble', 409.

complex and deeply researched ideas may not appeal to them, given their individualistic orientation and lack of enthusiasm for institutional religion.

However, Lynn Schofield Clark's research concerning the religious and spiritual beliefs of American teenagers reveals that even confused and contradictory beliefs held by people who are largely ignorant of the original context of the teaching (such as Christian teens who profess to believe in reincarnation, but know nothing of Buddhism or Hinduism) may still assist them to refine their personal identity and orient themselves ethically and spiritually in their lives.[115] Regarding fans and spiritual quests, Park has further observed that:

> [a]nime's distinctive quality in its descriptions of religious and spiritual realms – integrating symbols, themes, doctrines, and mythologies from various religious traditions – is a cultural manifestation of the Japanese integrative spirituality, which would provide a valuable explanation of why some American young people, who are characterised as spiritual seekers, are fascinated by the cultural artefacts. Yet, I have to point out that…even though they are interested in anime's spirituality, this might not be the only reason for their love of anime.[116]

While there is interest in the religious and spiritual aspects of anime, it is worth noting how Hayao Miyazaki described Lady Eboshi from *Princess Mononoke* in an interview: 'I think of her as the most modern character because she has no interest in the salvation of her soul'. He added, 'I think that for many modern people who no longer believe in the power of redemption, she's a very compelling character'.[117]

These comments are fascinating to scholars of contemporary religion, who are familiar with the statistical decline of all religious institutions and the exponential growth in 'personal spiritualities' in the West.[118] The distinguishing characteristic of such spiritual positions is that an individual can reject the supernatural world entirely yet assert that he or she is 'spiritual', while another individual performs Pagan rituals to the elves from J. R. R. Tolkien's *Lord of the Rings* novels which he or she asserts actually exist. Yet others derive their ultimate values from Marvel superhero comics, passionately supporting the Manchester United football team,

---

115. Lynn Schofield Clark, *From Angels to Aliens: Teenagers, the Media, and the Supernatural* (Oxford: Oxford University Press, 2003).

116. Park, 'Creating My Own Cultural and Spiritual Bubble', 409.

117. Miyazaki, quoted in Elisabeth Vincentelli, 'Bittersweet Sympathies: For a Japanese Animator, Grown-up Messages are Kid Stuff', *The Village Voice* (1999), at http://www.villagevoice.com/1999-10-26/film/bittersweet-sympathies (accessed 10 May 2011).

118. Lyon, *Jesus in Disneyland*.

or engaging in projects of self-transformation (the gym, plastic surgery, or fandom activities like cosplay). Thus, the fact that many great anime creators are not personally religious, yet their work is suffused with spiritual concerns, should not be viewed as an insurmountable contradiction, but rather typical of late-modern consumer capitalist religiosity and spirituality. Miyazaki is opposed to institutional religion. He told Elisabeth Vincentelli that religion, *per se*, has no part in his filmmaking. Rather, he has a personal religion, which 'has no practice, no Bible, no saints, only a desire to keep certain places and my own self as pure and holy as possible. That kind of spirituality is very important to me'.[119] Therefore, despite Miyazaki's indifference to religion, his spiritual concern for nature, and the ideal of spiritual purity and holiness are prominent interests among both fan groups and contemporary spiritual seekers in the West. Concerning Miyazaki's *oeuvre*, religion and Western audiences, Jolyon Baraka Thomas has noted that:

> Miyazaki's films serve as religious texts that inspire and exhort people to alterations in behavior; they are sometimes used ritually (repetitively, as liturgical texts, as scripture) for edification as well as entertainment. Furthermore, the cosmology and mythology of the films comes [sic] to be interpreted and applied to reality after the films end [sic]. At times this results in audience members recreating rituals in reality that they learned through the film narrative; audience members may also identify certain physical places as sacred because they were the alleged inspiration for sacred places found within the narrative realms of the films themselves... Just as *anime* deploys religious motifs, religious institutions and individuals deploy *anime* as a method of affecting audience outlook and behavior.[120]

Thomas here makes insightful and important points with regards to aficionados and the far-reaching influence that the spiritual and religion content of anime can have on their lives, as a philosophy or an ethical code to guide their decision-making and guide them in life choices.

In this section anime's attraction for Western audiences has been detailed. Particular attention has been given to Park's argument regarding the religious and spiritual content of anime. It has also been argued that this content in anime (borrowed from the major religions) is frequently stripped of sacred meaning and value, so that anime aficionados may devise personal understandings of that content. Yet, some anime may still inspire curiosity in aficionados to investigate particular religious and spiritual elements of the narratives they view. Thus, the

---

119. Miyazaki, quoted in Vincentelli, 'Bittersweet Sympathies'.
120. Jolyon Baraka Thomas, '*Shūkyō Asobi* and Miyazaki Hayao's *Anime*', *Nova Religio: The Journal of Alternative and Emergent Religions* 10.3 (2007): 80.

religious and spiritual content of anime can be understood as a double-edged sword with reference to the Western anime audience. Finally, the attitude of 'spiritual seekership' which has become increasingly common in Western culture since approximately 1980 (though it is detectable from the 1950s onwards) has been established as highly compatible with the religious and spiritual concerns of anime, in that such seekers create their own rituals (which, arguably, is one way to describe cosplay) and combine eclectic beliefs to suit their vision of who they are. Anime aficionados are deeply engaged with the project of creating self-identity and group identity, both of which are key spiritual quests among modern Western seekers.

Anime Pilgrimage

The intimate relationship between pilgrimage (often understood to be a journey specifically mandated within the context of traditional religion) and tourism (often understood to be a journey for personal pleasure and secular pursuits) is widely acknowledged by scholars who work in the field of travel studies. In the context of anime, a phenomenon often referred to as 'anime pilgrimage' or 'anime tourism' has emerged only recently. This activity involves anime aficionados taking time out to travel to the particular places in Japan that feature in anime. This section discusses how these places have become the focus of interest for aficionados, and argues that these trips share a similarity with cosplay performance in the sense that both activities enable fans to experience anime narratives in more immediate and self-transformational ways. Victor Turner's anthropological model of pilgrimage is utilized to interpret 'anime tourism', which will be defined and described, with reference to a range of sites that have become focal points for this fan behaviour. Traditionally, travel has been viewed as an educational and developmental activity, with visits to historical sites, places of natural beauty, and other culturally significant cities or institutions as the important destinations, whereas pilgrimage has been understood to exist only within the context of religion. Yet, as Leah Watkins has observed, the distinction between pilgrimage and tourism is difficult to sustain in Japan, because 'the divisions between sacred and profane, the godly and the worldly, are much less clearly defined'.[121] In contemporary times, new types of tourism have developed, including 'pop-culture

---

121. Leah Watkins, 'Japanese Travel Culture: An Investigation of the Links between Early Japanese Pilgrimage and Modern Japanese Travel Behaviour', *New Zealand Journal of Asian Studies* 10.2 (2008): 93.

tourism, sex tourism, study tourism and ecotourism'.[122] Anime tourism is a subcategory of pop culture tourism. Benjamin Ng, who studied young Hong Kong Chinese fans of Japanese popular culture who travelled to Japan, argues that these tourists were interested in 'locations featured in popular movies, novels, television dramas or other forms of popular culture'.[123]

The respected anime scholar Susan Napier has noted that American youth go on anime tours of Japan, 'visiting such sacred sites as Studio Ghibli or buying the Meiji candy drops highlighted in the anime *Grave of the Fireflies*'.[124] In Australia an 'Otaku-Anime Adventure Program' tour of Tokyo was advertised which included sites such as the Ghibli Museum and Tokyo International Anime Fair.[125] Thus organized tours specifically designed to fulfil the desires of devoted anime aficionados have been developed in response to market demand. Erik Cohen contended that, '[m]odern tourists are sometimes perceived as secular pilgrims in search of authentic experiences, a secular surrogate of the sacred, which they hope to encounter in the course of sightseeing trips'.[126] This is particularly appropriate to anime fans and their special trips to Japan, as they desire to experience something extraordinary that will transform their quotidian lives.

According to Victor Turner, pilgrimage is best understood as a rite of passage, where pilgrims separate from the community and enter a liminoid stage in which they experience sacredness and *communitas*, a special camaraderie among groups of pilgrims.[127] When they re-integrate into the community, the pilgrims (like initiates) have a changed status due to the ritual they have undergone. In the late twentieth and early twenty-first centuries, religiosity and spirituality have been de-coupled from religious institutions, and ritual has become individualistic and focused on self-transformation, through activities that may include participation in anime fandom, including cosplay, fansubbing and anime pilgrimage. Recent scholarship has emphasized that 'spiritual tourism' is a growing phenomenon among Westerners, as they understand journeying to certain destinations (chief among which is India) to be crucial

---

122. Benjamin Wai-ming Ng, 'Hong Kong Young People and Cultural Pilgrimage to Japan: The Role of Japanese Popular Culture', in Janet Cochrane (ed.), *Asian Tourism: Growth and Change* (Amsterdam, Boston and London: Elsevier, 2008), 183.

123. Ng, 'Hong Kong Young People', 183.

124. Napier, 'When Godzilla Speaks', 13.

125. Anon, 'Otaku-Anime Adventure Program', *JTB Global Marketing & Travel Inc.* (2007), flyer.

126. Erik Cohen, 'Pilgrim', in Jafar Jafari (ed.), *Encyclopedia of Tourism* (New York: Routledge, 2000), 438.

127. Turner, 'The Centre Out There', 191-92.

to spiritual development and the project of self-transformation.[128] Thus, Takayoshi Yamamura's statement that anime aficionados consider the sites they visit to be 'holy places' makes perfect sense in the context of contemporary spirituality.[129]

Occasionally, and in harmony with the aims of traditional religious pilgrimage, anime aficionados may contribute to community initiatives through their travels. Anime related trips, therefore, can also be beneficial for the target region as well as personally satisfying for the anime pilgrims. For example, the town of Washimiya (merged with two other towns into already existing city of Kuki, Saitama prefecture) experienced a significant rise in visits after a publicity campaign about 'the town as the "sacred place" for [the] *Lucky Star*' anime.[130] Due to aficionados visiting this place, six characters from *Lucky Star*, the Hiiragi family, were given 'certificates of residence' in 'a special ceremony', which demonstrates how far communities are willing to go to make aficionados happy, and reap the benefits of their presence.[131] The release of the anime *Yosuga no Sora* had a significant impact on tourism in the Ashikaga region.[132] These areas in Japan, which are portrayed in anime and have become a place of allure to aficionados, are termed 'Mecca[s] for Anime Fans'.[133] Other places of noteworthy anime pilgrimage in Japan include: Nishinomiya city, featured in *The Melancholy of Haruhi Suzumiya*; Nanto city, featured in the *True Tears* anime; and Ōmachi city (Nagano Prefecture), featured in the *Please Teacher* and *Please Twins* anime.[134] Jolyon Baraka Thomas notes that a small Hikawa Shrine in Tokyo, 'the model for a homophonous shrine... featured in the Sailor Moon series has become the focus of fans' religious devotion'.[135] Anime pilgrimage sites are thus scattered around the whole of the Japanese archipelago. It is recognized that certain anime (for example, Miyazaki's *Porco Rosso*, which is set in Europe) are located in places other than Japan. However, to date there is no anime pilgrimage to any site situated outside of Japan.

---

128. Alex Norman, *Spiritual Tourism: Travel and Religious Practice in Western Society* (London and New York: Continuum, 2011).
129. Yamamura, 'Anime Pilgrimage and Local Pilgrimage Promotion', 4.
130. Yamamura, 'Anime Pilgrimage and Local Pilgrimage Promotion', 4.
131. Yamamura, 'Anime Pilgrimage and Local Pilgrimage Promotion', 5.
132. Felicity Hughes, 'Anime Fan Pilgrimages Help Boost Tourism', *Japan Times Online* (*Japan Pulse*) (2010), at http://blog.japantimes.co.jp/japan-pulse/anime-fan-pilgrimages-help-boost-tourism (accessed 9 February 2012).
133. Takeshi Okamoto, 'A Study on Impact of Anime on Tourism in Japan: A Case of "Anime Pilgrimage"', *Web-Journal of Tourism and Cultural Studies* 013 (2009): 1, at http://hdl.handle.net/2115/38539 (accessed 7 May 2011).
134. Okamoto, 'A Study on Impact of Anime on Tourism in Japan', 2.
135. Thomas, *Drawing on Tradition*, 76.

Nobuharu Imai has drawn attention to a particular problem that arises for anime aficionados who desire to visit sites regarded as sacred in Japan. Often, anime (which are, after all, animated fictions) are not set in easily identifiable 'real' places, and fans must exercise considerable imaginative energy in determining the precise locations of their pilgrimage journeys:

> [f]ilm tourism is generally organized through travel agencies; however, this is not the case for 'sacred journeys' in *Otaku* culture as locations of animation works are not usually divulged to the general public. *Otaku*, therefore, must look for the location by themselves. On this point, as it is difficult to single-handedly identify a location, *Otaku* rely upon the help of their internet networks... [A]fter an animation is broadcast, *Otaku* exchange their impressions and discuss the location of the work in their personal blogs, bulletin board systems or Social Network Services.[136]

Yet certain pilgrimages popular with anime fans are assisted by official bodies, such as the Japan National Tourism Organization (JNTO), which promotes a 'Japan Anime Map' featuring various anime-related destinations of significance.[137] However, these sites tend not to be the specific settings of anime series and films, but are rather museums, galleries and theme parks that celebrate and archive the imaginative works of anime *auteurs*, such as 'Osamu Tezuka...Shigeru Mizuki, the Hello Kitty brand and, of course, Studio Ghibli's Art Museum'.[138]

Museums are an important part of anime aficionados' travel, as are events such as Expo 2005, at which one of the attractions was a replica of the house in which the characters Satsuki, Mei and their father, from Hayao Miyazaki's *My Neighbour Totoro* (1988), lived.[139] This expo was held seventeen years after that film was released, which is a testimony to the strength and long-lasting popularity of Miyazaki's work. The JNTO markets other opportunities for aficionados to engage with the series or films of their choice. For example, on the JNTO website it is stated: 'The Melancholy of Haruhi Suzumiya is mainly set in various places in Kansai region including Nishinomiya City, Hyōgo Prefecture. Many locales are found especially around the stations of Hankyu Railway', and

---

136. Nobuharu Imai, 'The Momentary and Placeless Community: Constructing a New Community with regards to Otaku Culture', *Inter Faculty* 1 (2010), at https://journal.hass.tsukuba.ac.jp/interfaculty/article/viewFile/9/25 (accessed 18 May 2011).

137. Anon, 'Japan Anime Map', *Japan National Tourism Organization* (n.d.), at http://www.jnto.go.jp/eng/animemap (accessed 7 February 2012).

138. Rayna Denison, 'Anime Tourism: Discursive Construction and Reception of the Studio Ghibli Art Museum', *Japan Forum* 22.3-4 (2010): 547.

139. Anon, '2005 World Exposition, Aichi, Japan Video Clips', *The Ministry of Foreign Affairs of Japan* (English language) (2005), at http://www.mofa.go.jp/j_info/expo2005/video.html (accessed 6 February 2012).

offered as a specific attractant the information that in Nishinomiya City cosplayers can be encountered at certain locations.[140] The website further advertises another particular place: '[t]he outdoor stage in Kabutoyama Forest Park (Kabutoyama Shinrin-koen) where Yuki Nagato and Mikuru Asahina, two SOS Brigade members, battled for the first time is well-known among the fans', as a site that has the potential to be meaningful for aficionados.[141] It is emphasized to fans that anime creators have found inspiration for their work in many unusual places; in the case of *Spirited Away* (2001), Miyazaki 'visited the Edo-Tokyo Tatemono-en (Open Air Architectural Museum) in western Tokyo's Koganei Park. He found magic in its snippets of the city's built history, from 200-year-old farmhouses to a 1960s streetcar'.[142] Aficionados, too, can be inspired by the assemblage of historical buildings at the museum, which is presented very much like a film studio, filled with 'sets' from different periods of Japan's history.

The argument of this section is that the aficionados' visits to these places is motivated by the desire to enter the fictional world of anime narratives that often contain magical elements. This contention is supported by the JNTO website, on which it is noted that '[t]he main thrill that visitors derive from going to such locations is the feeling of blending right in to the story when they see the actual scenery or buildings depicted in anime'.[143] This is analogous to the desire of traditional religious pilgrims to connect with the events and personalities from their religion associated with the place of pilgrimage (for example, Christians becoming immersed in the Greco-Roman era and focused on personages from the New Testament when visiting the Middle East and the Holy Land in particular). The Japanese word *junrei* (pilgrimage)[144] is usually used by aficionados in the combined term *seichi junrei*, meaning 'sacred pilgrimage'.[145] Although the sites visited in anime pilgrimage 'are not

---

140. Anon, 'Pilgrimage to Sacred Places – Anime, Manga & Games: The Melancholy of Haruhi Suzumiya', *Japan National Tourism Organization* (n.d.), at http://www.jnto.go.jp/eng/indepth/cultural/pilgrimage/haruhi.html (accessed 6 February 2012).

141. Anon, 'Pilgrimage to Sacred Places – Anime, Manga & Games'.

142. John McGee, 'Edo-Tokyo Open Air Architectural Museum', *Metropolis* (*Japan's Number 1 English Magazine*) (n.d.), at http://archive.metropolis.co.jp/tokyo/497/art.asp (accessed 7 February 2012).

143. Anon, 'Exotic Experience – Scenery Look Familiar? Visiting Locations for Famous Anime', *Japan National Tourism Organization* (n.d.), at http://www.jnto.go.jp/eng/indepth/exotic/JapanesQue/amusing/201102_indight.html (accessed 8 February 2012).

144. Frank Brinkley, *Brinkley's Japanese-English Dictionary*, vol. 1 (Cambridge: W. Heffer and Sons, 1963), 512.

145. Takamasa Sakurai, 'Looking East: Making the Otaku Pilgrimage', *The Daily*

traditional holy sites',[146] these travels nevertheless have a very special meaning. In many anime supernatural and transformative events occur in ordinary settings, for instance a high school. In Chapter 2 it was argued that the profane everyday world and the sacred supernatural world are closely linked in Japan, due to the pervasiveness of Shintō, a religious tradition that teaches that everything is alive, suffused with divinity, and interconnected. Anime protagonists are often ordinary teenagers who may have supernatural powers or be chosen for a special role, often as a saviour. This type of protagonist, a teenage boy or girl, is a relevant role model for many young members of the anime audience. Consequently, visiting places in Japan that are locations in anime featuring this type of protagonist can be one of the motivating factors in the quest to merge, symbolically speaking, with the diegetic world of the anime story.

Dōgo Onsen is a famous hot springs complex in Ehime Prefecture on the island of Shikoku that has been in use for over a thousand years. This bathhouse complex was featured in Miyazaki's *Spirited Away* (2001), when the heroine Chihiro visits the hot spring,[147] causing it to become an attractive site for anime aficionados. Hiromasa Yonebayashi's film, *The Secret World of Arrietty* (2010), was scripted by Miyazaki and is based on the children's novel *The Borrowers*, published in 1952 by the English author Mary Norton. The setting for this anime was based on Seibien in Hirakawa, Aomori Prefecture, which was completed in 1911 by Moriyoshi Seitou, 'a powerful local figure and landowner'.[148] The architectural style of the building, called the Seibikan, is a combination of 'pure Japanese sukiya style' (on the lower level) and the Western Renaissance style on the upper level.[149] Fourteen thousand tourists came to Seibien estate in 2009, but after the release of *The Secret World of Arrietty* fourteen thousand visitors arrived in one twenty-day period, according to the estate manager Katsuhiko Kasai.[150]

Anime aficionados who journey to the real settings of anime films and series are uniquely able to appreciate various aspects of Japanese heritage in immediate and experiential ways. Hideaki Anno's *Neon Genesis Evangelion* (1995–1996) is one of the best-known and influential anime series for Western viewers, and it also has pilgrimage locations. The futuristic site

---

Yomiuri (2011), at http://www.yomiuri.co.jp/dy/features/arts/T110506004050.htm (accessed 8 February 2012).

146. Sakurai, 'Looking East'.

147. Anon, 'Anime in Real Time', *Official Tourism Guide for Japan Travel* (n.d.), at http://www.japantravelinfo.com/popculture/anime.php?a=1 (accessed 8 February 2012).

148. Anon, 'Exotic Experience'.

149. Anon, 'Exotic Experience'.

150. Anon, 'Exotic Experience'.

Tokyo-3, where much of the story of NGE takes place, is based on '[t]he Sengokubara district in the northwest corner of Hakone', a hot springs resort which is not far from Tokyo.[151] For anime aficionados interested in locations that feature in Neon Genesis Evangelion there is even 'an English-language map of actual places that appear in the anime':[152]

> [t]he map describes 19 famous locations in Hakone: beautiful Lake Ashi; Hakone Shrine, with its red *torii* gate reflected in the calm lake waters; Owakudani, a barren region of steam fissures and boiling ponds that is living evidence of volcanic eruptions from 400,000 years ago; the Hakone Cable Car and the Hakone Tozan Train that carry visitors through the air and up and down mountain slopes. This is where the story of giant robot Evangelions and the mysterious enemy Angels unfolds and where they carry out their epic battles.[153]

Visiting such sites has the potential to have a long-lasting impression on devoted fans. There are institutional reasons why the travels of anime aficionados are so readily characterized as pilgrimages. Ian Reader, a scholar of Japanese religious pilgrimage, particularly the Shikoku circuit, argues that the contemporary Japanese media reports on pilgrimage only when:

> pilgrimage is treated, in media terms, as a cultural community and an aspect of Japanese heritage. As such, media interest and positive reporting of pilgrimage occurs in a context in which pilgrimage has been discreetly detached from religion as an organised, faith-centred entity, and assigned to the realm of culture.[154]

This can be demonstrated with reference to Internet forums where anime aficionados discuss their special journeys, answering each other's questions and giving advice about these journeys.

One representative website is *Punynari's Island Adventures*, which is a travel blog set in Hawai'i and Japan established in 2008 by a male anime aficionado in his late twenties. Punynari is passionate about anime and travel, with a penchant for the supernatural, and describes himself as having 'always had a "spirit of an adventurer" – to climb the highest mountain, to explore the darkest cave, to venture into the unknown, to investigate ghost stories, to go everywhere to say "I have been there"'.[155] His anime pilgrimages are recorded in extensive photographic essays in

---

151. Anon, 'Exotic Experience'.
152. Anon, 'Exotic Experience'.
153. Anon, 'Exotic Experience'.
154. Ian Reader, 'Positively Promoting Pilgrimage: Media Representations of Pilgrimage in Japan', *Nova Religio* 10.3 (2006): 27.
155. Punynari, 'Anime Pilgrimages', *Punynari's Island Adventures* (2012), at http://punynari.wordpress.com/anime-pilgrimages (accessed 21 December 2012).

which he posts scenes from certain of his favourite anime and recreates those scenes in photographs taken on his travels; that is he has found the exact locations that the animators have drawn and memorialized them through photography (which is congruent with the documentation of cosplay performance in photographs discussed earlier). There is no doubt that these journeys are personally and spiritually important to him; he states that '[b]y going on these pilgrimages, I feel closer to the anime characters because it feels like I have entered their world'. One example will be given here of an anime pilgrimage. Punynari enthuses that:

> *Evangelion* was the first anime I have ever watched and till this day, it remains my favorite anime of all time. I was actually watching *Eva* before dvds and even before fansubs. I actually had to order the fan-subbed vhs tapes through the mail back in the day. Needless to say, I am what you would call an *Evangelion* fanboy... So, naturally, when I heard Tokyo 3 was based in the Hakone area I decided to undertake the daunting *Evangelion* anime pilgrimage a bit at a time.[156]

The pilgrimage he undertook is chronicled in a lengthy, lavishly illustrated three-part essay, which covers actual physical locations, maps and aids for the Western fan, and a detailed account of the theme park 'Evangelion World'. There he photographed cosplay girls and experienced 'geek' moments, as he entered the world of his favourite anime:

> I could hear Eva Unit 01 roaring and shaking the walls. It was time to see Unit 01 with my own eyes. The same feelings of excitement that I had when viewing the life-sized *Gundam* were with me now. Although, the excitement was greater then [sic] with *Gundam*. I am only lightly into *Gundam*, but am in love with the *Evangelion* series and the world that they live in (as troublesome as it is).[157]

Punynari's dedication to anime is revealed by the extensive pilgrimages he has made (on his blog to date there are seventeen distinct anime on which he has built devotional travel).

Many sites in Japan attract anime aficionados such as Punynari. With regards to Miyazaki's *Princess Mononoke,* the Aomori area's archaic woodlands feature in this work and in order to depict such typical Japanese landscape there were organized '[s]ketching sessions' for the artists in the Shirakami Mountains.[158] This is another example of pilgrimage destination for anime aficionados that is a site of great natural beauty. It is interesting to note that as well as Aomori area's ancient forests, Yakushima

---

156. Punynari, 'Anime Pilgrimages'.
157. Punynari, 'Anime Pilgrimages'.
158. Anon, 'Anime in Real Time'.

(Island), south 'of the Osumi Peninsula in the Kagoshima prefecture' also features in *Princess Mononoke*.[159] Anime artists may seek sources for their works closer to everyday life: Naoko Takeuchi, the creator of *Sailor Moon* and a Tokyo resident, drew upon the Azabu Jūban district of Tokyo for inspiration, and the female characters from *Sailor Moon* also spend time together in the affluent Roppongi district, a culturally distinctive 'social center of Japan'.[160] Shintō shrines also become targets for anime pilgrimage. In the anime *Kure-nai* (English 'Crimson', 2008) the Maruho Shrine is featured; this shrine was based on the Kaichu Inari Shrine in Shinjuku, Tokyo. Similarly, the Raifuku Shrine from *Kamichu!* (English 'Teenage Goddess') was based on two shrines, the Misode Tenmangu Shrine and the Ushitora Shrine; while *Please Twins!* featured a shrine based on the Kamisuwa Shrine in the Nagano Prefecture.[161] The importance of Shintō shrines was discussed in Chapter 2.

Nerima City is another important location, because, as Toshirō Shimura (the Mayor of Nerima City) has stated, both the *Astro Boy* series and the film *Legend of the White Serpent* (1958) were produced in Nerima, where there are over ninety anime studios.[162] However, as yet Nerima has attracted few pilgrims. The Toei Animation Gallery, a project of Tōei Dōga studios (Toei Animation Co., Ltd.), is one venue suggested for anime pilgrimage in Nerima.[163] Other venues that are listed as sites of interest to anime pilgrimage are galleries, museums and similar institutions. Ghibli Studio (in Mitaka), Osamu Tezuka World (in Kyōto), Osamu Tezuka Memorial Hall (in Takarazuka City), and Ishinomaki Mangattan Museum (in Ishinomaki City) are all recommended as sites of potential transformative power.[164] Furthermore, in Japan there are sites where large sculptures of anime characters, such as Tetsujin 28 (Gigantor), Laputa Sentinel and Mobile Suite Gundam RX-78, have been erected,[165] and these are also places that hold a particular interest for aficionados. The statues of Tetsujin 28 and Mobile Suit Gundam RX-78 are a little over 18 metres tall, while LaPuta

---

159. Anon, 'Anime in Real Time'.
160. Anon, 'Anime in Real Time'.
161. Anon, 'Visit Anime Spots', *att. Japan* 45 (2009), at http://www.att-japan.net/modules/tinyd1/rewrite/tc_84.html (accessed 25 February 2012).
162. Toshirō Shimura, 'Greeting – Birthplace of Japanese Animation, Nerima City', Nerima Animation Site (2010), at http://www.animation-nerima.jp/eng/greeting.html (accessed 9 February 2012).
163. Anon, 'Animania Festival'.
164. Anon, 'An Invitation to an "Otaku" Tour – Visiting the Great Masters of Japanese Animation', *Japan National Tourism Organization* (n.d.), at http://www.jnto.go.jp/eng/indepth/exotic/animation/d4_great.html (accessed 9 February 2012).
165. Matt Alt, 'Make a Pilgrimage to Robot Mecha', *Wired* (2009), at http://www.wired.com/magazine/tag/robots (accessed 8 February 2012).

Sentinel from Miyazaki's *oeuvre* is nearly 5 metres high.[166] Matt Alt has stated that Tetsujin 28 is in 'Wakamatsu Park, in the Nagata ward of Kobe', while Laputa Sentinel is in '[t]he Ghibli Museum in a Tokyo suburb', and Mobile Suit Gundam RX-78 is in 'Fuji-Q Highland park, near Mount Fuji'.[167] For those anime aficionados who travel to see the Mobile Suit Gundam RX-78 statue, '[i]f fans complete a data-collecting game, they are granted access to nerdvana (the cockpit in its chest)'.[168] Thus, the trip to see this anime character offers an additional special experience. Punynari, discussed above, has recorded that he has viewed this large Gundam statue.

Reflecting on personal anime pilgrimage experience Takamasa Sakurai explained that, '[v]isiting a real location that was featured in an animated series makes me feel like I'm standing at the intersection of the two- and three-dimensional worlds. I think this is the charm of such pilgrimages'.[169] Sakurai gives credit for this special experience to the artists who created the work, by acknowledging that those who enabled aficionados to 'partake in this unusual feeling' at the pilgrimage venues are 'the artistic talents' that stand behind the work.[170] It is interesting to note how strongly aficionados can empathise with anime characters. That is, while it appears that it may be easier to empathise with a human actor than a cartoon character, anime aficionados have found a way to do it with ease, indicating that anime narrative has considerable potential to make a special impression on its audience.

As at traditional religious pilgrimage sites various objects that have a special meaning for pilgrims (pictures, and so on) are available for purchase; similarly, there are also items that are available for purchase by anime aficionados during their anime pilgrimages. Akihabara is one of the most popular neighbourhoods where anime aficionados can purchase items of interest. Various anime-related items are often available to aficionados: for example, '[a] limited-edition K-On! Choco Snack' was marketed to fans of the anime *K-On!* along with many other inexpensive items including, 'special *yaki-soba* sandwiches, cold cocoa drinks, sticker sets and caramel corn. Fan can also accumulate points by buying Gogo no Kocha drinks, which then qualifies them to win lottery prizes that include T-shirts, K-On! figurines and a custom-made electric guitar'.[171] Traditional religious souvenirs are part of consumer culture, like the fan-oriented merchandise beloved of anime aficionados,

---

166. Alt, 'Make a Pilgrimage to Robot Mecha'.
167. Alt, 'Make a Pilgrimage to Robot Mecha'.
168. Alt, 'Make a Pilgrimage to Robot Mecha'.
169. Sakurai, 'Looking East'.
170. Sakurai, 'Looking East'.
171. Felicity Hughes, 'Some Konbeni Snacks with Your Favourite Anime?', *Japan*

but such purchases could be understood as a means to take away a tiny piece of a special location, which will serve as a reminder of the pilgrimage journey, and thus helps create the special connection between the devotee and that place.

The word 'pilgrimage' traditionally refers to the sacred journeys and visits of a religious devotee to places that have spiritual meaning because they were associated with a particular holy person or an event important to the religion. These religious devotees experience past events related to those places through the activity of visiting. They also visit such places in search of spiritual purification, healing, prayer and forgiveness. Anime 'pilgrimage' is not pilgrimage in that traditional sense. Yet, visiting locations portrayed in anime has the potential, symbolically speaking, to bring anime aficionados to the alternative world of anime. They recall what anime character(s) did at that particular place, how they felt in the situation they experienced at that time in the story, and so on. This encounter crosses the boundaries of time, space, the real and unreal; it is not an everyday or mundane experience. Thus, it is more helpful to think about religious pilgrimage and touristic activities as points along a continuum, which may be more or less spiritual, depending on the pilgrim or tourist. The sociologist Erik Cohen has suggested that the basic issue for evaluating the travel was 'the degree to which [the traveller's] journey represents a "quest for the centre," and the nature of that centre'.[172] He developed a typology of the tourist experience which detailed five possible attitudes to the 'centre': (1) the Recreational tourist is committed to his or her own culture as the centre and travel is just an enjoyable 'vacation' from it; (2) the Diversionary tourist is less committed to his or her own culture as centre, and travel is 'the meaningless pleasure of a centre-less person';[173] (3) the Experiential tourist is alienated from his or her culture and seeks to 'recapture meaning by a vicarious, essentially aesthetic, experience of the authenticity of others'; (4) the Experimental tourist 'is in "search of himself," insofar as...he seeks to discover that form of life which elicits a resonance in himself... His is essentially a religious quest, but diffuse'; and (5) the Existential tourist is committed to an elective 'centre', and may:

> live in two worlds: the world of their everyday life, where they follow their practical pursuits, which for them is devoid of deeper meaning; and the world of their 'elective' centre, to which they will depart on periodical pilgrimage to derive spiritual sustenance... the tourist

---

Times Online (Japan Pulse) (2010), at http://blog.japantimes.co.jp/japan-pulse/some-konbeni-snacks-with-your-favorite-anime (accessed 9 February 2012).

172. Erik Cohen, 'A Phenomenology of Tourist Experiences', *Sociology* 13 (1979): 183.
173. Cohen, 'A Phenomenology of Tourist Experiences', 186.

travelling in the existential mode is phenomenologically analogous to a pilgrimage.[174]

Existential tourists are therefore in exile when they are not living in their elective centre. Thus Cohen equated existential tourism with pilgrimage and a religious or spiritual quest, which is realized through finding one's true 'self' via experiences of authenticity, all of which is entirely congruent with the process of anime pilgrimage described in this chapter. The fact that anime aficionados travel specifically to see special places indicates how much they are drawn to that particular anime story, its events and characters, and the importance they attach to having authentic experiences in Japan itself.

This section has discussed anime aficionados' travel activities, referred to by scholars and fans alike as 'anime tourism', 'anime pilgrimage' and *seichi junrei* ('sacred pilgrimage'). The use of 'pilgrimage' signifies that these trips are not ordinary holidays for anime aficionados, but possess spiritual meaning and value for them, although not in a strict, institutionally religious sense. Similarly to the experience of cosplay discussed earlier, it is here argued that aficionados' pilgrimage also can represent, symbolically, the breaking of the boundaries between the diegetic and non-diegetic worlds, offering fans the possibility to merge into the alternative reality in which the anime characters live. However, as noted previously, aficionados are not only drawn to characters, but also the events and situations that anime characters experience, which may have some otherworldly, supernatural dimension. The empathy with the anime characters and the story, which aficionados experience during their pilgrimage, is not only stimulated through the sense of sight and hearing that is experienced while watching anime on screen.

Thus far this chapter has considered the influence of anime on Western aficionados, and the comparative research concerning *Star Trek* similarly has focused on Western fans. In conclusion, the reverse scenario will be briefly sketched. Jeff Greenwald's research for *Future Perfect: How Star Trek Conquered Planet Earth* (1998) took him to Japan, where Torekkis (Japanese Trekkies) discussed frankly their love of the series and the films, and the ways in which *Star Trek* (for them) exemplifies Japanese values. Shigenobu Ito tells Greenwald that the atmosphere on the 'Enterprise' reflects the Japanese notion of *wa* (the balance between stability, *dou*, and action, *sei*). In *The Original Series* these values were expressed in Spock and Kirk, respectively, whereas in *Next Generation* they are incarnated in Picard and Riker.[175] Many fans informed him that android Data

---

174. Cohen, 'A Phenomenology of Tourist Experiences', 190.
175. Greenwald, *Future Perfect*, 209.

(played by Brent Spiner) has a 'Japanese personality', 'looks Japanese', and in his longing to be human parallels the Japanese desire 'to follow Western ways... [though] we are not Western'.[176] The Torekkis' love of technology, space travel and the 'Enterprise' specifically elicited one profound conversation between Greenwald and Torekki Mr Murata that effectively summarizes the argument of this book:

> It has been said, Murata elaborates poetically, that over eight million gods live in Japan. Everything, every object, holds a bit of god within. 'There is a Japanese expression: "After ninety-nine years of use, a thing becomes alive." Thus, there is the idea that the *Enterprise* itself is alive. That is because love causes a thing to live. In the case of the *Enterprise*, it is the love of the captains – and of engineers Scotty and Geordi LaForge – that brings the ship to life'. A sweet sentiment, I reflect, but vaguely disturbing. 'What you just said now, about things becoming alive, after ninety-nine years...' I lean across the now-empty beef platter. 'Is the same thing true of plastic sushi?' Murata leans towards me in turn, and furrows his brow. '*Especially* of plastic sushi'.[177]

This remarkable exchange identified a profound difference between Japanese fans of *Star Trek* and the anime aficionados discussed in this chapter. When Japanese Torekkis view the Western popular cultural product that is *Star Trek*, they read it through the lens of Shintō, Buddhism, and Japanese culture, and discover that it powerfully embodies their own value systems. When anime aficionados lose themselves in the alternative world of anime, it is precisely this strangeness, the Japanese emphasis on the divine life present in everything and the blurred boundaries between the natural, supernatural, technological, flesh and machinery that attracts them. They do not view anime through the lens of Western or Christian values, but rather are embracive of the religious and spiritual values that pervade Japanese culture.

Conclusion

This chapter has focused on the devotion of Western anime aficionados, arguing that its momentum and strength have continuously increased. A considerable amount of credit for this goes to the aficionados themselves and a range of unconventional initiatives they pioneered from the 1980s onwards. Over time, anime has acquired a high level of recognition and acceptance as an art form and as entertainment, and it is likely that its cultural penetration of the West will continue to grow in the twenty-first century. A number of fan activities have also been analysed.

---

176. Greenwald, *Future Perfect*, 203-205.
177. Greenwald, *Future Perfect*, 203.

It has been argued that cosplay can be interpreted as an expression of the desire on the part of aficionados to enter into the diegetic world of anime, their narratives and events, which are often supernatural or otherworldly. This signals that one of the reasons for the popularity of anime is their religious and spiritual content. In the West, so-called 'spiritual seekers' search for re-enchantment and an escape from the mundane world. Popular culture often informs such quests, and the chapter discussed *Star Trek* fandom as a phenomenon analogous to the fan behaviours of anime aficionados, and as a similar type of imaginative devotion that may create individual and communal meaning.

While it is acknowledged that many anime aficionados develop personal understandings of religious motifs and spiritual traditions in anime that do not reflect the teachings of the actual religions (Christianity, Shintō, Buddhism and so on), some fans become immersed in the Japanese language and culture and become well-informed about the mythological and folkoric content of the films and television series they love. Many fans travel to Japan in order to visit the real locations that are portrayed in anime. These journeys possess special meaning for anime aficionados, and are often referred to as 'anime pilgrimages'. It has been argued that this type of travel, similarly to the act of cosplaying, represents the desire to enter the alternative reality of anime, and to experience their otherworldly events and remarkable characters.

Conclusion:
Profane and Sacred Worlds in Anime

> Ohana Matsumae: '[a] wish card?' Enishi Shijimia (Ohana's uncle): '[i]f you write your wish on it and tie it to the *bonbori*, a god will use it to illuminate his path home back to Izumo, and in return, he'll grant you your wish' (from anime series *Blossoms for Tomorrow*, episode 'A Tearful Chef Romance').

It should come as no surprise that Japan's rich spiritual and religious traditions have contributed significantly to the development of the anime art form, which is now one of the most prestigious global artistic forms in the early twenty-first century. Yet the mosaic of the anime world is built up largely from elements of specifically Japanese spiritual and religious traditions, mythology and folklore, and depicts settings and eras of time that are recognizable as originating in Japan.[1] These settings include the historical past and the imagined future; they may be realistic and mundane, or fantastic and supernaturally-oriented. The references to religion and spirituality are often portrayed in an implicit and subtle way, rather than in an explicit fashion, and focus on the natural world or the notion that everything in existence possesses life and personhood. Some directors do employ explicit religious references, borrowing from various world religions and indigenous traditions, for instance Christianity, Judaism, Hinduism, Buddhism and Shintō. Often the spiritual content that manifests combines elements from a number of traditions, just as the visual style and narratives of anime may also draw upon Western sources; the importance of American cartoons (like Walt Disney's *Mickey Mouse*), and stories drawn from European literature (including Victor Hugo's *Les Misérables*) being just two examples.

The dialogue from *Blossoms for Tomorrow* (2011) quoted above references an anime explicitly engaged with the religious beliefs and practices of Shintō. Activities performed at the Izumo Shrine, religious occasions such as the Bonbori Festival, and a range of cultural references that would be familiar to every Japanese child are manifested in the tale of Ohana Matsumae and her relationship with her grandmother the innkeeper. Viewing this anime is an educational experience

---

1. Thomas, *Drawing on Tradition*, 8-12.

for Western anime audiences, to whom the Shintō religion is unfamiliar. Mamoru Oshii's *Angel's Egg* (1985) has been analysed as a mysterious, minimalist anime in which biblical texts (particularly the account of Noah's survival of the Great Flood from the Old Testament) are charged with significance, and which also presents a world in which religion and faith are absent, or diminished. In Shōji Kawamori's anime series *Arjuna* (2001), the tale of schoolgirl Juna who possesses a special quality called 'Earth Sympathy' and has a mission to help the planet, the telepath called Cindy speaks of an ancient priest who shared Juna's ability to tune into the experiences of the Earth:

> Long ago, in ancient times…one of those chosen as a priest of the gods… set out alone into the catacombs…below the shrine of the goddess of fertility. He survived for many days without water or food. And during that time…his duty was to report all of the happenings…in the world that he sensed by resonating with the planet (episode 'Tears of the Forest').

These are but a few examples of the great richness of religious and spiritual motifs and themes in anime, which often feature plots that are apocalyptic and protagonists with supernatural powers whose destiny it is to save the planet, humanity, or indeed the whole universe through courage and heroism.[2]

Chapter 1 argued that Japanese art styles, both religious and secular, which developed over approximately a thousand years, contributed to the aesthetic of both modern manga and anime. After Japan opened to the West in the mid-nineteenth century, Japanese cartoonists became familiar with Western comic books. While it is acknowledged that Western influence is noticeable in modern manga and anime, the main sources of inspiration are of Japanese origin, and these include the animistic sensibility of Shintō and specifically Japanese forms of Buddhism. Chapter 1 concluded with a brief discussion of contemporary religion and spirituality, and how these new spiritual forms related to popular culture and consumerism. It was argued that as the West 'Easternises', the East is engaged in a parallel process of 'Westernisation',[3] which is reflected in popular culture such as anime (which is produced in Japan but appeals powerfully to Western audiences, as well as to fans in Asia).

Chapter 2 briefly discussed motifs and themes from Buddhism, Christianity and new religions, while special attention was given to Shintō and its profound contribution to Japanese culture. The *kami*, that is, divine spirits, and the supernatural in general are the focus of Shintō, and references to them frequently appear in manga and anime. Animism and

---

2. Garnar, 'It's the End of the Species as We Know It', 287-99.
3. Campbell, 'Easternisation of the West', 35-49.

anthropomorphism were used as methodological lenses to comprehend the use of supernatural material in manga and anime, such as animal transformations and the attribution of life or divine presence in inanimate objects such as rocks, mountains and dolls, and also in machines and technological innovations, including robots and the Internet. A range of supernatural creatures and mythological beings (including extraterrestrials, angels, *kappa*, *oni*, and others) were documented in terms of the roles they play in anime plots.

Chapter 3 identified numerous genres and subgenres that feature in anime, and the formation of generic hybrids that is now the norm in anime. Generic hybrids increase the likelihood that certain anime will appeal to many different audiences. It was further argued that in multiple genres and generic hybrids, there are elements present of the supernatural, suggesting that this subgenre is a favourite with audiences. The elements of this subgenre borrow substantially from world religions and mythologies. It was noted that the presence of a supernatural subgenre is detectable even in anime with realistic subject matter, such as tragedy. It was contended that these supernatural elements may function as a metaphor for the celebration of the human spirit despite misfortunes, or as a symbol with soteriological overtones. Chapter 3 has also compared the Japanese sun goddess Amaterasu and the Western nature goddess, and the child protagonist in anime and the 'divine child' of mythology, with particular reference to the works of Mamoru Oshii and Hayao Miyazaki.

Numerous anime aficionados are today found in the Western world, and they were the focus of Chapter 4. Anime can trigger an interest among fans in the language and culture of Japan. Two activities of anime aficionados were given particular attention: cosplaying and travel to 'sacred' sites in Japan that are portrayed in anime. In this context it was argued that both of these activities fulfil the desire of anime aficionados to enter into the alternative reality of anime, to be transformed as individuals and to experience a world beyond mundane everyday life. While watching anime, aficionados empathise with the story and going on pilgrimage visits to anime sacred sites has the potential to enrich that experience through physically encountering the 'real' world of anime. Research on *Star Trek* fandom was compared to similar studies of anime aficionados, with strong parallels being noted and analysed.[4] Western 'spiritual seekers' are attracted to the religious content of anime, even when they know little about the religions in question (chiefly Buddhism, Shintō, and Christianity), and they tend to construct highly personal and individualized meaning from the religious motifs and themes,

---

4. Jindra, '*Star Trek* Fandom', 27-51.

usually related to their individual identity or to the identity of the fan community to which they belong.

This study has approached anime from the point of view of both producers and consumers, analysing the employment of spiritual and religious motifs by directors, and the reception of this content by fans. The mutual imbrication of the profane and sacred worlds in anime, along with the profound reciprocal relationship between 'Eastern' (Japanese) and 'Western' (chiefly American) culture in the development of the anime artistic form, form the twin narrative arcs of the book. The appeal of anime to aficionados is, broadly speaking, the appeal of the spiritual in a post-religious world, in which personal identity and meaning in life may be crafted from popular cultural texts which offer an immersive and enchanting experience that, for many in the modern world, is more thrilling and authentic than 'real life'. In the past, religions posited that after human existence on earth had ceased, the individual soul would be reincarnated again, or perhaps would reside in heaven. In the early twenty-first century, spiritual seekers still ardently desire a life beyond that of everyday reality, and just as passionately believe in the existence of other worlds and the afterlife. However, the other worlds are the fantasy landscapes and outer-space settings of anime (and other popular cultural forms), and the afterlife the digital circuitry and electronic impulses of the Internet. These important new understandings of religion and the spiritual underpin anime's status as a major site of new religious and spiritual inspiration in the West, and, indeed, the world.

Bibliography

Abbitt, Erica Stevens. 'Androgyny and Otherness: Exploring the West through the Japanese Performative Body'. *Asian Theatre Journal* 18.2 (2001): 249-56.
Addison, James Thayer. 'Religious Life in Japan'. *Harvard Theological Review* 18.4 (1925): 321-56.
Addiss, Stephen. *Zenga and Nanga: Paintings by Japanese Monks and Scholars*. New Orleans: New Orleans Museum of Art, 1976.
Allison, Anne. *Millennial Monsters: Japanese Toys and the Global Imagination*. Berkeley, Los Angeles and London: University of California Press, 2006.
Alt, Matt. 'Make a Pilgrimage to Robot Mecha'. *Wired* (2009), at http://www.wired.com/magazine/tag/robots (accessed 8 February 2012).
Anderson, Richard. 'Vengeful Ancestors and Anima Spirits: Personal Narratives of the Supernatural in a Japanese New Religion'. *Folklore* 54.2 (1995): 112-40.
Anon. 'Pilgrimage to Sacred Places – Anime, Manga & Games: The Melancholy of Haruhi Suzumiya'. *Japan National Tourism Organization* (n.d.), at http://www.jnto.go.jp/eng/indepth/cultural/pilgrimage/haruhi.html (accessed 6 February 2012).
Anon. 'Exotic Experience – Scenery Look Familiar? Visiting Locations for Famous Anime'. *Japan National Tourism Organization* (n.d.), at http://www.jnto.go.jp/eng/indepth/exotic/JapanesQue/amusing/201102_indight.html (accessed 8 February 2012).
Anon. 'An Invitation to an "Otaku" Tour – Visiting the Great Masters of Japanese Animation'. *Japan National Tourism Organization* (n.d.), at http://www.jnto.go.jp/eng/indepth/exotic/animation/d4_great.html (accessed 9 February 2012).
Anon. 'Japan Anime Map'. *Japan National Tourism Organization* (n.d.), at http://www.jnto.go.jp/eng/animemap (accessed 7 February 2012).
Anon. 'Animania Festival'. *About Animania* (n.d.), at http://animania.net.au/2011/animania (accessed 28 April 2011).
Anon. 'Anime in Real Time'. *Official Tourism Guide for Japan Travel* (n.d.), at http://www.japantravelinfo.com/popculture/anime.php?a=1 (accessed 8 February 2012).
Anon. 'Anime'; 'Manga', 'Hokusai'. *The Macquarie Dictionary Online* (n.d.). Sydney: Macquarie Dictionary Publishers, at http://www.macquariedictionary.com.au (accessed 30 December 2011).
Anon. 'Anthropomorphism, n.'; 'Metamorphosis, n.'; 'Androgyny, n.'. *Oxford English Dictionary* (n.d.). Oxford: Oxford University Press, at http://www.oed.com (accessed 3 October 2010).
Anon. 'Anthropomorphous'. *Oxford Dictionaries* (n.d.), at http://oxforddictionaries.com/definition/english/anthropomorphous (accessed 27 December 2012).
Anon. 'The Animerica Interview: Takahata and Nosaka – Two Grave Voices in Animation'. *Animerica: Anime and Manga Monthly* 2.11 (1994): 6-11. Originally published in *ANIMAGE Magazine* (1987).

Anon. 'Ichiban'. *Wired* 9.09 (2001): 120-25.
Anon. '2005 World Exposition, Aichi, Japan Video Clips'. *The Ministry of Foreign Affairs of Japan* (English language) (2005), at http://www.mofa.go.jp/j_info/expo2005/video.html (accessed 6 February 2012).
Anon. 'Japan Launches International Manga Award – A "Nobel Prize in Manga"'. *ICv2* (25 May 2007), at http://www.icv2.com/articles/news/10648.html (accessed 2 November 2013).
Anon. 'Otaku-Anime Adventure Program'. *JTB Global Marketing & Travel Inc.*, flyer, 2007.
Anon. 'GONG, the UK Based Japanese Animation Channel Launches in Over 30 Countries'. *PR Newswire Europe Including UK Disclose.* New York, 2007.
Anon. 'Visit Anime Spots'. *att. Japan* 45 (2009), at http://www.att-japan.net/modules/tinyd1/rewrite/tc_84.html (accessed 25 February 2012).
Anon. 'Kusanagi'. *Encyclopædia Britannica Online* (2012), at http://www.britannica.com/EBchecked/topic/325455/Kusanagi (accessed 23 February 2012).
Antoni, Klaus. '*Yasukuni-Jinja* and Folk Religion: The Problem of Vengeful Spirits'. *Asian Folklore Studies* 47.1 (1988): 123-36.
—'Momotarō (The Peach Boy) and the Spirit of Japan: Concerning the Function of a Fairy Tale in Japanese Nationalism of the Early Showa Age'. *Asian Folklore Studies* 50.1 (1991): 155-88.
Armstrong, Thomas. *The Radiant Child.* Wheaton, IL: Theosophical Publishing House, 1985.
Arnold, Michael. 'Japanese Anime and Animated Cartoons'. *Midnight Eye: Visions of Japanese Cinema* (2004), at http://www.midnighteye.com/features/japanese-anime-and-the-animated-cartoon (accessed 16 November 2007).
Ashikaga, Ensho. 'The Festival for the Spirits of the Dead in Japan'. *Western Folklore* 9.3 (1950): 217-28.
Ashkenazi, Michael. *Handbook of Japanese Mythology.* Oxford and New York: Oxford University Press, 2003.
Aston, William George. 'Japanese Myth'. *Folklore* 10.3 (1899): 294-324.
—*Shinto: The Way of the Gods.* Bristol and Tokyo: Ganesha Publishing and Oxford University Press, 1997 [1905].
Avramides, Anita. 'Descartes and Other Minds'. *Teorema* XVI/I (1996): 27-46.
Baer, Elizabeth R. *The Golem Redux: From Prague to Post-Holocaust Fiction.* Detroit, MI: Wayne State University Press, 2012.
Baisley, Sarah. 'U.S. Born and Raised Anime Series *Kappa Mikey* Takes to Worldwide Waves'. *Animation World Network* (2006), at http://www.awn.com/news/us-born-raised-anime-series-kappa-mikey-takes-worldwide-waves (accessed 8 October 2014).
Barkman, Adam. 'Anime, Manga and Christianity: A Comprehensive Analysis'. *Journal for the Study of Religions and Ideologies* 9.27 (2010): 25-45.
—'Did Santa Die on the Cross?'. In *Anime and Philosophy: Wide-Eyed Wonder*, ed. Josef Steiff and Tristan D. Tamplin, 105-120. Chicago and La Salle, IL: Open Court Publishing, 2010.
Barks, Coleman. *A Year with Rumi: Daily Readings.* New York: Harper Collins, 2006.
Barnouw, Erik. *Documentary: A History of the Non-Fiction Film*, 2nd edn. Oxford: Oxford University Press, 1993.
Beck, Jerry (gen. ed.). *Animation Art: From Pencil to Pixel, the History of Cartoon, Anime & CGI.* New York: Harper Design International, 2004.

Beck, Jerry. *The Animated Movie Guide*. Chicago, IL: A Capella Books, 2005.
Belk, Russell W. 'Material Values in the Comics: A Content Analysis of Comic Books Featuring Themes of Wealth'. *Journal of Consumer Research* 14.1 (1987): 26-42.
Berger, Peter. *The Social Reality of Religion*. London: Faber and Faber, 1969 [1967].
Beyman, Rebecca and Jürgen W. Kremer. 'The Spirit of Integration: Mythic Androgyns and the Significance of Shamanic Trance'. *Revision* 26.1 (2003): 40-48.
Birberick, Anne Lynn. *Reading Undercover: Audience and Authority in Jean de La Fontaine*. Cranbury, NJ: Associated Universities Press, 1998.
Bird-David, Nurit. '"Animism" Revisited: Personhood, Environment, and Relational Epistemology' [and Comments and Reply]. *Current Anthropology* 40 (1999): S67-S91.
Blacker, Carmen. 'The Divine Boy in Japanese Buddhism'. *Asian Folklore Studies* 22 (1963): 77-88.
—'Supernatural Abductions in Japanese Folklore'. *Asian Folklore Studies* 26.2 (1967): 111-47.
—*The Catalpa Bow: A Study of Shamanistic Practices in Japan*. London: Allen and Unwin, 1975.
Bowie, Theodore R. 'A Note on the Skeleton in Japanese Art'. *Art Journal* 21.1 (1961): 16-18.
Boyd, Ian DeWeese. '*Shōjo* Savior: Princess Nausicaä, Ecological Pacifism, and the Green Gospel'. *Journal of Religion and Popular Culture* 21.2 (2009), at www.usask.ca/relst/jrpc/pdfs/art21(2)-ShōjoSavior.pdf (accessed 10 December 2010).
Boyd, James W. and Tetsuya Nishimura. 'Shinto Perspectives in Miyazaki's Anime Film "Spirited Away"'. *Journal of Religion and Film* 8.2 (2004), at http://www.unomaha.edu/jrf/Vol8No2/boydShinto.htm (accessed 10 December 2010).
Brenner, Robin E. *Understanding Manga and Anime*. Westport, CN: Libraries Unlimited, 2007.
Brinkley, Frank. *Brinkley's Japanese-English Dictionary*, vol. 1. Cambridge: W. Heffer and Sons, 1963.
—*Brinkley's Japanese-English Dictionary*, vol. 2. Cambridge: W. Heffer and Sons, 1963.
Broderick, Michael. 'Superflat Eschatology: Renewal and Religion in Anime'. *Animation Studies – Animated Dialogues 2007* (2007): 29-45.
Bruno, Michael. 'Cosplay: The Illegitimate Child of SF Masquerades'. *Glitz and Glitter*. Millennium Costumers Guild (2002), at http://millenniumcg.tripod.com/glitzglitter/1002articles.html (accessed 6 July 2010).
Buljan, Katharine. 'Animated Film: Genres and Audiences – Western and Japanese Animated Films'. *Lumina: Australian Journal of Screen Arts and Business* 4 (2010): 193-208.
Bunce, William K. (ed.). *Religions in Japan: Buddhism, Shinto, Christianity*, rev. edn. Rutland, VT: Tuttle, 1967.
Bush, Laurence C. *Asian Horror Encyclopedia: Asian Horror Culture in Literature, Manga and Folklore*. San Jose, CA: Writers Club Press, 2001.
Callis, Cari. 'Nothing that Happens is Ever Forgotten'. In *Anime and Philosophy: Wide-Eyed Wonder*, ed. Josef Steiff and Tristan D. Tamplin, 93-104. Chicago and La Salle, IL: Open Court, 2010.
Campbell, Colin. 'The Easternisation of the West'. In *New Religious Movements: Challenge and Response*, ed. Bryan Wilson and Jamie Cresswell, 35-49. London and New York: Routledge, 1999.
—*The Romantic Ethic and the Spirit of Modern Consumerism*. York: Alcuin Academic, 2005.

Casal, U. A. 'The Goblin Fox and Badger and Other Witch Animals of Japan'. *Folklore Studies* 18 (1959): 1-93.
Cavallaro, Dani. *The Cinema of Mamoru Oshii: Fantasy, Technology and Politics*. Jefferson, NC and London: McFarland, 2006.
—*Anime and the Art of Adaptation: Eight Famous Works from Page to Screen*. Jefferson, NC: McFarland, 2010.
Chapin, Helen B. 'The Gion Shrine and the Gion Festival'. *Journal of the American Oriental Society* 54.3 (1934): 282-89.
Clark, Lynn Schofield. *From Angels to Aliens: Teenagers, the Media, and the Supernatural*. Oxford: Oxford University Press, 2003.
Clements, Jonathan and Helen McCarthy. *The Anime Encyclopedia: A Guide to Japanese Animation Since 1917*, rev. edn. Berkeley, CA: Stone Bridge Press, 2006.
Clift, Wallace B. 'Child'. In *The Encyclopedia of Religion*, chief editor Mircea Eliade, 243-45, vol. 3. New York: MacMillan, 1987.
Cohen, Erik. 'A Phenomenology of Tourist Experiences'. *Sociology* 13 (1979): 179-201.
—'Pilgrim'. In *Encyclopedia of Tourism*, ed. Jafar Jafari, 438. New York: Routledge, 2000.
Coleman, Samuel. *Family Planning in Japanese Culture: Traditional Birth Control in a Modern Culture*. Princeton, NJ: Princeton University Press, 1992.
Condry, Ian. 'Dark Energy: What Fansubs Reveal about the Copyright Wars'. *Mechademia* 5 (2010): 193-208.
Cooper-Chen, Anne M. *Cartoon Cultures: The Globalization of Japanese Popular Media*. New York: Peter Lang, 2010.
Coppa, Francesca. 'A Brief History of Media Fandom'. In *Fan Fiction and Fan Communities in the Age of the Internet: New Essays*, ed. Karen Hellekson and Kristina Busse, 41-59. Jefferson, NC: McFarland, 2006.
Covell, Stephen Grover. *Japanese Temple Buddhism: Worldliness in a Religion of Renunciation*. Honolulu: University of Hawai'i Press, 2005.
—'The Price of Naming the Dead: Posthumous Precept Names and Critiques of Contemporary Japanese Buddhism'. In *Death and the Afterlife in Japanese Buddhism*, ed. Jacqueline Stone and Mariko Namba Walters, 293-324. Honolulu: University of Hawai'i Press, 2009.
—'Religious Culture'. In *The Cambridge Companion to Modern Japanese Culture*, ed. Yoshio Sugimoto, 147-65. Melbourne: Cambridge University Press, 2009.
Crafton, Donald. *Before Mickey: The Animated Film 1898-1928*. Cambridge, MA and London: MIT Press, 1982.
Crusader. '*Kannazuki no Miko* (Redux): The Greatest Love Story Ever Told in Mecha'. *That Anime Blog* (2008), at http://www.thatanimeblog.com/index.php/2008/07/kannazuki-no-miko-redux-the-greatest-love-story-ever-told-in-mecha (accessed 3 October 2010).
Cubbison, Laurie. 'Anime Fans, DVDs, and the Authentic Text'. *The Velvet Light Trap* 56 (2005): 45-57.
Curti, Giorgio Hadi. 'The Ghost in the City and a Landscape of Life: A Reading of Difference in Shirow and Oshii's *Ghost in the Shell*'. *Environment and Planning D: Society and Space* 26 (2008): 87-106.
Cusack, Carole M. 'Konkokyo (Golden Light Teachings) and Modernity: A Test of the Faivre-Hanegraaff Six-Point Typology of Western Esotericism'. *Australian Religion Research Review* 20.3 (2007): 317-33.
—*Invented Religions: Imagination, Fiction and Faith*. Farnham and Burlington, VT: Ashgate, 2010.

—'Sport'. In *Religion and Everyday Life and Culture*, ed. Richard D. Hecht and Vincent F. Biondo III, 915-43. Westport, CT: Praeger, 2010.
—'The Western Reception of Buddhism: Celebrity and Popular Cultural Media as Agents of Familiarisation'. *Australian Religion Studies Review* 24.3 (2011): 297-316.
Daliot-Bul, Michal. '*Asobi* in Action: Contesting the Cultural Meanings and Cultural Boundaries of Play in Tokyo from the 1970s to the Present'. *Cultural Studies* 23.3 (2009): 355-80.
Darley, Andrew. 'Bones of Contention: Thoughts on the Study of Animation'. *Animation: An Interdisciplinary Journal* 2.1 (2007): 63-76.
Darlington, Tanja. 'The Queering of Haruhi Fujioka: Cross-Dressing, Camp and Commoner Culture in *Ouran High School Host Club*'. *ImageTextT: Interdisciplinary Comics Studies* 4.3 (2009), at http://www.english.ufl.edu/imagetext/archives/v4_3/darlington/?print (accessed 2 October 2009).
Dawson, Lorne L. and Douglas E. Cowan. 'Introduction'. In *Religion Online: Finding Faith on the Internet*, ed. Lorne L. Dawson and Douglas E. Cowan, 1-16. New York and London: Routledge, 2004.
Del George, Dana. *The Supernatural in Short Fiction of the Americas: The Other World in the New World*. Westport, CN: Greenwood Press, 2001.
Denison, Rayna. 'Anime Tourism: Discursive Construction and Reception of the Studio Ghibli Art Museum'. *Japan Forum* 22.3-4 (2010): 545-63.
Dewdney, Christopher. *Acquainted with the Night: Excursions through the World after Dark*. London: Bloomsbury, 2010.
Do Rozario, Rebecca-Anne. 'Reanimating the Animated: Disney's Theatrical Productions'. *Drama Review* 48.1 (2004): 164-77.
Drazen, Patrick. *Anime Explosion! The What? Why? And Wow! of Japanese Animation*. Berkeley, CA: Stone Bridge Press, 2003.
Dreifus, Claudia. 'A Passion to Build a Better Robot, One with Social Skills and a Smile'. *New York Times* (10 June 2003), at http://www.philosophicalturn.net/intro/Consciousness/Emotional_Robots.pdf (accessed 5 October 2010).
Duncan, Randy and Matthew J. Smith. *The Power of Comics: History, Form and Culture*. London and New York: Continuum, 2009.
Dunlap, Kathryn and Carissa Wolf. 'Fans Behaving Badly: Anime Metafandom, Brutal Criticism, and the Intellectual Fan'. *Mechademia* 5 (2010): 267-83.
Earhart, H. Byron. *Japanese Religion: Unity and Diversity*, 4th edn. Victoria, Australia and Belmont, CA: Thomson/Wadsworth, 2004.
Ebert, Roger. 'Grave of the Fireflies (1988)'. *Chicago Sun-Times* (2000), at http://rogerebert.suntimes.com/apps/pbcs.dll/article?AID=/20000319/REVIEWS08/3190301/1023 (accessed 10 May 2012).
—'My Neighbor Totoro (1993)'. *Chicago Sun-Times* (2001), at http://rogerebert.suntimes.com/apps/pbcs.dll/article?AID=/20011223/REVIEWS08/112230301/1023 (accessed 23 August 2012).
Eder, Matthias. 'Reality in Japanese Folktales'. *Asian Folklore Studies* 28.1 (1969): 17-25.
Eggert, Brian. 'My Neighbour Totoro (1988)'. *Deep Focus Review* (2010), at http://www.deepfocusreview.com/reviews/myneighbortotoro.asp (accessed 24 August 2012).
Eisenstein, Sergei M. *Eisenstein on Disney*, ed. J. Leyda. London: Methuen, 1988.
Eliade, Mircea. *The Sacred and the Profane: The Nature of Religion*. New York: Harcourt Brace Jovanovich, 1987 [1959].
Evans, Jonathan. 'The Repetition of Haruhi Suzumiya'. *The Comics Grid: Journal of Comics Scholarship* (2012), at http://www.comicsgrid.com (accessed 18 November 2012).

Evans, Tom and Mary Anne Evans. *Shunga: The Art of Love in Japan*. New York: Paddington Press, 1975.

Fagan, Bryan D. and Jody Condit Fagan. *Comic Book Collections for Libraries*. Santa Barbara, CA: ABC-CLIO, 2011.

Fairchild, William P. 'Shamanism in Japan'. *Folklore Studies* 21 (1962): 1-122.

Ferguson, George Wells. *Signs and Symbols in Christian Art*. Oxford: Oxford University Press, 1961 [1954].

Fingarette, Herbert. *Confucius: The Secular as Sacred*. San Francisco: Harper and Row, 1972.

Fischer, Ann. 'Flexibility in an Expressive Institution: Sumō'. *Southwestern Journal of Anthropology* 22.1 (1966): 31-42.

Fischer, Felice. 'Japanese Buddhist Art'. *Philadelphia Museum of Art Bulletin* 87.369 (1991): 1-27.

Fishelov, David. *Metaphors of Genre: The Role of Analogies in Genre Theory*. University Park, PA: Pennsylvania State University Press, 1993.

Fisher, Mary Pat. *Religions Today: An Introduction*. London: Routledge, 2002.

Foster, Michael D. 'The Metamorphosis of the *Kappa*: Transformation of Folklore to Folklorism in Japan'. *Asian Folklore Studies* 57 (1998): 1-24.

—*Pandemonium and Parade: Japanese Monsters and the Culture of Yōkai*. Berkeley, Los Angeles and London: University of California Press, 2009.

Freud, Sigmund. 'Mourning and Melancholia'. In *On Metapsychology, The Theory of Psychoanalysis: Beyond the Pleasure Principle, the Ego and the Id, and Other Works*, general ed. and trans. James Strachey, ed. Angela Richards, 245-68. Harmondsworth, Middlesex: Penguin Books, 1984 [1917].

—*Totem and Taboo*. London: Routledge, 2003 [1950].

Fukunaga, Natsuki. '"Those Anime Students": Foreign Language Literacy Development through Japanese Popular Culture'. *Journal of Adolescent and Adult Literacy* 50.3 (2006): 206-222.

Fukushima Jr, Dennis H. 'The Lost Fireflies'. *Fukushima Review* (n.d.), at http://www.willamette.edu/~rloftus/jfilm/hotarurev.html (accessed 10 May 2012).

Fusanosuke, Natsume. 'Japanese Manga Encounter the World'. *Japan Echo* (Tokyo) 29.3 (2002): 63-66.

Galbraith, Patrick. 'Akihabara: Conditioning a Public "Otaku" Image'. *Mechademia* 5 (2010): 210-230.

Galbraith, Patrick and Thomas Lamarre. 'Otakuology: A Dialogue'. *Mechademia* 5 (2010): 360-74.

Garnar, Andrew Wells. 'It's the End of the Species as We Know It, and I Feel Anxious'. In *Anime and Philosophy: Wide-Eyed Wonder*, ed. Josef Steiff and Tristan D. Tamplin, 287-99. Chicago and La Salle, IL: Open Court, 2010.

Geoghegan, Tom. 'What Was *Monkey Magic* All About?' *BBC News Magazine* (2008), at http://news.bbc.co.uk/1/hi/magazine/7520243.stm (accessed 15 October 2010).

Gerbert, Elaine. 'Images of Japan in the Digital Age'. *East Asia: An International Quarterly* 19.1-2 (2001): 95-122.

—'Laughing Priests in the Atsuta Shrine Festival'. In *Humour and Religion: Challenges and Ambiguities*, ed. Hans Geybels and Walter Van Herck, 54-65. London and New York: Continuum, 2011.

Gier, Nicholas F. *Spiritual Titanism: Indian, Chinese and Western Perspectives*. Albany, NY: State University of New York Press, 2000.

Glum, Peter. 'Divine Judgement in Bosch's Garden of Earthly Delights'. *Art Bulletin* 58.1 (1976): 45-54.
Goldberg, Ellen. 'The Re-orientation of Buddhism in North America'. *Method and Theory in the Study of Religion* 11 (1999): 340-56.
Goldstein, Diane E., Sylvia Ann Grider and Jeannie Banks Thomas. *Haunting Experiences: Ghosts in Contemporary Folklore*. Logan, UT: Utah State University Press, 2007.
González, Luis Pérez. 'Fansubbing Anime: Insights into the "Butterfly Effect" of Globalisation on Audiovisual Translation'. *Perspectives: Studies in Translatology* 14.4 (2006): 260-77.
Graham, Patricia J. 'A Heterodox Painting of "Shussan Shaka" in Late Tokugawa Japan: Part II'. *Artibus Asiae* 52.1-2 (1992): 131-45.
Grant, Barry Keith. *Film Genre: From Iconography to Ideology*. London and New York: Wallflower, 2007.
Gravett, Paul. *Manga: Sixty Years of Japanese Comics*. London: Laurence King Publishing, 2004.
Greenwald, Jeff. *Future Perfect: How Star Trek Conquered Planet Earth*. New York and London: Penguin Books, 1998.
Grigsby, Mary. '*Sailormoon: Manga* (Comics) and *Anime* (Cartoon) Superheroine Meets Barbie: Global Entertainment Commodity Comes to the United States'. *Journal of Popular Culture* 32.1 (1998): 59-80.
Gunsaulus, Helen C. 'A Painted Scroll of the Early *Ukiyo-é* School'. *Bulletin of the Art Institute of Chicago* 24.4 (1930): 44-46.
Gymnich, Marion and Alexandro S. Costa. 'Of Humans, Pigs, Fish, and Apes: The Literary Motif of Human-Animal Metamorphosis and its Multiple Functions in Contemporary Fiction'. *L'Esprit Créateur* 46.2 (2006): 68-88.
Haas, Daniel. 'Why Nice Princesses Don't Always Finish Last'. In *Anime and Philosophy: Wide-Eyed Wonder*, ed. Josef Steiff and Tristan D. Tamplin, 121-30. Chicago and La Salle, IL: Open Court, 2010.
Hairston, Marc. 'A Cocoon with a View: *Hikikomori, Otaku*, and *Welcome to the NHK*'. *Mechademia* 5 (2010): 311-23.
Hamabato, Matthews Masayuki. *Crested Kimono: Power and Love in the Japanese Business Family*. Ithaca, NY: Cornell University Press, 1990.
Hanly, Charles. 'Pragmatism, Tradition, and Truth'. *American Imago* 63.3 (2006): 261-82.
Harada, Violet. 'The Badger in Japanese Folklore'. *Asian Folklore Studies* 35.1 (1976): 1-6.
Hardacre, Helen. 'Creating State Shintō: The Great Promulgation Campaign and the New Religions'. *Journal of Japanese Studies* 12.1 (1986): 29-63.
Hart, Christopher. *Manga Mania: How to Draw Japanese Comics*. New York: Watson-Guptill Publications, 2001.
—*Manga Mania Shoujo: How to Draw the Charming and Romantic Characters of Japanese Comics*. New York: Watson-Guptill Publications, 2004.
Harvey, Graham. 'The Roots of Pagan Ecology'. *Religion Today* 9.3 (1994): 38-41.
—*Animism: Respecting the Living World*. Kent Town, SA and London: Wakefield Press and C. Hurst and Co., 2005.
Hashimoto, Miyuki. 'Visual Kei Otaku Identity: An Intercultural Analysis'. *Intercultural Communication Studies* 16.1 (2007): 87-99.
Hatcher, Jordan S. 'Of Otakus and Fansubs: A Critical Look at Anime Online in Light of Current Issues in Copyright Law'. *SCRIPT-ed* 2.4 (2005): 544-71.

Hearn, Lafcadio. *Japan's Religions; Shinto and Buddhism*, ed. K. Kato. New Hyde Park, NY: University Books, 1966.
Heinricy, Shana. 'Take a Ride on the Catbus'. In *Anime and Philosophy: Wide-Eyed Wonder*, ed. Josef Steiff and Tristan D. Tamplin, 3-11. Chicago and La Salle, IL: Open Court, 2010.
Herbert, Jean. *Shintō: At the Fountain-Head of Japan*. London: Allen and Unwin, 1967.
Hildburgh, Walter L. 'Some Magical Applications of Brooms in Japan'. *Folklore* 30.3 (1919): 169-207.
Hill, Michael. *Slave to the Rhythm: Animation at the Service of the Popular Music Industry*. Unpublished MA thesis. Sydney: University of Technology, Sydney, 1995.
—'Anime, Art and Design', public lecture, Arts and Asia Lecture Series. Sydney: Art Gallery of New South Wales, 2003.
—*A Study of Contemporary Australian Alternative Comics 1992-2000 with Particular Reference to the Work of Naylor, Smith, Danko and Ord*. Unpublished PhD thesis. Sydney: Macquarie University, 2003.
—'Understanding Anime and Manga Character Design of the Magic Kingdom', public lecture in association with the exhibition 'Japan: Kingdom of Characters'. Sydney: The Japan Foundation, 2011.
Hjorth, Larissa. 'Game Girl: Re-imagining Japanese Gender and Gaming via Melbourne Female Cosplayers'. *Intersections: Gender and Sexuality in Asia and the Pacific* 20 (2009), at http://intersections.anu.edu.au/issue20/hjorth.htm (accessed 1 July 2011).
Holtom, Daniel C. *The National Faith of Japan: A Study in Modern Shintō*. London: Paul, Trench, Trubner, 1938.
Hozumi, Nobushige. *Ancestor-Worship and Japanese Law*. Charleston, SC: BiblioBazaar, 2008.
Hughes, Felicity. 'Anime Fan Pilgrimages Help Boost Tourism'. *Japan Times Online* (*Japan Pulse*) (2010), at http://blog.japantimes.co.jp/japan-pulse/anime-fan-pilgrimages-help-boost-tourism (accessed 9 February 2012).
—'Some Konbeni Snacks with Your Favourite Anime?' *Japan Times Online* (*Japan Pulse*) (2010), at http://blog.japantimes.co.jp/japan-pulse/some-konbeni-snacks-with-your-favorite-anime (accessed 9 February 2012).
Hugo, Victor. *Les Misérables*, trans. Lee Fahnestock and Norman MacAfee. New York: Signet Classics, 1987.
Hume, David. *A Dissertation on the Passions and the Natural History of Religions*, ed. T. L. Beauchamp. Oxford: Clarendon Press, 2006 [1757].
Idema, Wilt L. *The White Snake and Her Son: A Translation of the Precious Scroll of Thunder Peak*. Indianapolis, IN: Hackett, 2009.
Ideta, Minoru and Rosemary Iwamura. 'Otomo Interview'. In *Kaboom! Explosive Animation from America and Japan*, 137-40. Sydney: Museum of Contemporary Art, 1994.
Iglehart, Charles W. 'Current Religious Trends in Japan'. *Journal of Bible and Religion* 15.2 (1947): 81-85.
Iida, Yumiko. 'Between the Technique of Living an Endless Routine and the Madness of Absolute Degree Zero: Japanese Identity and the Crisis of Modernity in the 1990s'. *Positions* 8.2 (2000): 423-64.
Imai, Nobuharu. 'The Momentary and Placeless Community: Constructing a New Community with regards to Otaku Culture'. *Inter Faculty* 1 (2010), at https://

journal.hass.tsukuba.ac.jp/interfaculty/article/viewFile/9/25 (accessed 18 May 2011).
Imamura, Taihei. 'Japanese Art and the Animated Cartoon'. *Quarterly of Film and Television* 7.3 (1953): 217-22.
Irving, Paul M. C. Forbes. *Metamorphosis in Greek Myths*. Oxford: Clarendon Press, 1990.
Ito, Kinko. 'A History of Manga in the Context of Japanese Culture and Society'. *Journal of Popular Culture* 38.3 (2005): 456-75.
Ito, Mizuko. 'Japanese Media Mixes and Amateur Cultural Exchange'. In *Digital Generations: Children, Young People, and New Media*, ed. David Buckingham and Rebekah Willett, 49-66. Mahwah, NJ: Lawrence Erlbaum Associates, 2006.
Iwabuchi, Koichi. 'Undoing Inter-national Fandom in an Age of Brand Nationalism'. *Mechademia* 5 (2010): 87-96.
Jamieson, Teddy. 'Orient Excess'. *Sunday Herald* (8 November 2009): 10-15.
Jay, Elisabeth. *Faith and Doubt in Victorian Britain*. Houndsmills: Macmillan Education, 1986.
Jenkins, Henry. 'Pop Cosmopolitanism: Mapping Cultural Flows in an Age of Media Convergence'. In *Globalization: Culture and Education in the New Millennium*, ed. Marcelo M. Suárez-Orozco and Desirée Baolian Qin-Hilliard, 114-40. Berkeley, CA: University of California Press, 2004.
—'When Piracy Becomes Promotion: How Unauthorized Copying Made Japanese Animation Profitable in the United States'. *Reason* 38.7 (2006): 78-79.
Jindra, Michael. '*Star Trek* Fandom as a Religious Phenomenon'. *Sociology of Religion* 55.1 (1994): 27-51.
—'"*Star Trek* to Me is a Way of Life": Fan Expressions of *Star Trek* Philosophy'. In *Star Trek and Sacred Ground: Explorations of Star Trek, Religion, and American Culture*, ed. Jennifer E. Porter and Darcee L. McLaren, 217-30. Albany, NY: State University of New York Press, 1999.
Josephson, Jason Ānanda. 'When Buddhism Became a "Religion": Religion and Superstition in the Writings of Inoue Enryō'. *Japanese Journal of Religious Studies* 33.1 (2006): 143-68.
Jung, Carl Gustav. *Four Archetypes*. London: Routledge, 2006 [1969].
Kalland, Arne. 'Holism and Sustainability: Lessons from Japan'. *Worldviews* 6.2 (2002): 145-58.
Kalsched, Donald. *The Inner World of Trauma: Archetypal Defenses of the Personal Spirit*. London and New York: Routledge, 1996.
Kamstra, Jeffrey. 'Japanese Monotheisms and New Religions'. In *Japanese New Religions in the West*, ed. Peter B. Clarke and Jeffrey Somers, 104-117. Sandgate, Kent: Japan Library, 1994.
Kasulis, Thomas P. *Shinto: The Way Home*. Honolulu: University of Hawai'i Press, 2004.
Katō, Genchi. *A Study of Shintō: The Religion of the Japanese Nation*. Tokyo: Meiji Japan Society, 1926.
Kaufmann, Thomas DaCosta. *Arcimboldo: Visual Jokes, Natural History, and Still-Life Painting*. Chicago, IL: University of Chicago Press, 2009.
Kelsey, W. Michael. 'The Raging Deity in Japanese Mythology'. *Asian Folklore Studies* 40.2 (1981): 213-36.
Kelts, Roland. 'Japanamerica: Stray Ambassadors'. *3:AM Magazine* (2010), at http://www.3ammagazine.com/3am/japanamerica-stray-ambassadors (accessed 19 March 2012).

Kennedy, Malcolm D. *A Short History of Japan*. New York: New American Library, 1964.
Kern, Adam L. *Manga from the Floating Word: Comicbook Culture and the Kibyōshi of Edo Japan*. Cambridge, MA: Harvard University Asia Center, 2006.
—'Manga versus Kibyōshi'. In *A Comics Studies Reader*, ed. Jeet Heer and Kent Worcester, 236-43. Jackson, MS: University Press of Mississippi, 2009.
Kimbrough, R. Keller. 'Preaching the Animal Real in Late Medieval Japan'. *Asian Folklore Studies* 65.2 (2006): 179-206.
Kirby, Danielle. 'Readers, Believers, Consumers and Audiences: Complicating the Relationship between Consumption and Contemporary Narrative Spiritualities'. *Australian Journal of Communication* 39.1 (2012): 119-31.
Kitagawa, Joseph M. 'Some Remarks on Shintō'. *History of Religions* 27.3 (1988): 227-45.
Klaus, Carl H. et al. (eds). *Elements of Literature: Essay, Fiction, Poetry, Drama, Film*, 4th edn. New York: Oxford University Press, 1991.
Knapp, Bettina Liebowitz. *Women in Myth*. Albany, NY: State University of New York Press, 1997.
Kobayashi, Tadashi. *Ukiyo-e: An Introduction to Japanese Woodblock Prints*. New York: Kodansha America, Inc., 1997 [1982].
Koizumi, Tetsunori. 'Traditional Japanese Religion and the Notion of Economic Man'. *Journal of Cultural Economics* 1.2 (1977): 35-46.
Koyama-Richard, Brigitte. *One Thousand Years of Manga*. Paris: Flammarion, 2007.
Krikke, Jan. 'Computer Graphics Advances the Art of Anime'. *IEEE Computer Graphics and Applications* 26.3 (2006): 14-19.
Kristeva, Julia. *Black Sun: Depression and Melancholia*, trans. Leon S. Roudiez. New York: Columbia University Press, 1989.
Kühn, Herbert. *The Rock Pictures of Europe*, trans. Alan Houghton Brodrick. London: Sidgwick and Jackson, 1956.
Kuroda, Toshio. 'Shinto in the History of Japanese Religions'. *Journal of Japanese Studies* 7.1 (1981): 1-21.
Lacey, Nick. *Narrative and Genre: Key Concepts in Media Studies*. Basingstoke: Macmillan, 2000.
Lamarre, Thomas. *The Anime Machine: A Media Theory of Animation*. Minneapolis: University of Minnesota Press, 2009.
Lambert, Yves. 'Religion in Modernity as a New Axial Age: Secularization or New Religious Forms?' *Sociology of Religion* 60.3 (1999): 303-333.
Lamont-Brown, Raymond. 'Japan's New Spirituality'. *Contemporary Review* 275.1603 (1999): 70-73.
Lawson, Kede. 'Aso's "Manga Museum" Plan Cool with Aussies'. *Japan Times Online* (*Kyodo News*) (2009), at http://www.japantimes.co.jp/news/2009/07/14/national/asos-manga-museum-plan-cool-with-aussies/#.VLcF7caG7hc (accessed 20 February 2012).
Leonard, Sean. 'Progress against the Law: Anime and Fandom, with the Key to the Globalization of Culture'. *International Journal of Cultural Studies* 8.3 (2005): 281-305.
Lester, Paul Martin. *Visual Communication: Images with Messages*, 4th edn. Belmont, CA: Thomson Wadsworth, 2006.
Levi, Antonia. *Samurai from Outer Space: Understanding Japanese Animation*. Chicago, IL: Open Court, 1996.
—'New Myths for the Millennium: Japanese Animation'. In *Animation in Asia and the Pacific*, ed. John A. Lent, 33-50. Eastleigh, UK: John Libbey, 2001.

—'The Americanization of Anime and Manga: Negotiating Popular Culture'. In *Cinema Anime: Critical Engagements with Japanese Animation*, ed. Steven T. Brown, 43-63. New York: Palgrave Macmillan, 2006.
Lévi-Strauss, Claude. *The Savage Mind*. London: Weidenfeld and Nicholson, 1966.
Lillehoj, Elizabeth. 'Man-made Objects as Demons in Japanese Scrolls'. *Asian Folklore Studies* 54.1 (1995): 7-34.
Lin, Irene H. 'Child Guardian Spirits (*Gohō Dōji*) in the Medieval Japanese Imaginaire'. *Pacific World: Journal of the Institute of Buddhist Studies*. Third Series 6 (2004): 153-80.
Lings, Martin. 'Sufi Answers to Questions on Ultimate Reality'. *Studies in Comparative Religion* 13.3-4 (1979): 1-11.
Looser, Tom. 'Gothic Politics: Oshii, War, and Life without Death'. *Mechademia* 4 (2009): 55-73.
Lyon, David. *Jesus in Disneyland: Religion in Postmodern Times*. Cambridge: Polity Press, 2002 [2000].
Manhire, Toby. 'Hobbit Tourism Scatters More of Tolkien's Magic across New Zealand'. *The Observer* (13 October 2012), at http://www.guardian.co.uk/world/2012/oct/13/hobbit-new-zealand-tourism (accessed 21 December 2012).
Maringer, Johannes. 'Clay Figurines of the Jomon Period: A Contribution to the History of Ancient Religion in Japan'. *History of Religions* 14.2 (1974): 128-39.
Masanao, Amano (ed.). *Manga Design*. Köln, London, Los Angeles, Madrid, Paris and Tokyo: Taschen, 2004.
Mason, Joseph W. T. *The Meaning of Shinto: The Primaeval Foundation of Creative Spirit in Modern Japan*. New York: E. P. Dutton, 1935.
Maxwell, Catherine. 'Interview – Mamoru Oshii'. *Omusubi* (Sydney: The Japan Foundation) 4-5 (2004), at http://www.jpf.org.au/06_newsletter/oshii-ishikawa_interview_omusubi_02.pdf (accessed 24 February 2012).
McBlane, Angus. 'Just a Ghost in a Shell?' In *Anime and Philosophy: Wide-Eyed Wonder*, ed. Josef Steiff and Tristan D. Tamplin, 27-38. Chicago and La Salle, IL: Open Court, 2010.
McCarthy, Helen. *Hayao Miyazaki: Master of Japanese Animation. Films, Themes, Artistry*. Berkeley, CA: Stone Bridge Press, 1999.
—'The Development of the Japanese Animation Audience in the United Kingdom and France'. In *Animation in Asia and the Pacific*, ed. John A. Lent, 73-84. Eastleigh, UK: John Libbey Publishing, 2001.
—*500 Manga Heroes and Villains*. London: Collins and Brown, 2006.
—*The Art of Osamu Tezuka: God of Manga*. New York: Abrams ComicArts, 2009.
McFarland, H. Neill. *Rush Hour of the Gods*. New York: Harper Collins, 1970 [1967].
McGee, John. 'Edo-Tokyo Open Air Architectural Museum'. *Metropolis* (*Japan's Number 1 English Magazine*) (n.d.), at http://archive.metropolis.co.jp/tokyo/497/art.asp (accessed 7 February 2012).
McKenzie, Caroline. 'Ponyo'. *Reverse Shot- Reviews* (2009), at http://www.reverse-shot.com/reviews/entry/376/ponyo, accessed 10 May 2012.
McLelland, Mark. 'A Short History of "*Hentai*"'. *Intersections: Gender, History and Culture in the Asian Context* 12 (2006), at http://intersections.anu.edu.au/issue12/mclelland.html (accessed 14 October 2010).
McNeill, David. 'A Scholarly Home for Manga'. *Chronicle of Higher Education* 55.24 (2009): A6.

Mihara, Shigeyosho. '*Ukiyo-e*: Some Aspects of Japanese Classical Picture Prints'. *Monumenta Nipponica* 6.1-2 (1943): 245-61.
Mills, Alice. 'Harry Potter and the Terrors of the Toilet'. *Children's Literature in Education*. 37.1 (2006): 1-13.
Misaka, Kaoru. 'The First Japanese Manga Magazine in the United States'. *Publishing Research Quarterly* 19.4 (2004): 23-30.
Miya, Tsugio. 'Chōjū Giga, Scroll of Frolicking Animals'. In *Japanese Scroll Paintings Chōjyū Giga*, ed. Shin'ichi Tani, 1-3. Tokyo: Kadokawa Shoten, 1976.
Miyake, Lynne K. 'Graphically Speaking: Manga Versions of *The Tale of Genji*'. *Monumenta Nipponica* 63.2 (2008): 359-92.
Miyao, Daisuke. 'Before Anime: Animation and the Pure Film Movement in Pre-War Japan'. *Japan Forum* 14.2 (2002): 191-209.
Moore, Albert C. *Iconography of Religions: An Introduction*. Philadelphia, PA: Fortress Press, 1977.
Moore, Pauline. 'When Velvet Gloves Meet Iron Fists: Cuteness in Japanese Animation'. In *The Illusion of Life II: More Essays on Animation*, ed. Alan Cholodenko, 119-51. Sydney: Power Publications, 2007.
Morgan, Joyce. 'Superheroes for a Complex World'. *Sydney Morning Herald: Spectrum* (10-11 February 2007): 8-9.
Morris, Ivan. *The World of the Shining Prince: Court Life in Ancient Japan*. New York: Kodansha America, Inc., 1994 [1964].
Motz, Lotte. *The Faces of the Goddess*. New York: Oxford University Press, 1997.
Mouer, Ross and Craig Norris. 'Exporting Japan's Culture: From Management Style to Manga'. In *The Cambridge Companion to Modern Japanese Culture*, ed. Yoshio Sugimoto, 352-68. Melbourne: Cambridge University Press, 2009.
Murfin, Ross C. and Supryia M. Ray. *The Bedford Glossary of Critical and Literary Terms*, 2nd edn. Basingstoke: Palgrave Macmillan, 2003.
Nagata, Kazuaki. 'Market for Mobile "Manga" Taking Off'. *The Japan Times* (11 July 2008), at http://www.japantimes.co.jp/news/2008/07/11/business/market-for-mobile-manga-taking-off/#.VLcLJcaG7hc (accessed 30 December 2011).
Nakamura, Karen and Hisako Matsuo. 'Female Masculinity and Fantasy Spaces: Transcending Genders in the Takarazuka Theatre and Japanese Popular Culture'. In *Men and Masculinities in Contemporary Japan: Dislocating the Salaryman Doxa*, ed. James E. Roberson and Nobue Suzuki, 59-76. London and New York: RoutledgeCurzon, 2003.
Napier, Susan Jolliffe. *Anime from Akira to Princess Mononoke: Experiencing Contemporary Japanese Animation*. New York: Palgrave Macmillan, 2001.
—'The Problem of Existence in Japanese Animation'. *Proceedings of the American Philosophical Society* 149.1 (2005): 72-79.
—'Matter Out of Place: Carnival, Containment and Cultural Recovery in Miyazaki's *Spirited Away*'. *Journal of Japanese Studies* 32.2 (2006): 287-310.
—'When Godzilla Speaks'. In *In Godzilla's Footsteps: Japanese Pop Culture Icons on the Global Stage*, ed. William M. Tsutsui and Michiko Ito, 9-19. New York: Palgrave Macmillan, 2006.
Nash, Eric P. *Manga Kamishibai: The Art of Japanese Paper Theater*. New York: Abrams ComicArts, 2009.
Navok, Jay and Sushil K. Rudranath. *Warriors of Legend: Reflections of Japan in Sailor Moon*, 2nd edn. North Charleston, SC: BookSurge, LLC, 2005.

Newitz, Annalee. 'Magical Girls and Atomic Bomb Sperm'. *Film Quarterly* 49.1 (1995): 2-15.
Ng, Benjamin Wai-ming. 'Hong Kong Young People and Cultural Pilgrimage to Japan: The Role of Japanese Popular Culture'. In *Asian Tourism: Growth and Change*, ed. Janet Cochrane, 183-92. Amsterdam, Boston and London: Elsevier, 2008.
Norman, Alex. *Spiritual Tourism: Travel and Religious Practice in Western Society*. London and New York: Continuum, 2011.
Nornes, Abé Mark. 'For an Abusive Subtitling'. *Film Quarterly* 52.3 (1999): 17-34.
Norris, Craig. 'Manga, Anime and Visual Art Culture'. In *The Cambridge Companion to Modern Japanese Culture*, ed. Yoshio Sugimoto, 236-60. Melbourne: Cambridge University Press, 2009.
Norris, Craig and Jason Bainbridge. 'Selling *Otaku*? Mapping the Relationship between Industry and Fandom in the Australian Cosplay Scene'. *Intersections: Gender and Sexuality in Asia and the Pacific* 20 (2009), at http://intersections.anu.edu.au/issue20/norris_bainbridge.htm (accessed 29 December 2011).
Nosco, Peter. *Remembering Paradise: Nativism and Nostalgia in Eighteenth-Century Japan*. Cambridge, Mass.: Council on East Asian Studies, Harvard University, distributed by Harvard University Press, 1990.
Nye, Joseph. *Soft Power: The Means to Success in World Politics*. New York: Public Affairs, 2004.
Odell, Colin and Michel le Blanc. *Studio Ghibli: The Films of Hayao Miyazaki and Isao Takahata*. London: Kamera Books, 2009.
Ohnuki-Tierney, Emiko. *The Monkey as Mirror: Symbolic Transformations in Japanese History and Ritual*. Princeton, NJ: Princeton University Press, 1987.
Okamoto, Takeshi. 'A Study on Impact of Anime on Tourism in Japan: A Case of "Anime Pilgrimage"'. *Web-Journal of Tourism and Cultural Studies* 013 (2009): 1-9, at http://hdl.handle.net/2115/38539 (accessed 7 May 2011).
Okamoto, Yoshitomo. *The Namban Art of Japan*. New York and Tokyo: John Wetherill Inc. and Heibonsha, 1972.
Okuhara, Rieko. 'Walking Along with Nature: A Psychological Interpretation of *My Neighbour Totoro*'. *The Looking Glass: New Perspectives on Children's Literature* 10.2 (2006), at http://www.lib.latrobe.edu.au/ojs/index.php/tlg/article/view/104/100 (accessed 15 October 2010).
O'Leary, Stephen D. 'Cyberspace as Sacred Space: Communicating Religion on Computer Networks'. In *Religion Online: Finding Faith on the Internet*, ed. Lorne L. Dawson and Douglas E. Cowan, 37-58. New York and London: Routledge, 2004.
Olivier, Marco. 'Nihilism in Japanese Anime'. *South African Journal of Art* 22.3 (2007): 55-67.
Ono, Sokyo. *Shinto: The Kami Way*. Rutland, VT: Tuttle, 1976.
Ono, Yoko. 'Nostalgia and Futurism in Contemporary Japanese Sci-Fi Animation'. *Asiascape.net Occasional Paper Series* 3 (2008): 1-9.
Ooka, Dianne T. 'Ike-no Taiga: Paintings in the Collection'. *Philadelphia Museum of Art Bulletin* 66.305 (1971): 28-44.
Opler, Morris E. and Robert Seido Hashima. 'The Rice Goddess and the Fox in Japanese Religion and Folk Practice'. *American Anthropologist* (New Series) 48.1 (1946): 43-53.
Orbaugh, Sharalyn. 'Emotional Infectivity: Cyborg Affect and the Limits of the Human'. *Mechademia* 3 (2008): 150-72.

Orloff Matsunaga, A. 'The Land of Natural Affirmation, Pre-Buddhist Japan'. *Monumenta Nipponica* 21.1-2 (1966): 203-209.

Orr, Tamra. *Manga Artists*. New York: Rosen, 2009.

Ortega-Brena, Mariana. 'Peek-a-boo I See You: Watching Japanese Hard-core Animation'. *Sexuality & Culture* 13.1 (2008): 17-31.

Ouwehand, Cornelius. 'Some Notes on the God Susa-no-o'. *Monumenta Nipponica* 14.3-4 (1959): 384-407.

Page, Tony. *Buddhism and Animals: A Buddhist Vision of Humanity's Rightful Relationship with the Animal Kingdom*. London: UKAVIS, 1999.

Pandey, Rajyashree. 'The Medieval in Manga'. *Postcolonial Studies* 3.1 (2000): 19-32.

Park, Jin Kyu. '"Creating My Own Cultural and Spiritual Bubble": Case of Cultural Consumption by Spiritual Seeker Anime Fans'. *Culture and Religion: An Interdisciplinary Journal* 6.3 (2005): 393-413.

Patten, Fred. 'A Capsule History of Anime'. *Animation World Magazine* 1.5 (1996), at http://www.awn.com/mag/issue1.5/toc1.5.html (accessed 30 August 2010).

—'Anime in the United States'. In *Animation in Asia and the Pacific*, ed. John A. Lent, 55-72. Eastleigh, UK: John Libbey Publishing, 2001.

—'Early Asian Animation'. In Beck (ed.), *Animation Art*, 30-31.

—'The Slide Toward War'. In Beck (ed.), *Animation Art*, 52-53.

—'The War Clouds Thicken'. In Beck (ed.), *Animation Art*, 76-77.

—'Commercial vs. Artistic'. In Beck (ed.), *Animation Art*, 174-75.

—'An Animation Industry Begins'. In Beck (ed.), *Animation Art*, 196-97.

—'An Explosion of Anime'. In Beck (ed.), *Animation Art*, 236-37.

—'Sci-Fi & Puppets'. In Beck (ed.), *Animation Art*, 260-61.

—'Growth in All Directions'. In Beck (ed.), *Animation Art*, 294-95.

—'Anime in the 1990s'. In Beck (ed.), *Animation Art*, 330-31.

—'Small-Screen Success'. In Beck (ed.), *Animation Art*, 368-69.

Pellitteri, Marco et al. *The Dragon and the Dazzle: Models, Strategies, and Identities of Japanese Imagination – A European Perspective*, trans. Roberto Branca. Latina, Italy: Tunué, 2010.

Penicka-Smith, Sarah. 'Cyborg Songs for an Existential Crisis'. In *Anime and Philosophy: Wide-Eyed Wonder*, ed. Josef Steiff and Tristan D. Tamplin, 261-74. Chicago and La Salle, IL: Open Court, 2010.

Perper, Timothy and Martha Cornog. 'Eroticism for the Masses: Japanese Manga Comics and their Assimilation into the U.S.'. *Sexuality & Culture* 6.1 (2002): 3-126.

Pfeiffer, William Sanborn. 'Mahikari: New Religion and Japanese Popular Culture'. *Journal of Popular Culture* 34.2 (2000): 155-68.

Phillips, William H. *Film: An Introduction*, 3rd edn. New York: Bedford/St Martins, 2005.

Picard, Martin. 'Haunting Backgrounds: Transnationality and Intermediality in Japanese Survival Horror Video Games'. In *Horror Video Games: Essays on the Fusion of Fear and Play*, ed. Bernard Perron, 95-120. Jefferson, NC: McFarland, 2009.

Picone, Mary. 'Lineaments of Ungratified Desire: Rebirth in Snake Form in Japanese Popular Religion'. *RES: Anthropology and Aesthetics* 5 (1983): 105-113.

Piggott, Joan R. '*Mokkan*: Wooden Documents from the Nara Period'. *Monumenta Nipponica* 45.4 (1990): 449-70.

Piggott, Juliet. *Japanese Mythology*. London, New York, Sydney and Toronto: Paul Hamlyn, 1969.

Pinkerton, Penny. 'Themes in *Naruto* Manga and Anime are Lessons in Japanese Culture'. *Examiner.Com* (2010), at http://www.examiner.com/anime-in-national/

themes-naruto-manga-and-anime-are-lessons-japanese-culture (accessed 16 October 2010).
Poitras, Gilles. *Anime Essentials: Every Thing a Fan Needs to Know*. Berkeley, CA: Stone Bridge Press, 2001.
Poole, Adrian. *Tragedy: A Very Short Introduction*. Oxford and New York: Oxford University Press, 2005.
Porter, Jennifer E. 'Pilgrimage and the IDIC Ethic: Exploring *Star Trek* Convention Attendance as Pilgrimage'. In *Intersecting Journeys: The Anthropology of Pilgrimage and Tourism*, ed. Ellen Badone and Sharon R. Roseman, 160-79. Urbana and Chicago, IL: University of Illinois Press, 2004.
Possamai, Adam. *Religion and Popular Culture: A Hyper-Real Testament*. Brussels: Peter Lang, 2005.
—'Yoda Goes to the Vatican: Youth Spirituality and Popular Culture'. *Charles Strong Lecture* (Charles Strong Trust, 2007), at http://users.esc.net.au/~nhabel/lectures/Yoda_Goes_to_the_Vatican.pdf (accessed 20 October 2010).
Pounds, W. 'Enchi Fumiko and the Hidden Energy of the Supernatural'. *Journal of the Association of Teachers of Japanese* 24.2 (1990): 167-83.
Power, Natsu Onoda. *God of Comics: Osamu Tezuka and the Creation of Post-World War II Manga*. Jackson, MS: University Press of Mississippi, 2009.
Prebish, Charles. *Luminous Passage: The Practice and Study of Buddhism in America*. Berkeley and Los Angeles, CA: University of California Press, 1999.
Price, Shinobu. 'Cartoons from Another Planet: Japanese Animation as Cross-Cultural Communication'. *Journal of American & Comparative Cultures* 24.1-2 (2001): 153-69.
Punynari. 'Anime Pilgrimages'. *Punynari's Island Adventures* (2012), at http://punynari.wordpress.com/anime-pilgrimages (accessed 21 December 2012).
Rauch, Eron and Christopher Bolton. 'A Cosplay Photography Sampler'. *Mechademia* 5 (2010): 176-90.
Reader, Ian. *Religion in Contemporary Japan*. Honolulu: University of Hawai'i Press, 1991.
—'Positively Promoting Pilgrimage: Media Representations of Pilgrimage in Japan'. *Nova Religio* 10.3 (2006): 13-31.
Reider, Noriko T. 'Transformation of the Oni: From the Frightening and Diabolical to the Cute and Sexy'. *Asian Folklore Studies* 62.1 (2003): 133-57.
—'*Onmyōji* Sex, Pathos, and the Grotesquery in Yumemakura Baku's *Oni*'. *Asian Folklore Studies* 66 (2007): 107-124.
Robertson, Jennifer. 'The Politics of Androgyny in Japan: Sexuality and Subversion in the Theatre and Beyond'. *American Ethnologist* 19.3 (1992): 419-42.
Robinet, Isabelle. *Taoism: Growth of a Religion*, trans. Phyllis Brooks. Stanford, CA: Stanford University Press, 1997.
Rommens, Aarnoud. 'Manga Story-telling/Showing'. *Image [&] Narrative: Online Magazine of the Visual Narrative* 1 (2000), at http://www.imageandnarrative.be/narratology/aarnoudrommens.htm (accessed 29 September 2009).
Rosmarin, Adena. *The Power of Genre*. Minneapolis, MN: University of Minnesota Press, 1985.
Ruh, Brian. 'Transforming U.S. Anime in the 1980s: Localisation and Longevity'. *Mechademia* 5 (2010): 31-49.
Sabin, Roger. *Adult Comics: An Introduction*. London: Routledge, 1993.
Sakurai, Takamasa. 'Looking East: Making the Otaku Pilgrimage'. *The Daily Yomiuri*

(2011), at http://www.yomiuri.co.jp/dy/features/arts/T110506004050.htm (accessed 8 February 2012).

Sanger, Keith. *The Language of Drama*. London and New York: Routledge, 2000.

Saunders, E. Dale. 'Japanese Mythology'. In *Mythologies of the Ancient World*, ed. Samuel Noah Kramer, 409-442. Garden City, NY: Anchor Books/Doubleday, 1961.

Schattschneider, Ellen. 'Family Resemblances: Memorial Images and the Face of Kinship'. *Japanese Journal of Religious Studies* 31.1 (2004): 141-62.

Schodt, Frederik L. *Manga! Manga! The World of Japanese Comics*, rev. edn. Tokyo and New York: Kodansha International, 1986.

—*Dreamland Japan: Writings on Modern Manga*. Berkeley, CA: Stone Bridge Press, 1996.

—*An Interview with Masamune Shirow* (1998), at http://www.jai2.com/MSivu.htm (accessed 31 December 2011).

—*The Astro Boy Essays: Osamu Tezuka, Mighty Atom, and the Manga/Anime Revolution*. Berkeley, CA: Stone Bridge Press, 2007.

Schwartz, Adam and Elaine Rubinstein-Avila. 'Understanding the Manga Hype: Uncovering the Multimodality of Comic-Book Literacies', *Journal of Adolescent & Adult Literacy* 50.1 (2006): 40-49.

Schwöbel, Christoph. 'Divine Agency and Providence'. *Modern Theology* 3.3 (1987): 225-44.

Screech, Timon. *Sex and the Floating World: Erotic Images in Japan, 1700–1820*. London: Reaktion Books, 1999.

Seo, Audrey Yoshiko and Stephen Addiss. *The Sound of One Hand: Paintings and Calligraphy by Zen Master Hakuin*. Boston, MA: Shambhala Publications Inc., 2010.

Shelley, Rex, Teo Chuu Yong and Russell Mok. *Japan*. Singapore: Times Books International, 1990.

Shillony, Ben-Ami. 'The Princess of the Dragon Palace: A New Shinto Sect is Born'. *Monumenta Nipponica* 39.2 (1984): 177-82.

Shimura, Toshirō. 'Greeting – Birthplace of Japanese Animation, Nerima City'. *Nerima Animation Site* (2010), at http://www.animation-nerima.jp/eng/greeting.html (accessed 9 February 2012).

Shipman, Hal. 'Grave of the Child Hero'. In *Anime and Philosophy: Wide-Eyed Wonder*, ed. Josef Steiff and Tristan D. Tamplin, 193-202. Chicago and La Salle, IL: Open Court, 2010.

Silvio, Carlo. 'Refiguring the Radical Cyborg in Mamoru Oshii's *Ghost in the Shell*'. *Science Fiction Studies* 26 (1999): 54-72.

Simes, Amy. 'Children of the Gods: The Quest for Wholeness in Contemporary Paganism'. In *Women as Sacred Custodians of the Earth? Women, Spirituality and the Environment*, ed. Alaine M. Low and Soraya Tremayne, 219-37. New York: Berghahn Books, 2001.

Simmons, Pauline. 'Artist Designers of the Tokugawa Period'. *Metropolitan Museum of Art Bulletin* (New Series) 14.6 (1956): 133-48.

Simpson, John A. and Edmund S. C. Weiner (eds). *The Oxford English Dictionary*, 2nd edn, vol. 6. Oxford: Clarendon Press; Oxford; New York: Oxford University Press, 1989.

—*The Oxford English Dictionary*, 2nd edn, vol. 17. Oxford: Clarendon Press; Oxford; New York: Oxford University Press, 1989.

Smith, Christian and Melinda Lundquist Denton. *Soul Searching: The Religious and Spiritual Lives of American Teenagers*. Oxford and New York: Oxford University Press, 2005.

Smith, Robert. 'On Certain Tales of the *Konjaku Monogatari* as Reflections of Japanese Folk Religion'. *Asian Folklore Studies* 25 (1966): 221-33.

Smyers, Karen A. '"My Own Inari": Personalization of the Deity in Inari Worship'. *Japanese Journal of Religious Studies* 23.1-2 (1996): 85-116.

Snodgrass, Judith. *Presenting Japanese Buddhism to the West: Orientalism, Occidentalism, and the Columbian Exposition*. Chapel Hill, NC: University of North Carolina Press, 2003.

Snow, Jean. 'Akihabara Nerds Rally Behind Likely Japanese PM'. *Wired* (2008), at http://www.wired.com/gamelife/2008/09/japan-pm-candid (accessed 19 March 2012).

Somerville, Jane. 'Japanese *Manga*: Not Just Funny Pictures for Children'. *Look: Art Gallery Society of New South Wales* (February 2007): 38-39.

Stadler, Jane. *Screen Media: Analysing Film and Television*. Crows Nest, NSW: Allen and Unwin, 2009.

Staemmler, Birgit. 'Virtual *Kamikakushi*: An Element of Folk Belief in Changing Times and Media'. *Japanese Journal of Religious Studies* 32.2 (2005): 341-52.

Stefansson, Halldor. 'Earth-Gods in Morimachi'. *Annals of Human Sciences* 6 (1985): 28-44.

Strecher, Matthew C. 'Magical Realism and the Search for Identity in the Fiction of Murakami Haruki'. *Journal of Japanese Studies* 25.2 (1999): 263-98.

Surhone, Lambert M., Mariam T. Tennoe and Susan F. Henssonow. *World Masterpiece Theatre: Anime*. Saarbrücken: Betascript, 2010.

Suter, Rebecca. 'From *Jusuheru* to *Jannu*: Girl Knights and Christian Witches in the Work of Miuchi Suzue'. *Mechademia* 4 (2009): 241-56.

Tanabe Jr, George J. 'Playing with Religion'. *Nova Religio: The Journal of Alternative and Emergent Religions* 10.3 (2007): 96-101.

Tani, Shin'ichi, ed. *Japanese Scroll Paintings Chōjyū Giga*, 1-3. Tokyo: Kadokawa Shoten, 1976.

Tatsumi, Yoshihiro. *Good-Bye*. Montreal: Drawn & Quarterly, 2008.

—*A Drifting Life*. Montreal: Drawn & Quarterly, 2009.

Thomas, Jolyon Baraka. '*Shūkyō Asobi* and Miyazaki Hayao's *Anime*'. *Nova Religio: The Journal of Alternative and Emergent Religions* 10.3 (2007): 73-95.

—*Drawing on Tradition: Manga, Anime, and Religion in Contemporary Japan*. Honolulu: University of Hawai'i Press, 2012.

Thompson, Christopher S. 'The Ochiai Deer Dance: A Traditional Dance in a Modern World'. *Journal of Popular Culture* 38.1 (2004): 129-48.

Thompson, Jason. *Manga: The Complete Guide*. New York: Ballantine Books/Del Rey, 2007.

Thomsen, Harry. *The New Religions of Japan*. Rutland, VT: Charles E. Tuttle Co., 1963.

Thouny, Christophe. 'Waiting for the Messiah: The Becoming-Myth of *Evangelion* and *Densha otoko*'. *Mechademia* 4 (2009): 111-29.

Toku, Masami. 'What is Manga? The Influence of Pop Culture in Adolescent Art'. *Art Education* 54.2 (2001): 11-17.

Tom, Patricia Vettel. 'Felix the Cat as Modern Trickster'. *American Art* 10.1 (1996): 65-87.

Torrance, Richard. 'Literacy and Literature in Osaka, 1890–1940'. *Journal of Japanese Studies* 31.1 (2005): 27-60.

Tsurumi, Shunsuke. 'Edo Period in Contemporary Popular Culture'. *Modern Asian Studies* 18.4 (1984): 747-55.
—*A Cultural History of Postwar Japan*. London: Kegan Paul, 1990.
Tudor, Andrew. 'Genre'. In *Film Genre: Theory and Criticism*, ed. Barry Keith Grant, 16-23. Metuchen, NJ: Scarecrow Press, 1977.
Turner, Victor. 'The Centre Out There: Pilgrim's Goal'. *History of Religions* 12.3 (1972): 191-92.
Tylor, Edward B. *Primitive Culture: Researches into the Development of Mythology, Philosophy, Religion, Language, and Art, and Custom*, 4th and rev. edn, vol. 1. London: John Murray, 1903 [1871].
—*Primitive Culture: Researches into the Development of Mythology, Philosophy, Religion, Art and Custom*, vols. 1 and 2. New York: Gordon Press, 1974 [1871].
Ueno, K. 'Explanation of Plates'. In *Japanese Scroll Paintings Chōjyū Giga*, ed. Shin'ichi Tani. Tokyo: Kadokawa Shoten, 1976.
Van Straelen, Henry. 'The Japanese New Religions'. *Numen* 9.3 (1962): 228-40.
Vidal, Denis. 'Anthropomorphism or Sub-anthropomorphism? An Anthropological Approach to Gods and Robots'. *Journal of the Royal Anthropological Institute* (New Series) 13.4 (2007): 917-33.
Vincentelli, Elisabeth. 'Bittersweet Sympathies: For a Japanese Animator, Grown-up Messages are Kid Stuff'. *The Village Voice* (1999), at http://www.villagevoice.com/1999-10-26/film/bittersweet-sympathies (accessed 10 May 2011).
Watkins, Leah. 'Japanese Travel Culture: An Investigation of the Links between Early Japanese Pilgrimage and Modern Japanese Travel Behaviour'. *New Zealand Journal of Asian Studies* 10.2 (2008): 93-110.
Waugh, Coulton. *The Comics*. Jackson, MS: University Press of Mississippi, 1947.
West, Mark I. 'Invasion of the Japanese Monsters: A Home-Front Report'. In *The Japanification of Children's Popular Culture: From Godzilla to Miyazaki*, ed. Mark I. West, 17-24. Lanham, MD: Scarecrow Press, 2009.
Wigan, Mark. *Sequential Images*. Lausanne: AVA Publishing, 2008.
Wood, Andrea. '"Straight" Women, Queer Texts: Boy-Love Manga and the Rise of a Global Counterpublic'. *Women's Studies Quarterly* 34.1-2 (2006): 394-414.
Wood, Aylish. 'Re-Animating Space'. *Animation: An Interdisciplinary Journal* 1.133 (2006): 133-52.
Yamamura, Takayoshi. 'Anime Pilgrimage and Local Tourism Promotion: An Experience of Washimiya Town, the Sacred Place for Anime "Lucky Star" Fans'. *Web-Journal of Tourism and Cultural Studies* 14 (2009): 1-9, at http://hdl.handle.net/2115/38541 (accessed 7 May 2011).
Yamaori, Tetsuo. *Wandering Spirits and Temporary Corpses: Studies in the History of Japanese Religious Tradition*, ed. and trans. Dennis Hirota. Kyoto: International Research Center for Japanese Studies, 2004.
Yang, Jeff, Dina Gan and Terry Hong. *Eastern Standard Time: A Guide to Asian Influence on American Culture from Astro Boy to Zen Buddhism*. Boston and New York: Mariner Original, 1997.
Yates, Ronald E. *The Kikkoman Chronicles: A Global Company with a Japanese Soul*. New York: McGraw-Hill, 1998.
Yen, Alsace. 'Thematic Patterns in Japanese Folktales: A Search for Meanings'. *Asian Folklore Studies* 33.2 (1974): 1-36.
Yomota, Inuhiko. 'Stigmata in Tezuka Osamu's Works'. *Mechademia* 3 (2008): 97-109.
Yoshida, Reiji. '"Manga" Fans have been Won Over but What about the Rest of

Japan?'. *The Japan Times* (23 September 2008), at http://www.japantimes.co.jp/text/nn20080923a6.html (accessed 30 December 2011).

Yoshida, Teigo. 'The Stranger as God: The Place of the Outsider in Japanese Folk Religion'. *Ethnology* 20.2 (1981): 87-99.

Yoshinori, Sugano. 'Manga and Non-Photorealistic Rendering'. *ACM SIGGRAPH Computer Graphics* 33.1 (1999): 65-66.

Yuasa, Manabu. 'Japanese TV Animation in the Early Years: Animation and Animated Humans'. In *Kaboom! Explosive Animation from America and Japan*, 59-65. Sydney: Museum of Contemporary Art, 1994.

Zahlten, Alexander. 'Tokyo Godfathers'. In *Directory of World Cinema: Japan*, ed. John Berra, 82-83. Bristol: Intellect Books, 2010.

Zan. 'Zan's Profile'. *Cosplay.com* (n.d.), at http://www.cosplay.com/member/1663/costumes (accessed 21 December 2012).

Zoeteman, Kees. *Gaiasophy: The Wisdom of the Living Earth. An Approach to Ecology*, trans. Tony Langham and Plym Peters. Hudson, NY: Lindisfarne Press, 1991.

INDEX

Abbitt, Erica Stevens 87
abduction 109
Addiss, Stephen 101
advertising 38
Aerial Momotarō 123
Aeschylus 135
Aesop's fables 91, 122
Aetherius Society 52-53
afterlife 41, 138
   hell 94-95
   reincarnation 53, 55, 74, 84-85
   Shintō 84
   Yomi-no-Kuni 84-85
Akihabara 176, 186, 204
Akira 39, 127, 147, 157-59, 179
Alakazam the Great 124
Albarn, Damon 97
Alice in Wonderland 86, 99
   Disney animation 94
Allison, Anne 34-35, 58, 77
Amaterasu (sun-goddess) 7, 69, 71, 80, 114, 117, 129, 144, 160, 191
   Nausicaä of the Valley of the Wind 129-31, 133
Amazing Three (Wonder Three) 45, 68, 148
Ambassador Atom (Atomu Taishi) 31-32
amulets 72
   see also talismans
ancestor worship/veneration 68, 77, 109, 112
Andersen, Hans Christian 148
Ando, Masahiro
   Blossoms for Tomorrow 116, 135, 143-44, 146, 209
androgyny 34, 74, 86-88, 97
Angel Sanctuary 112

Angel's Egg 147, 149, 151, 159, 210
animal scrolls *see Chōjū Giga*
animal transformations 89-100
   Chōjū Giga 89-90
   metamorphosis 94-100
Animals' Olympics, The 123, 126
animated cartoons 13, 117
   metamorphosis 85-86, 92-93
   sound 92-93
anime 1-9
   academic studies 4
   cultural importance 3
   definition 2
   global penetration 3, 23-24, 125
   history 122-23, 165-66
   transition from manga 1-2, 37-48
anime aficionados 7-8, 163-208
   Australia 170
   conventions 163, 168, 170
   cosplay *see* cosplay
   diegesis 164, 181, 185, 200, 206, 208
   extreme fans/nerds *see otaku*
   fansubbing 171-73
   France 179
   Germany 170, 179
   Internet 178-80
   Italy 178-79
   Japanese culture/language 180-81
   pilgrimage *see* anime pilgrimage
   religio-spiritual content 56, 187-95
   spiritual seekers 164, 187-95, 208
   United Kingdom 170, 178
   United States 164, 168-70, 173, 178, 188-90

Index

Western aficionados 163-81, 188-90
see also Star Trek
anime pilgrimage 8, 164, 195-207
　diegesis 200, 206, 208
　Japan National Tourism Organization (JNTO) 198-99
　merchandise/souvenirs 204-205
　Punynari's Island Adventures 201-202
　religious pilgrimage compared 205
　sculptures of anime characters 203-204
　seichi junrei (sacred pilgrimage) 199, 206
　self-transformation 195-97
　tourism 195-97, 205-206
animism 46, 75-77, 79
　anthropomorphism 76-77, 79
　defining 75
　Shintō 35-6, 75, 78
　soul 75-77
　techno-animism 35, 58-59
　technology 78
Anno, Hideaki 174
　Neon Genesis Evangelion 74, 108, 112-14, 146, 174, 200-202
anthropomorphism 79-83, 94
　animism 76-77, 79
　Chōjū Giga 92
　defining 79-80
　deities 80
　Disney characters 80
　fables 91-92
　Shintō 80
Antoni, Klaus 85
Aoki, Yasunao 119
apocalypse 7, 74, 113-14, 158
Appleseed 46
Araki, Tetsurō 121
Arcimboldo, Giuseppe 92
Argentosoma 127
Arjuna 127, 210
Armstrong, Thomas 147

Arnold, Michael 165-66
Asahara, Shōkō 36
Ashikaga, Ensho 85
Asō, Tarō 12, 24, 176
Aston, William George 72, 80, 103
Astro Boy (*Tetsuwan Atomu*) 2-3, 31-35, 45, 59, 78-79, 108, 120, 146, 172, 178, 180, 188, 203
Atomu Taishi (*Ambassador Atom*) 31-33
Attack No. 1 124
Aum Shinrikyo 36
Australia 2, 24, 45, 96
　anime aficionados 170
　cosplay 182
　Otaku-Anime Adventure Program 196
Awabi Fisherwoman and Octopus 20, 31, 94
awatee ('panic pictures') 27

badgers 97-99
Bainbridge, Jason 185
baku ('eater of dreams') 102-103
Barefoot Gen 125
Barkman, Adam 112-13, 142
Battle of the Monkey and the Crab, The 122
Battle of the Planets 169
Beautiful Dreamer see Urusei Yatsura
Belk, Russell W. 38
Berger, Peter 49
Besson, Luc 125
Big Comic Strips manga magazine 13
bishōnen 43
Black Cat Hooray! 123
Black Dog (*Norakuro*) 123
Blacker, Carmen 70, 107-109
Blade Runner 33, 47
Blavatsky, Madame Helena 50-51
Bleach 39, 41-42, 128
Blossoms for Tomorrow 116, 135, 143-46, 209
　Ando, Masahiro 143
　kami 65

Boku no Songokū (*Songoku the Monkey*) 45
Bolton, Christopher 187
Bonbori festival 116, 144-45, 209
boredom 155-57, 177
Borrowers, The 200
Bosch, Hieronymus 95
Bowie, Theodore 108-109
Boyd, James W. 111
Brenner, Robin 15, 179
bricolage 56
Buddha, the 31, 82, 88-89
Buddhahood 77, 85
buddhas 107
   kami 65
Buddhism 5, 7, 14, 46, 63, 148
   America 52
   androgyny 87
   anthropomorphism 79, 81-82
   death 85, 89
   establishment in Japan 64
   impermanence, doctrine of 88-89
   influence in Japan 65
   Inoue, Enryō's 'modern Buddhism', 23, 50
   Mahayana Buddhism 107
   maya 58
   Meiji Restoration 23, 28, 50, 65-66
   Nichiren 65
   nirvana 89
   Noh (*Nō*) drama 20
   reincarnation 53, 55, 74, 84-85
   science 50-51
   self 60, 89
   sexuality 94
   shinbutsu shūgō 65
   Shingon 65
   Shintō 5, 28, 64-65
   theriomorphic transformation 81-82
   True Pure Land 65
   in the West 52, 55

World's Parliament of Religions 51-52
Zen *see* Zen Buddhism
zenga (Zen paintings) 6, 16
Burst Angel 127
Busch, Wilhelm 13, 86
Bush, Laurence C. 101-102, 112

Campbell, Colin 49, 53
Carroll, Lewis 86, 92, 99
Cartesian perception 91
Carus, Paul 52
Casal, U. A. 97-98
cats 97, 99
   Catbus 99, 152
   Japanese cat spirit (*bake neko*) 99
cave paintings 82
censorship 19
character types 39-40, 120-21, 125
Chikamatsu, Monzaemon 137
child/young adult protagonist 4, 7, 117-18
   abduction 109
   Christian symbolism/themes 150-51
   'divine child' motif 7, 118, 146-60
   resilience 137
   spiritual realm 108
   supernatural subgenre 146-59
   tragedy subgenre 137-38
Chōjū Giga (animal scrolls) 6, 15-16, 89-90
Christianity 5, 8, 16-17, 66, 164
   Angel's Egg 147, 149-51, 159
   the apocalypse 7, 74, 113-14, 158
   Christian imagery/motifs 46, 111, 142-43, 149-51, 158
   decline in institutional religion 49-50, 55, 58, 193
   as foreign religion 23, 66
   influence on *Princess Knight* 73
   influences 17, 73, 111-14
   Judeo-Christian references 149-51, 210

kakure Kirishitan (hidden
   Christians) 53, 66
Meiji Restoration 66
outlawed 16, 66
Protestant missions 23, 28
sexuality 94
shin shūkyō 53, 111
Sukyo Mahikari 111-12
themes in *Tokyo
   Godfathers* 142-43
World's Parliament of
   Religions 51-52
Chrno Crusade 112
Church of All Worlds 57
Church of Jesus Christ of Latter-
   day Saints 50
Church of Scientology 53
Cindi in Space 38
cinematic techniques 27, 41
CLAMP 37
Clark, Lynn Schofield 193
Clift, Wallace B. 160
Cohen, Erik 196, 205-206
comedy/humour 21, 119-20, 123-
   24, 126
comic books 6, 13-14, 43
comic strips 6, 13, 22, 24, 27-29,
   102
Comiket 181-82
communications technology 56-57,
   59
   mobile phones 43, 79
   see also Internet
Condry, Ian 173
Confucianism 5, 64-65, 147
Convention of Kanagawa 1854 27
conventions
   anime conventions 163, 168, 170
   cosplay conventions 56, 182-
      83, 187
   Star Trek conventions 56, 183
Cooling Off on the Boat 123
Cooper-Chen, Anne 178-79
Cornog, Martha 19
cosplay 2, 40, 162-64, 181-87, 199

Australia 182
cosplay conventions 56, 182-
   83, 187
digital technology 187
fansubbing compared 186
gender identity 186
Internet 187
personal transformation 184-85
photographic sessions 184, 202
ritual 185
Star Trek 182-85
Costa, Alexandre Segão 83
Covell, Stephen 36, 59
creation mythology, Shintō 69
Cubbison, Laurie 166
Curti, Giorgio 48
cyborgs 3-4, 60, 85, 191
   see also Ghost in the Shell

Daijin, Konkō 50, 53
Daliot-Bul, Michal 184-85
Daoism 5, 46, 64
   Shintō 64-65
   yin-yang principle 65
Darley, Andrew 86
Darwin, Charles 50
Day the Earth Stood Still, The 52
de Semlyen, André 180
death 84-85, 89
Deguchi, Nao 50
Del George, Dana 138, 157
Denshin-kyō (Religion of the
   Electricity God) 53
*Destiny of the Shrine Maiden
   (Priestesses of the Godless
   Month)* 71
*Detective Stories of Sabu and Ichi,
   The* 124
Dharmapala, Anagarika 51-52
Dick, Philip K. 33
diegesis 8, 127, 164, 181, 185, 200,
   206, 208
digital technology 59
   anime production 121
   cosplay 187

manga production 40, 42-43
Dirks, Rudolph 13
Disney animations 17, 22, 29, 34, 80, 86, 92, 94, 123-24, 209
Disney, Walt 3, 11, 33, 60, 92
'divine child' motif 7, 118, 146-60
dogs
   jinmenken ('human-faced dog') 100
   metamorphosis 95, 97
   Norakuro (*Black Dog*) 123
   tengu (dog-spirits) 95, 109
dōjinshi 24-25, 37, 39, 46, 57, 171
dolls 77-78, 81, 85, 123
drama genre 135, 140, 146

Earhart, H. Byron 68
Easternization 49, 53, 61
Ebert, Roger 153
ecological themes 130-35
Eder, Matthias 99
Edison, Thomas Alva 53
Edo period 6, 14, 16-18, 95
Eggert, Brian 152-53
Eightman series 124
Eisenstein, Sergei 86, 94
Eliade, Mircea 141-42
Emperor worship 30, 32
Engi Shiki (Detailed Laws of the Engi period) 64
Epic of Gilgamesh 134
erotica 2, 123
   hentai 20, 94
   shunga 6, 18-19, 23
Escaflowne 189
Evans, Jonathan 154-55
evolution, theory of 50

fables 91-92, 122
fans *see* anime aficionados; *otaku*
fansubbing 171-73
   cosplay compared 186
fantasy 122-24, 129
   sword and sorcery 125
female characters 7, 46, 117, 130

mahō shōjo (magical girl) genre 121, 124, 156
shōjo 26, 29, 31, 39, 45, 88, 128
Femme Nikita, La 125
Ferguson, George Wells 151
fireflies 138-39
Fischer, Ann 21
Fishelov, David 119
Fleischer, Max 17, 29, 33
floating world, the 17-18
folk tales 96, 105-106, 122-24, 128
   European 129
   Peach Boy *see* Peach Boy
Ford, John 70, 141
Foster, Michael Dylan 95, 100-101
foxes
   Blossoms for Tomorrow 145-46
   fox spirits 97-98
   metamorphosis 97
France 23, 165, 168, 170, 178-79
Freshly Baked!! Japan (*Yakitate!! Japan*) 119, 126
Freud, Sigmund 77, 156
Fuji (Mount) 16, 20, 69, 119, 204
Fukunaga, Natsuki 189
Fukushima, Dennis H. 138

Gaia (goddess) 7, 117, 130-31, 133, 135
Gaki Zoshi ('Hungry Demons') 108-109
Galbraith, Patrick 174, 186
Gan, Dina 41
Garo 41
GeGeGe No Kitarō 124
gekiga manga 26, 31, 39, 45
gender 43, 55
   androgyny 34, 74, 86-88, 97
   cosplay 186
   see also female characters; sexuality
generic hybrids 7, 117, 121-29
   derived from manga 127-28
   examples 127-28
   hybridity 127

shōnen/shōjo 128
    supernatural subgenre 128
Genji Monogatari ('Tale of Genji') 97
genres 7, 26, 31, 117-60
    animation techniques 121
    character types 120-21, 125
    children's anime 123-24
    comedy/humour 21, 119-20, 123-24, 126
    defining 118-19
    dōjinshi 24-25, 37, 39, 46, 57, 171
    drama 135, 140, 146
    erotica *see* erotica
    examples 121-22, 126-27
    fantasy 122-25
    film 118
    folk tales 122-24, 128
    gekiga 26, 31, 39, 45
    genre elements 120
    giant robots 124-25
    high-school fantasy 125
    horror 95, 120-21, 124
    housewives' market 124
    hybridity *see* generic hybrids
    literary criticism 118-19
    mahō shōjo (magical girl) 121, 124, 156
    mecha see *mecha*
    narrative 120, 125, 127
    redikomi 39
    samurai-ninja historical-adventure 124
    science fiction 126
    seijin 39
    shōjo *see* shōjo
    shōnen 39, 128
    sports 123-24
    styles 121
    supernatural *see* supernatural subgenre
    sword and sorcery 125
    tragedy *see* tragedy
    transformation 124
    war propaganda 45, 57, 123
    World War II drama 125, 136

yonkoma manga 39
Gerbert, Elaine 144
Germany
    anime aficionados 170, 179
    Star Trek fans 167
Getter Robo 168
Ghost in the Shell 3-4, 6, 11, 46-48, 56, 58, 61, 89, 109, 171, 191-92
    Ghost in the Shell 2: Innocence 81, 147, 191
    Kōkaku Kidōtai 46-47
    religious motifs 191
    see also Oshii, Mamoru
giant robots *see* robots
Gibson, William 47
Gigantor 45
girls' manga *see* shōjo
Godzilla (*Gojira*) 35
gohō ('protectors of the Law') 107-108
Gokusen 128
golem 191
GONG 180
González, Luis Pérez 171
Gotō, Shinpei 122
Grandville, J. J. 92
Grave of the Fireflies 135-39, 146, 196
Greenwald, Jeff 167-68, 177-78, 183-84, 206-207
Grigsby, Mary 29
Guanyin (Japanese Kannon) 148
guardian spirits 97, 107-108, 153
Gymnich, Marion 83

Hairston, Marc 175
Hakone Shrine 201
Hakuin, Ekaku 16
Hanahekonai's New Sword 122
Hanako of the Toilet 100-101
Hanasaku Iroha (*Blossoms for Tomorrow*) 116, 135, 143-46, 209
Hanly, Charles 76
Harada, Violet 98
Hardacre, Helen 54-55
Harry Potter novels 101

Hart, Christopher 40
Harvey, Graham 77, 131-32
Hasegawa, Machiko 32
Hashiguchi, Takashi 119
Hashima, Robert Seido 145
Hashimoto, Miyuki 173-74
Heinlein, Robert A. 57
hentai 94
    tentacle *hentai* 20, 94
Heraclitus 83
Herbert, Jean 69
Hergé (Georges Prosper Remi) 137
Heron Maiden, The 10
hierophany 141
High School of the Dead 121, 128
high-school romance 102-103, 107, 125, 154
    see also *Urusei Yatsura*
hikikomori ('recluse') 175-76
Hildburgh, Walter L. 81
Hill, Michael 80, 82
Hirata, Atsutane 28, 53
Hiroshige *see* Utagawa, Hiroshige
Hiroshima, bombing of *see* World War II
Hishikawa, Moronobu 18
Hitchcock, Alfred 34
Hobbit, The 164
Hogarth, William 13
Hokusai, Katsushika 6, 20, 31
    Awabi Fisherwoman and Octopus 20, 31, 94
    Mangwa 2, 20
homelessness 141-42
Homer 83, 130
homosexuality 19, 43
Honda, Ishirō 35
Honda, Toshiaki 53
Hong, Terry 41
horror genre 95, 120-21, 124
Howl's Moving Castle 162
Hozumi, Nobushige 109
Hubbard, L. Ron 53
Hugo, Victor 139, 209
Hume, David 76

humour *see* comedy/humour
Hungary 177-78

Ideta, Minoru 188
Imai, Nobuharu 198
Imakita, Kōsen 51-52
Imamura, Taihei 90
imperial cult 69, 84
Inari 87, 97, 145
Inari Ōkami 87
individualism 49, 54-55
Inoue, Enryō 23, 50
Internet 56-57, 59, 89
    anime aficionados 178-80
    cosplay 187
    online role-playing games 187
Inuyasha 39
Iron Man #28 124
Ise Grand Shrine 69, 84
Ishihara, Tatsuya 117-18, 147
    Melancholy of Haruhi Suzumiya, The ii, 147, 154-57, 159, 176-77, 186, 197-98
Islam 51, 66, 114
    Sufism 147, 154-57, 159
Italy 178-79
Ito, Kinko 13
Iwabuchi, Koichi 171, 180
Iwamura, Rosemary 188
Iwasa, Matabei Katsumochi 18
Iwasaka, Michiko 101
Izanagi-no-Mikoto ('He Who Invites') 69, 84, 85, 114, 133
Izanami-no-Mikoto ('She Who Invites') 69, 84, 85, 114, 133
Izumo 71, 144, 209
Izumo Taisha shrine 144, 209

Jackson, Peter 164
Japan Punch 21-22
Japaneseness 40, 188
Jesus
    Christian imagery in *Tokyo Godfathers* 142-43
    Sukyo Mahikari 111-12

Jiji Shinpō 22
Jindra, Michael 56, 182-83
jinmenken (human-faced dog) 100
Josephson, Jason Ānanda 73
Journey to the West 45, 96
Judaism 51, 66, 147, 191
    Judeo-Christian references 149-51, 210
Jung, Carl Gustav 82-83, 149
Jungeru Taitei/Jungle Taitei (*Kimba the White Lion*) 3, 22, 31, 45
Jurojin (god of Wisdom) 72

Kabuki theatre 17, 87-88
Kagu-tsuchi (fire deity) 84
kakure Kirishitan (hidden Christians) 53, 66
Kakuyū 89
Kaleido Star 121, 127
Kalsched, Donald 149
Kamakura period 16, 20, 65
kameko (amateur photographer) 184
kami 4, 7, 35, 66-71, 78, 96, 110-11, 114, 131
    androgyny 87
    Bonbori festival 144
    buddhas/bodhisattvas 65
    creation mythology 69
    female *kami* 131
    imperial ancestors 68-69
    Inari 87, 97, 145
    kappa 95
    nature of 5, 67
    Noh theatre 21
    war dead 28
Kamichu! ('Teenage Goddess') 203
kamishibai (paper theatre) 6, 30, 44
    story cards 44
Kamstra, Jeffrey 53
Kannazuki no Miko (*Priestesses of the Godless Month/ Destiny of the Shrine Maiden*) 71
kappa (water goblin) 95
Kappa Mikey 95-96

Kasulis, Thomas 65, 74
Kawajiri, Yoshiaki 125
Kawate, Bunjirō 50
Kayoko's Diary 125
Kern, Adam L. 19
Kewpie doll 33-34
kibyōshi ('yellow cover' books) 6, 14, 18-20, 23
Kiej'e, Nikolas 101
Kimba the White Lion (*Jungeru Taitei*) 3, 22, 31, 45
kimonos 18, 67
Kimura, Hakusan 123
King, George 52-53
Kirby, Danielle 186
Kisala, Robert 35
Kishimoto, Masashi 98
Kitagawa, Joseph 67
Kitano, Tsunetomi 10
Kitayama Eiga Seisakujo (Kitayama Movie Factory) 122
Kitayama, Seitarō 122, 165, 179
Kitazawa, Rakuten 27
Kiyochika Punch 22
Klingons *see Star Trek*
kodomo (*kodomo muke*) manga 39, 121
Kogoshūi (Gleanings from Ancient Stories) 64
Kojiki (Record of Ancient Matters) 5, 14, 64, 69, 72, 85, 114
Kōkaku Kidōtai (*Mobile Armoured Riot Police*) 46
komikkusu 24
Kon, Satoshi 125, 140-43
Konjaku Monogatari 101
Konkōkyō 50, 53
Kōuchi, Jun'ichi 122
Kōzanji (Kōzan-ji) Temple 15, 89
Kristeva, Julia 155
Kujiki (Chronicle of Old Events) 64
Kūkai 65
Kumano Mandala 94-95
Kunisada (Toyokuni lll Utagawa) 62
Kure-nai ('Crimson') 203

Kuroda, Toshio 64-65
*Kurosagi Corpse Delivery Service,
    The* 41-42
Kurosawa, Akira 70
Kurozumi, Munetada 50
Kurozumikyō 50
Kusanagi no Tsurugi (legendary
    sword) 72, 191
Kyne, Peter B. 141
Kyōdan, P. L. 53
Kyoto (Kyōto)
    Kōzanji (Kōzan-ji) Temple 15, 89
    Kyoto Seika University 3
    Osamu Tezuka World 203
    kyoyo manga 12

La Fontaine, Jean de 91-92
Lady Oscar 179
Lambert, Yves 54
Landells, Ebenezer 21
*Legend of the White Serpent/Panda
    and the Magic Serpent* 93-94,
    99-100, 124, 165, 178, 203
Les Misérables: Shōjo Cosette 135-36,
    139-40, 146
Levi, Antonia 172, 189
Lévi-Strauss, Claude 82
Lin, Irene H. 108
Lings, Martin 155
Little Mermaid, The 148
Little Norse Prince, The 124
*Little Prince and the Eight-Headed
    Dragon, The* 124
Lord of the Rings
    film 164
    novels 193
Lotus Sutra 53
*Love in the Genroku Era: Sankichi and
    Osayo* 123
Lucky Star 197
Lyell, Charles 50
Lyon, David 168

McCarthy, Helen 4, 37, 168
McManus, George 28

Madhouse 125
magic 60
    Shintō 72-74
    talismans 69, 71-72, 110
Magic Boy 124, 165
magical girl (*mahō shōjo*) 121, 124,
    156
Mahayana Buddhism 107
Mahikari *see* Sukyo Mahikari
mahō shōjo (magical girl) 121, 124,
    156
manga 1-6, 8-9
    academic studies 4
    cinematic techniques 27, 41
    cultural importance 3, 12-13
    definition 2
    digital technology 40, 42-43
    dōjinshi 24-25, 37, 39, 46, 57, 171
    emergence in twentieth
        century 23-36
    gekiga manga 26, 31, 39, 45
    generic hybrids derived
        from 127-28
    global penetration 3, 23-24
    graphic and narrative
        origins 12-23
    instructional device 37-38
    kodomo (*kodomo muke*) manga 39
    kyoyo manga 12
    library editions 39
    manga artists (*mangaka*) 24-26,
        31, 37-38, 43-44, 171
    mobile phones 43
    plots 43
    sales 1
    sci-fi 124
    transition to anime 1-2, 37-48
    types 39
    yonkoma manga 39
Mangwa 2, 20
Marine Boy 178
marketing 38
Marley, Bob 165
Masaoka, Kenzō 123
Massive Multiplayer Online

Role-Playing Games (MMORPGs) 186-87
Matrix, The 58
Matrixism 57
Matsumoto, Reiji 45
Matsuo, Hisako 88
Mayhew, Henry 21
Mazinger Z 125
mecha 125-26, 130
   sexuality 107
   techno-animism 35, 58-59
   see also robots
Meiji Restoration 6, 22-23, 27, 60
   Buddhism 23, 28, 50, 65-66
   Christianity 66
   industrialization/modernization 21-22, 27, 78
   religious consequences 23, 28, 50, 65-66
   shin shūkyō 28, 50, 66
   Shintō 28, 50, 65-66, 78
   Westernization 27
   Yasukuni Shrine 28
melancholy 155-56, 177
Melancholy of Haruhi Suzumiya, The ii, 147, 154-57, 159, 176-77, 186, 197-98
Menglong, Feng 93
metamorphosis 83, 85-86, 94-96
   animal transformations 94-100
   animation 85-86, 92-93
   badgers 97-99
   bakemono 97
   bakeru 97
   cats 97, 99
   death 84
   decomposition 84
   definition 83
   dogs 95, 97
   foxes 97-98
   hentai 94
   kappa 95
   monkeys 96-97
   raccoon-dog 98
   sexuality 94

Shintō 84, 96
miko (female shamans) 70-71
military/war propaganda 45, 57, 93, 123
Miyazaki, Hayao 3-4, 115, 117, 125, 147, 169-70
   auteur 147, 169
   child/young adult characters 118, 147-49
   Howl's Moving Castle 162
   My Neighbour Totoro 4, 78-79, 99, 147, 151-54, 156, 159, 198
   Nausicaä of the Valley of the Wind 3, 88, 129-35, 169
   Ponyo 147-49, 151-54, 156, 159
   Princess Mononoke 3, 78, 130, 133-5, 179, 189, 193, 202-203
   religion 78-79, 194
   Spirited Away 4, 78, 109-11, 146, 199-200
Miyazaki, Tsutomu 173
Miyazawa, Kiichi 13
Mizuki, Shigeru 44
Mobile Armoured Riot Police 46
mobile phones 43, 79
Mobile Suit Gundam 125
mokkan (wooden slips) 14-15
Momotarō see Peach Boy
monkeys
   Battle of the Monkey and the Crab, The 122
   Boku no Songokū (Songoku the Monkey) 45
   metamorphosis 96-97
   Saiyūki (Monkey) 96
   Sankichi the Monkey: Air Defense Military Exercise 123
Moore, Pauline 2
Motoöri, Norinaga 28, 67, 103
Motz, Lotte 134
Mount Fuji 16, 20, 69, 119, 204
Mrs Sazae 124
mu-kokuseki (absence of nationality) 40
Mukuzō Imokawa, The Concierge 122

multiculturalism 107
Murakami, Haruki 177
Muraoka, Tsunetsugu 73
Murata, Yasuji 123
Musashi: The Dream of the Last Samurai 127
musume-yaku ('the role of a woman') 88
My Baseball 123
My Neighbour Totoro 4, 78-79, 99, 147, 151-54, 156, 159, 198
mythology 148
  anthropomorphism 92
  Bonbori festival 144
  creation mythology 69
  kusanagi 191
  metaphor 80-81

Nagasaki, bombing of *see* World War II
Nagata, Kazuaki 43
Nagai, Gō 125
Nakamori, Akio 173
Nakamura, Karen 88
Nakano, Takao 123
Nakayama, Miki 50, 53
Nakazawa, Keiji 125
Namban (Nanban) art 17, 20
Nankivell, Frank Arthur 27
Napier, Susan Jolliffe 47, 110-11, 158-59, 196
Nara period 14
narrative 120, 125, 127
Naruto 39, 98
Nausicaä of the Valley of the Wind 3, 88, 129-35, 169
Navok, Jay 72
Neon Genesis Evangelion 74, 108, 112-14, 146, 174, 200-202
nerds *see* otaku
New Age movement 56, 66, 70
new religions 50
  bricolage 56
  Japan *see shin shūkyō*

New Age movement 56, 66
new new religions 36, 59, 70
  post-World War II 52-53
New Zealand 96, 164
Newitz, Annalee 107
newspapers 22, 28-29
  comic strips 6, 13, 22, 27-29, 102
Ng, Benjamin 196
Niccolo, Giovanni 17
Nichiren 65
Nihon ryōiki 101
Nihon Shoki/Nihongi (Chronicles of Japan) 5, 14, 64, 69, 84, 133
Ninigi-no-Mikoto 69, 134, 191
Ninja Resurrection 112
nirvana 89
Nishimura, Tetsuya 111
Noh (*Nō*) drama 20-21
Noir 125
Norakuro (*Black Dog*) 123
Nornes, Abé Mark 172
Norris, Craig 25, 185
Norton, Mary 200
Nosaka, Akiyuki 136-37
Nye, Joseph 34-35

Ohnuki-Tierney, Emiko 96
Oiwa, Kendi (Kenji Ōiwa) 175
Okada, Yoshikazu 111
Okamoto, Ippei 27
Okuhara, Rieko 99
Okuni 87
Olcott, Henry Steel (Colonel) 50-51
Oman, John Wood 157
Ōmotokyo (Great Origin Teachings) 50
oni (demons) 103-104, 106-107
Onoe Baiko as Spirit of Cherry Tree 62
Opler, Morris E. 145
origami 67
Original Anime Video (OAV) 42
original video animation (OVA) 107, 125
Orion 46

Orr, Tamra 39
Ortega-Brena, Mariana 94
Osaka 26, 30
Osaka Puck (Ōsaka pakku) 26
Oshii, Mamoru 3, 7, 11, 60, 115, 117, 120, 125
    Angel's Egg 147, 149-51, 159, 210
    auteur 147
    child/young adult characters 118
    emotional content of anime 188-89
    Ghost in the Shell see Ghost in the Shell
    Urusei Yatsura 2: Beautiful Dreamer 102-106, 154
otaku 8, 12, 56-57, 105, 165, 173-76, 198
    becoming manga artists 25
    definition 174
    gender identity 186
    hikikomori ('recluse') 175-76
    market 174
    perception of 174-75
    use of term 8, 173-75
    see also anime aficionados; cosplay
Otherkin, the 186-87
Otohime, Princess of the Dragon Palace 105, 148
otoko-yaku ('the role of a man') 88
Ōtomo, Katsuhiro 117, 188
    Akira 40, 127, 147, 157-59, 179
    young adult characters 118
ōtsu-e 6, 16, 22
Outcault, Richard Felton 13, 27
Overfiend, The 107
Ovid 83

Pagan ideas 7, 117, 129-35, 160
Palaephatus 83
Panda and the Magic Serpent/Legend of the White Serpent 93-94, 99-100, 124, 165, 178, 203

Pandey, Rajyashree 89
paper theatre *see kamishibai*
Park, Jin Kyu 8, 164, 187, 190, 192-94
Patten, Fred 163, 173
Peach Boy 45, 106, 146
    Aerial Momotarō 123
    Momotarō 165, 179
    Momotarō: Umi no Shinpei (Momotarō, Sacred Soldiers of the Sea) 45
    Momotarō Sea Eagles 106
    Tarō the Sentry: Submarine 122
    war propaganda 123
Penicka-Smith, Sarah 48
Pentecostal churches 66
Perper, Timothy 19
Perry, Matthew C. (Commodore) 21, 27, 60, 78
Picone, Mary 83-84
Piggott, Joan 14
pilgrimage *see* anime pilgrimage
Please Teacher 197
Please Twins 197, 203
Poitras, Gilles 119, 129
Pokémon 45
Ponyo 147-49, 151-54, 156, 159
Poole, Adrian 135
Porco Rosso 197
pornography 19, 94
    see also erotica; *hentai*
Pounds, Wayne 101
Power, Natsu Onoda 4, 27, 34
Prebish, Charles 51
Price, Shinobu 168
Priestesses of the Godless Month/ Destiny of the Shrine Maiden (Kannazuki no Miko) 71
Prince of Tennis 128
Princess Knight (Ribon no Kishi) 3, 29, 31, 34, 45, 73, 86, 88, 190-91
Princess Mononoke 3, 78, 130, 133-35, 179, 189, 193, 202-203
printing technology 19

woodblock printing 14, 17-18
propaganda
    military/war propaganda 45, 57, 93, 123
Prophet, Mark L. 53
Punch 14, 21
Punynari's Island Adventures (blog) 201-202

raccoon-dog (*tanuki*) 98
Rail of the Star 125
Ranma 1/2 39, 87, 128
Rauch, Eron 187
Reader, Ian 201
Record of Lodoss War 125
redikomi manga 39
Reider, Noriko 103-104, 106
reincarnation 53, 55, 74, 85
Reynaud, Charles-Émile 122
Ribon no Kishi (*Princess Knight*) 3, 29, 31, 34, 45, 73, 86, 88, 190-91
Richter, Ludwig 86
Rintaro (Shigeyuki Hayashi) 125
Risshō Kōsei Kai 53
Robertson, Jennifer 87
Robotech 169, 172
robots 3, 85, 120
    giant robots 124-26
    see also Astro Boy; mecha
Roddenberry, Gene 163, 166
Rowling, J. K. 101
'Rozen Asō' *see* Asō, Tarō
Rozen Maiden 12
Rubinstein-Avila, Elaine 43
Rudranath, Sushil K. 72
Ruh, Brian 169
Rūmī, Jalāl ad-Dīn Muhammad 147
Runel, Benoit 180
Ryōbu Shintō 65

Sadamoto, Yoshiyuki 112
Sailor Moon 29, 43, 45, 70-72, 179, 187, 197, 203
Saiyūki (*Monkey*) 96-97
Sakurai, Hiroaki 139

Sakurai, Takamasa 204
Sally the Little Witch 124
samurai families 22
samurai films 70, 123
    samurai-ninja historical-adventure genre 124
Sankichi the Monkey: Air Defense Military Exercise 123
Sasuke 124
Satō, Jun'ichi 121
Saunders, E. Dale 101
Sazae-san (*Mrs Sazae*) 181
Schodt, Frederik 19-20, 29, 33-34, 44, 46, 88
Schwartz, Adam 43
Schwöbel, Christoph 142-43
science fiction 60, 124
    fans 166-67
    films 52
    subgenres 126
    see also Astro Boy; mecha; robots
Scientology 53
Scott, Ridley 33, 47
scrolls 92
    Chōjū Giga (animal scrolls) 6, 15-16, 89-90
Second Life 186
Secret World of Arrietty, The 200
secularization 49
    decline in institutional religion 49, 50, 55, 58, 193
    definition 49
seijin manga 39
Seitou, Moriyoshi 200
self 56, 58-60
    Buddhism 60, 89
    decline of institutional religion 49, 58
self-transformation 56, 187, 194
    pilgrimage 195-97
Seo, Mitsuyo 123
Seven Gods of Good Luck 72
sexual ambiguity *see* androgyny
sexuality 19, 43
    androgyny 34, 74, 86-88, 97

Christianity 94
homosexuality 19, 43
mecha 107
metamorphosis 94
perversion 94
pornography 19, 94
see also erotica; *hentai*
Shaku, Sōen 51-52
shamanism 70-71
Shichi Fukujin (Seven Gods of Good Luck) 72
Shimokawa, Ōten 122
Shimura, Toshirō 203
shin shin shūkyō (new new religions) 36, 59, 70
shin shūkyō (new religions) 5, 23, 36, 50, 53-60, 66
   1960s and 1970s 55-56
   Aum Shinrikyo (Aum Supreme Truth), 36
   characteristics 36, 54, 66
   Christian influences 53, 111
   Internet 57
   Meiji Restoration 28, 50, 66
   modernity 54-55
   Shintō 28, 53, 70
   Sukyo Mahikari 111-12
shinbutsu shūgō 65
Shingon 65
Shinran 65
Shintō 5-7, 16, 35, 46, 48, 63-64, 138, 147-49, 200
   afterlife 84-85
   ancestor worship/veneration 68, 77, 109, 112
   androgyny 87
   animism 35, 75, 78
   anthropomorphism 80
   Bonbori festival 116, 144-45, 209
   Buddhism 5, 28, 64-65
   Christian influences 53
   creation mythology 69
   Daoism 64-65
   death 84-85, 89
   defining 66-67
   deities *see* Shintō deities
   Emperor worship 30, 32
   Engi Shiki 64
   guardian spirits 97, 107-108, 153
   imperial cult 69, 84
   imperial family 68-69
   kami see kami
   Kogoshūi 64
   Kojiki 5, 14, 64, 69, 72, 85, 114
   magic 72-74
   Meiji Restoration 28, 50, 65-66, 78
   metamorphosis 96
   miko 70-71
   nationalism 28, 79
   nature worship 78
   new religions 28, 53, 70
   Nihon Shoki/Nihongi 5, 14, 64, 69, 84, 133
   Noh theatre 21
   pollution/purification 110-11
   purity/impurity 84
   "religion" 73-74
   Ryōbu Shintō 65
   Sect Shintō 28
   sexuality 94
   shin shūkyō 28, 53
   shinbutsu shūgō 65
   shrines *see* Shintō shrines
   soul 77
   State Shintō 28
   sumō wrestling 21
   talismans 72
   three-tier cosmos 67, 84
   World War II 54
Shintō deities 80
   see also Amaterasu; *kami*
Shintō shrines 4, 21, 63, 65, 109, 145, 197, 210
   anime pilgrimage 203
   Hakone Shrine 201
   imperial cult 69, 84
   Inari shrines 145, 203
   Ise Grand Shrine 69, 84
   Izumo Taisha shrine 144, 209

nationalization 28
Yasukuni Shrine 28
Shipman, Hal 151
Shirato, Sanpei 44
Shirow, Masamune 11, 46-47, 59-61, 171
see also Ghost in the Shell
Shishi odori 82
Shōchan and the Squirrel 28
shōjo 26, 29, 31, 39, 45, 88, 128
mahō shōjo (magical girl) 121, 124, 156
shōnen 39, 128
shōnen-ai 43
bishōnen 43
Shōnen Sandee 102
Showa era 50
shrines see Shintō shrines
Shūkyō asobi (religious play) 79
shunga 6, 18-19, 23
see also erotica
Siddhārtha Gautama see Buddha
Sky Crawlers, The 147
Smyers, Karen A. 97
Snodgrass, Judith 51
Sōka Gakkai 53
Songoku the Monkey (Boku no Songokū) 45
soul
animism 75-77
sourds 43
Spider and the Tulip, The 123
Spirited Away 4, 78, 109-11, 146, 199-200
spiritual seekers 164, 187-95, 208
spiritual tourism 196-97
Spiritualism 50
sports 123-24
Spotlight is on Shinpei Gotō, The 122
Staemmler, Birgit 109
Stahl, Georg Ernst 76
Star Blazers 45, 172
Star Trek 56, 163, 166-69, 192
alternative philosophy/ religion 168, 183, 192

characters 166, 177, 183-84, 206-207
conventions 56, 183
cosplay 182-85
fans 167, 177-78, 181-85, 206, 208
Germany 167
Hungary 177-78
Klingons 167-68, 183, 186, 192
Next Generation 166, 206
The Original Series 166, 206
Star Wars 25, 45
Steiff, Josef 4
Studio Ghibli 196, 198, 203
subtitling see fansubbing
Sufism 147, 154-57, 159
Sukyo Mahikari 111-12
Summit Lighthouse 53
sumō wrestling 21
supernatural beings 69, 100-115
abduction by 109
baku 102-103
gohō 107
oni 103-104, 106-107
yōkai 100
see also kami
Su no kamisama 112
supernatural subgenre 7, 128
beings see supernatural beings
boredom/melancholy 155-57
child/young adult
characters 146-59
Christian symbolism/ themes 142-43, 150-51
'divine child' motif 7, 118, 146-60
realistic subject matter 135-46
religious themes 141-43, 147
Sufism 147, 154-57, 159
tragedy 135-39
Western Pagan ideas 7, 117, 129-35, 160
Susanoo no Mikoto 71-72, 114, 124, 144, 191-92
Suzuki, Bunshirō 28

Suzuki, Daisetz (Daisetsu) Teitarō 52
Swinnerton, James 27
sword and sorcery 125

Takahashi, Nobuyuki (Nov) 182
Takahashi, Rumiko 102, 104
   Ranma 1/2 39, 87, 128
   see also *Urusei Yatsura*
Takahata, Isao
   Grave of the Fireflies 135-39, 146, 196
Takarazuka Theatre 30, 34, 88
Takenouchi documents 111
Takeuchi, Naoko
   Sailor Moon 29, 43, 45, 70-72, 179, 187, 197, 203
Takimoto, Tatsuhiko 175-76
Tale of Genji 97
talismans 69, 71-72, 110
Tamplin, Tristan D. 4
Tanabe, George J. 78-79
tanuki (raccoon-dog) 98
Taoism *see* Daoism
Tarō the Sentry: Submarine 122
Tatsumi, Yoshihiro 26
techno-animism 35, 58-59
technology
   Japanese culture 35
   see also digital technology; printing technology
tengu (dog-spirits) 95, 109
Tenrikyō 50, 53
tentacle *hentai* 20, 94
Tetsuwan Atomu (Astro Boy) 2-3, 31-35, 45, 59, 78-79, 108, 120, 146, 172, 178, 180, 188, 203
Tezuka, Osamu 2-3, 6, 11, 22, 25-26, 28-36, 44, 46, 60, 115, 120, 179
   Amazing Three/Wonder Three 45, 68, 148
   animation studio 45
   Astro Boy 2-3, 32-35, 45, 59, 78-79, 108, 120, 146, 172, 178, 180, 188, 203

Atomu Taishi (Ambassador Atom) 31-33
Boku no Songokū 45
cinematic techniques 34, 41
Disney 86
Kimba the White Lion 3
Princess Knight 3, 29, 31, 34, 45, 72-73, 86, 88, 190-91
Saiyūki (Monkey) 96
sex education manga 37
theatre
   Kabuki theatre 87-8
   Noh (Nō) drama 20-21
   Takarazuka Theatre 88
Theosophy 50
theriomorphic transformation 81-82
Thomas, Jolyon Baraka 9, 79, 194, 197
Thomsen, Harry 53-54, 66
Toba 15
Toei Animation Gallery 203
Tōei Dōga 45, 124, 129, 165, 168, 180, 203
Toelken, Barre 101
Tokugawa, Ieyasu 16-17, 66
Tokyo 17, 27, 30, 32, 122, 175
   Akihabara 176, 186, 204
   Akira 157
   Aum Shinrikyo sarin gas attacks 36
   comic market 173
   commuters 43
   Edo-Tokyo Tatemonoen (Open Air Architectural Museum) 199
   Hikawa Shrine 197
   Kaichu Inari Shrine 203
   Kure-nai 203
   Neon Genesis Evangelion 201, 202
   Otaku-Anime Adventure Program tour 196
   otaku retail district 186
   Sailor Moon 203
   Sazae-san (Mrs Sazae) 181

Tokyo International Anime
    Fair 196
Tokyo University 23
Welcome to the NHK 175
Yasukuni Shrine 28
Tokyo Godfathers 135, 140-43, 146
Tokyo Punch 22
Tom, Patricia Vettel 92
Tomino, Yoshiyuki 125
Tomorrow's Joe 124
Töpffer, Rodolphe 6, 13
Toriyama, Akira 98
Tortoise and the Hare, The 122-23
tourism 195-97, 205-206
    see also anime pilgrimage
Toyotomi, Hideyoshi 16, 66
tragedy 117, 125, 135-36, 146
    child/young adult
        protagonist 137-38
    error of judgment
        (hamartia) 137, 139
    Grave of the Fireflies 135-39, 146,
        196
    the human spirit 117, 135-36,
        138-40, 146
    supernatural elements 135-36,
        138-39
    tragic flaw 137
transformation genre 124
Trekkies/Trekkers see Star Trek
Trinity Blood 74
True Pure Land 65
True Tears 197
Tsuge, Yoshiharu 30-31
Tsukiyomi 114
Tsurumi, Shunsuke 14, 28, 32
Turner, Victor 185-86, 195-96
Tylor, Edward Burnett 75-77, 79

Uchū Senkan Yamato 45
ukiyo-e 6, 17-18, 20, 22, 29, 62
    shunga 18-19
Ukiyo, Matabei 18
United Kingdom 45, 96, 168
    anime aficionados 170, 178

United States 23-24, 45, 94-95
    anime aficionados 164, 168-70,
        173, 178, 188-90
    arrival of anime in 179, 188
    Buddhism 52
    Cindi in Space 38
    comics 43
    cosplaying 182
Urashima, Tarō 105, 148
Urusei Yatsura 70, 102-107, 125,
    154, 166
    cosplay 181-82
    oni 103-104, 106-107
    *Urusei Yatsura 2: Beautiful
        Dreamer* 3, 102-105, 154
Utagawa, Hiroshige 21, 136-37
    *One Hundred Famous Views of
        Edo* 21-22
Utagawa, Toyokuni III
    (Kunisada) 62

Vatican, the 179
Vincentelli, Elisabeth 194
Vivekananda, (Swami) 51
Voltron 169

Walt Disney see Disney animations;
    Disney, Walt
war/military propaganda 45, 57,
    93, 123
Warriors of the Wind 169
Watkins, Leah 195
Welcome to the NHK 175-76
Western appearance of
    characters 29
Western Pagan ideas 7, 117, 129-
    35, 160
Westernization 22, 49, 60-61
    Meiji Restoration 27
Wired 1
Wirgman, Charles 21
Wise, Robert 52
Witch Hunter Robin 125
Wonder Three/Amazing Three 45, 68,
    148

woodblock printing 14, 17-18
World of Power and Women, The 123
World War II 3, 14, 22, 25, 29-30, 32, 34, 52, 107
  Allied forces 104
  dramas *see* World War II dramas
  Hiroshima and Nagasaki bombings 25, 32, 35, 113, 125
  Momotarō 106
  propaganda 45, 57, 93, 123
  religious freedom 66
  Shintō 79
World War II dramas 125-26, 136
  Grave of the Fireflies 135-39, 146, 196
World of Warcraft 187
World's Parliament of Religions 51-52
Wu, Cheng-en 45, 96

X-Files, The 126
Xavier, Francis 16, 66
Xuanzang 96

Yakitate!! Japan 119, 126
Yakushima island 202-203
Yamaori, Tetsuo 87

Yamata no orochi (eight-headed and eight-tailed serpent) 71
Yang, Jeff 41
Yasakani no Magatama (legendary jewel) 72
Yasukuni Shrine 28
Yata no Kagami (legendary mirror) 72
yōkai (monster-spirits) 95, 100
yokoana ('tomb') 137
Yokoyama, Mitsuteru 45
Yomi-no-Kuni ('land of eternal night') 84-85
Yomota, Inuhiko 31-32
Yonezawa, Yoshihiro 173-74
yonkoma manga 39
Yoshida, Teigo 104
Yoshinori, Sugano 40, 42
young adults *see* child/young adult protagonist

Zeami, Motokiyo 20
Zen Buddhism 6, 16, 30, 52, 70
  kōan system (Zen riddle) 16
  Noh theatre 20
zenga 6, 16

www.ingramcontent.com/pod-product-compliance
Lightning Source LLC
Chambersburg PA
CBHW060948230426
43665CB00015B/2107